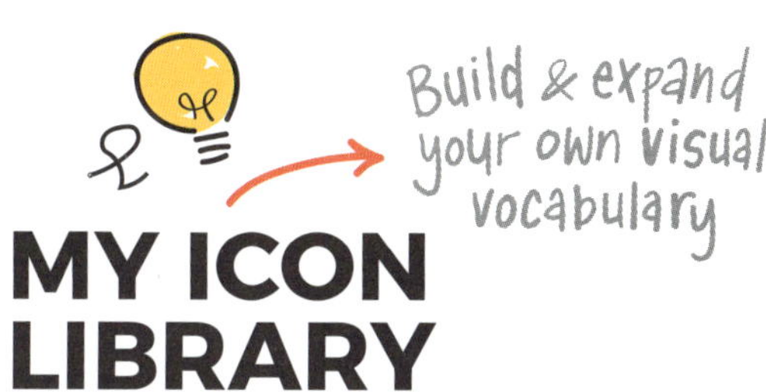

MY ICON LIBRARY

Willemien Brand

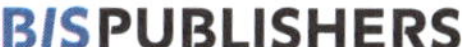

MY ICON LIBRARY

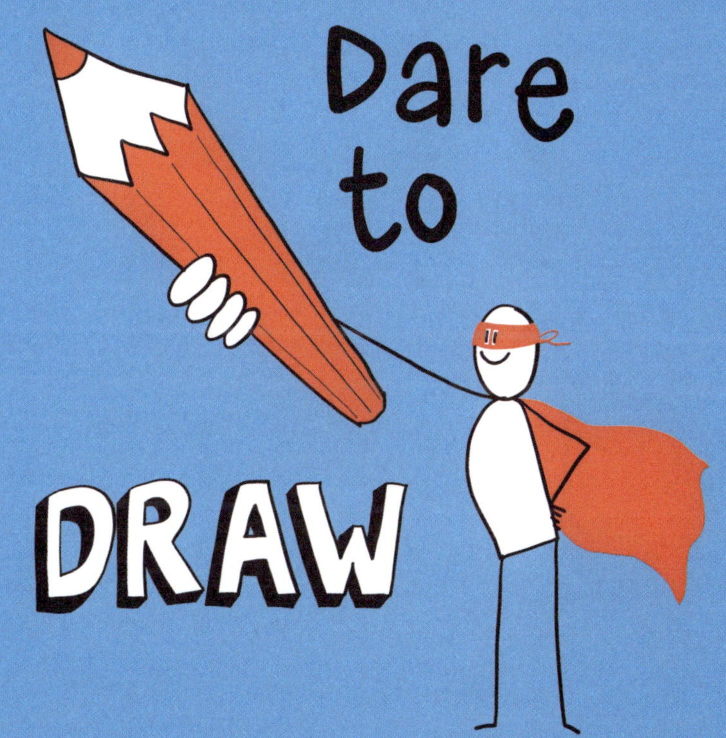
Dare to DRAW

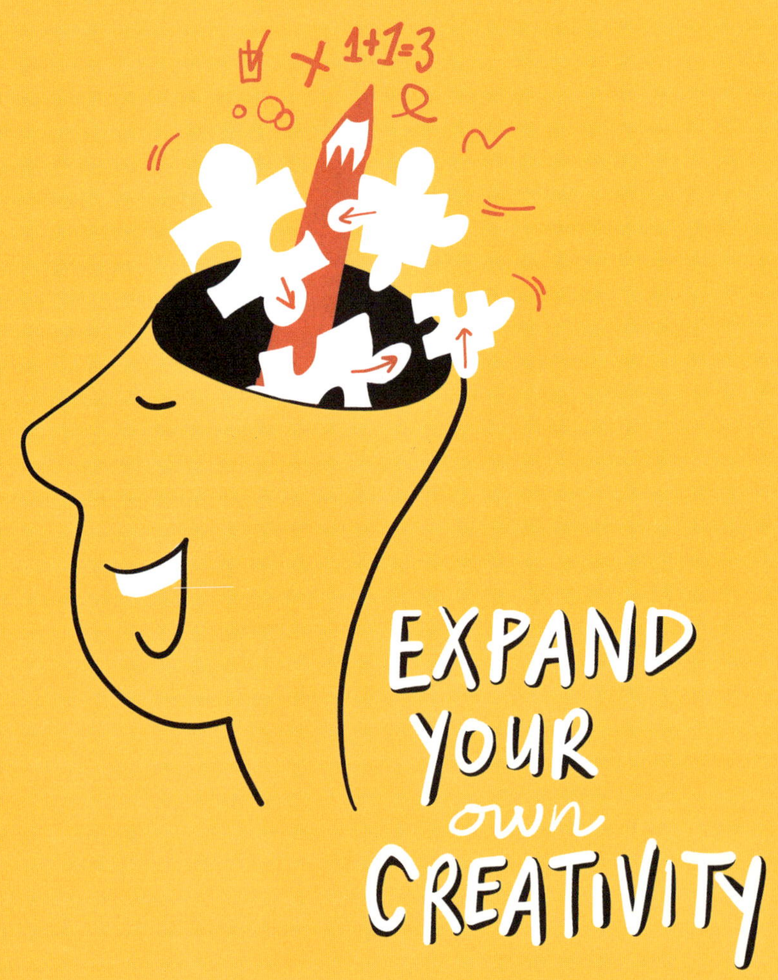

EXPAND
YOUR
own
CREATIVITY

WHY WE MADE THIS BOOK

Ever since we started our Visual Thinking/Business Drawing training sessions we have dreamt of compiling a collection of all the icons (more or less) frequently suggested by participants who wanted to know how they could visualize certain words or concepts. You could say that all the curious and creative people we've had the privilege of working with over the past twenty years have helped us create this book!

So, without further ado, here are the most common, interesting, weird and wonderful concepts in icon form. You will find sections on themes including 'finance', 'technology' and 'way of working'. They are further broken down into concepts such as 'cost-cutting, 'co-creation' and 'social innovation', all visualized in different ways.

These are not meant to be finished visual products. I want them to spark your creativity and inspire you to make your own icons, instead of plucking generic icons from the internet that often don't accurately express your story. And remember that every story has its own quirks and context, and therefore its own blend of icons and visuals. Keep practicing, keep expanding your icon library, so you will have the courage to tell your own visual story.

Enjoy!

Willemien Brand,
founder of Buro BRAND.

HOW TO USE THIS BOOK

We made this book to inspire you and to provide a resource that is easy to browse whenever you need it. That's why we made it more or less pocket-sized. You can now have icons at your fingertips wherever you go!

The main part of the book contains pages that each explain a certain word or concept.

These pages start with basic icons we designed ourselves or found online. We track down icons online by Googling a combination of words and then adding the word 'icon', 'illustration' or 'vector'.

The middle of the page shows four variations capturing different contexts of the word.

The bottom part contains a 'how to draw' area highlighting a rather difficult or interesting combined icon. Sometimes we chose to only draw a detail or a part of an icon, so you can fully understand it and use it as a base for your own icons.

At the beginning of the book there is an index, based on specific categories. If you are looking for a specific word or icon, use the alphabetic index at the back of the book!

We hope this book inspires you to come up with new ideas for your own visual jargon and icons and how to apply these.

PAGE STRUCTURE

ACTION

BASIC ICONS

DAILY WORK

COMBINED ICONS

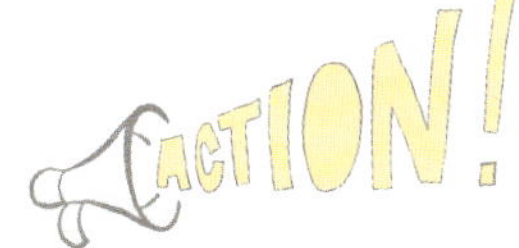

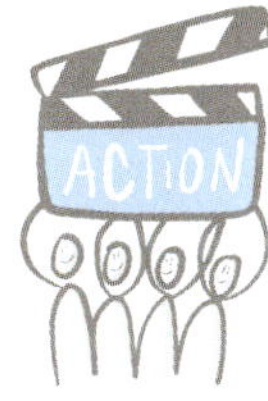

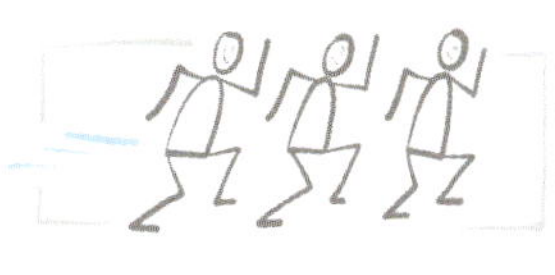

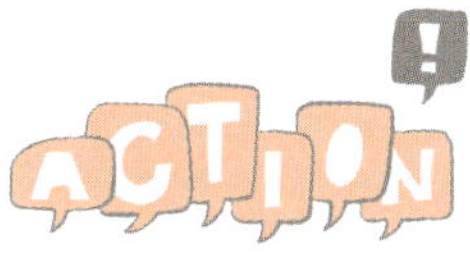

HOW TO DRAW

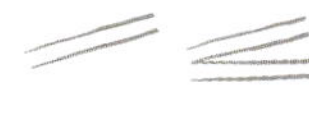

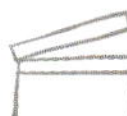

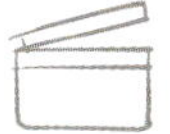

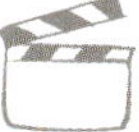

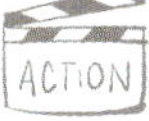

MATERIALS

We recommend using these pens, so that you can draw all of the icons shown here as an example.

NB. We drew all the icons on an iPad Pro, using adobe sketch.

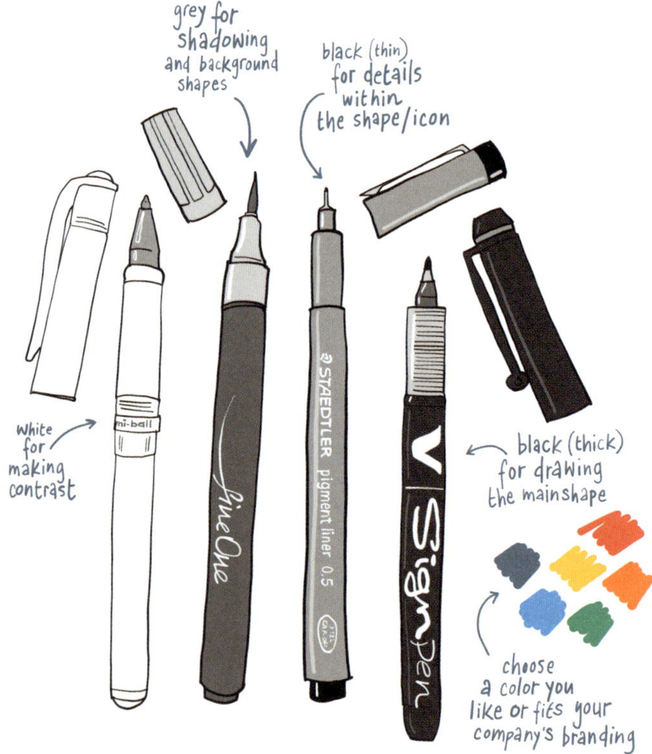

BASIC ICONS

We have noticed that people challenged to draw a concept can often express themselves visually even if they only know some basic icons. That's why we believe it is very useful to master some essential icons that fit almost every environment.

They are effective on their own, but you will also see them popping up in a lot of combined icons. They are a foundation for your creativity. Build on them!

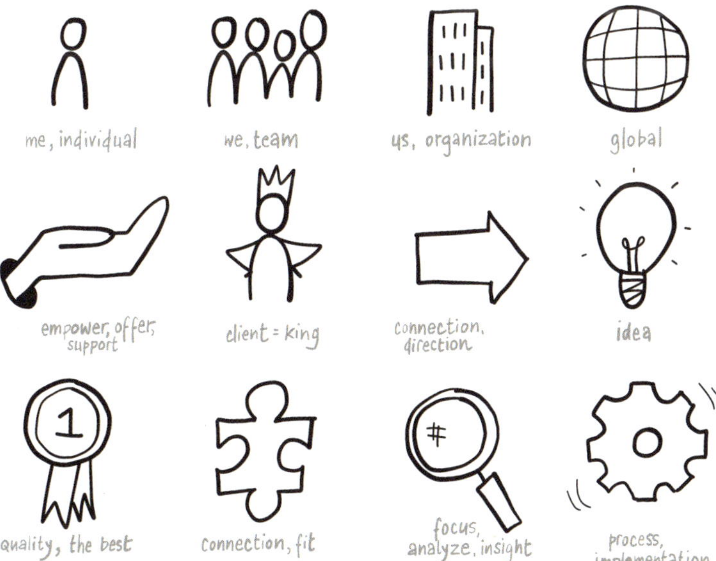

COMBINED ICONS

Combining icons is a way of adding your own meaning to the visual. That's why we don't like copying icons directly from internet; it's too generic!

You want to express yourself and your idea/concept as well and clearly as possible. To do that you can take several steps:

1. What concept do you want to visualize? What does it mean, what words do you associate it with? What characteristics does your concept have? Think about it for a while and write down the words (e.g. in a word cloud) if you like.
2. Google is your friend! Not only to search for icons for your main concept, but also to hunt for icons that could express all words related to your concept. Be inspired and optionally draw the icons you come across that you like.
3. Mix it up! Make combinations. And then make some more. Depending on the importance of your drawing, you should always experiment with visual hierarchy (size, order or 'reading'), compositions and contrast (thick lines/thin lines, black/gray/color). A simple trick to see whether it is coherent and balanced is to draw a rectangle around your drawing and look at it from a distance. Don't focus only on the drawing but also the white spaces.

Good to realize: using text or using visuals is not binary, it's a scale. Ask yourself where you feel comfortable, what is necessary or easiest in the given situation.

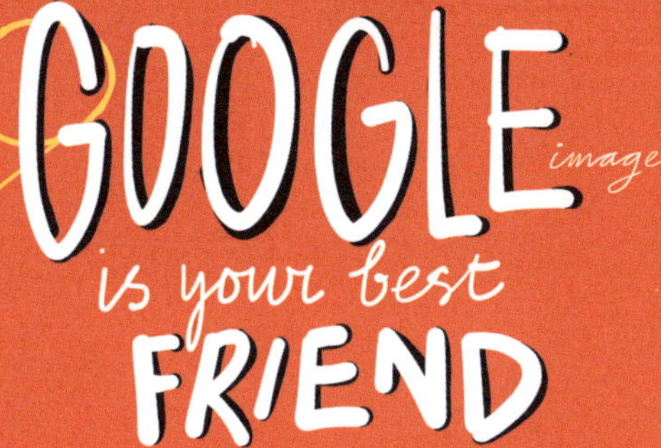

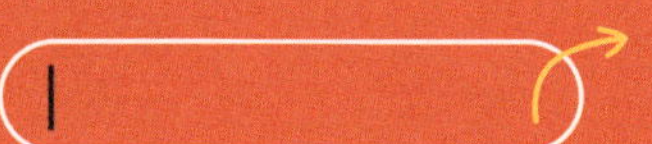

add 'icon'
'vector' or
'illustration'

Or just visit:
thenounproject.com
iconfinder.com

search on keywords

looking for inspiration

see the combination to tell your visual story

team

direction

goal

team alignment

BUSINESS ORGANIZATION

HOW ARE WE ORGANIZED?

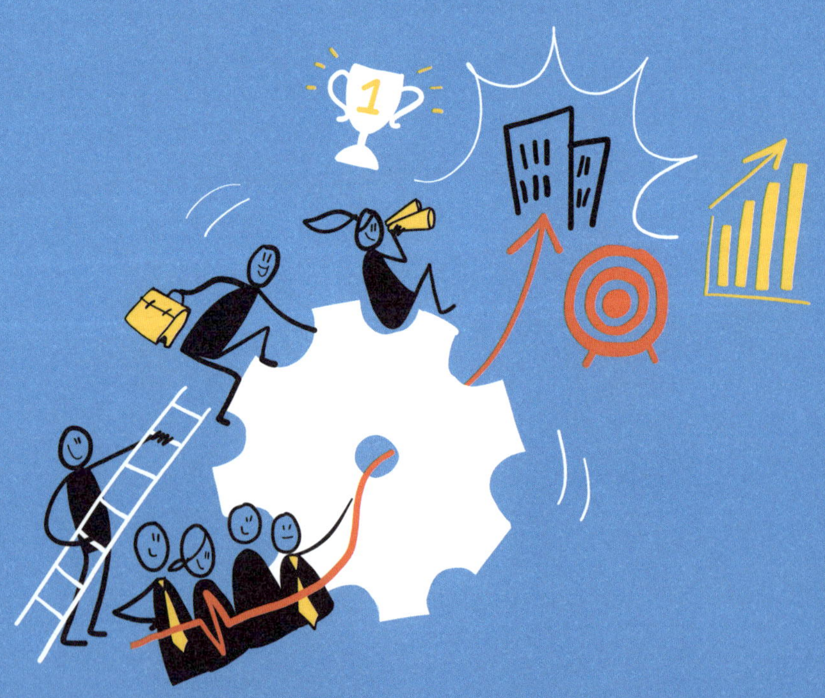

BUSINESS CASE

BASIC ICONS

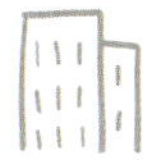
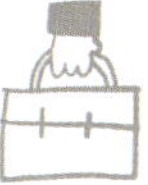
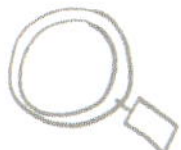
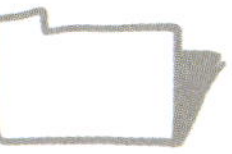
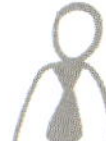
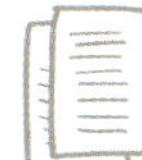

COMBINED ICONS

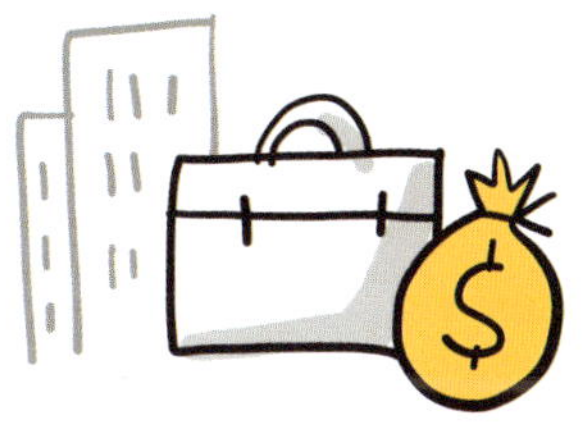
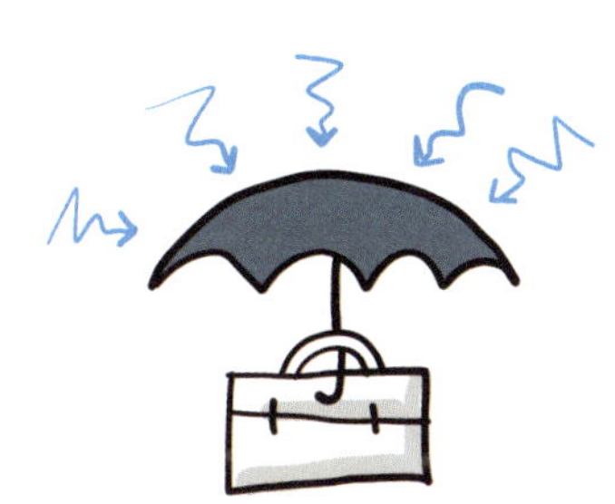
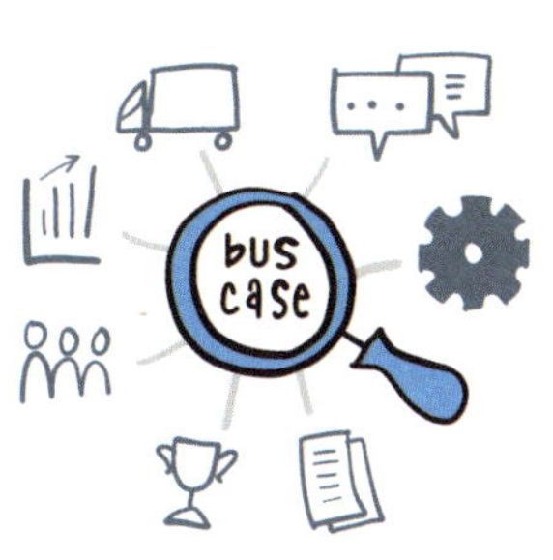

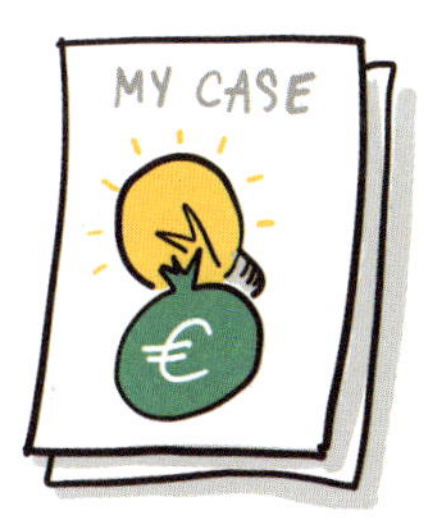

HOW TO DRAW

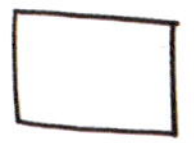
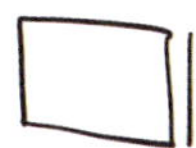
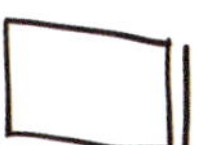
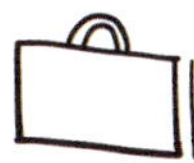
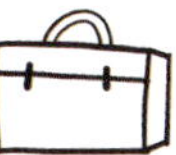

COMPLIANCE

BASIC ICONS

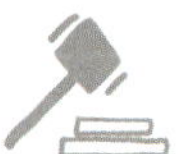

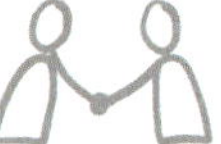
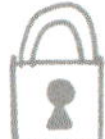

COMBINED ICONS

HOW TO DRAW

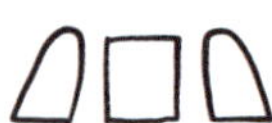
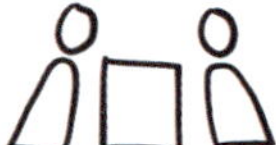
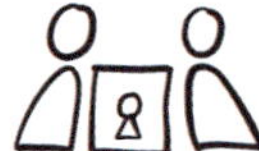

CONSULTANCY

BASIC ICONS

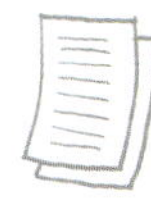
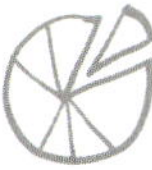
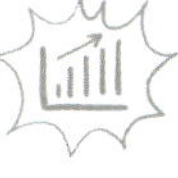
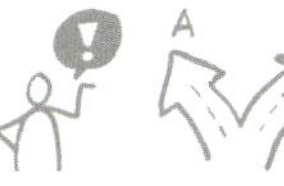

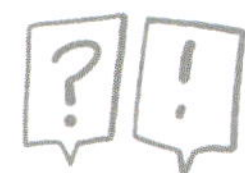

COMBINED ICONS

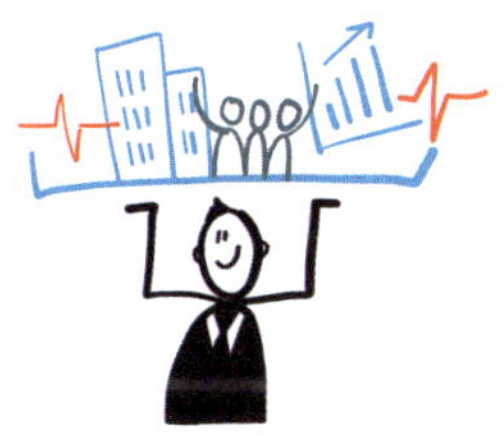

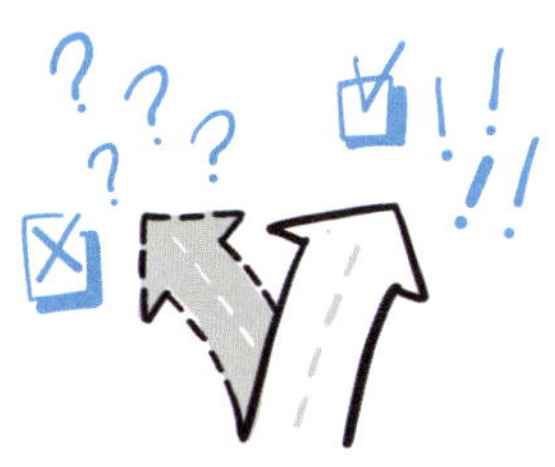
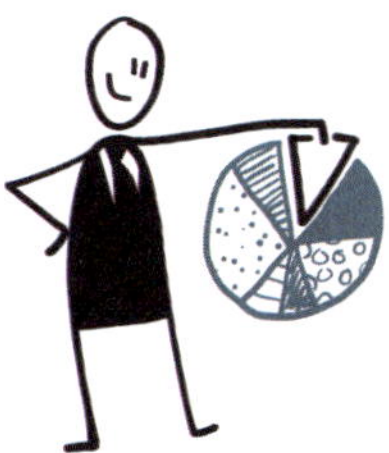

HOW TO DRAW

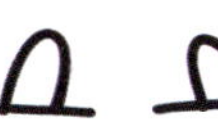
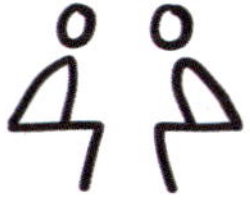
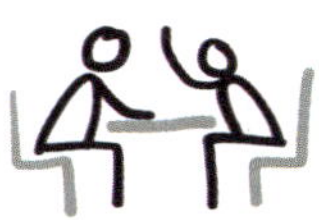

CORE VALUES

BASIC ICONS

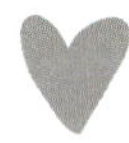 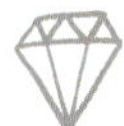 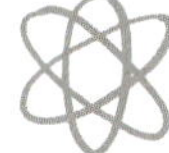 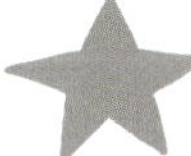 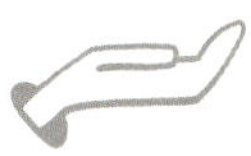 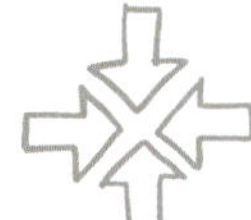

COMBINED ICONS

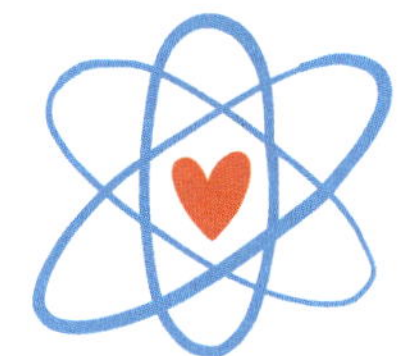

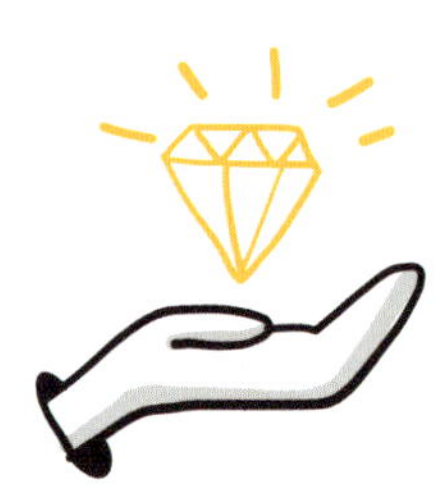

HOW TO DRAW

GOALS

BASIC ICONS

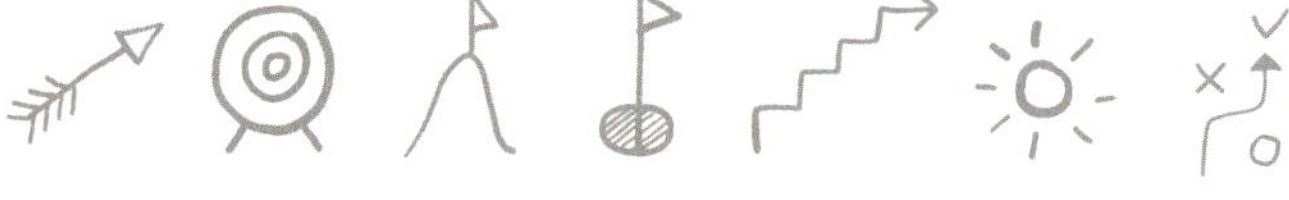

COMBINED ICONS

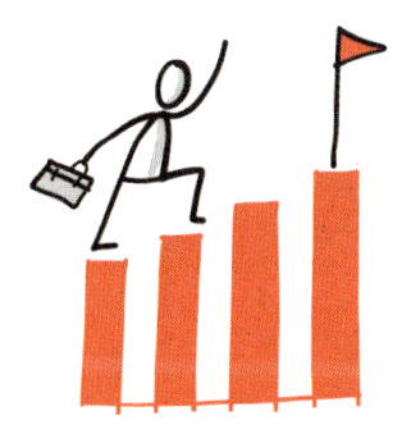

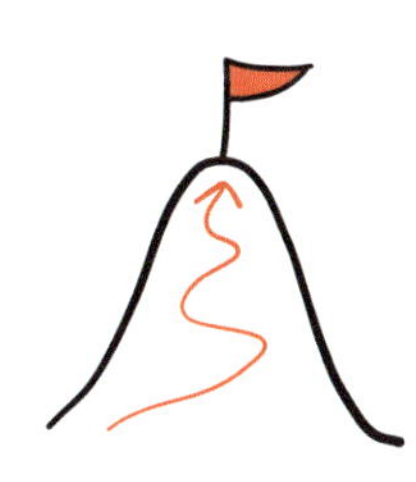

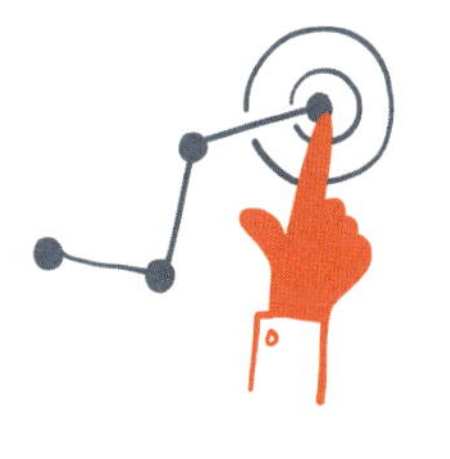

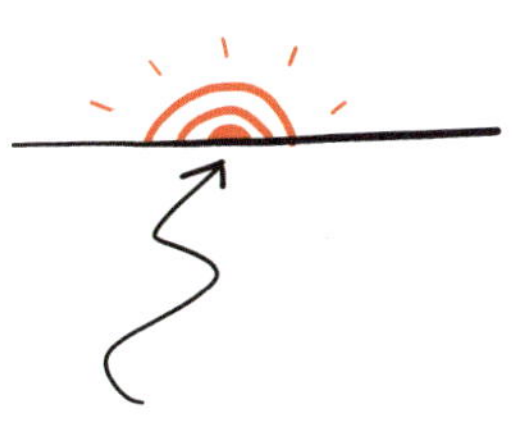

HOW TO DRAW

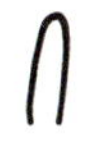

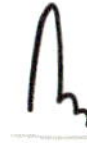

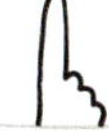

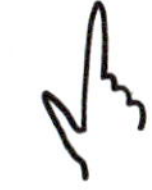

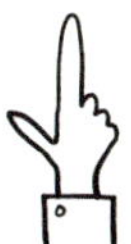

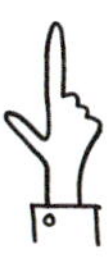

GOVERNMENT

BASIC ICONS

dutch government building icon

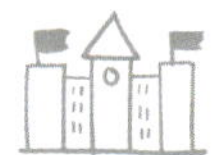 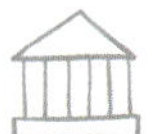 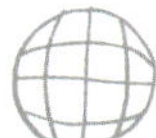 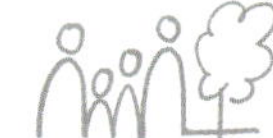 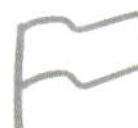 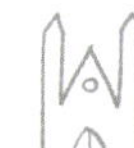

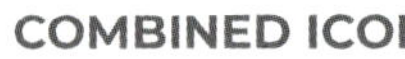

COMBINED ICONS

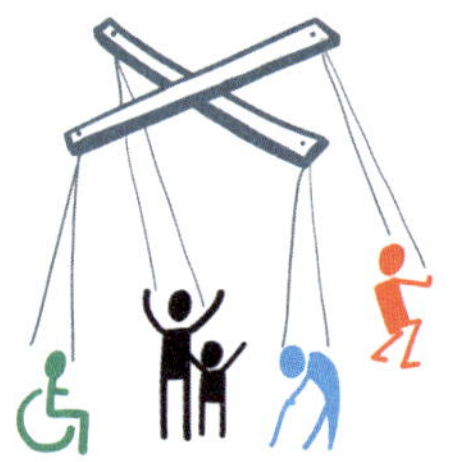

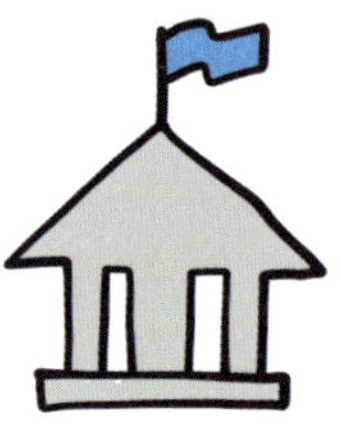

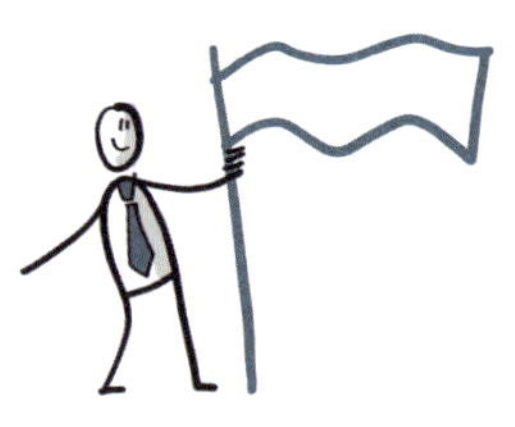

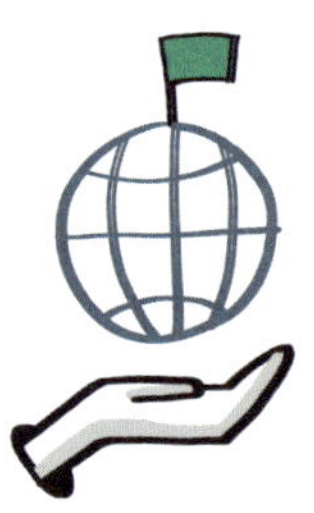

HOW TO DRAW

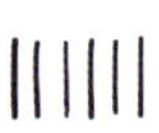 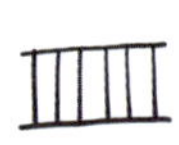 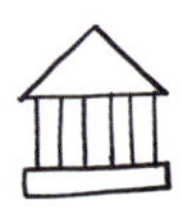 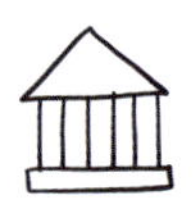 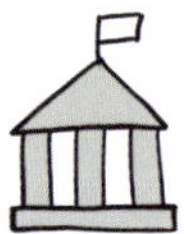

KEY RESOURCES

BASIC ICONS

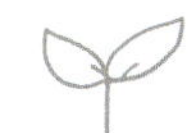
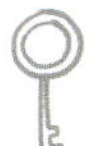
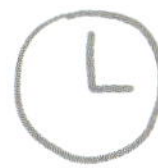
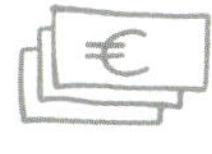
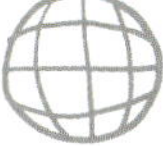
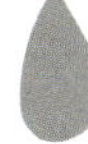
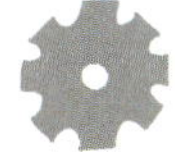

COMBINED ICONS

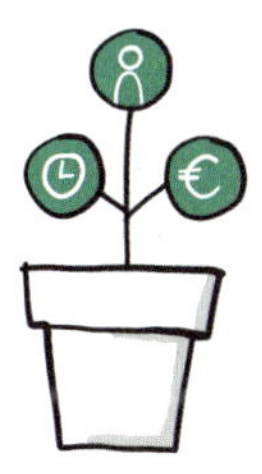
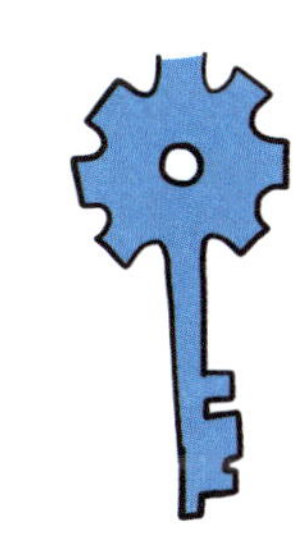
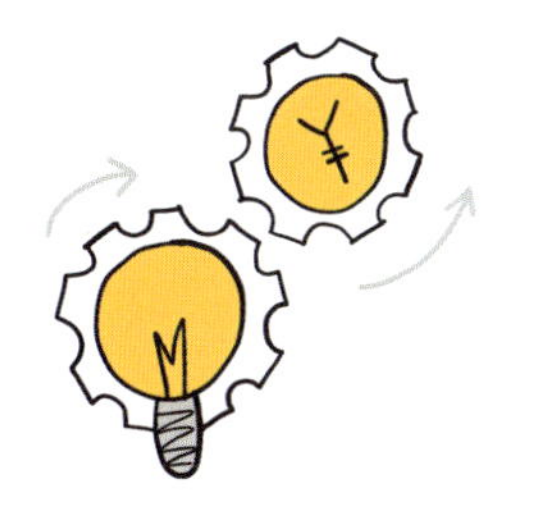
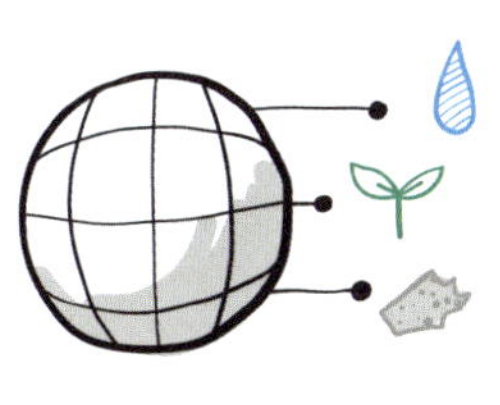

HOW TO DRAW

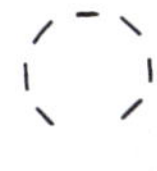
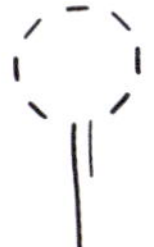
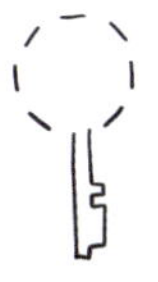
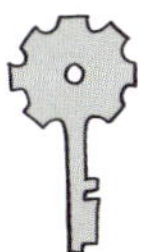

KEY PERFORMANCE INDICATORS (KPI)

BASIC ICONS

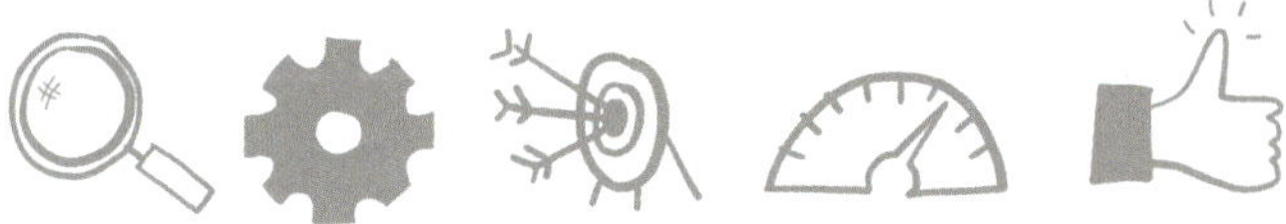

COMBINED ICONS

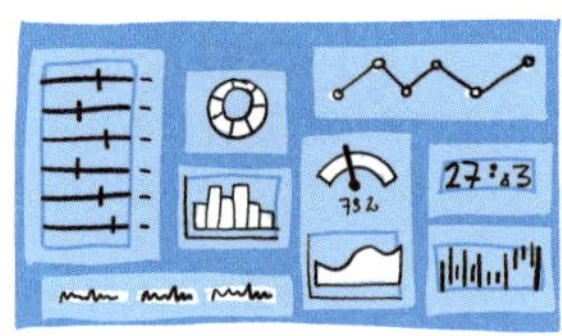

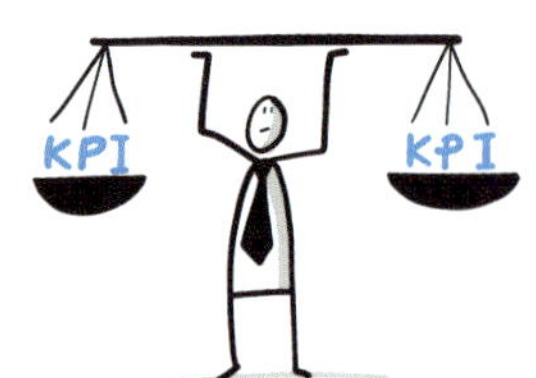

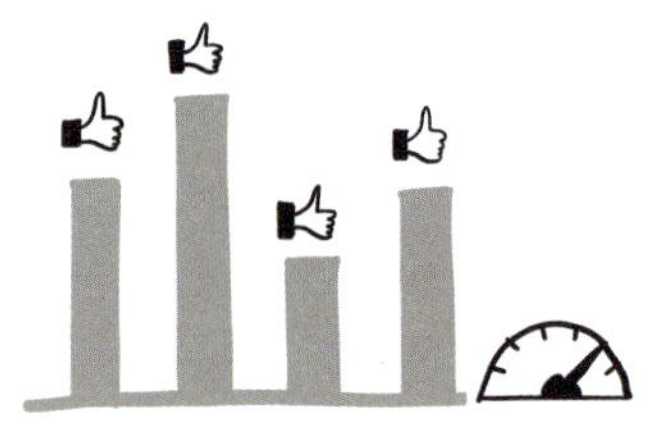

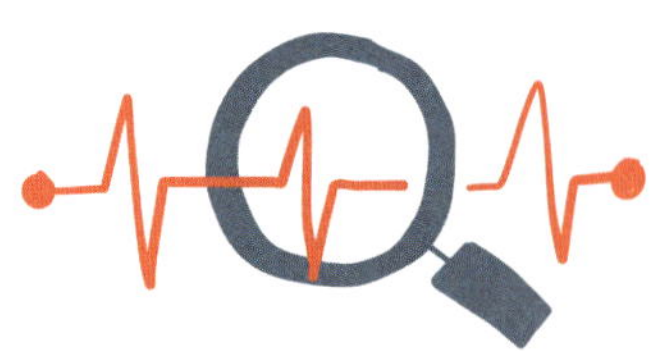

HOW TO DRAW

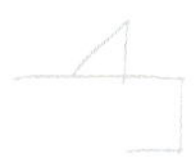

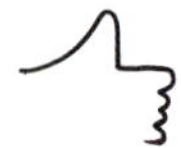

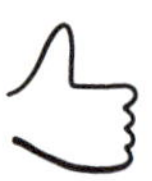

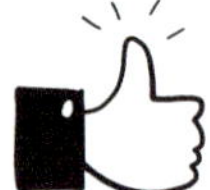

MANAGEMENT

BASIC ICONS

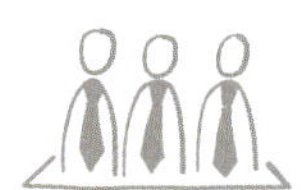
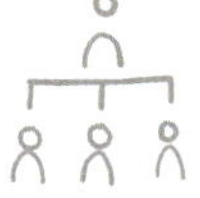
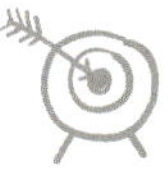
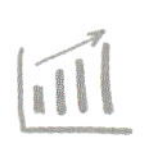

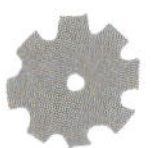

COMBINED ICONS

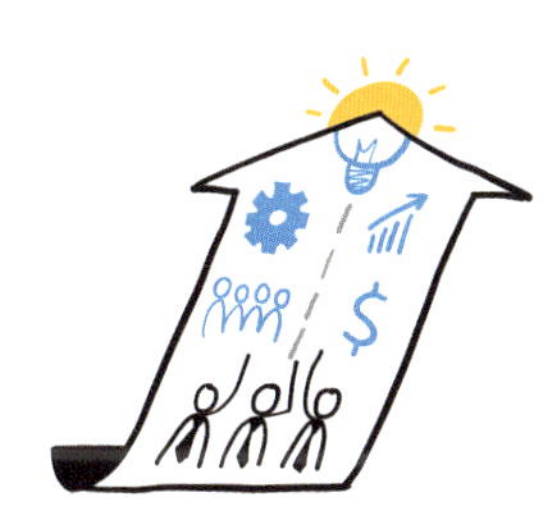

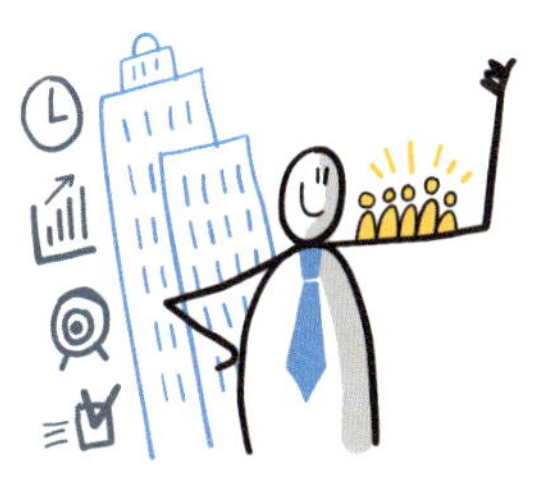
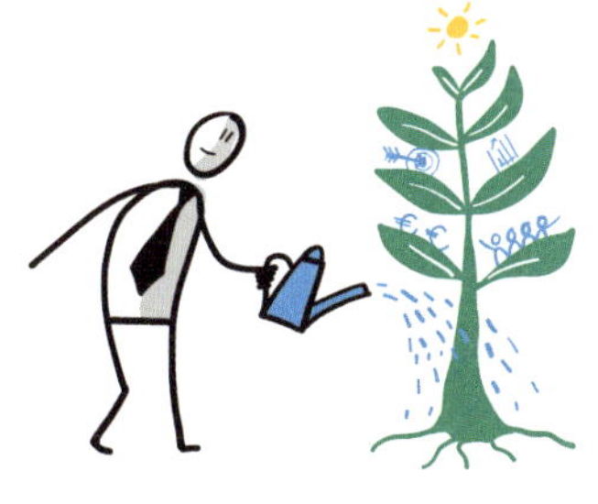

HOW TO DRAW

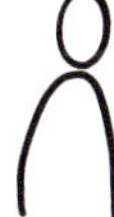
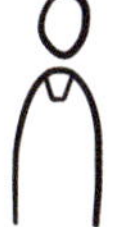
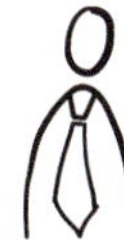
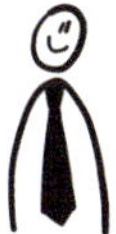

MISSION

BASIC ICONS

COMBINED ICONS

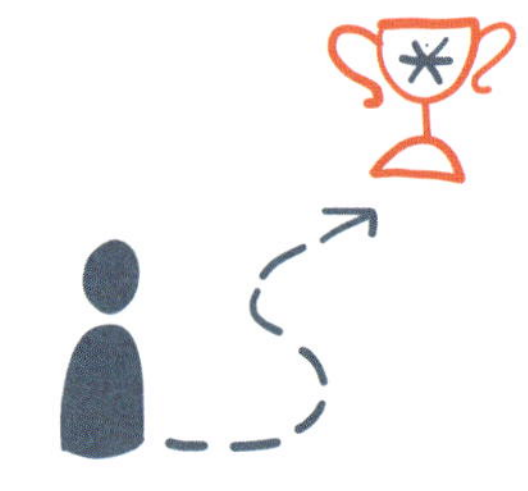

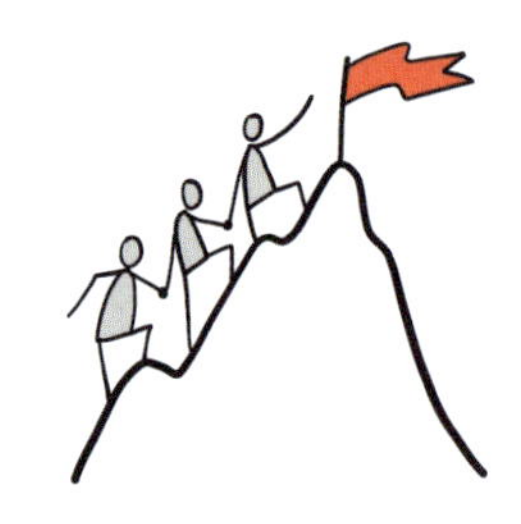

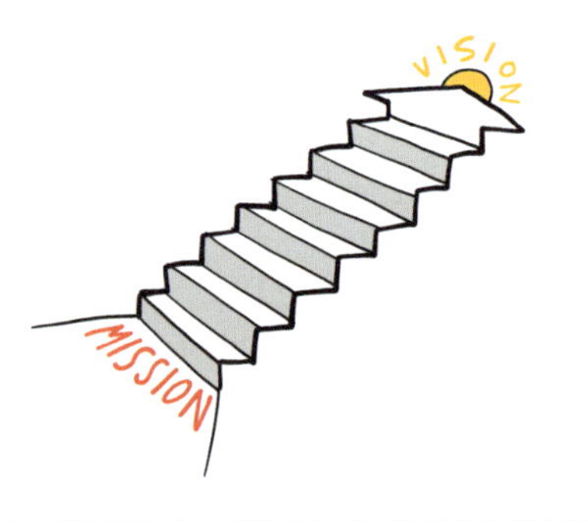

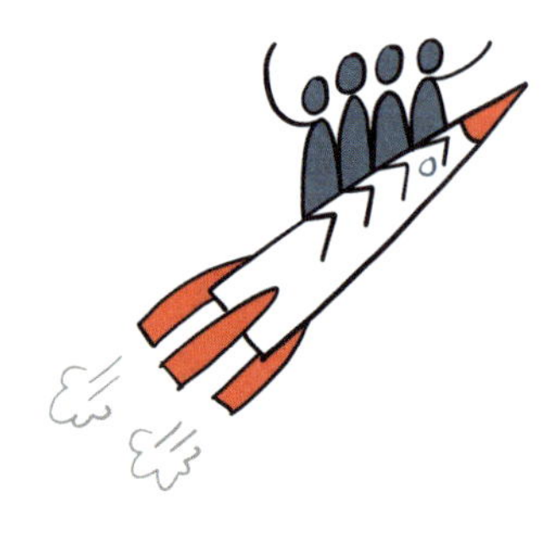

HOW TO DRAW

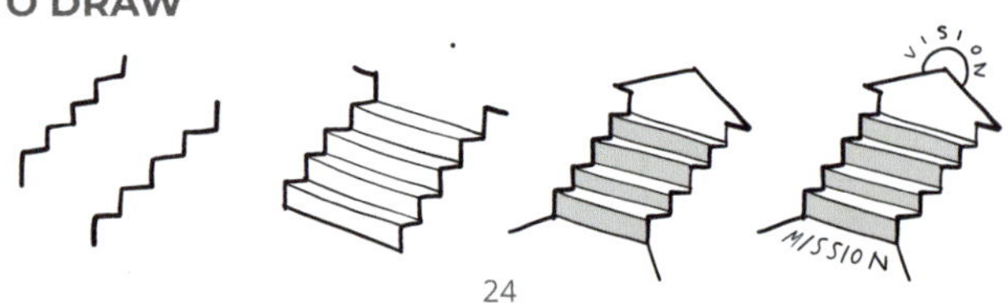

NETWORK

BASIC ICONS

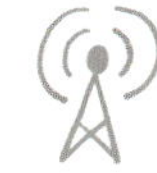
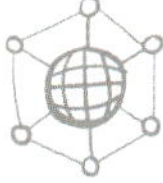
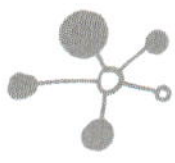
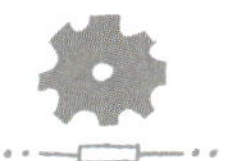
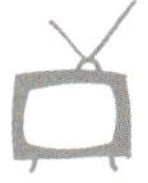
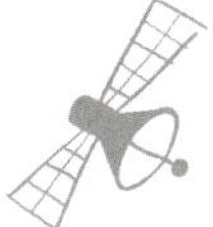

COMBINED ICONS

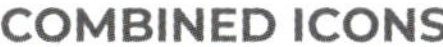

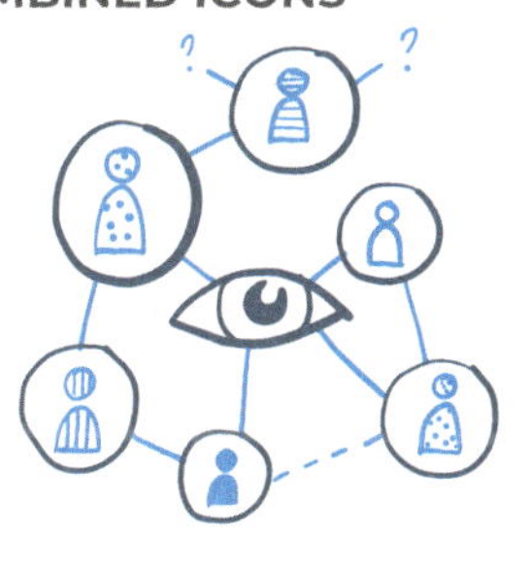

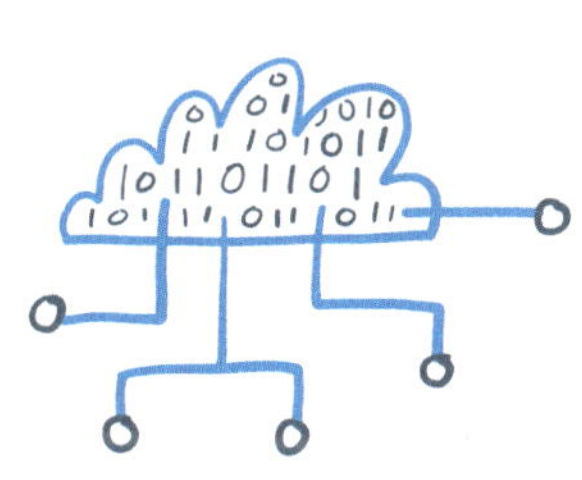

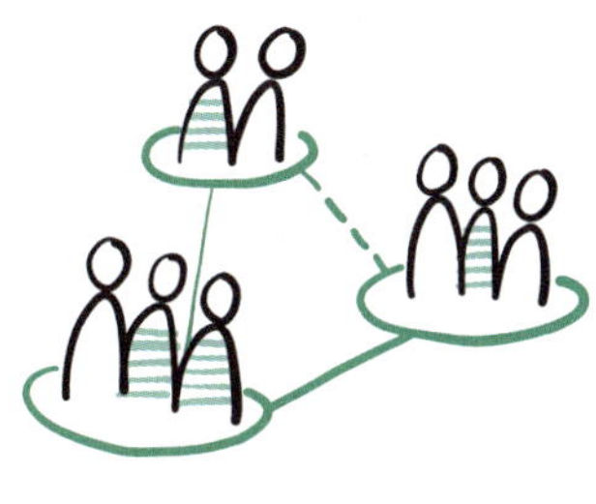

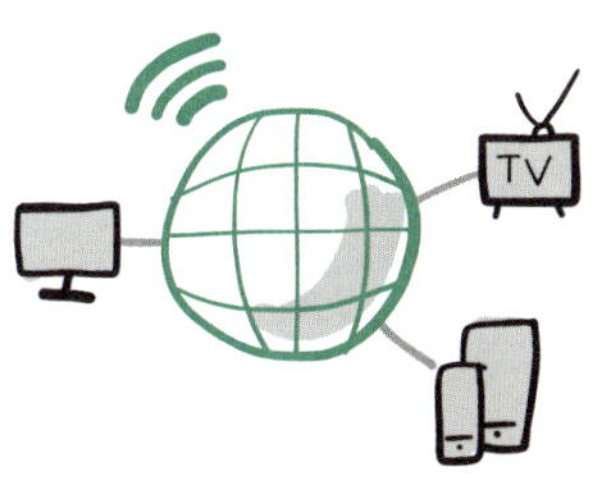

HOW TO DRAW

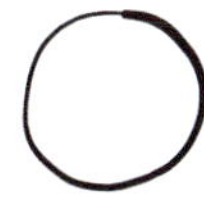
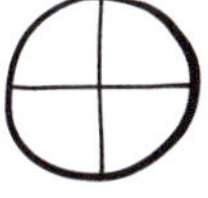
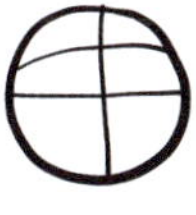
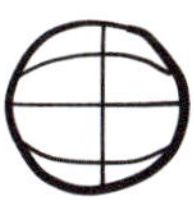
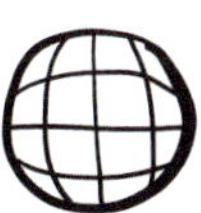

POLICY

BASIC ICONS

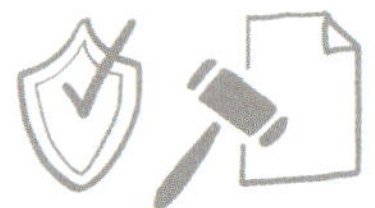
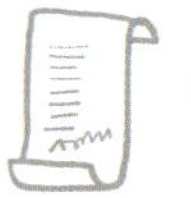

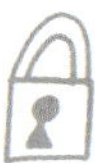
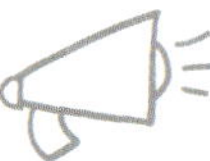

COMBINED ICONS

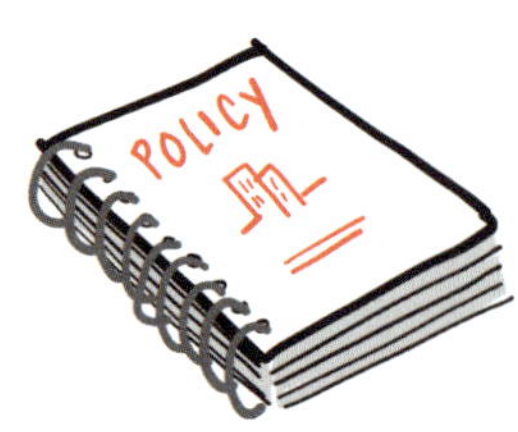

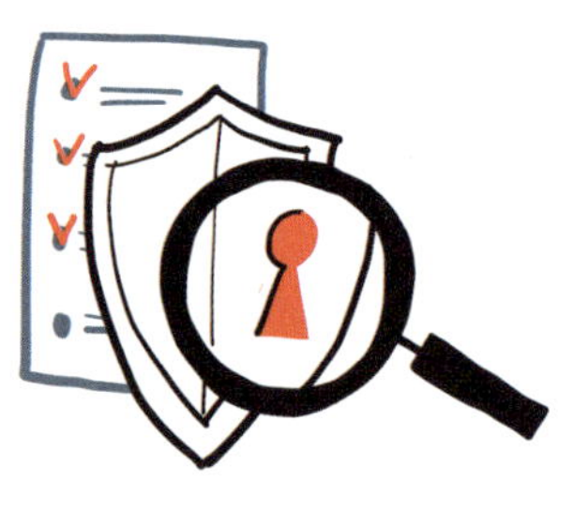

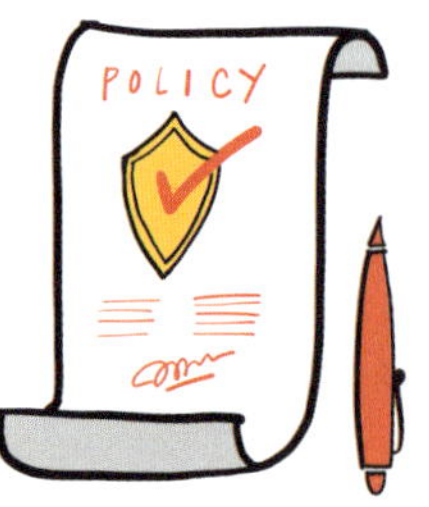

HOW TO DRAW

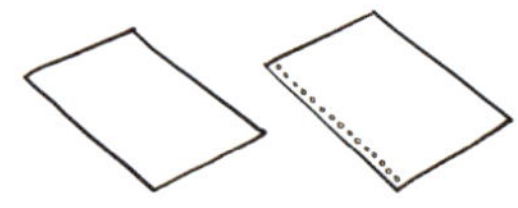
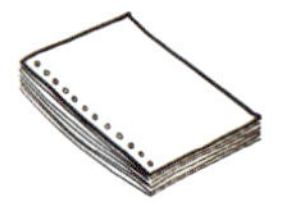
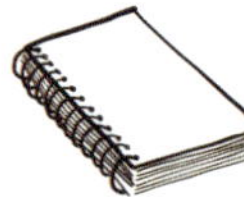
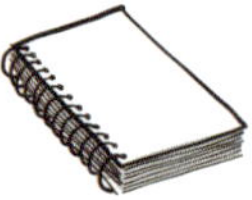

PURPOSE

BASIC ICONS

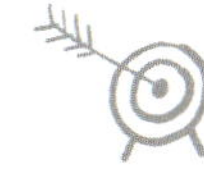
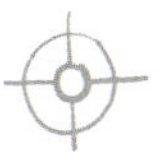
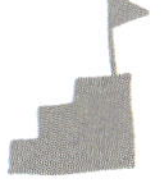
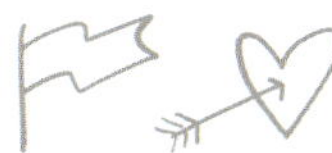

COMBINED ICONS

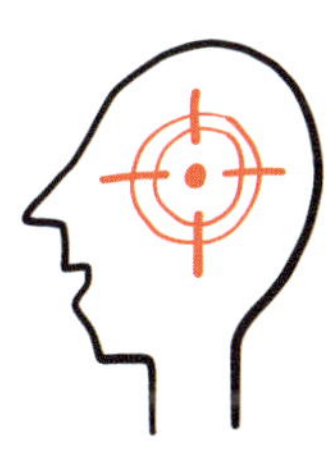
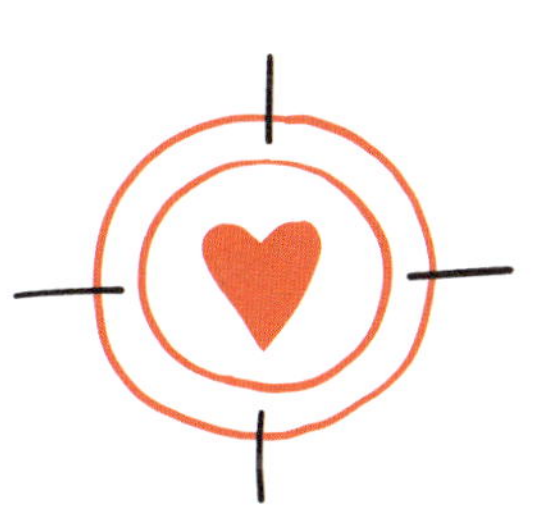

HOW TO DRAW

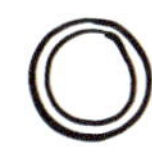

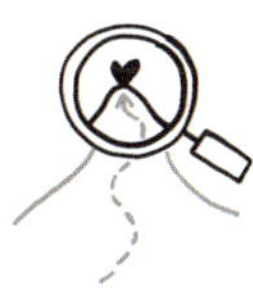

REPORTING (ANALYTICS)

BASIC ICONS

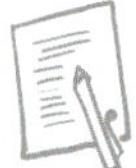
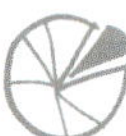
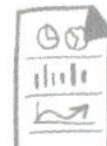
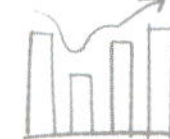
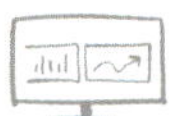
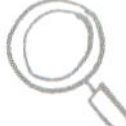

COMBINED ICONS

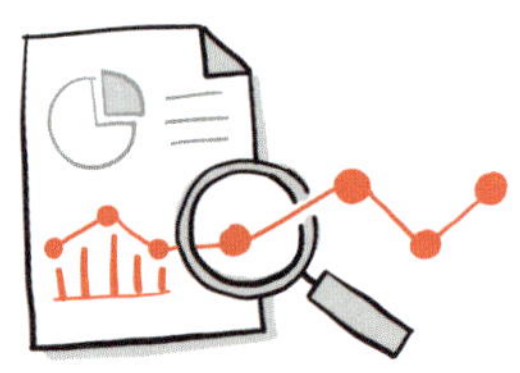
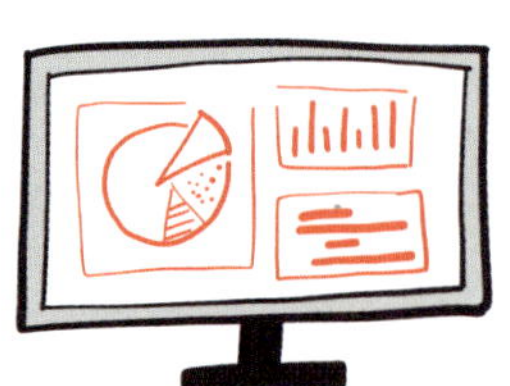
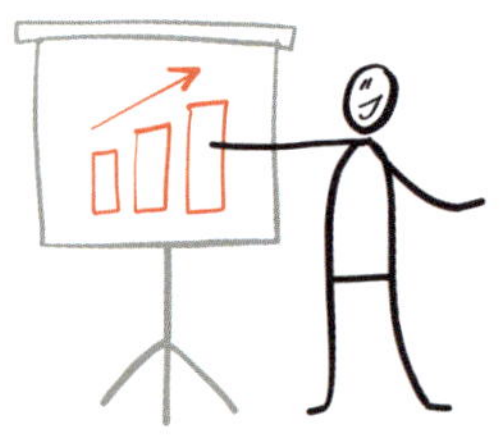
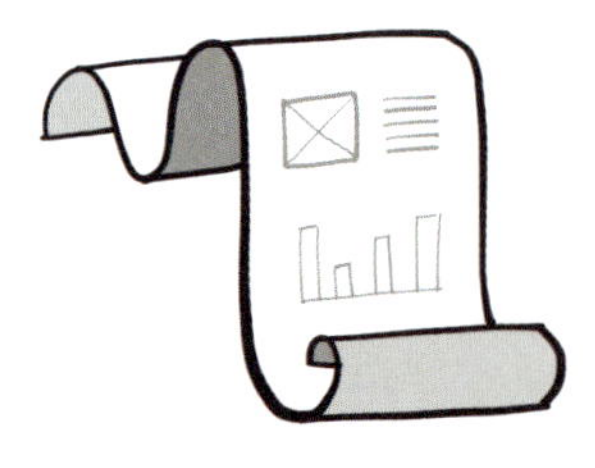

HOW TO DRAW

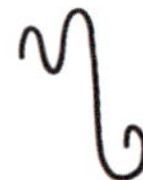
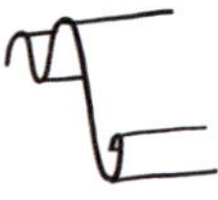
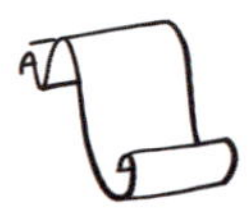
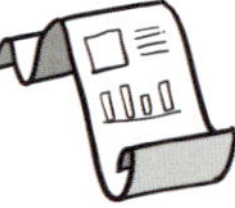

ROADMAP

BASIC ICONS

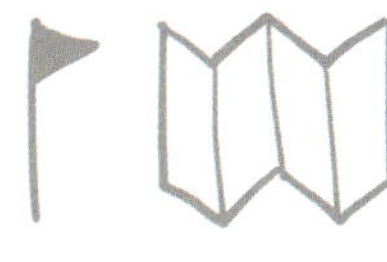

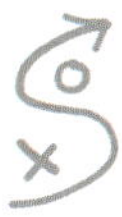
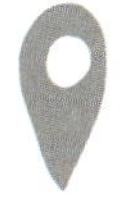
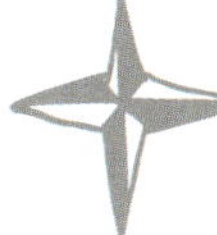

COMBINED ICONS

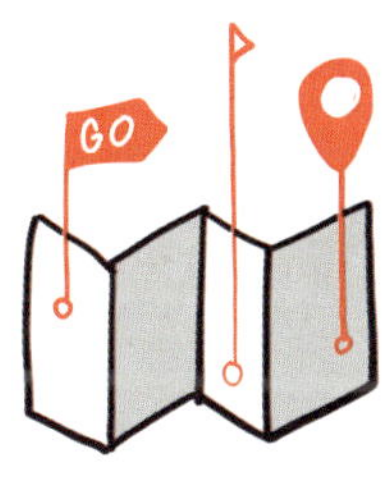

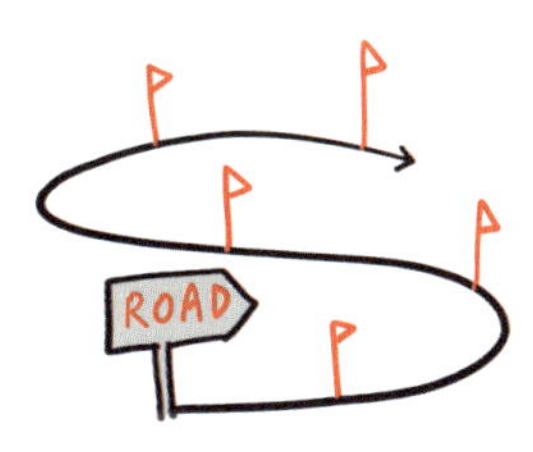

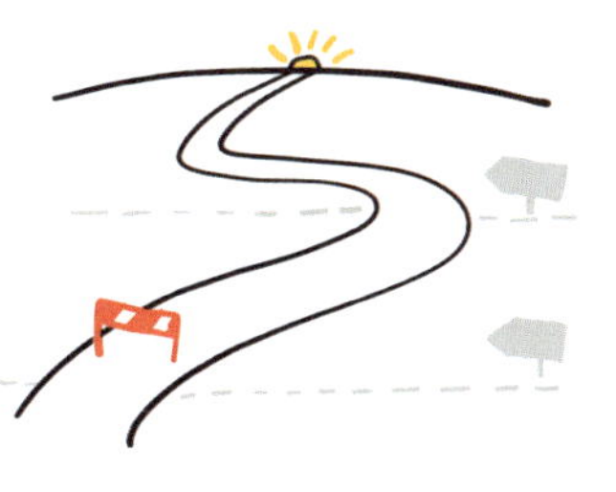

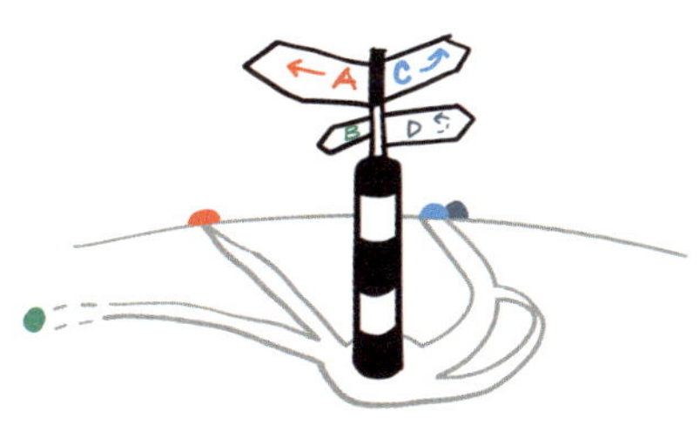

HOW TO DRAW

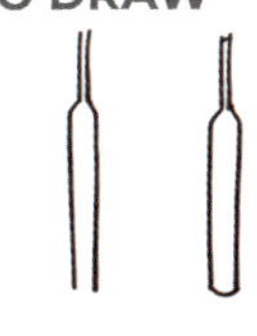
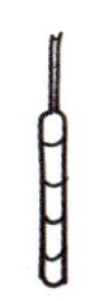
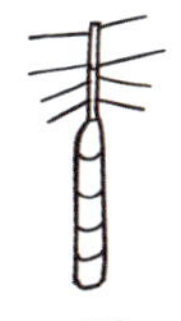
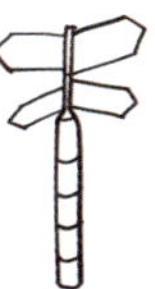
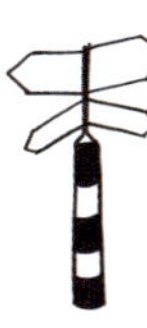

SOCIAL RESPONSIBILITY

BASIC ICONS

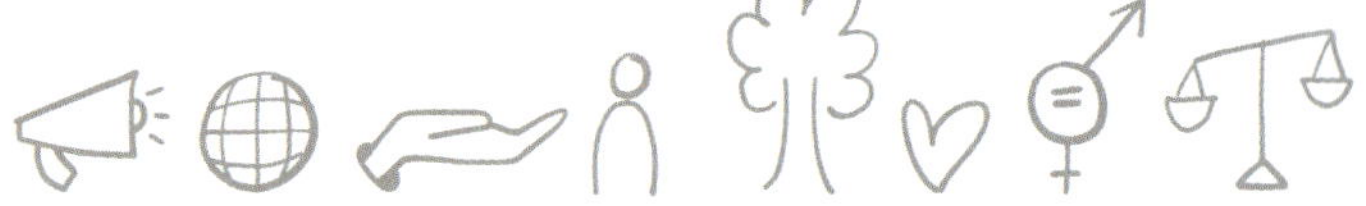

COMBINED ICONS

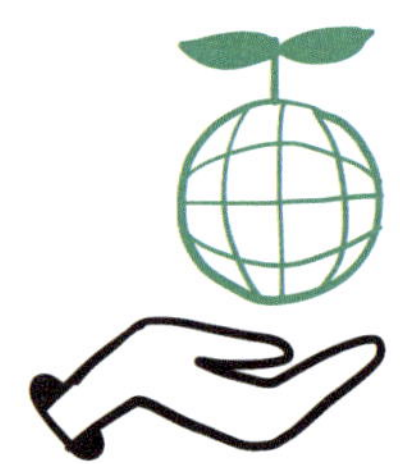

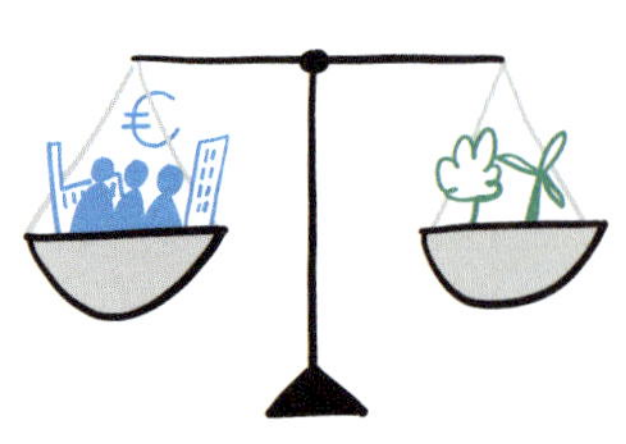

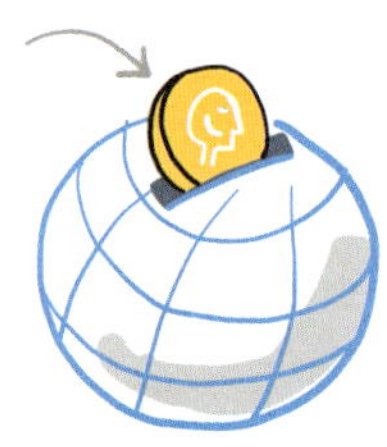

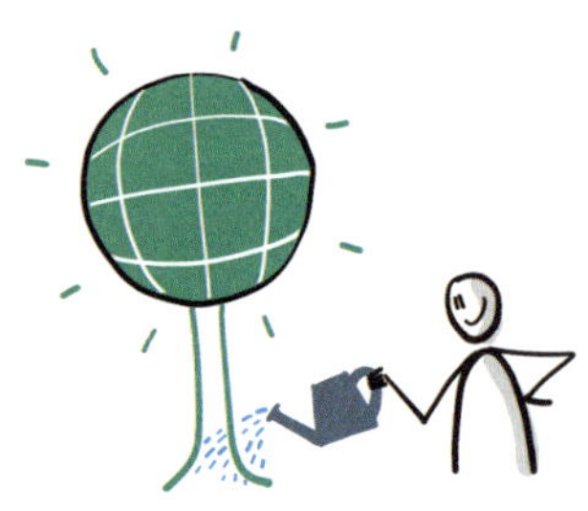

HOW TO DRAW

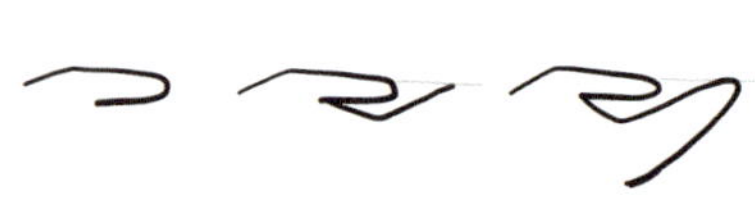

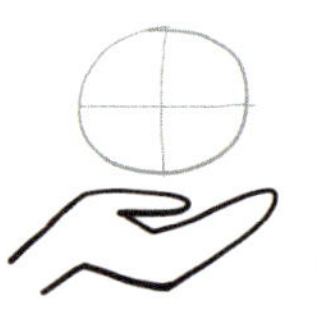

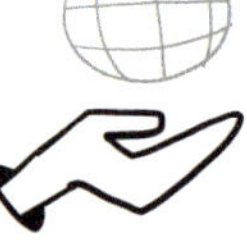

STAKEHOLDERS

BASIC ICONS

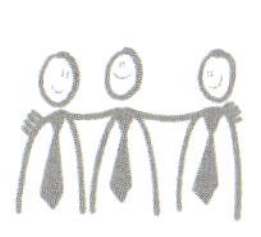
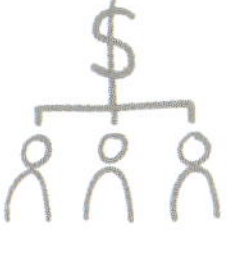

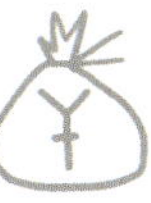

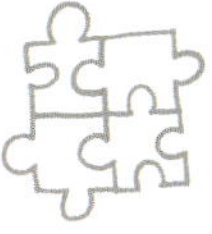
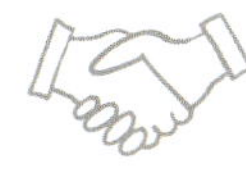

COMBINED ICONS

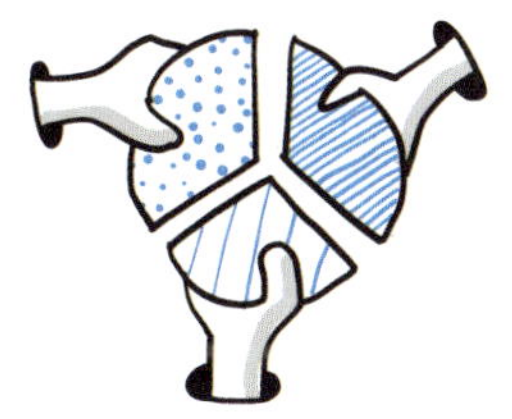
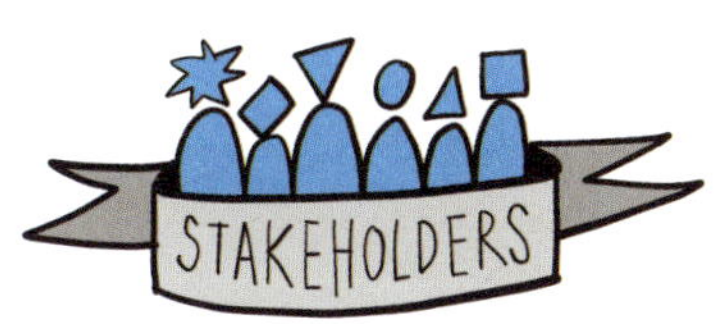

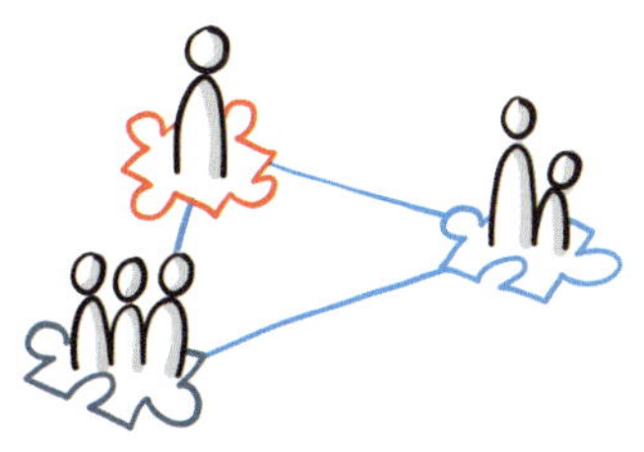

HOW TO DRAW

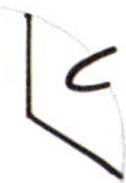
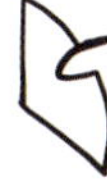
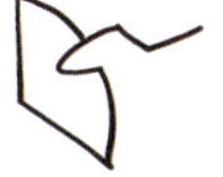
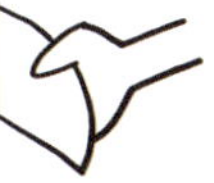
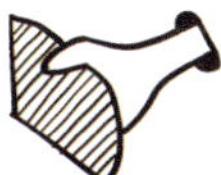

STRATEGY

BASIC ICONS

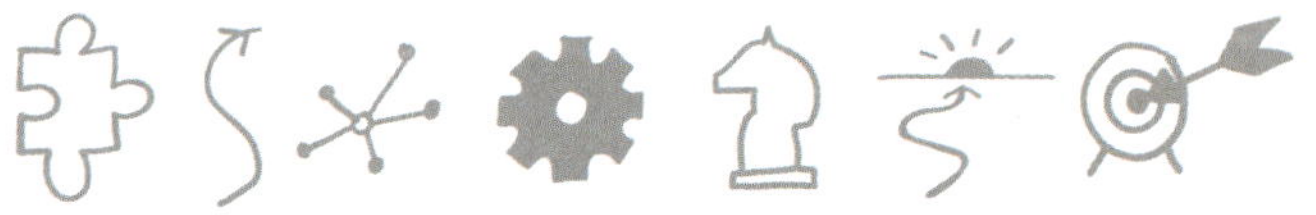

COMBINED ICONS

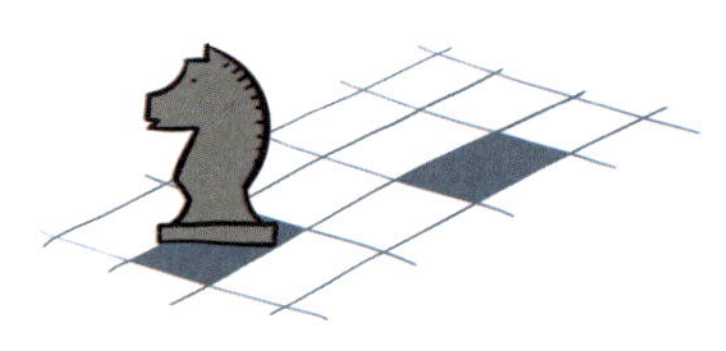

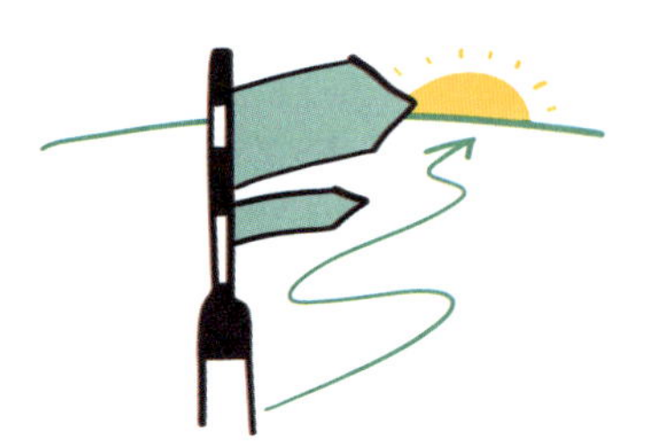

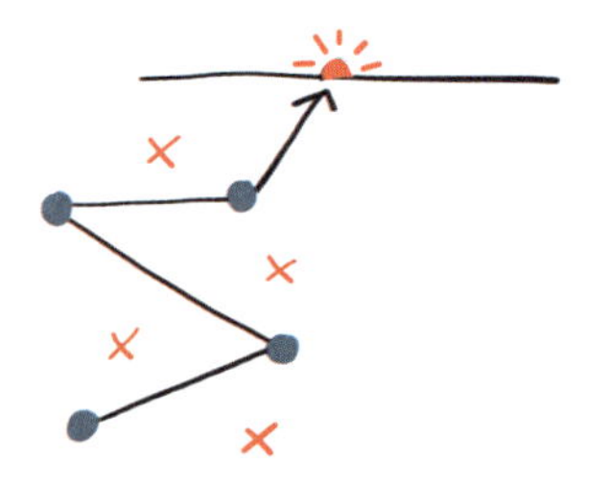

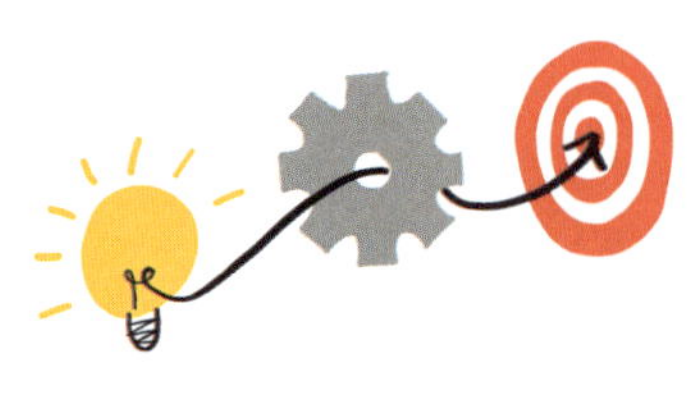

HOW TO DRAW

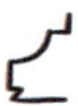

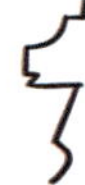

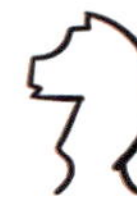

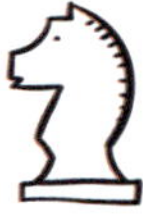

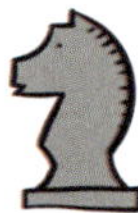

SUCCESS

BASIC ICONS

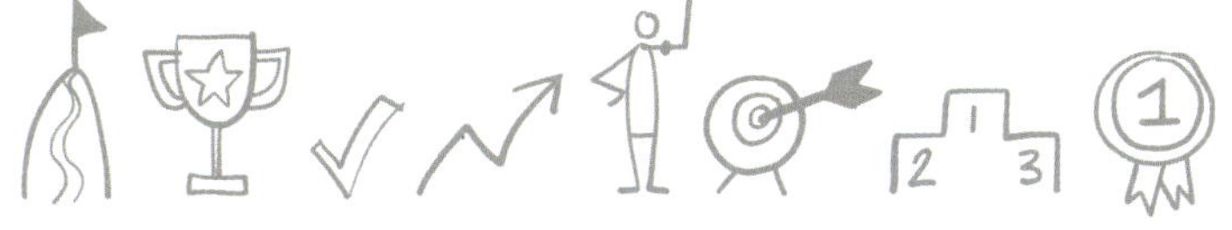

COMBINED ICONS

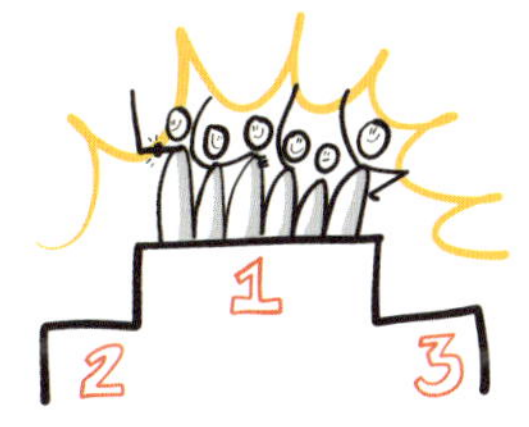

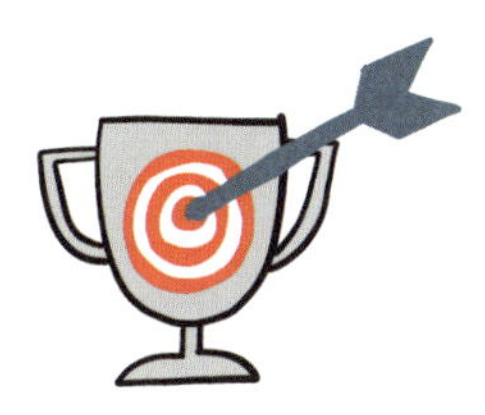

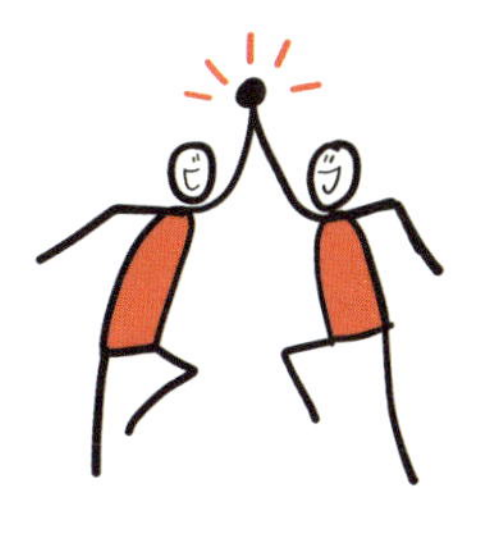

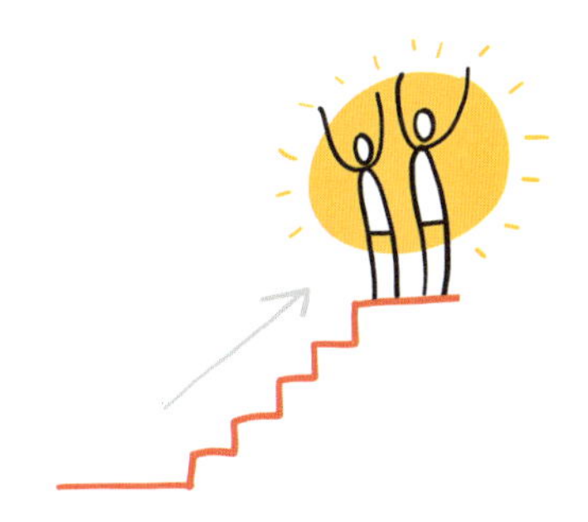

HOW TO DRAW

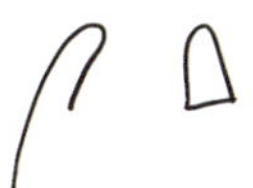

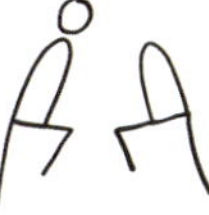

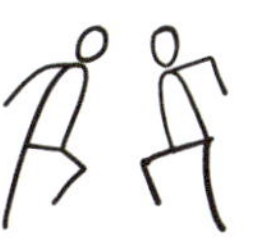

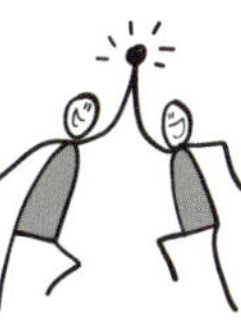

SUSTAINABLE DEVELOPMENT

BASIC ICONS

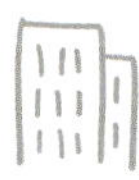

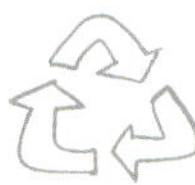
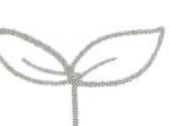
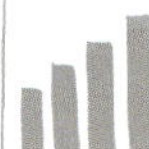
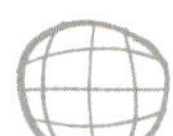
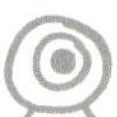

COMBINED ICONS

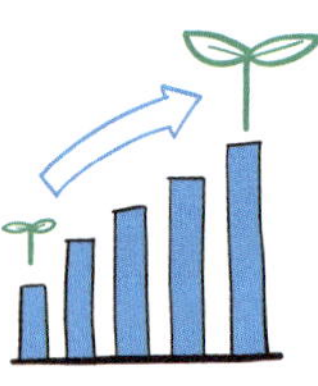
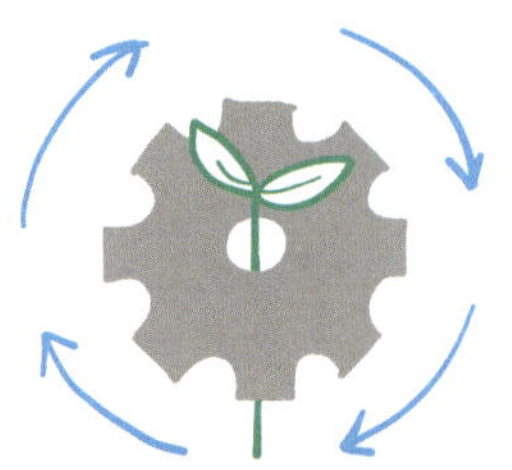
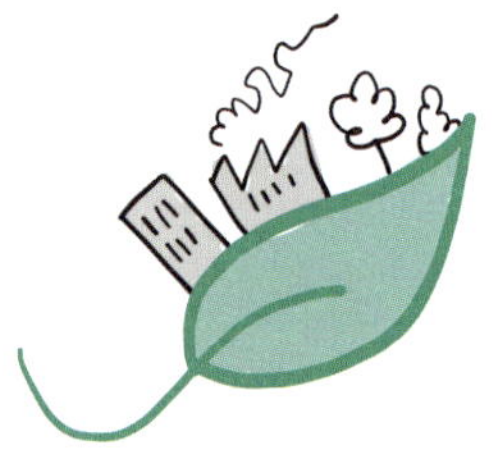
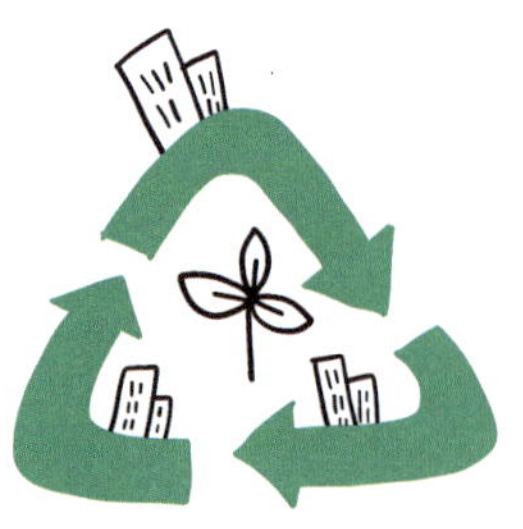

HOW TO DRAW

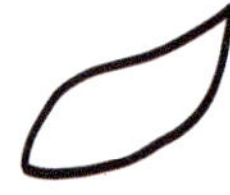
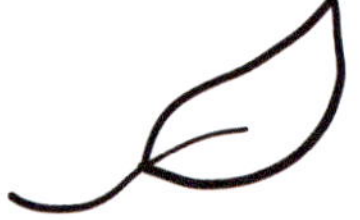
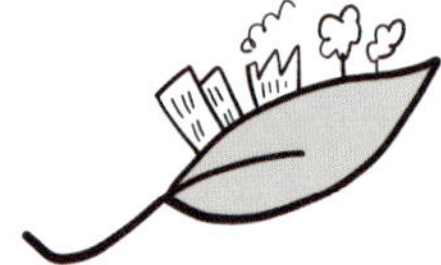

THREAT

BASIC ICONS

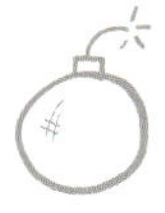
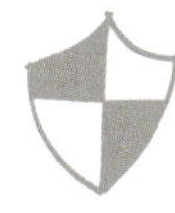
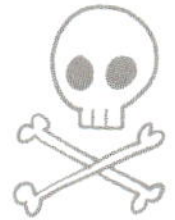
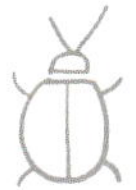
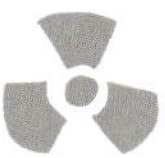

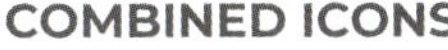

COMBINED ICONS

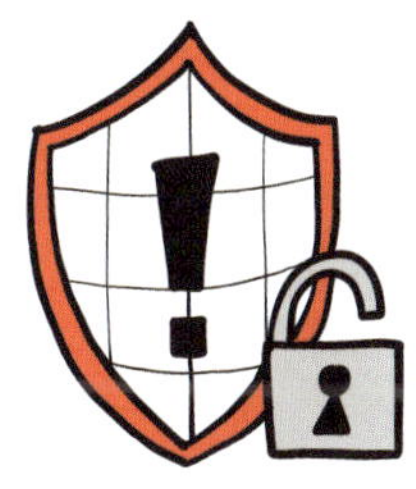
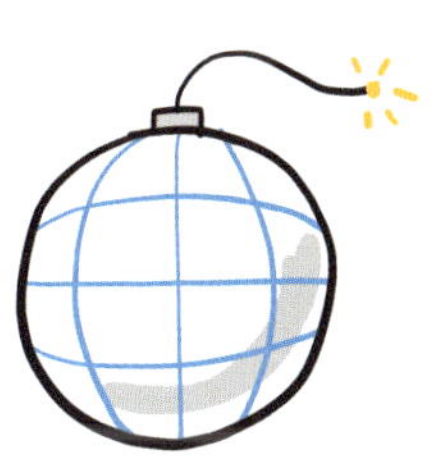

HOW TO DRAW

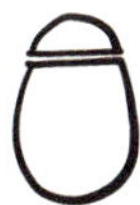
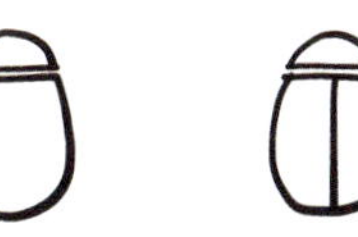
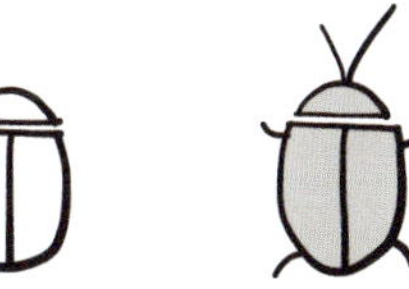

TRANSFORMATION, TRANSITION

BASIC ICONS

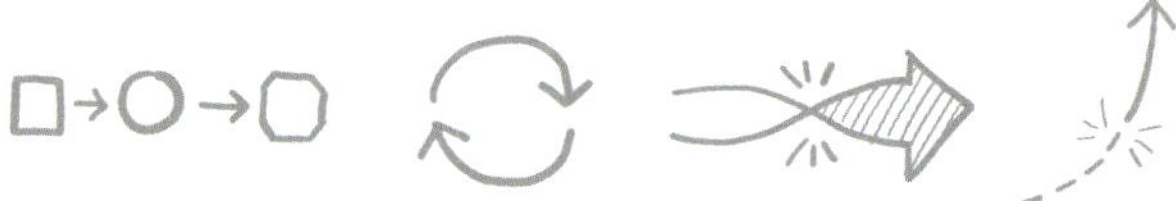

COMBINED ICONS

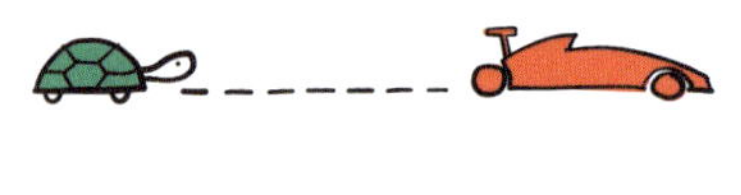

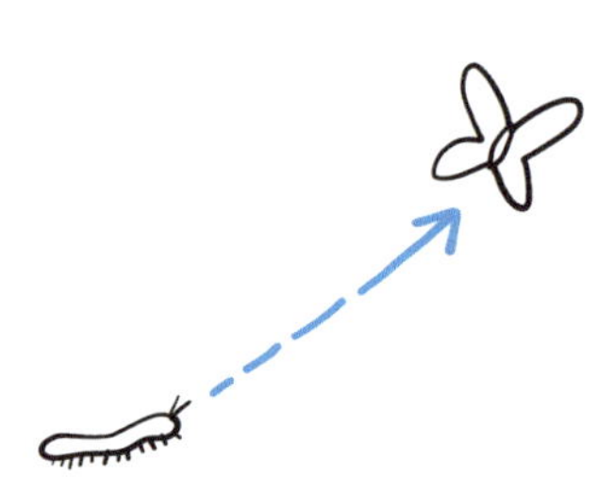

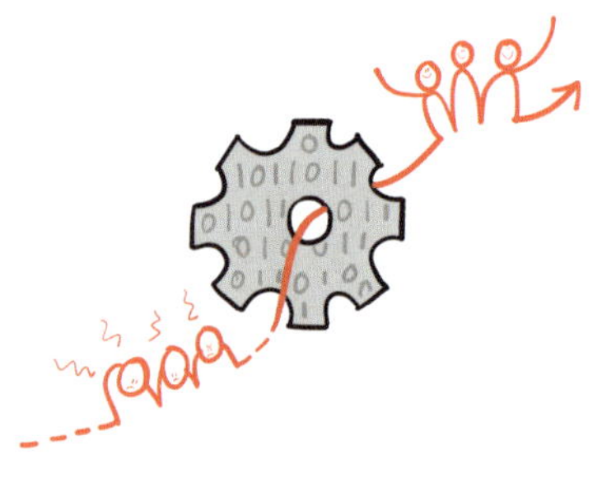

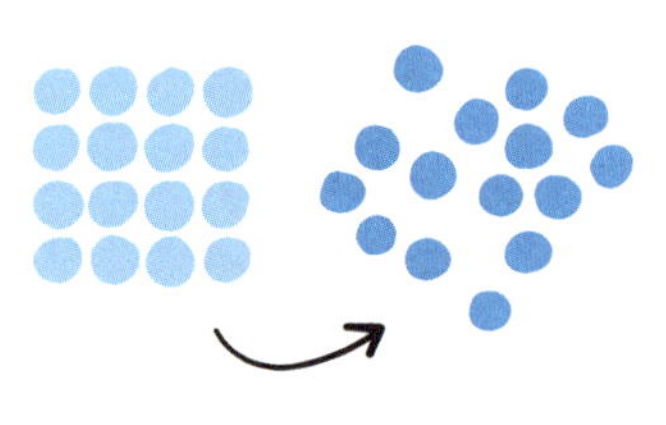

HOW TO DRAW

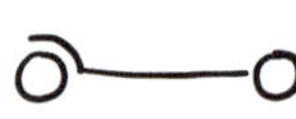

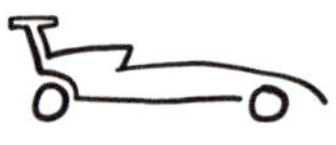

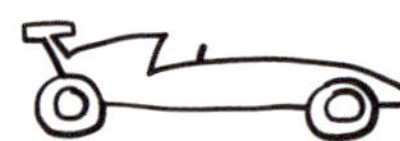

VISION

BASIC ICONS

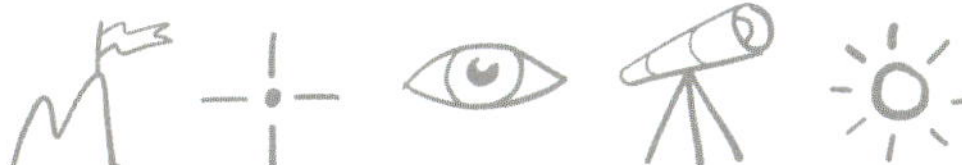

COMBINED ICONS

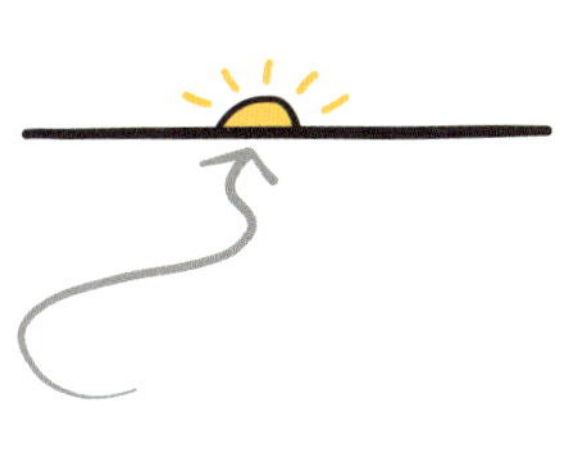

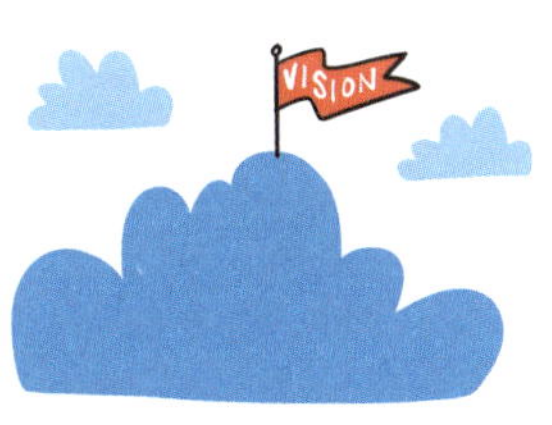

HOW TO DRAW

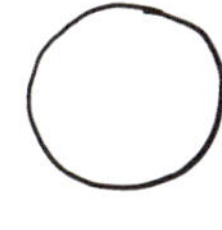

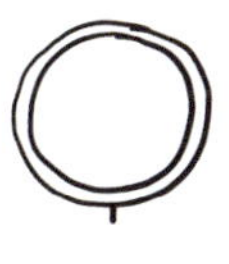

COMPETENCES

OUR SKILLS AND QUALITIES

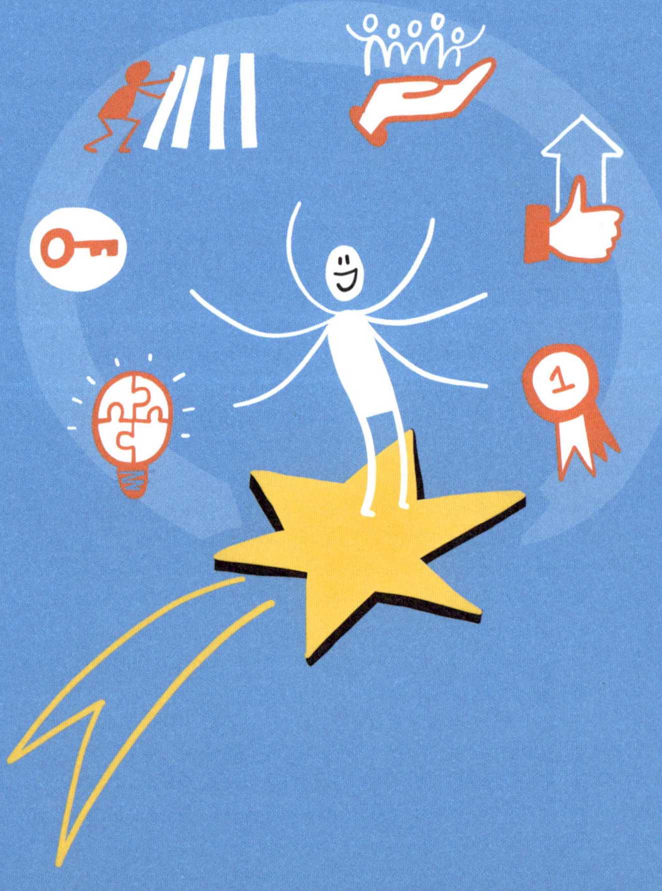

AMBITION

BASIC ICONS

COMBINED ICONS

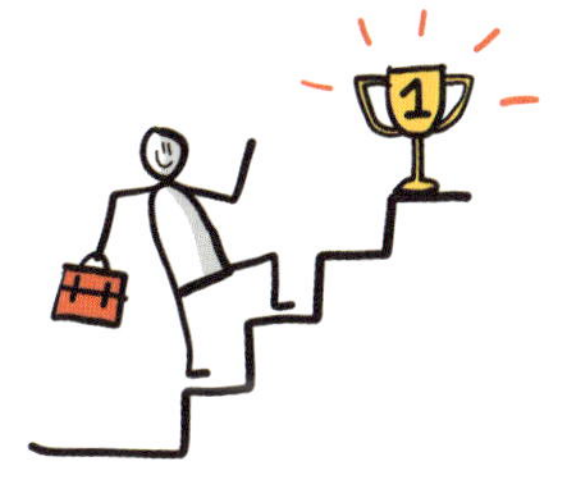

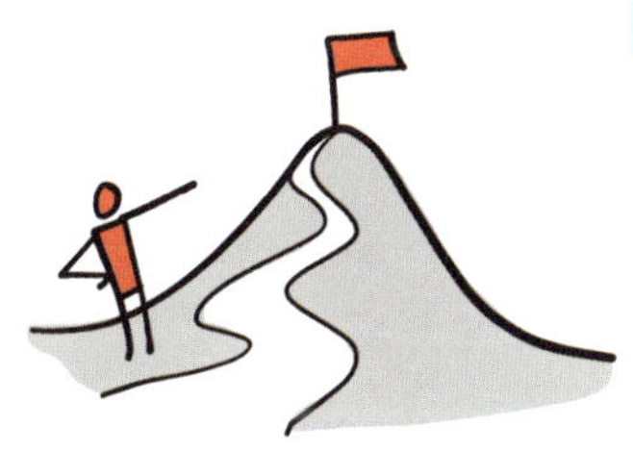

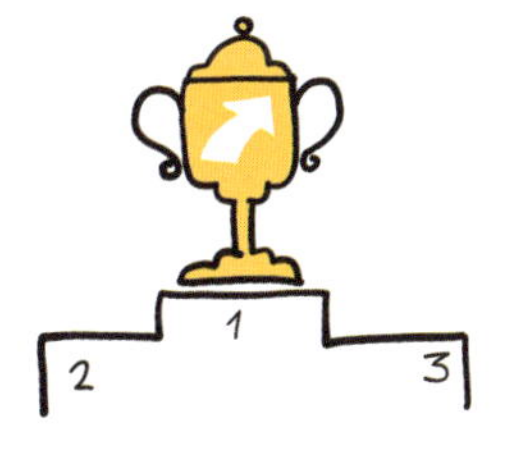

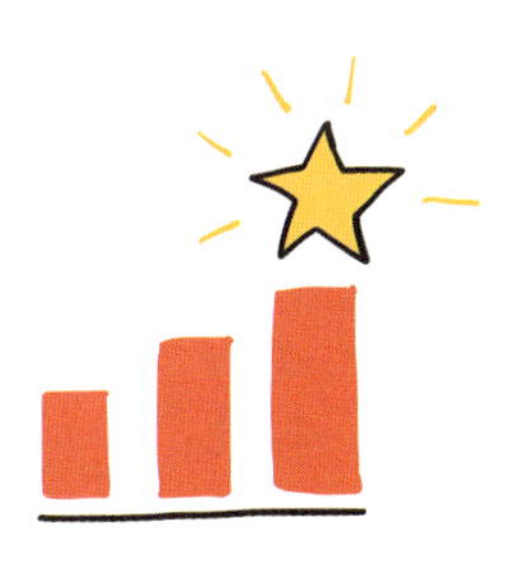

HOW TO DRAW

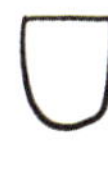
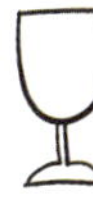
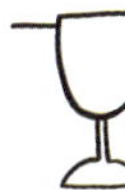

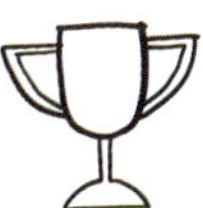

COLLABORATION

BASIC ICONS

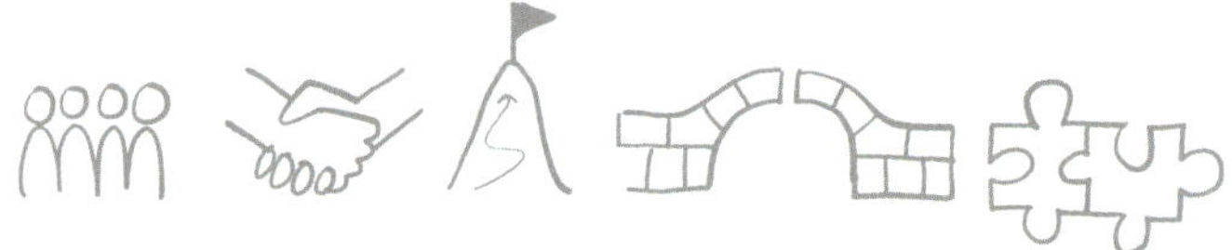

COMBINED ICONS

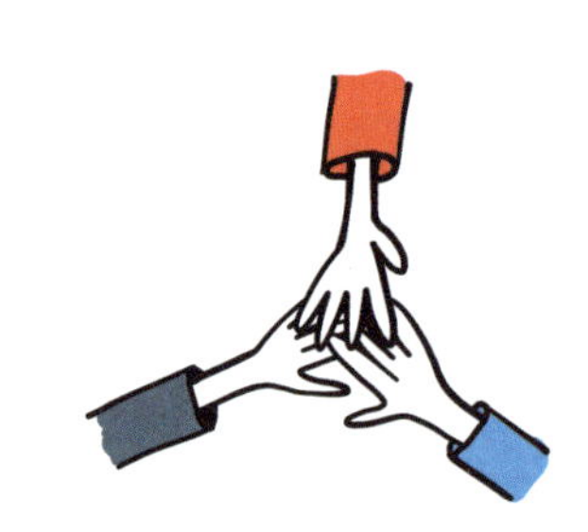

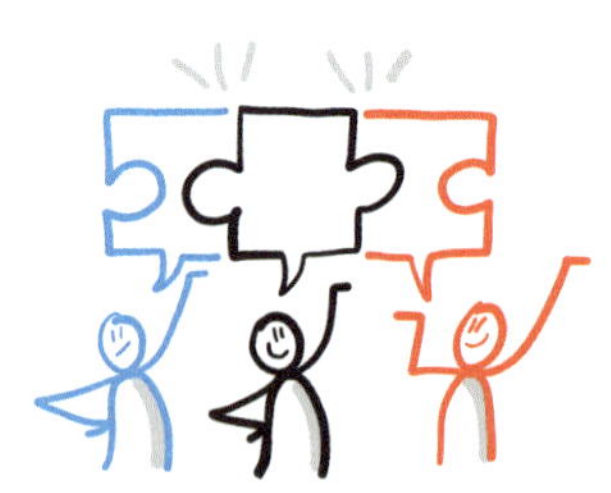

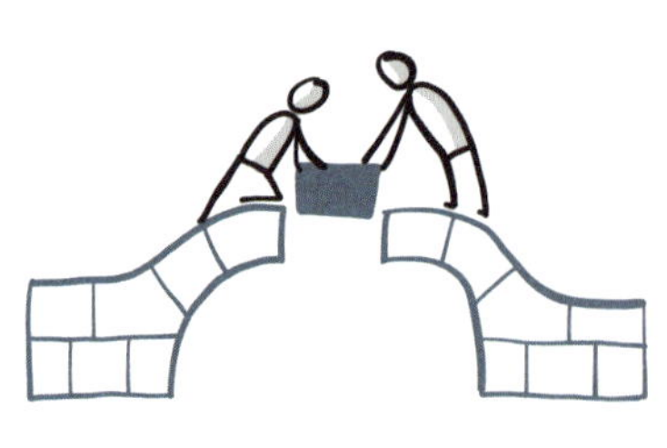

HOW TO DRAW

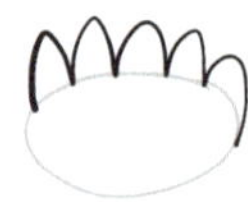

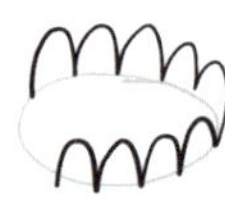

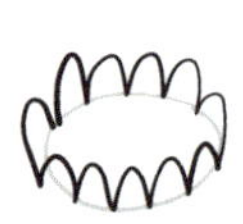

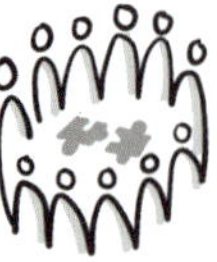

EMPATHY

BASIC ICONS

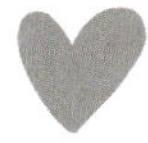

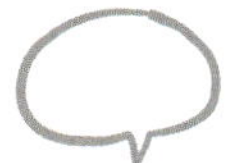
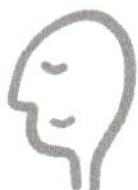
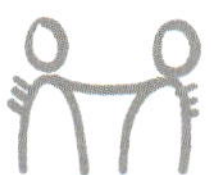

COMBINED ICONS

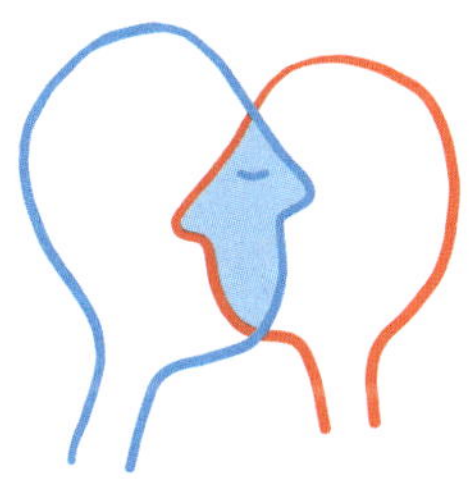

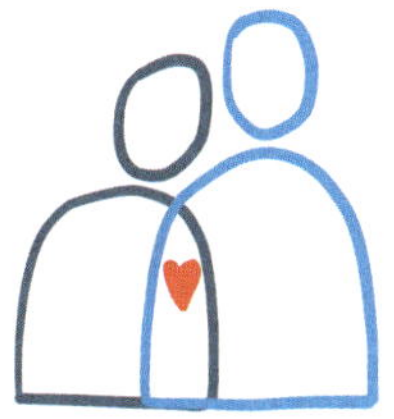

HOW TO DRAW

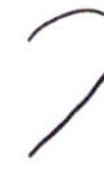
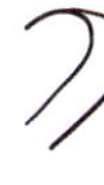
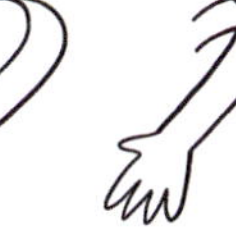
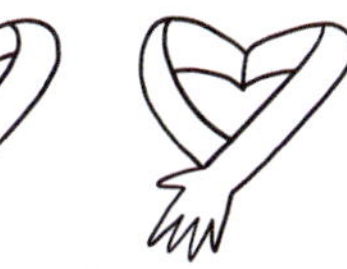

ENGAGEMENT

BASIC ICONS

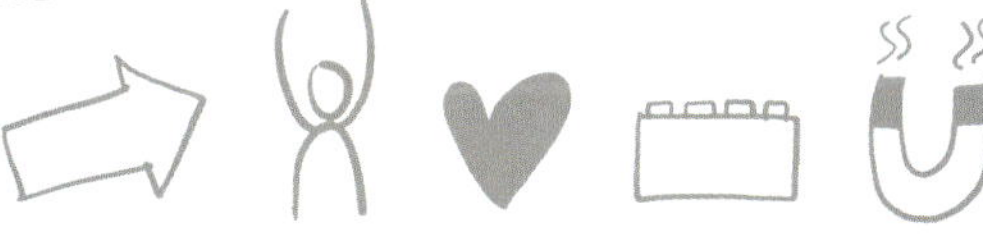

COMBINED ICONS

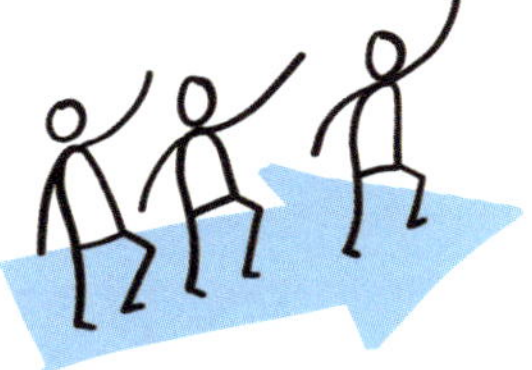

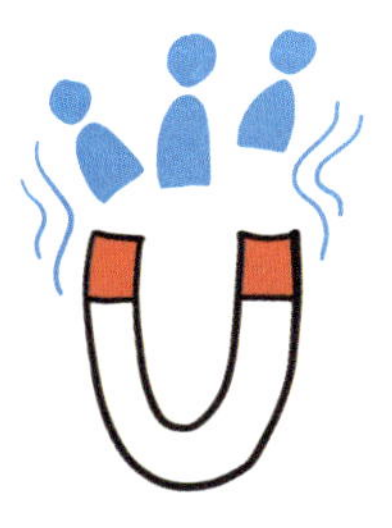

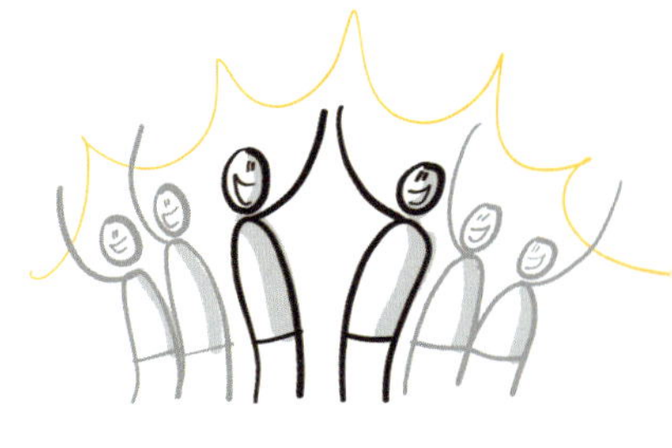

HOW TO DRAW

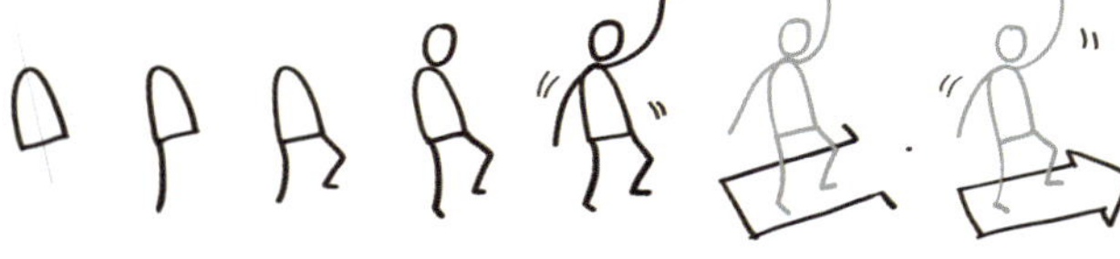

ENTREPRENEURIAL

BASIC ICONS

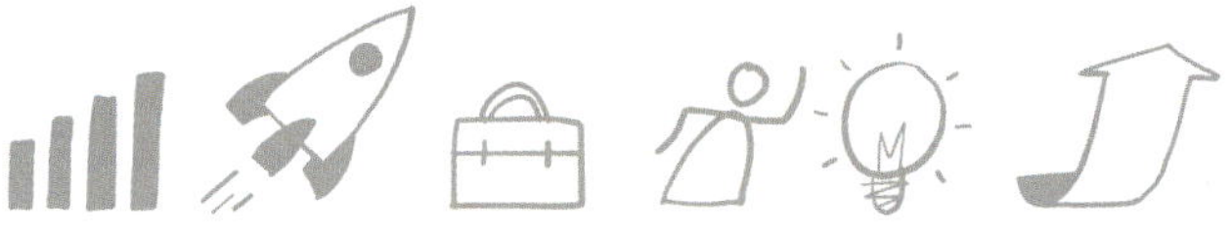

Competences

COMBINED ICONS

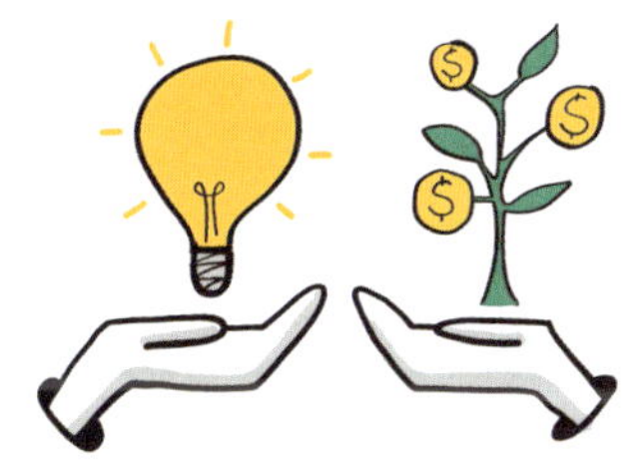

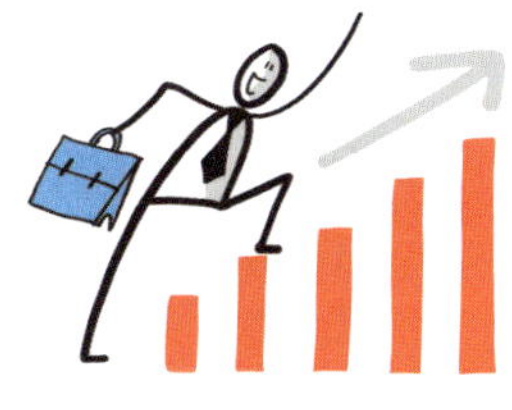

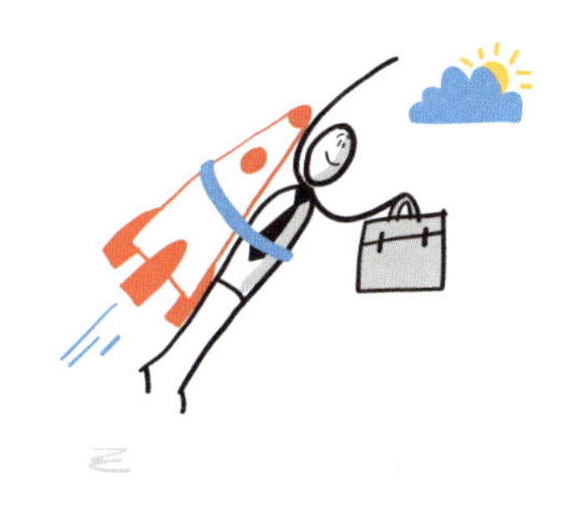

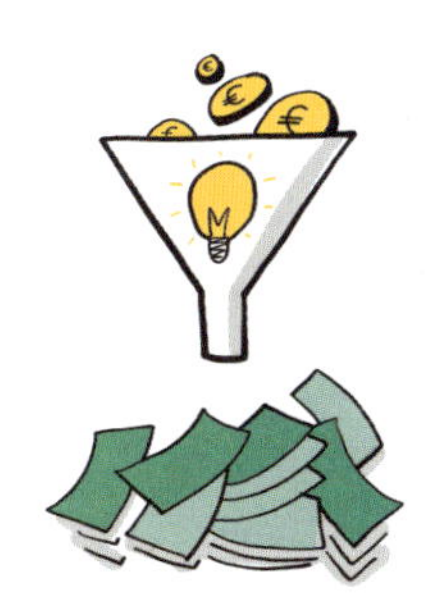

HOW TO DRAW

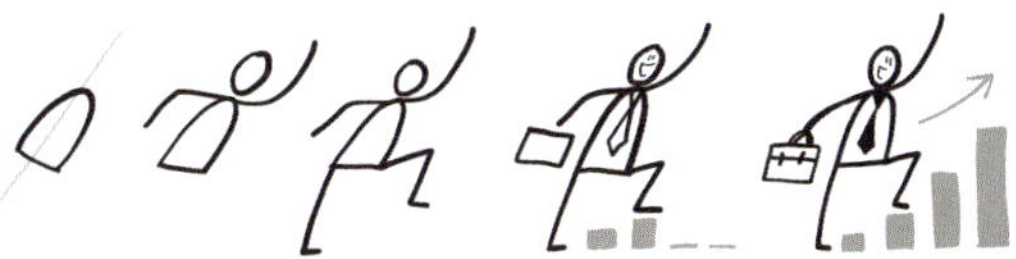

ENVIRONMENTAL RESPONSIBILITY

BASIC ICONS

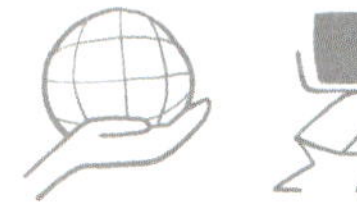
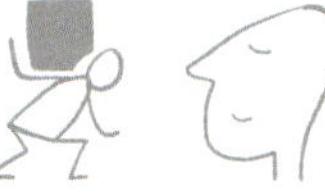
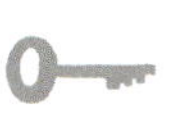
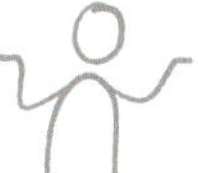

COMBINED ICONS

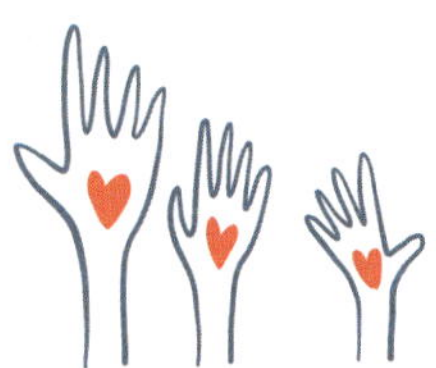
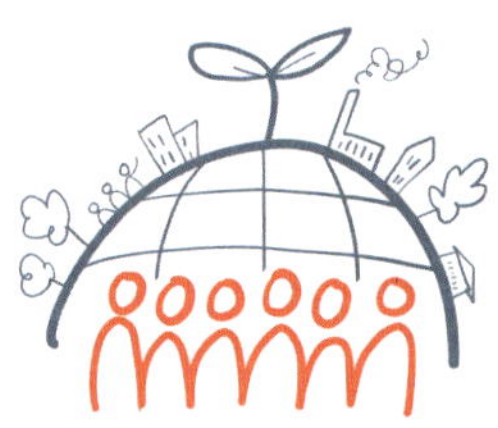
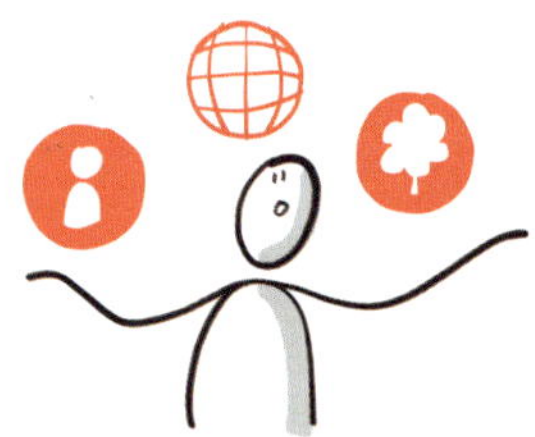
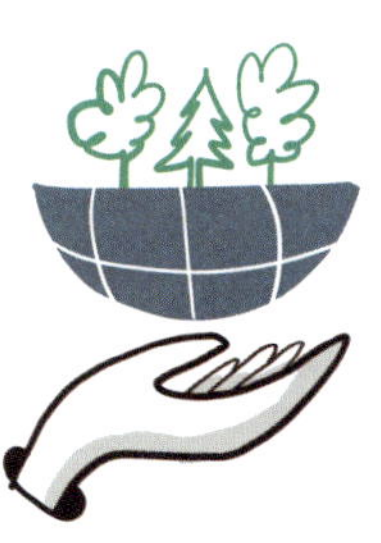

HOW TO DRAW

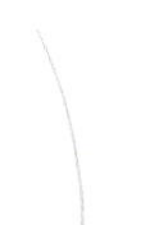
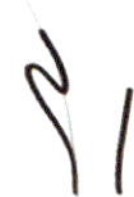
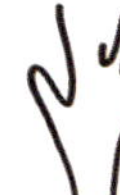
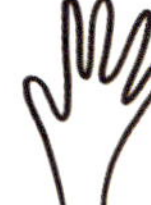
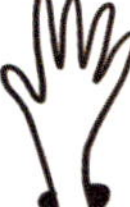

EXCELLENCE

BASIC ICONS

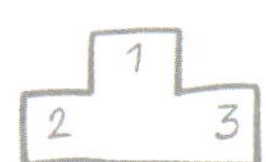

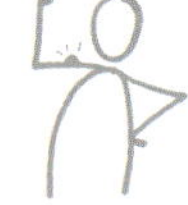
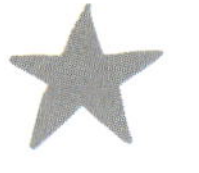
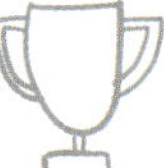
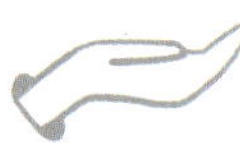

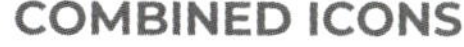

COMBINED ICONS

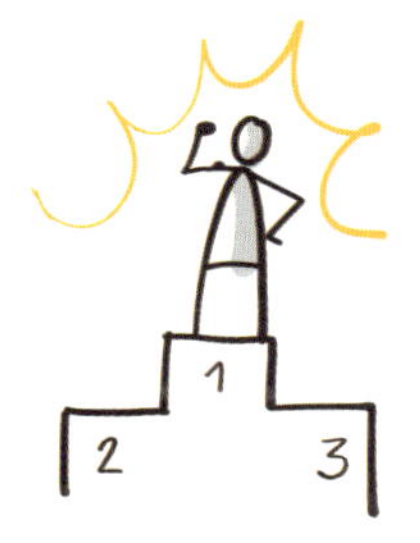

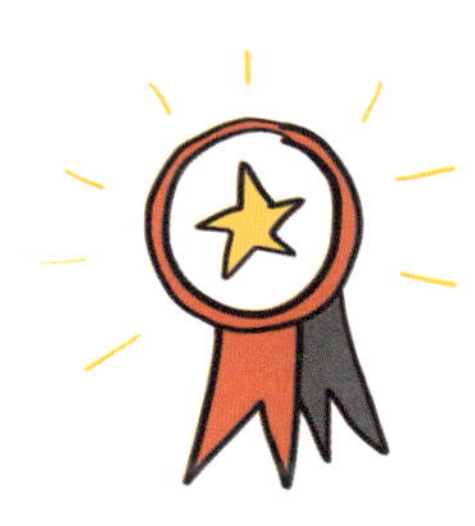
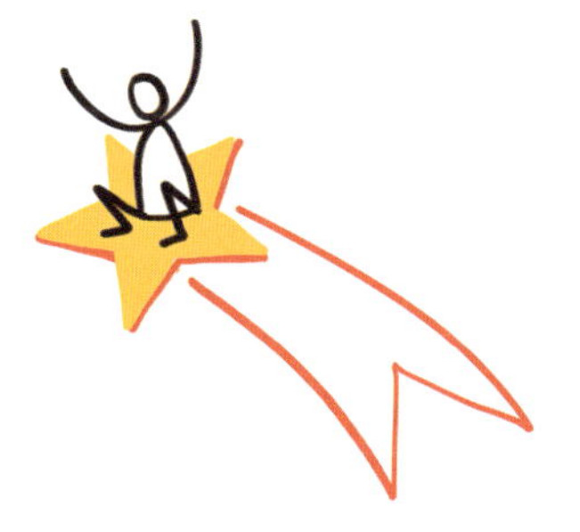
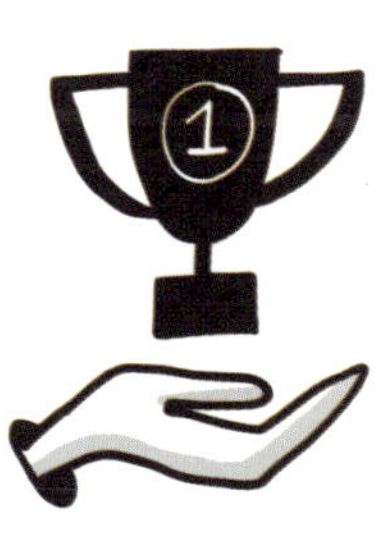

HOW TO DRAW

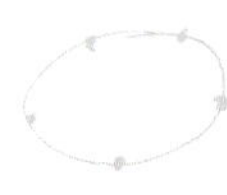
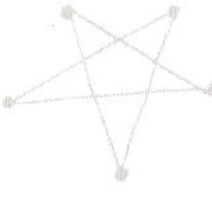

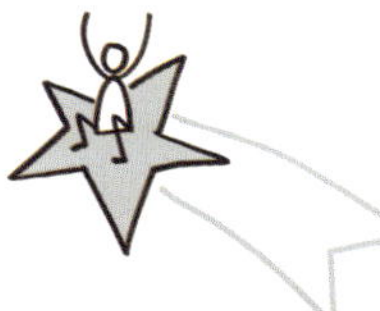

EXPERTISE, KNOWLEDGE

BASIC ICONS

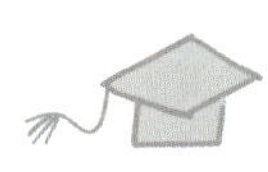 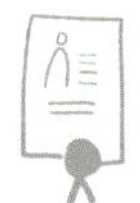 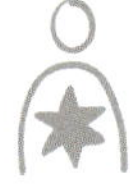 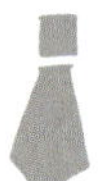 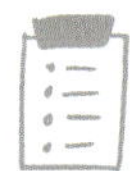 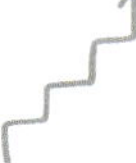 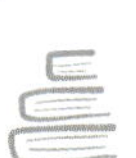

COMBINED ICONS

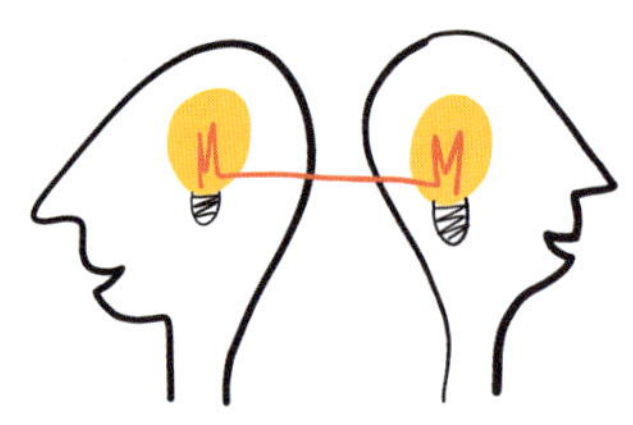

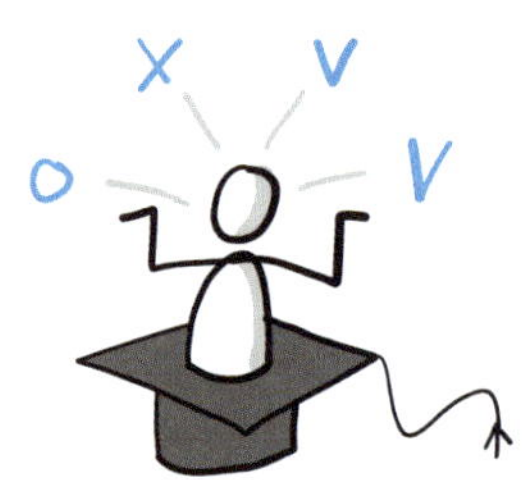

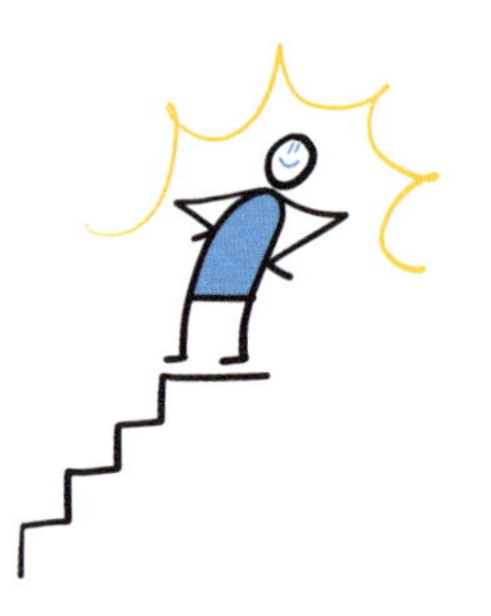

HOW TO DRAW

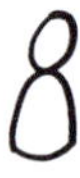   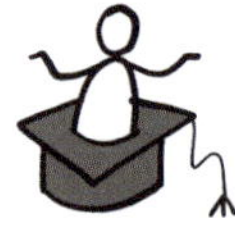

FLEXIBILITY

BASIC ICONS

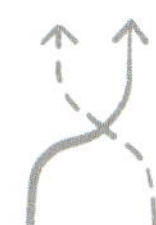 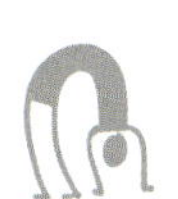 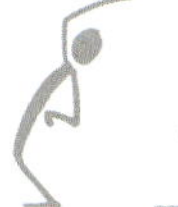  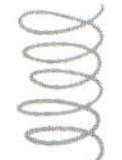 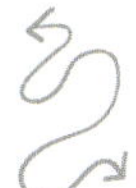

Competences

COMBINED ICONS

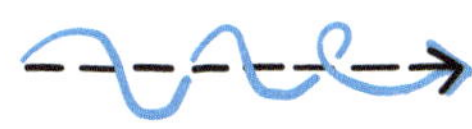

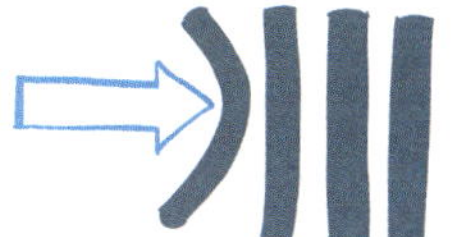

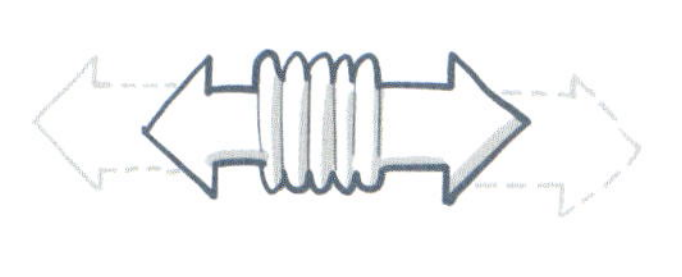

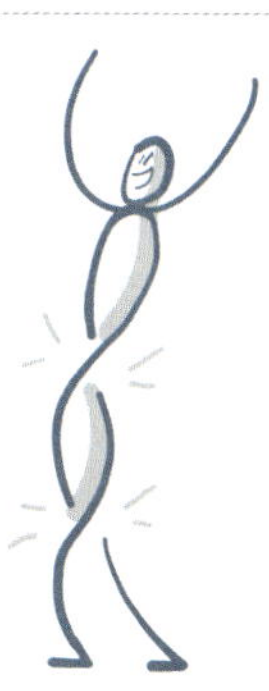

HOW TO DRAW

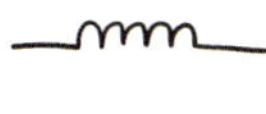

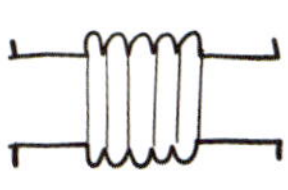

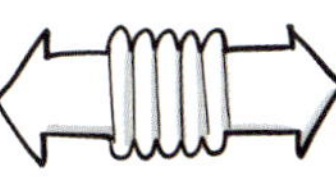

HELPING OTHERS

BASIC ICONS

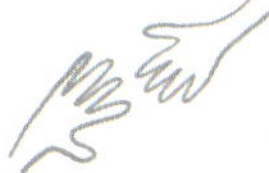

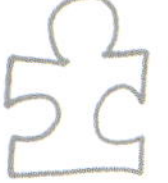
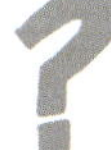
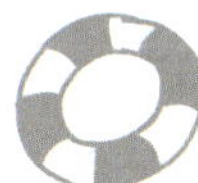

COMBINED ICONS

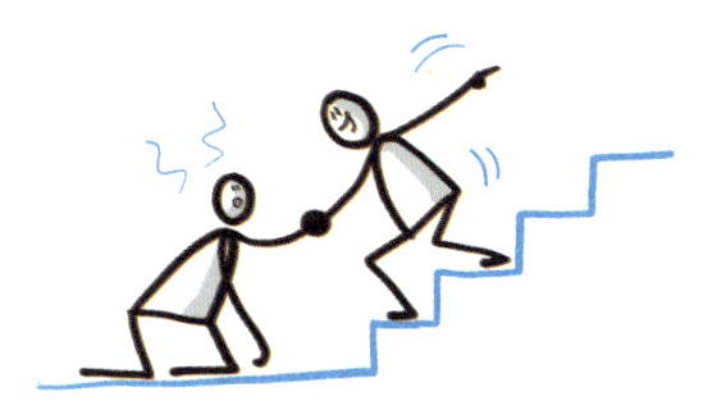
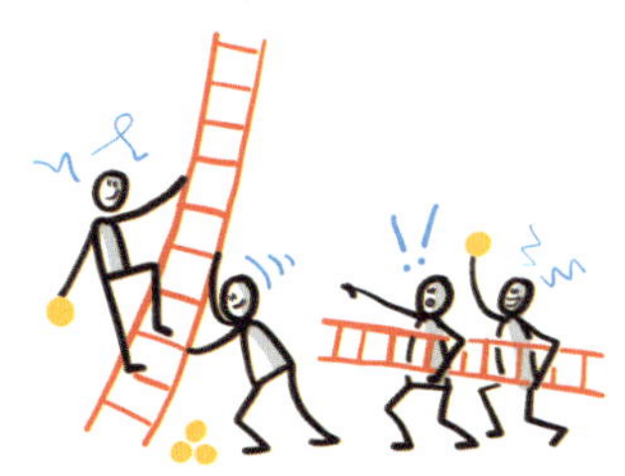
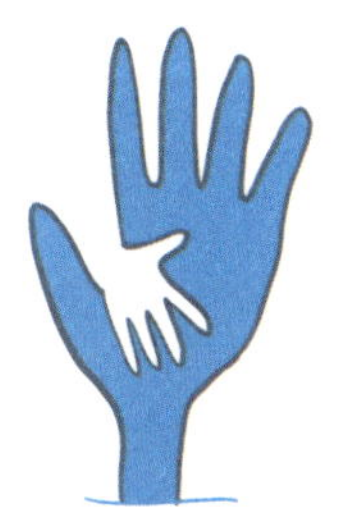

HOW TO DRAW

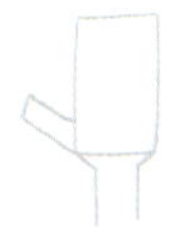
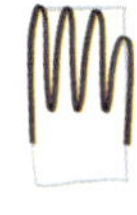
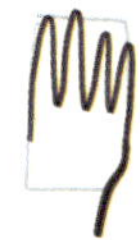
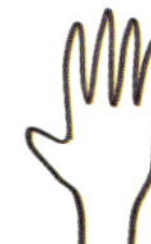
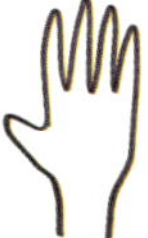
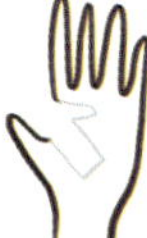
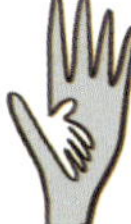

INTEGRITY

BASIC ICONS

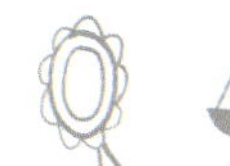
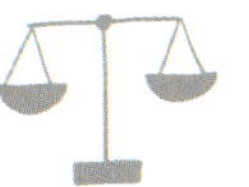
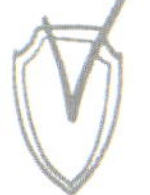
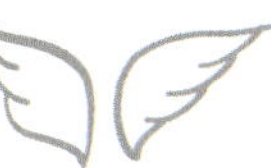
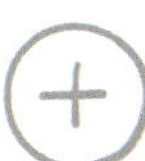
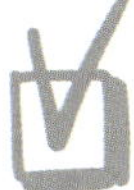

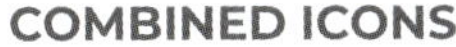

COMBINED ICONS

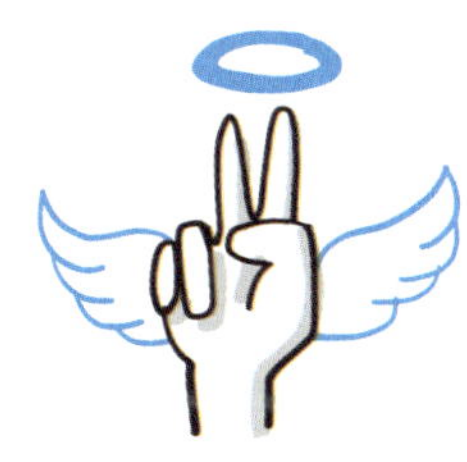
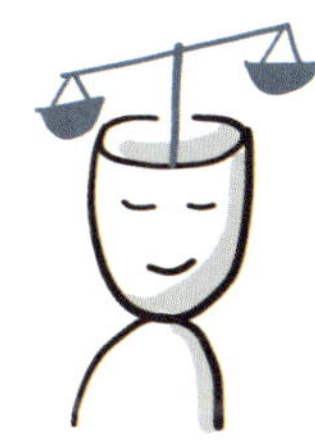
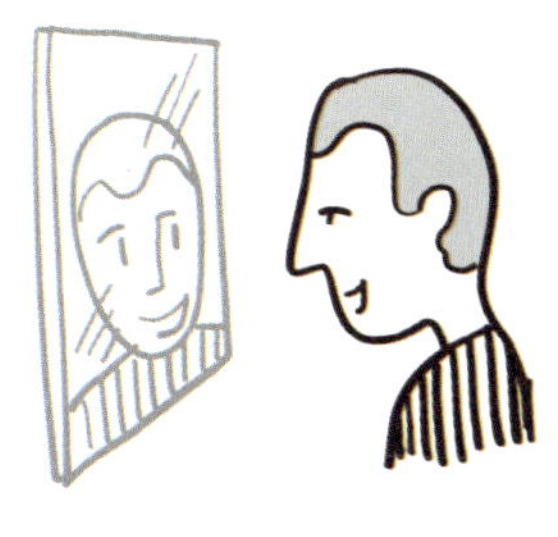
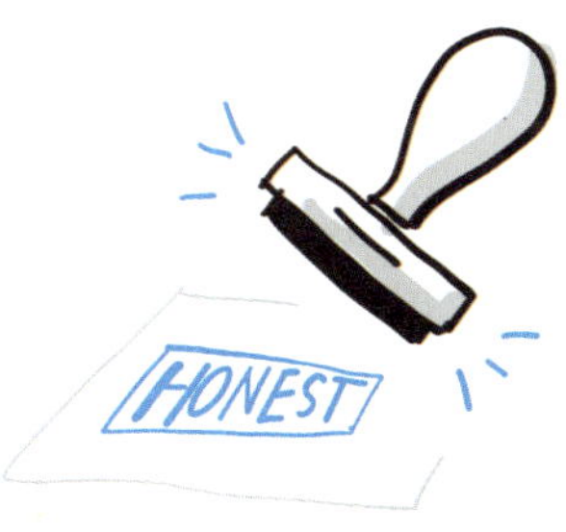

HOW TO DRAW

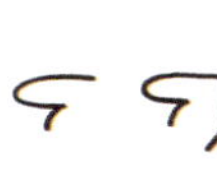
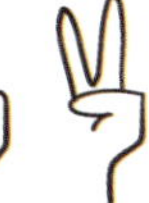
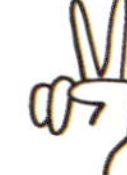
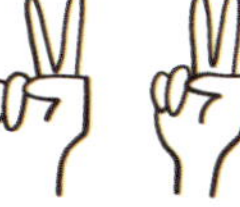
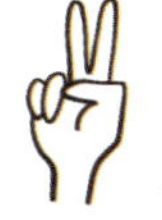
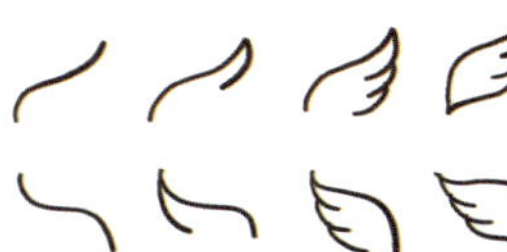

JOY, HAPPINESS

BASIC ICONS

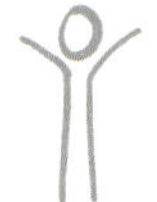

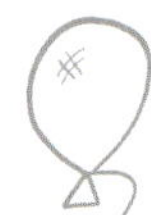

COMBINED ICONS

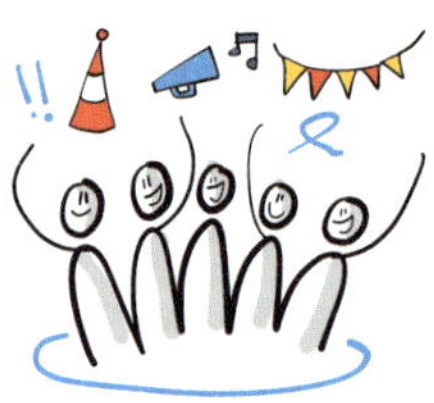

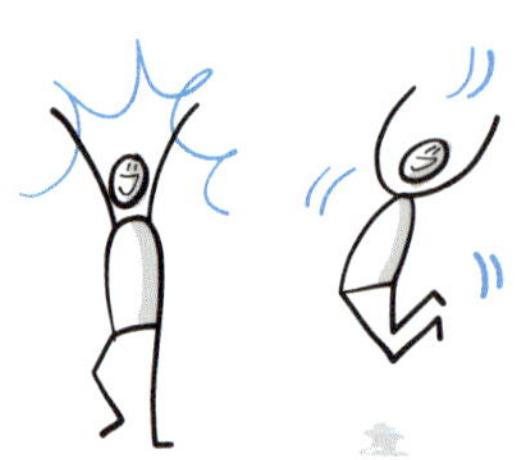
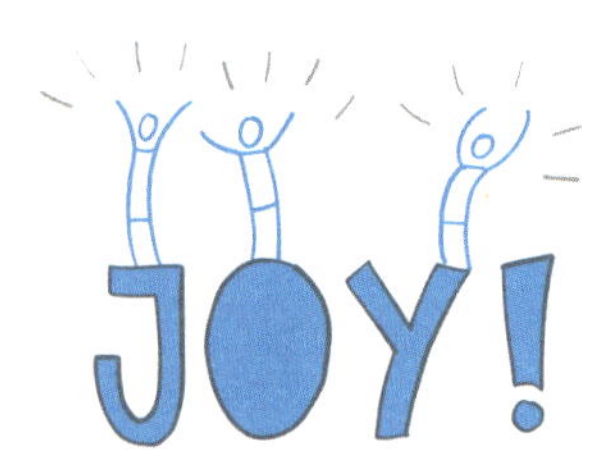

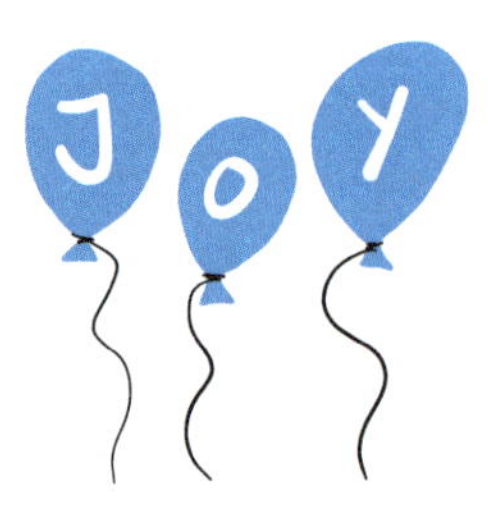

HOW TO DRAW

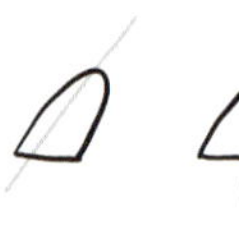
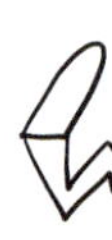
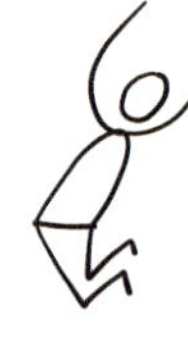
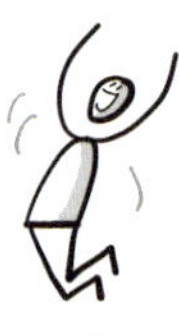

LEADERSHIP

BASIC ICONS

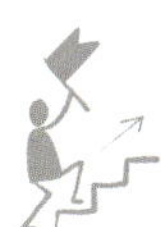
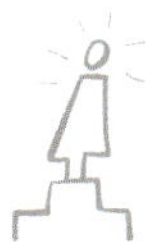
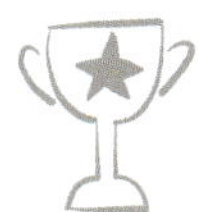
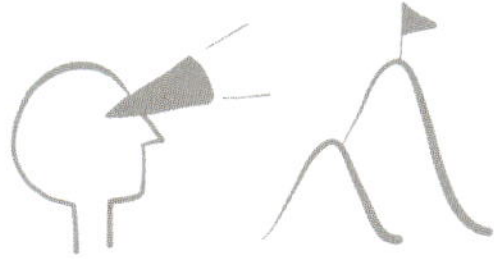

COMBINED ICONS

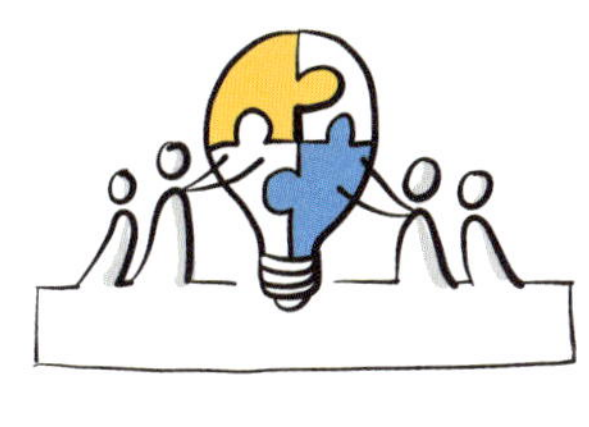

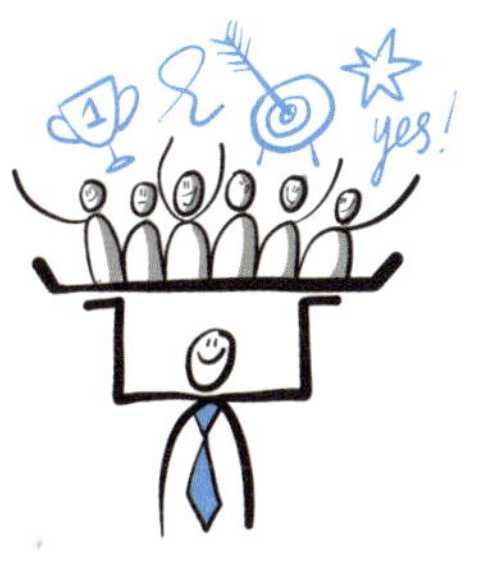

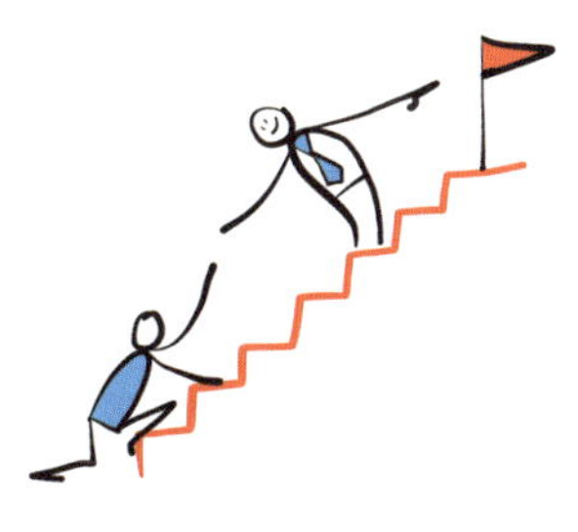

HOW TO DRAW

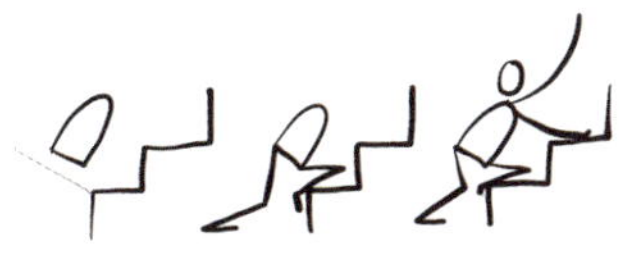

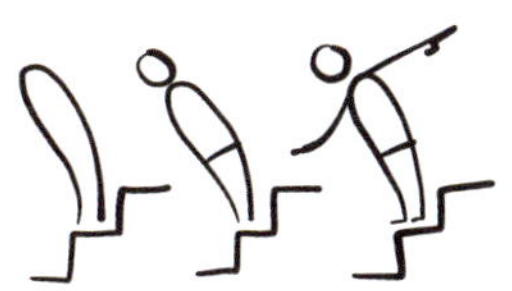

LOYALTY

BASIC ICONS

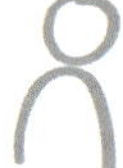
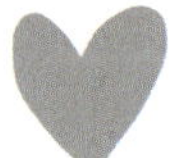

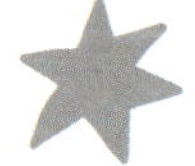
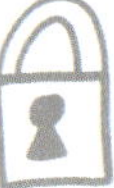
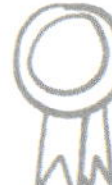
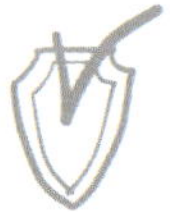

COMBINED ICONS

HOW TO DRAW

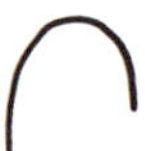
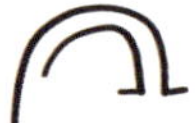
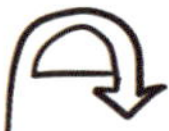
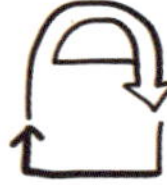

MOTIVATION

BASIC ICONS

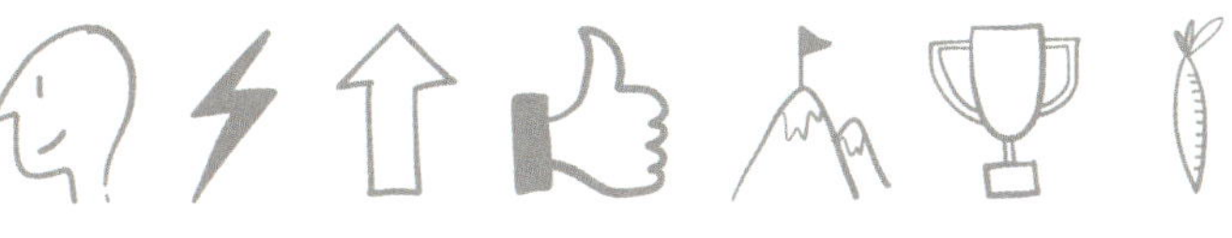

Competences

COMBINED ICONS

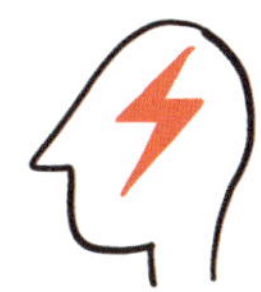

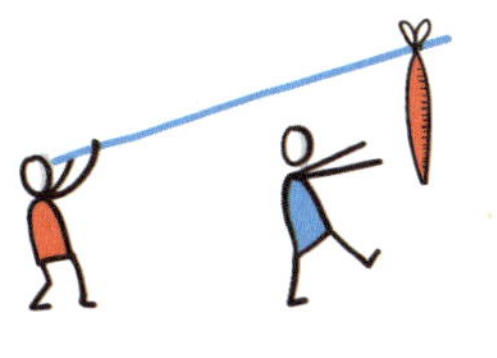

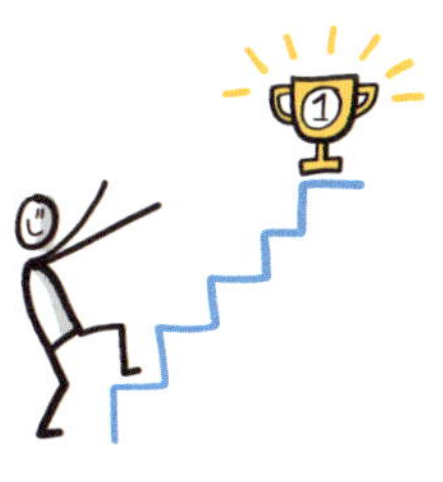

HOW TO DRAW

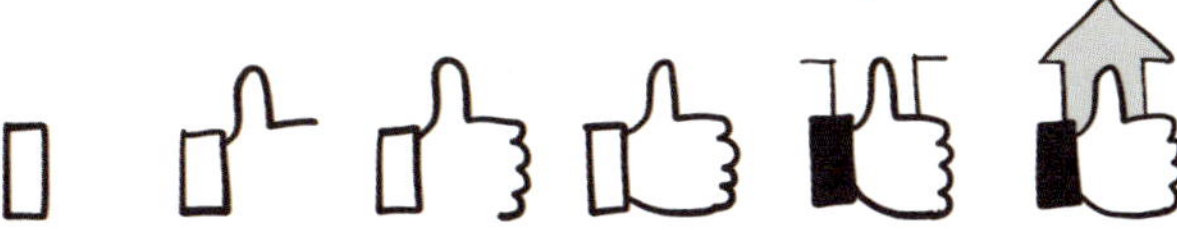

PASSION

BASIC ICONS

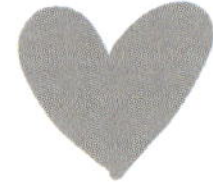

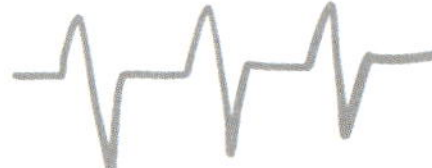

COMBINED ICONS

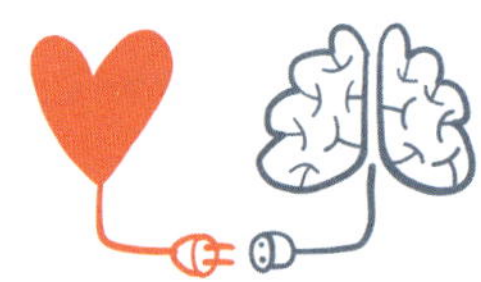
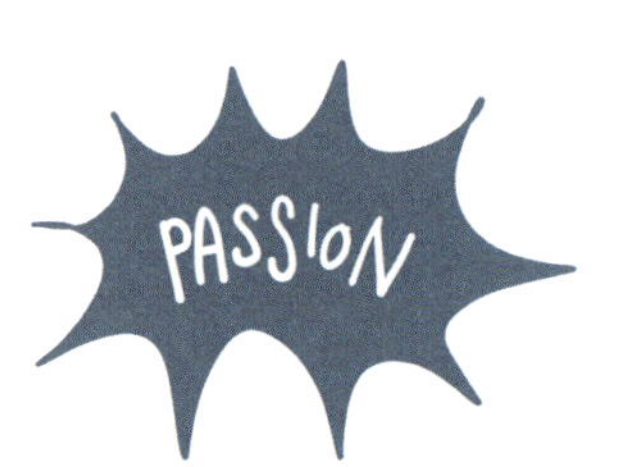

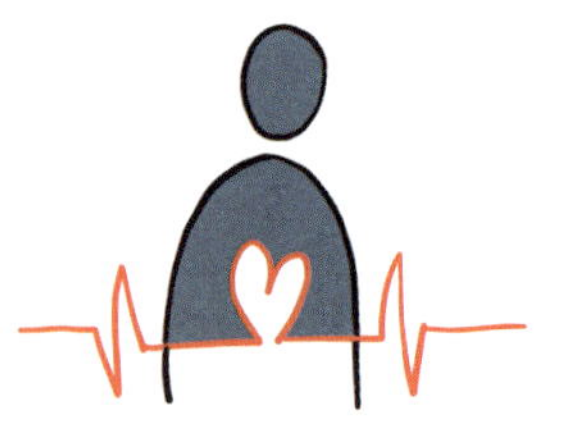
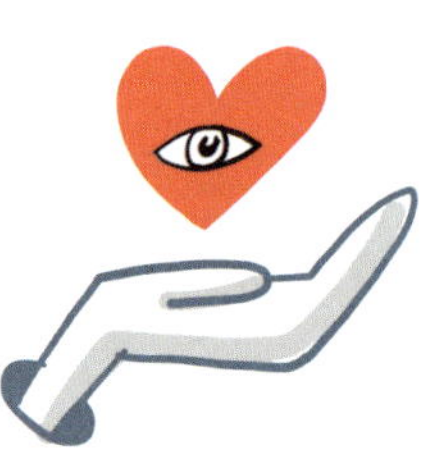

HOW TO DRAW

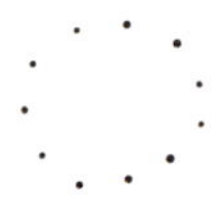
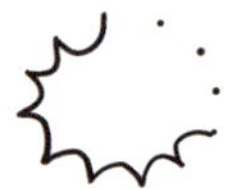
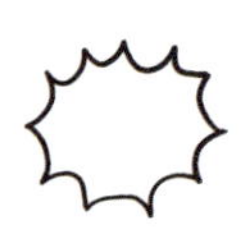
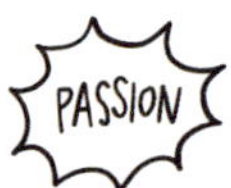

PROFESSIONAL

BASIC ICONS

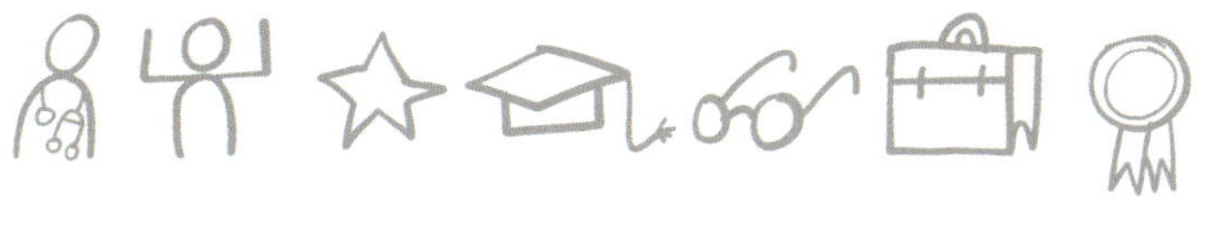

COMBINED ICONS

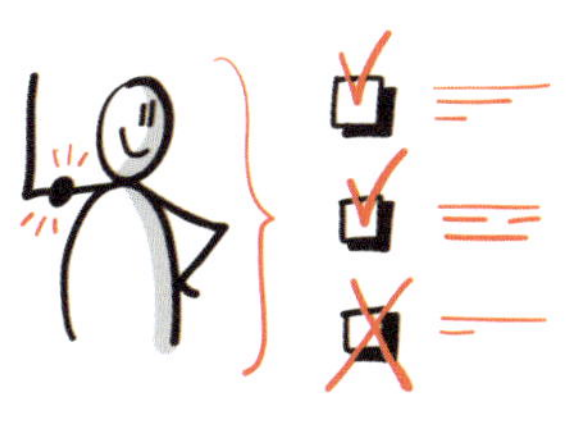

HOW TO DRAW

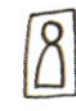

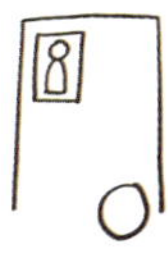

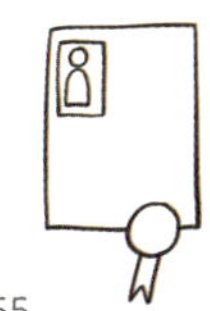

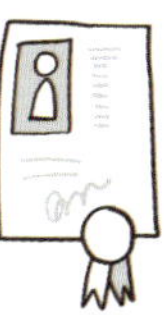

SHOWING INITIATIVE, PROACTIVE

BASIC ICONS

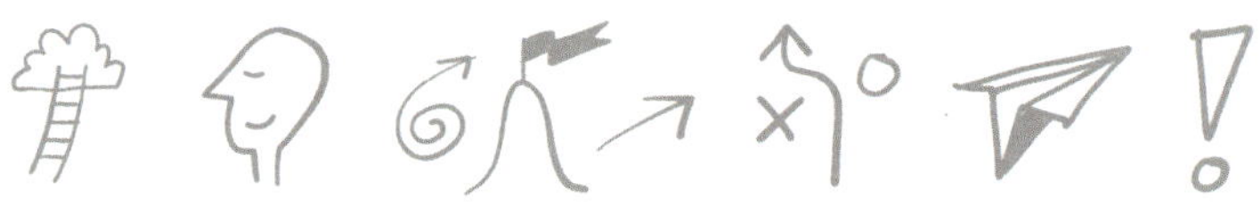

COMBINED ICONS

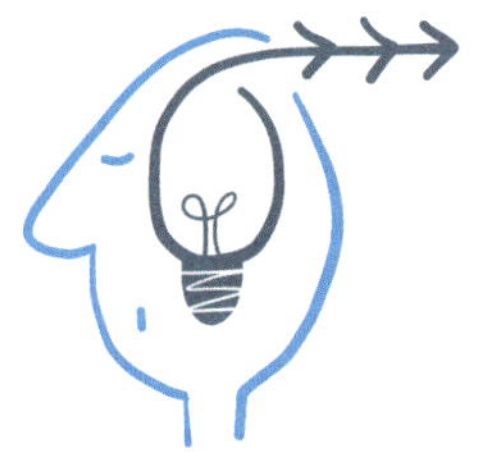

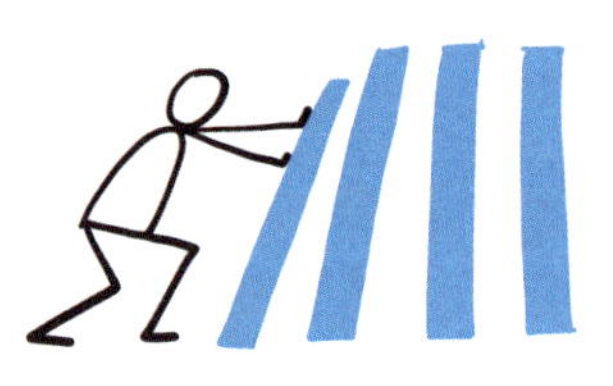

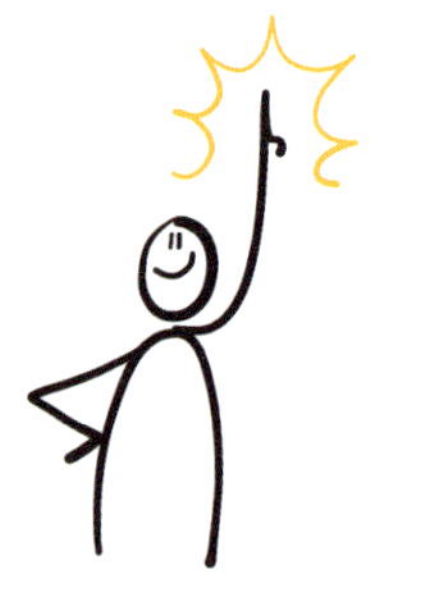

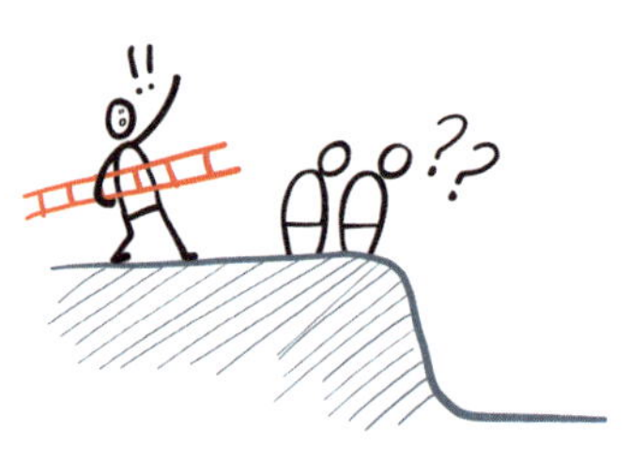

HOW TO DRAW

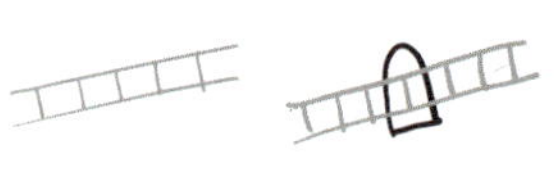

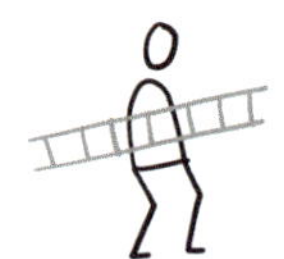

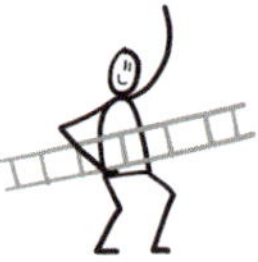

SOFT SKILLS

BASIC ICONS

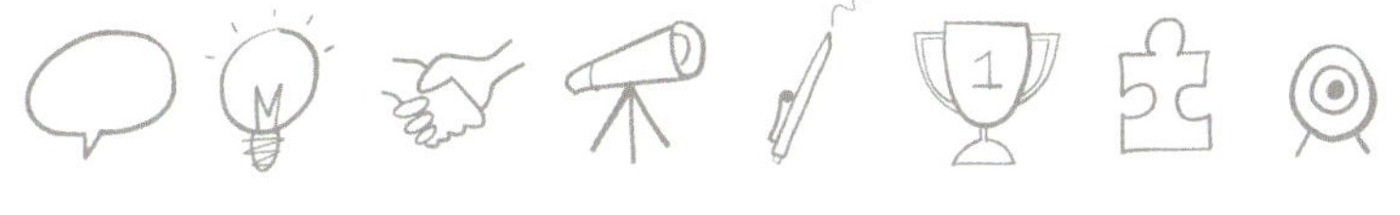

Competences

COMBINED ICONS

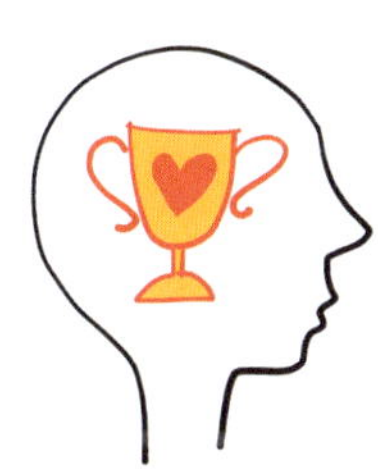

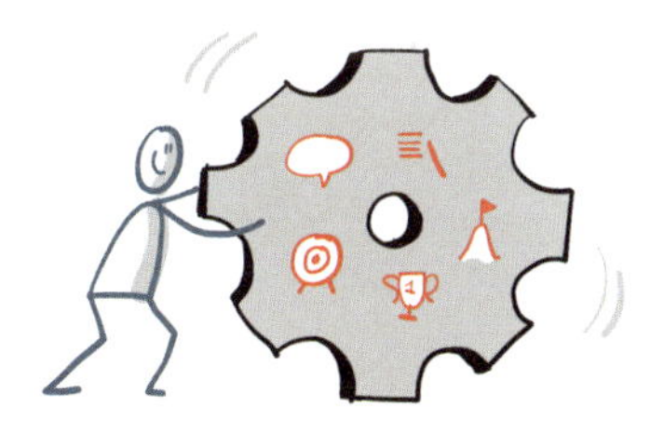

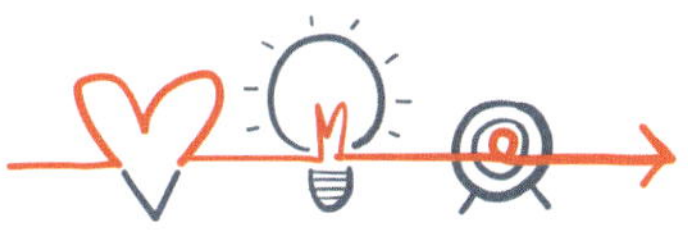

HOW TO DRAW

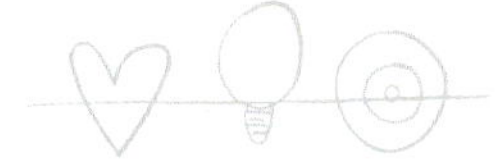

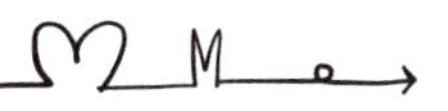

SUPPORTIVE

BASIC ICONS

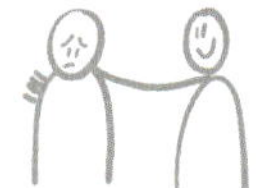 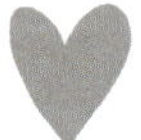 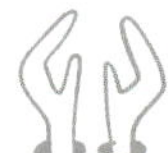 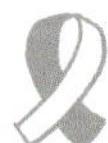 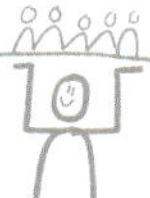  

COMBINED ICONS

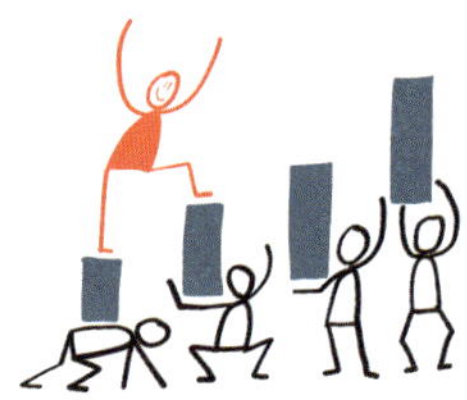

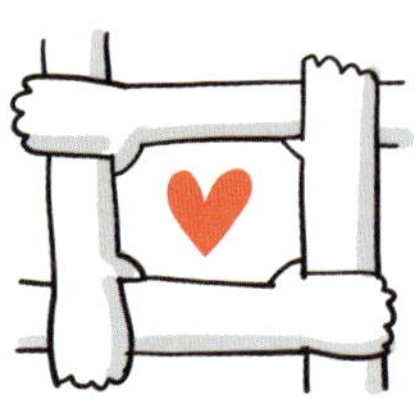

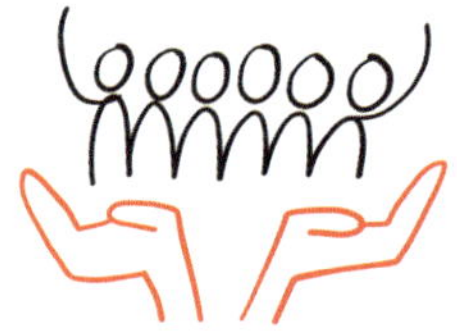

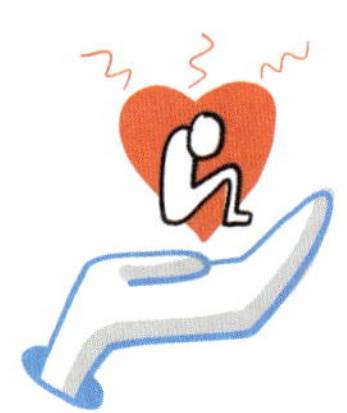

HOW TO DRAW

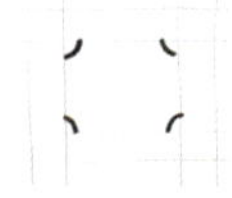 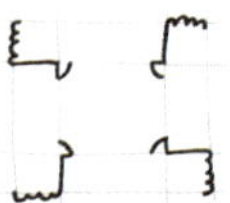 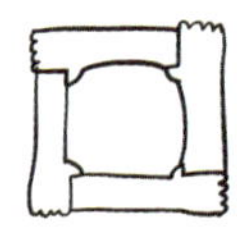 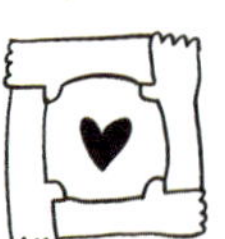

TRANSPARENCY

BASIC ICONS

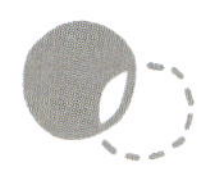
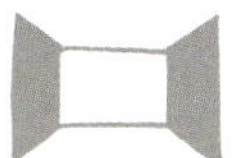
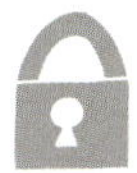
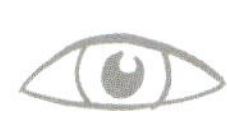
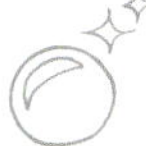
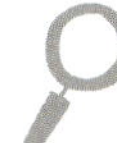

Competences

COMBINED ICONS

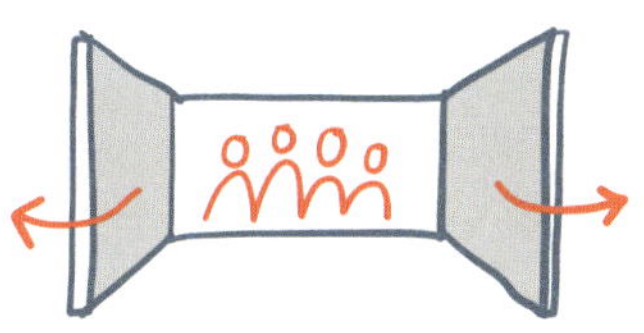

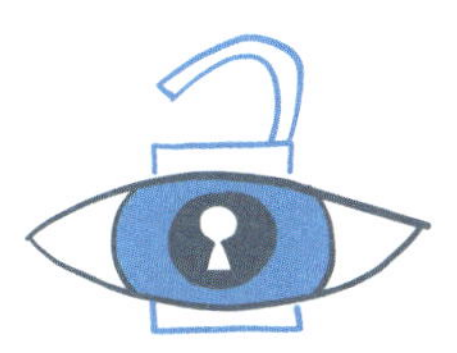

HOW TO DRAW

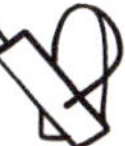
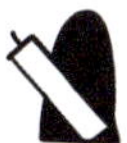

DAILY WORK

WHAT WE DO ALL DAY

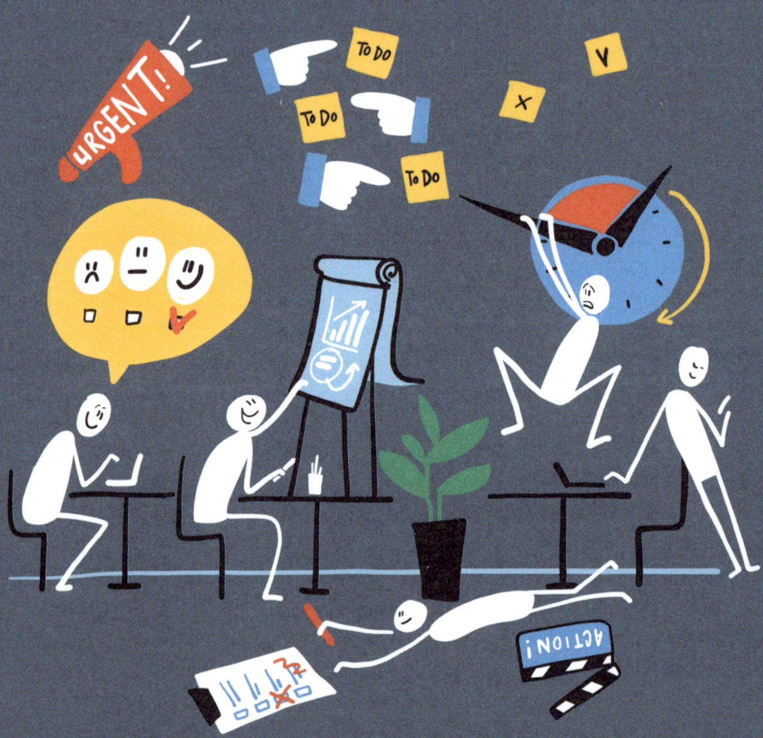

ACHIEVEMENT

BASIC ICONS

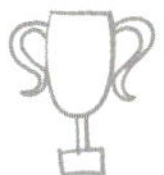
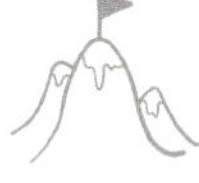
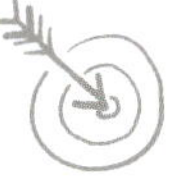
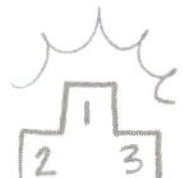

COMBINED ICONS

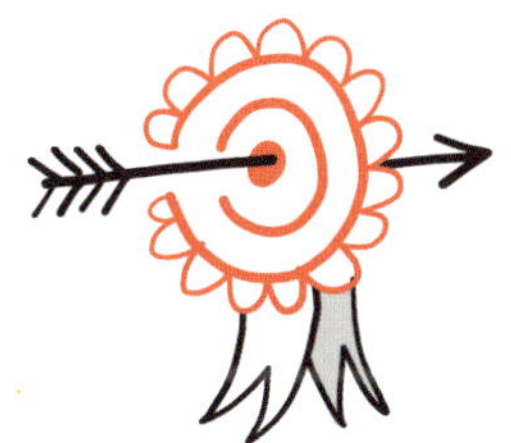
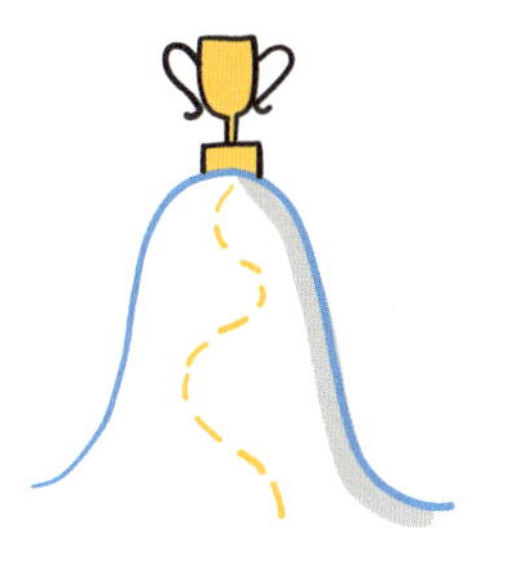
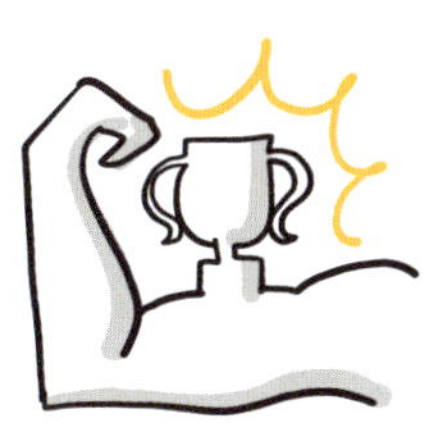

HOW TO DRAW

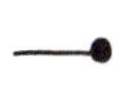
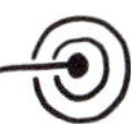
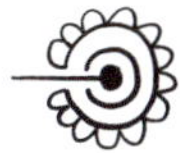

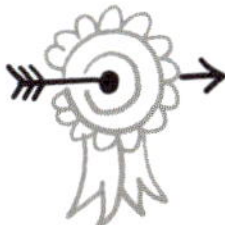

ACTION

BASIC ICONS

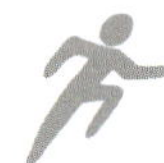
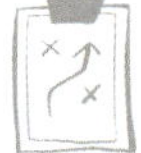

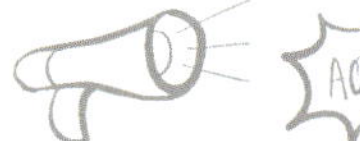
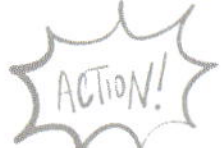

COMBINED ICONS

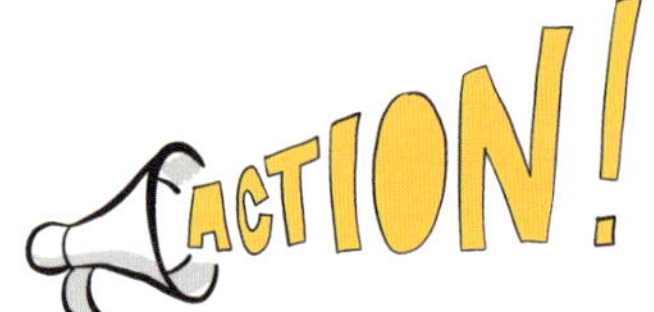

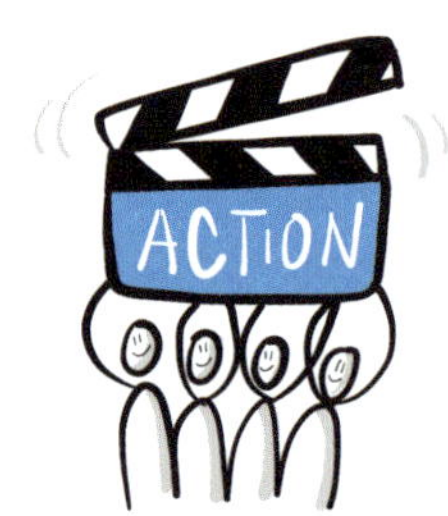

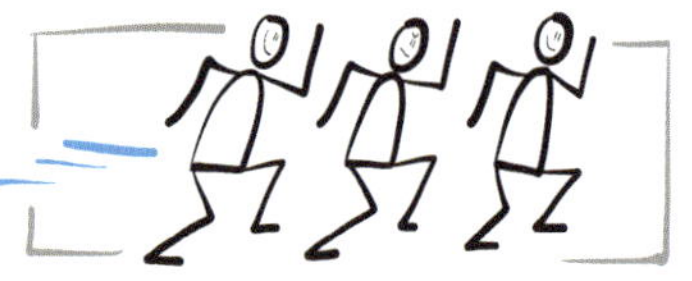

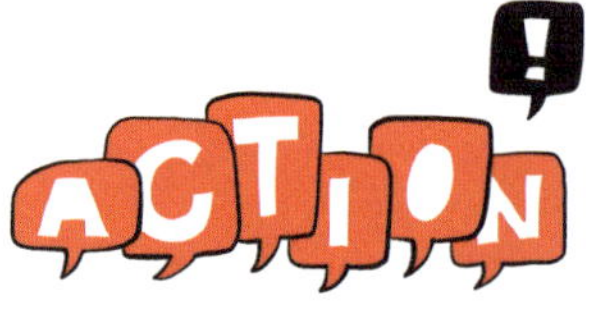

HOW TO DRAW

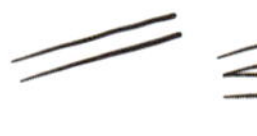
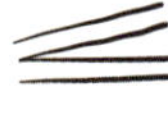
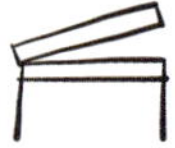
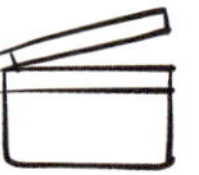

CO-CREATION

BASIC ICONS

COMBINED ICONS

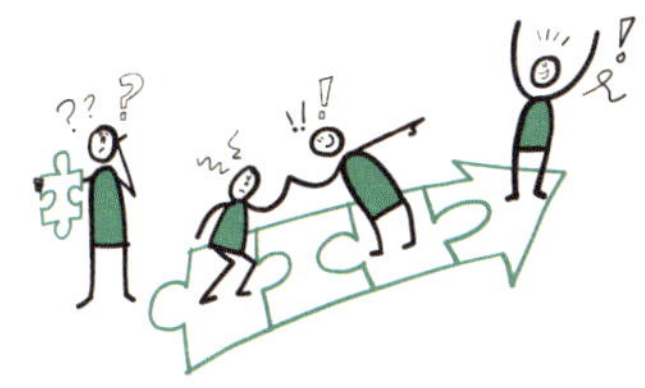

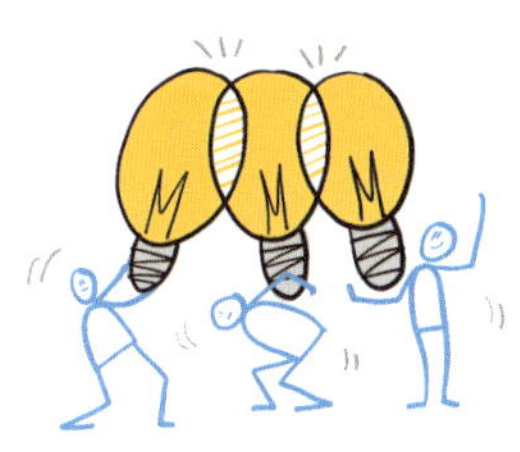

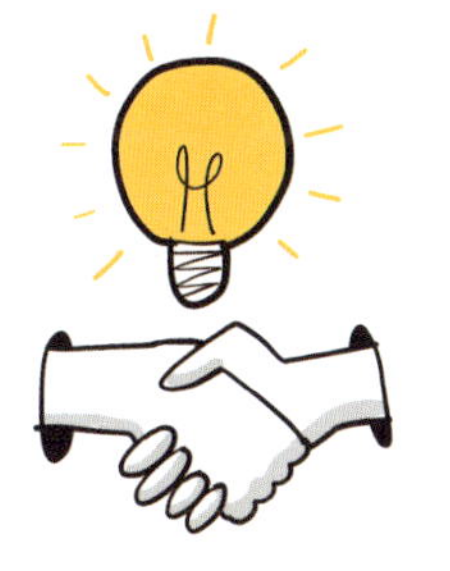

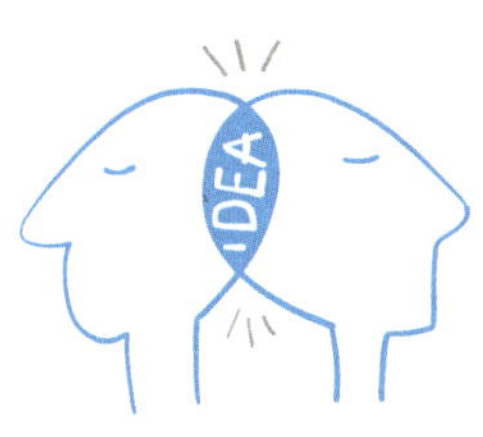

HOW TO DRAW

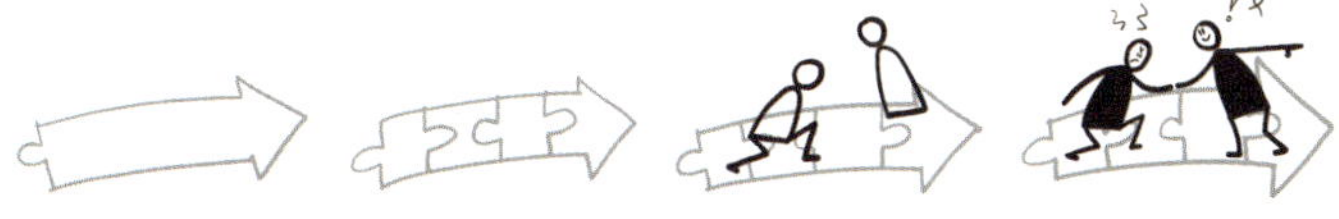

Daily work

COMPARING OPTIONS

BASIC ICONS

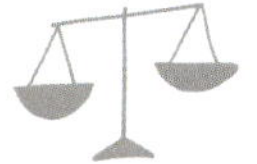

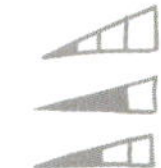
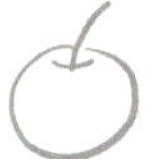
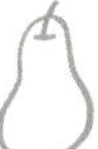
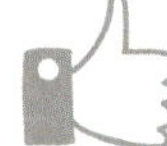
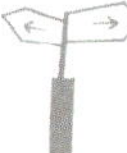

COMBINED ICONS

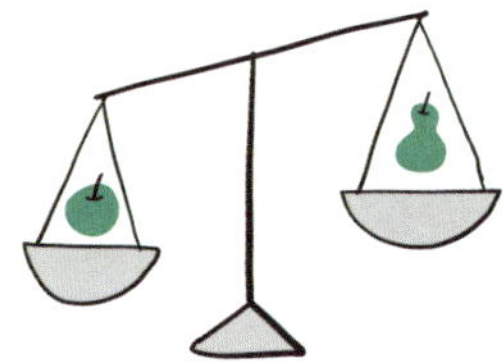
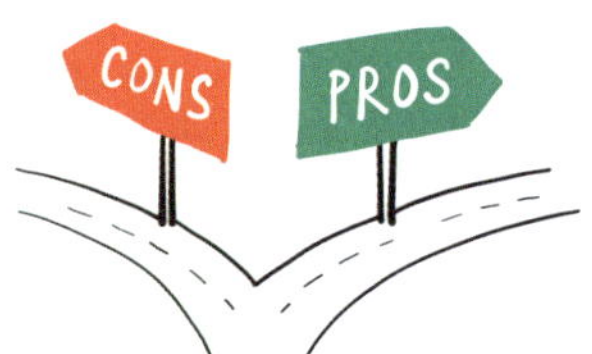

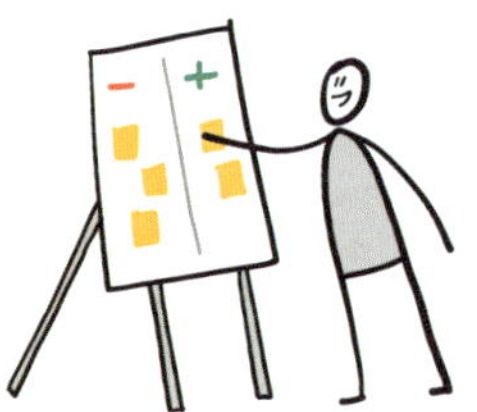

HOW TO DRAW

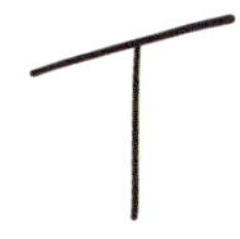
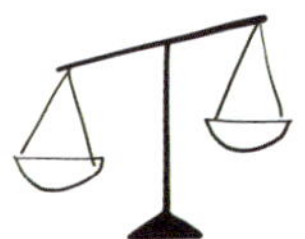
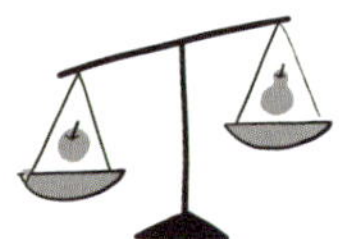

DECISION MAKING

BASIC ICONS

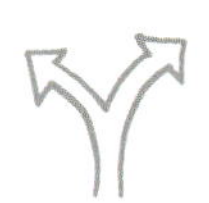
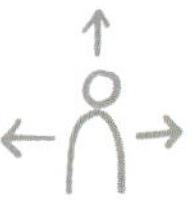
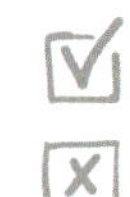
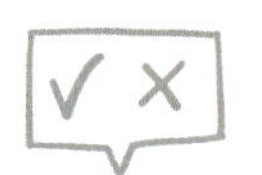
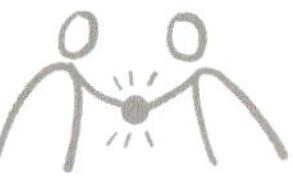

COMBINED ICONS

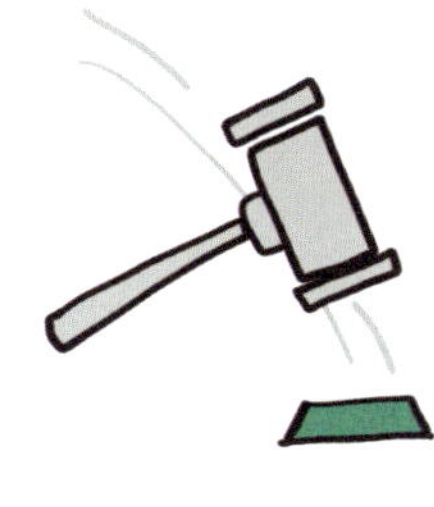
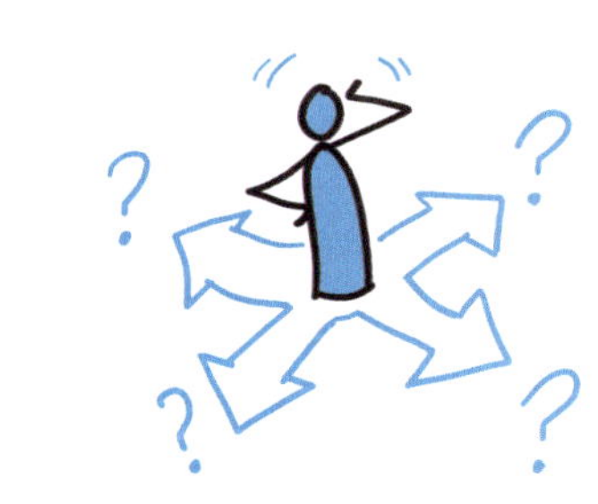
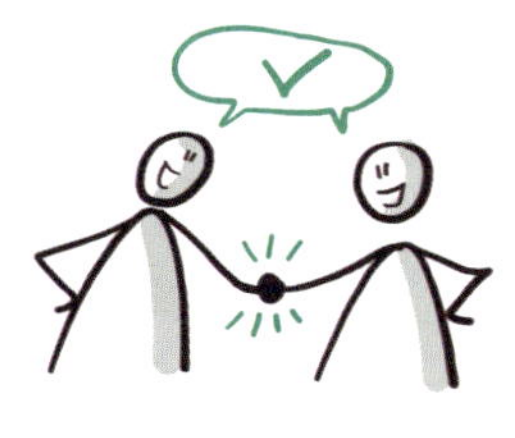
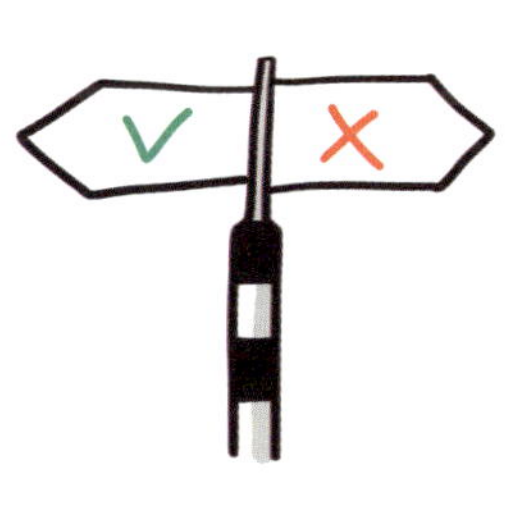

HOW TO DRAW

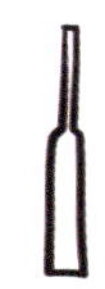
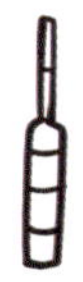
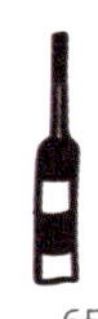
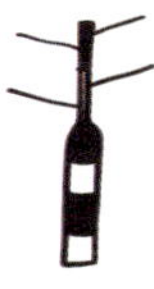
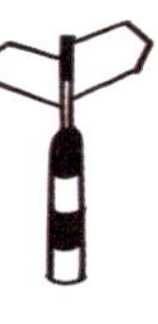

EFFICIENCY

BASIC ICONS

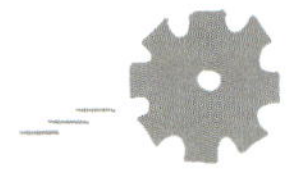

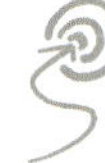
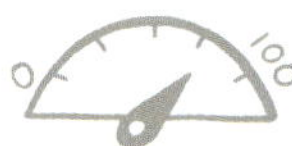
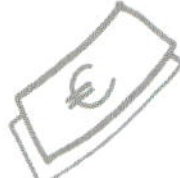
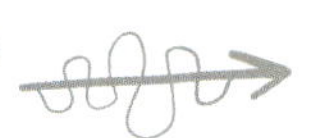

COMBINED ICONS

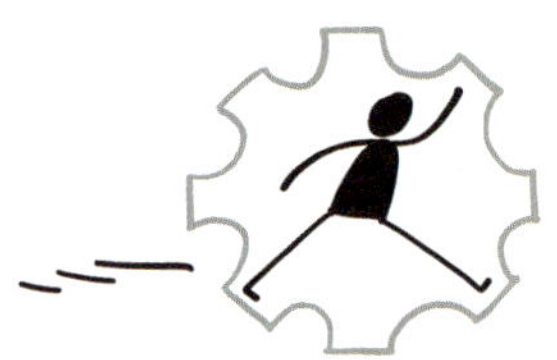
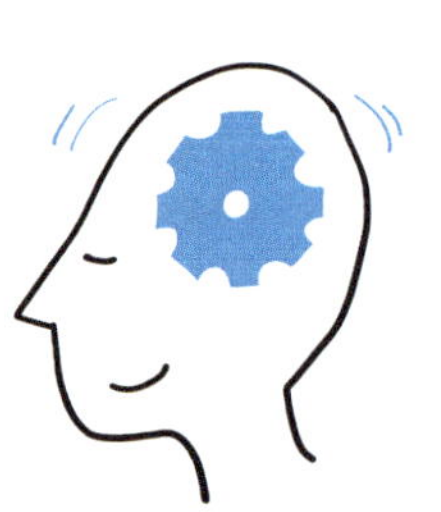
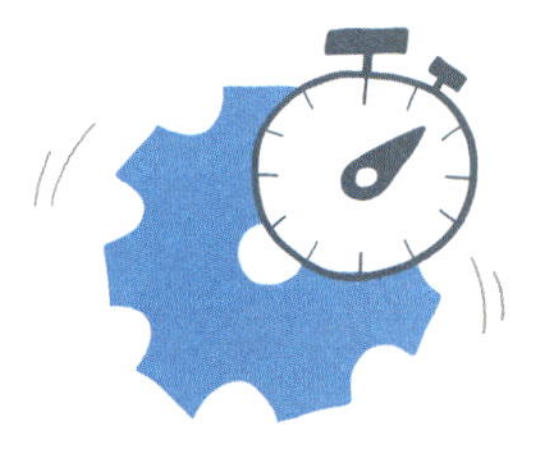
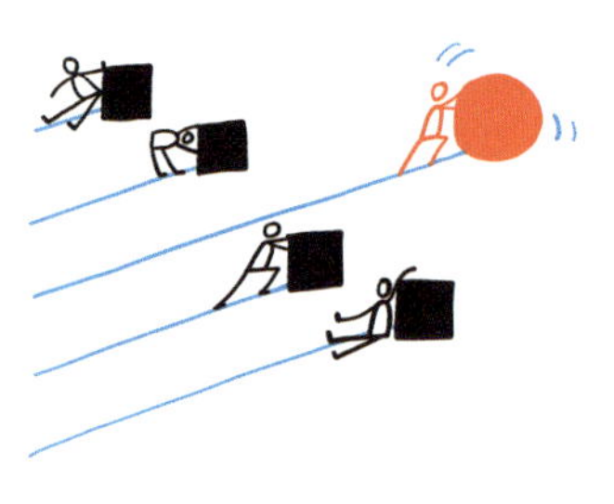

HOW TO DRAW

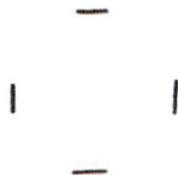
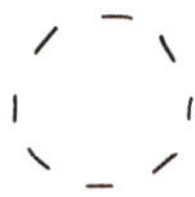
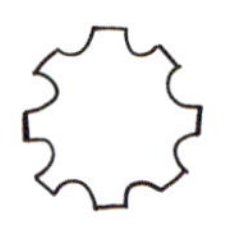
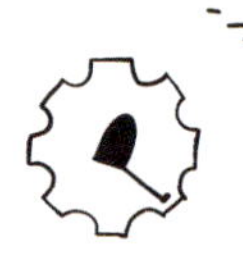
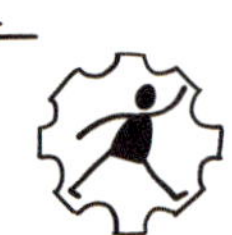

FEEDBACK

BASIC ICONS

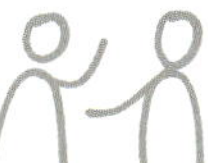

COMBINED ICONS

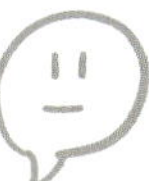

HOW TO DRAW

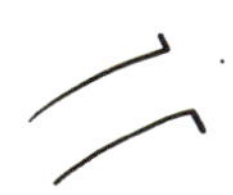
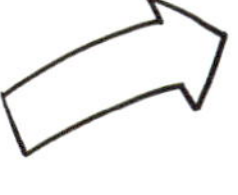
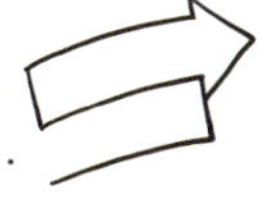
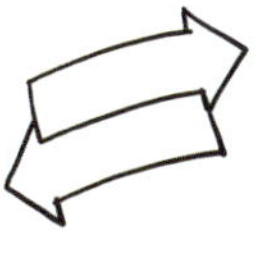
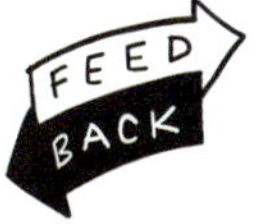

IMPORTANCE

BASIC ICONS

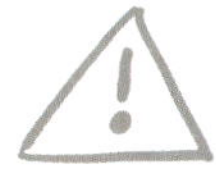
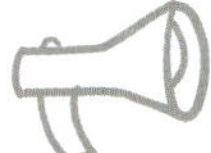
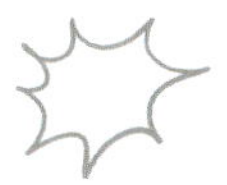
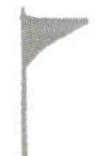

COMBINED ICONS

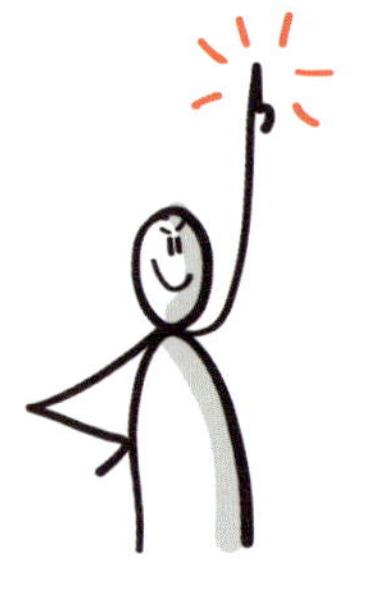

HOW TO DRAW

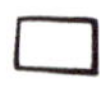
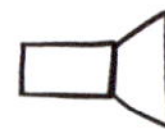
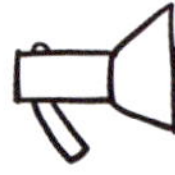
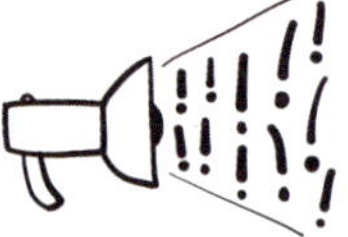

INFORMATION SHARING

BASIC ICONS

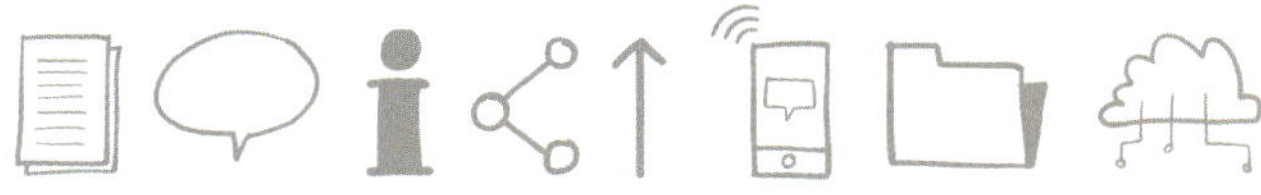

COMBINED ICONS

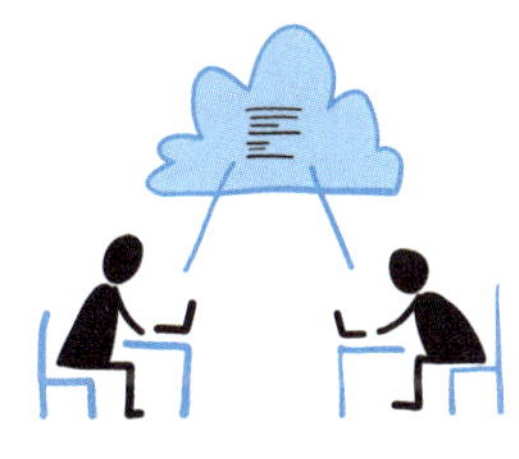

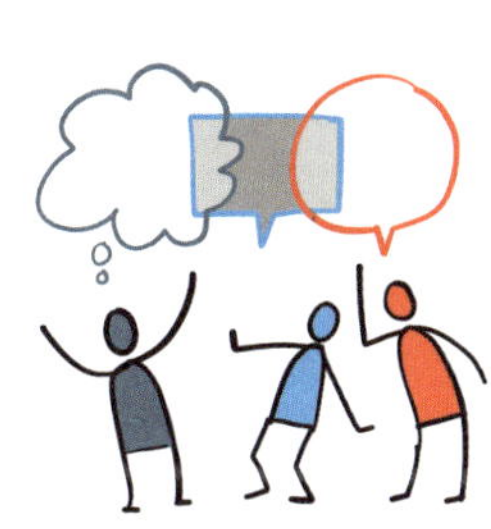

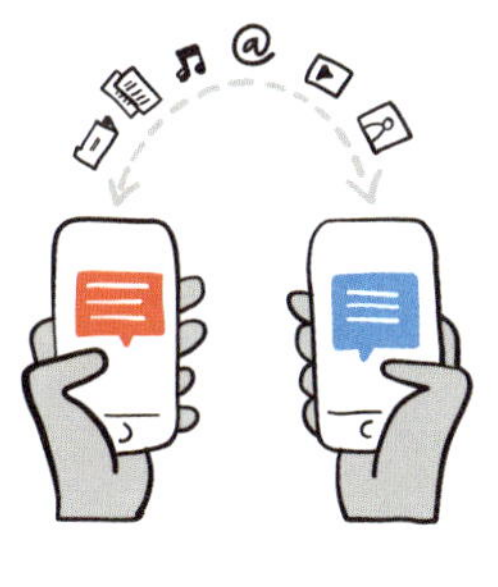

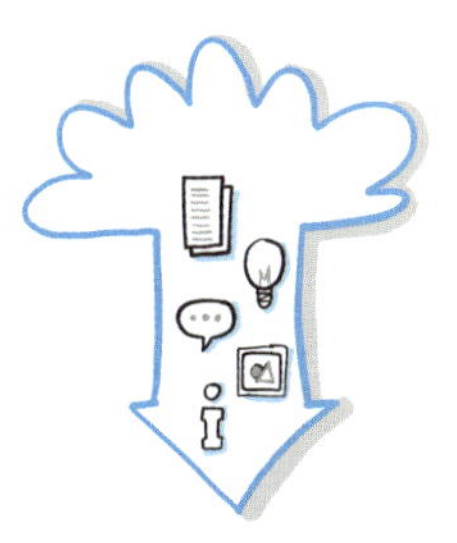

HOW TO DRAW

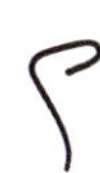

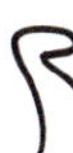

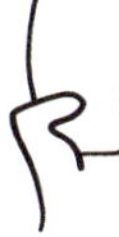

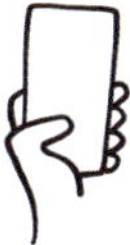

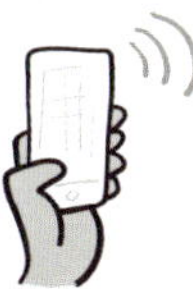

INPUT

BASIC ICONS

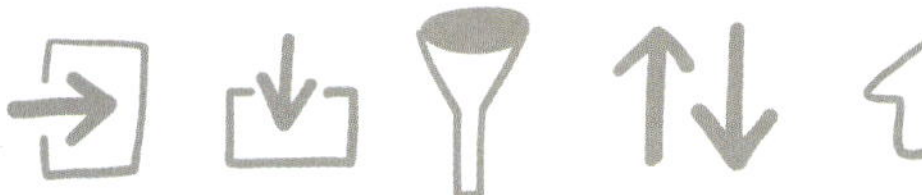

COMBINED ICONS

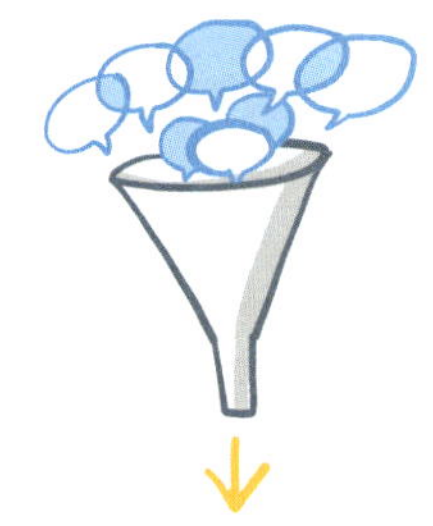

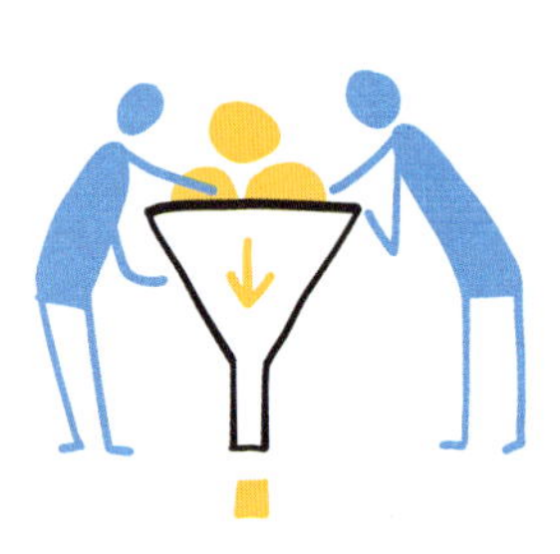

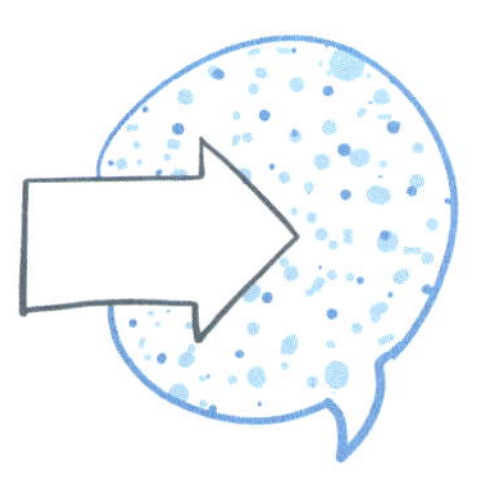

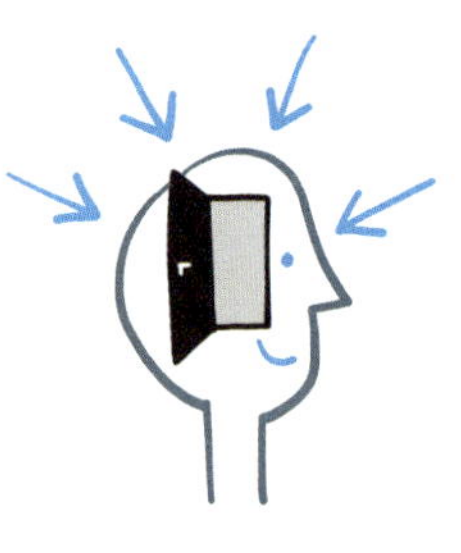

HOW TO DRAW

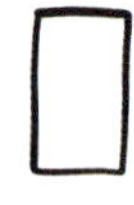

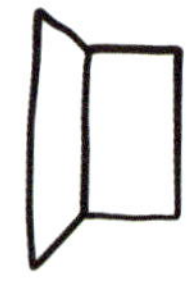

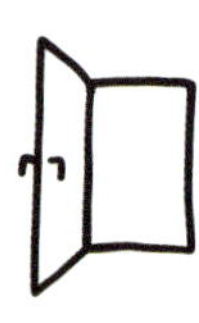

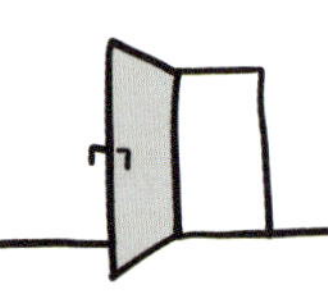

LOGISTICS

BASIC ICONS

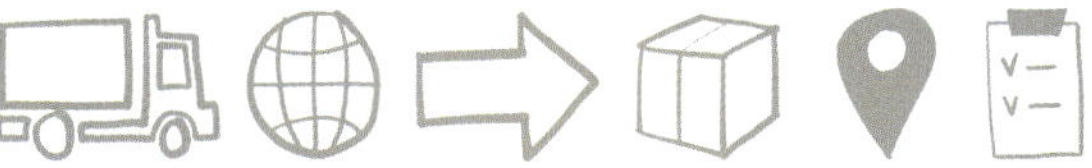

COMBINED ICONS

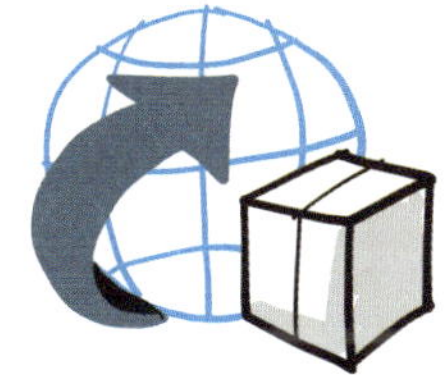

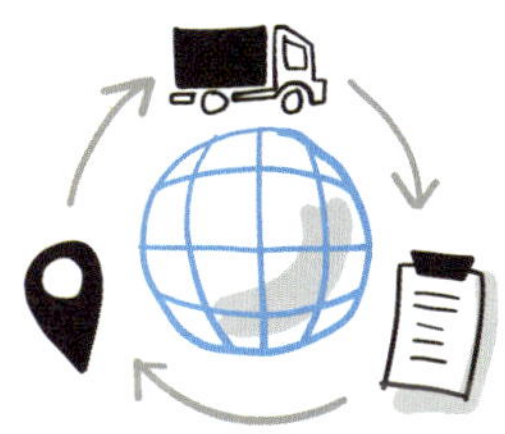

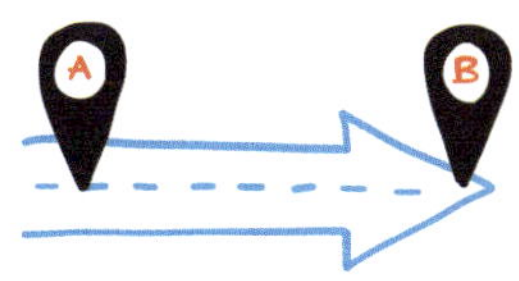

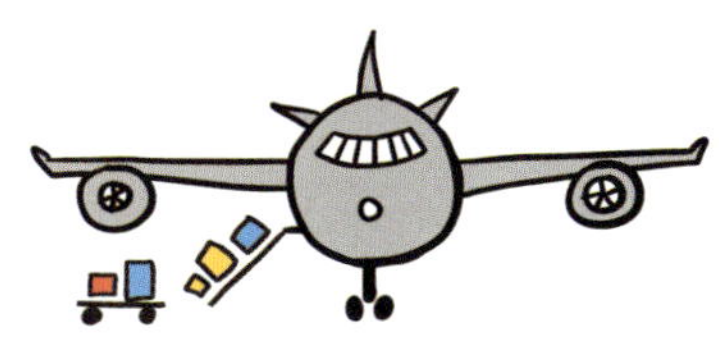

HOW TO DRAW

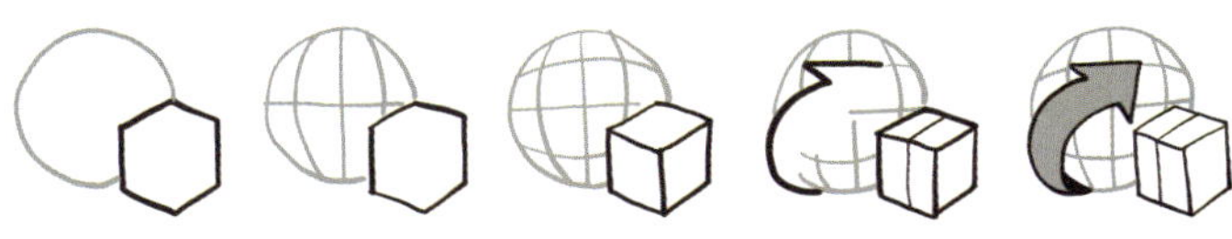

Daily work

MEET A DEADLINE

BASIC ICONS

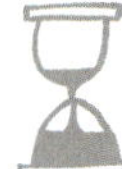
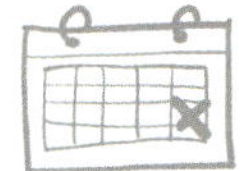

COMBINED ICONS

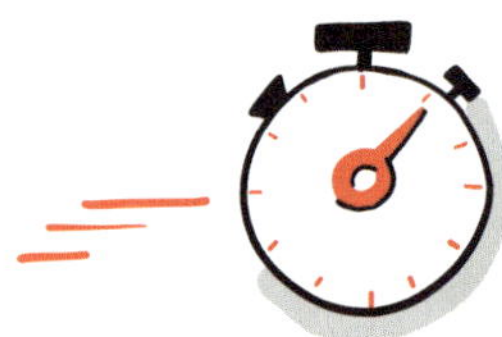
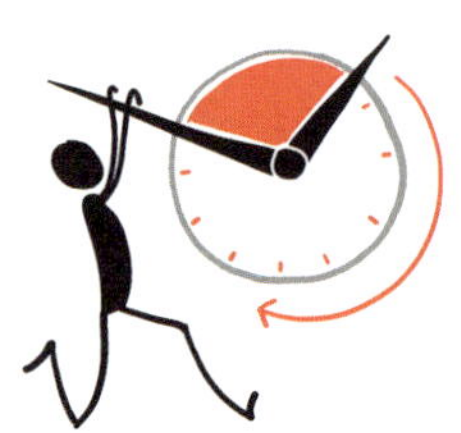
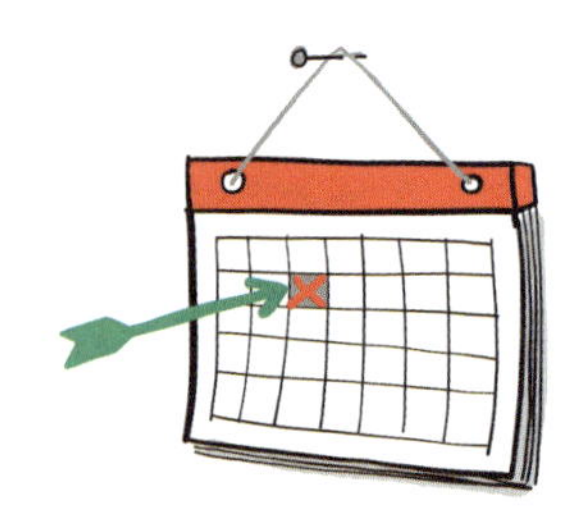
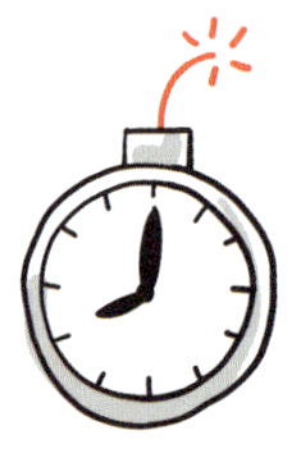

HOW TO DRAW

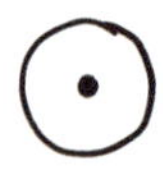
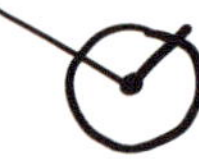
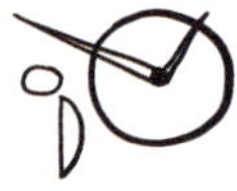
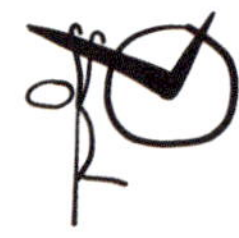
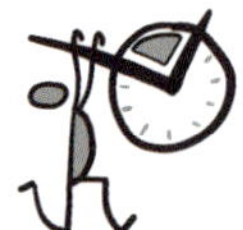

MEETING

BASIC ICONS

 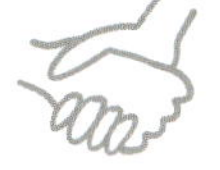 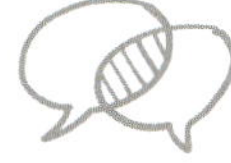 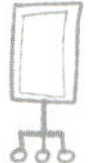 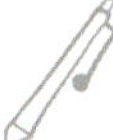 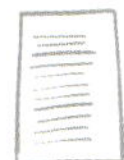

COMBINED ICONS

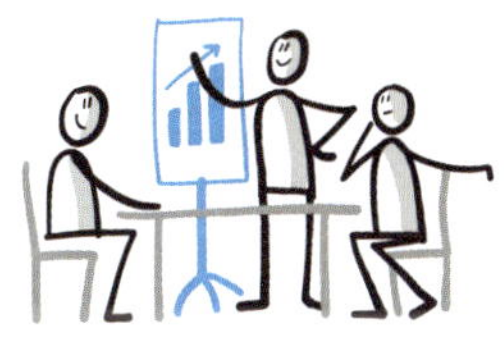

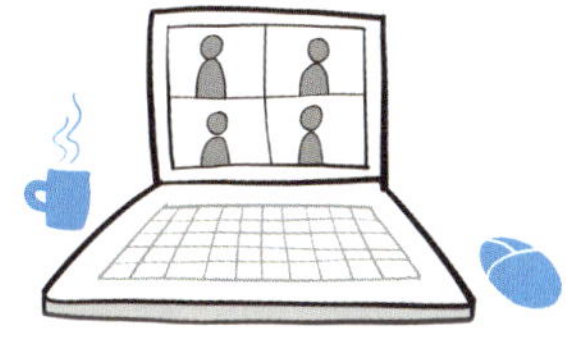

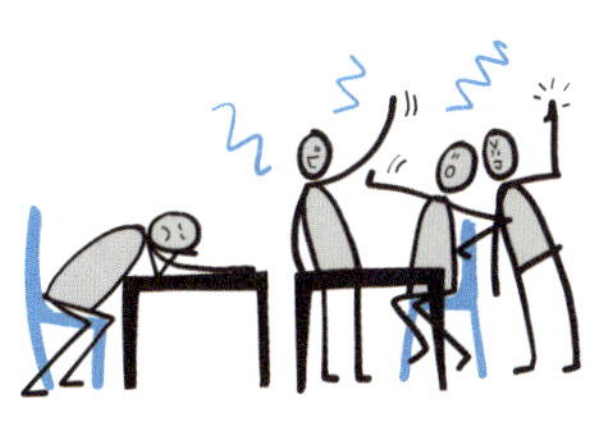

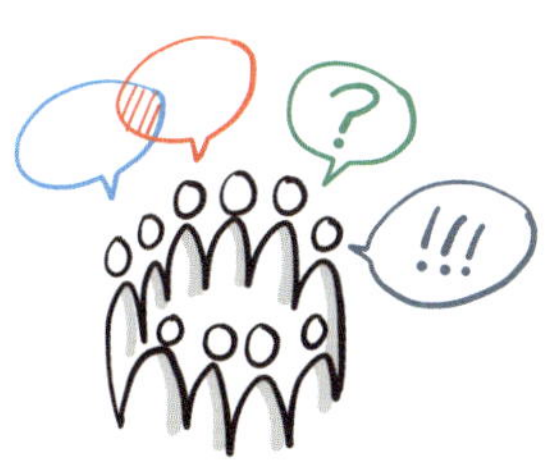

HOW TO DRAW

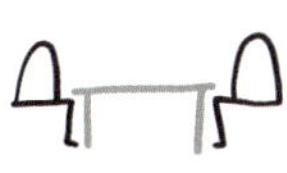 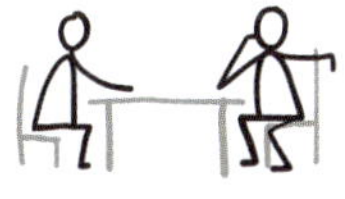 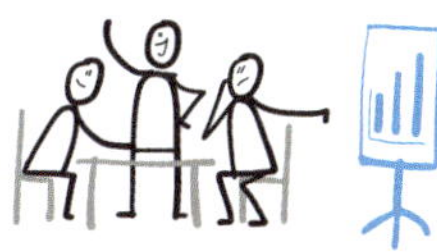

PANDEMIC

BASIC ICONS

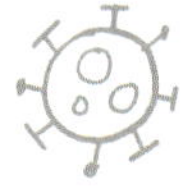
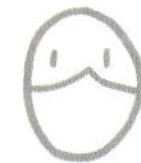

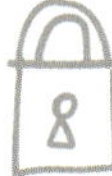
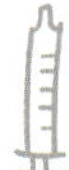
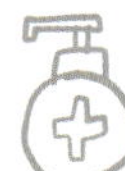
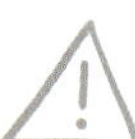

COMBINED ICONS

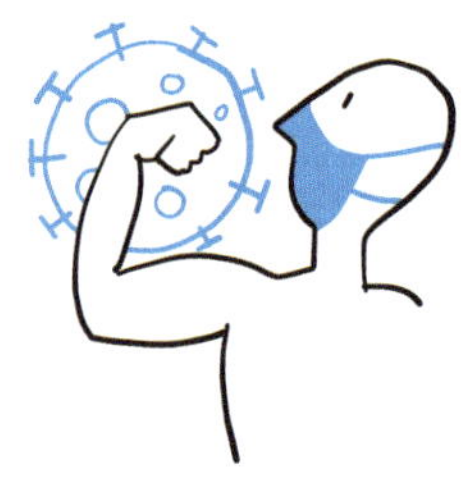
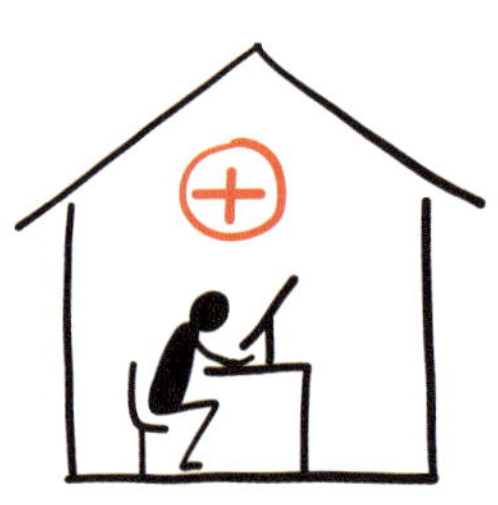

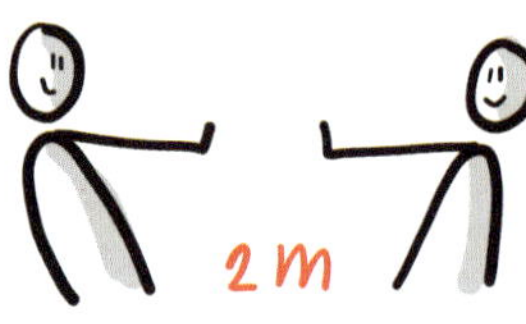

HOW TO DRAW

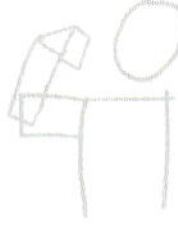
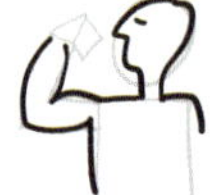
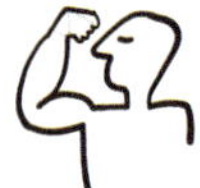
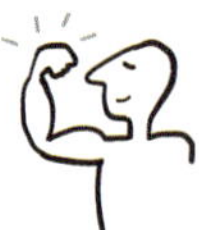

PLANNING

BASIC ICONS

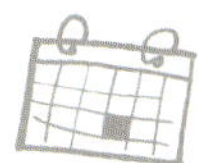
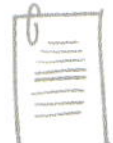
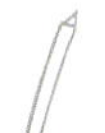

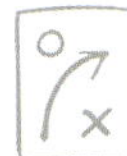
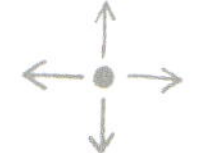

Daily work

COMBINED ICONS

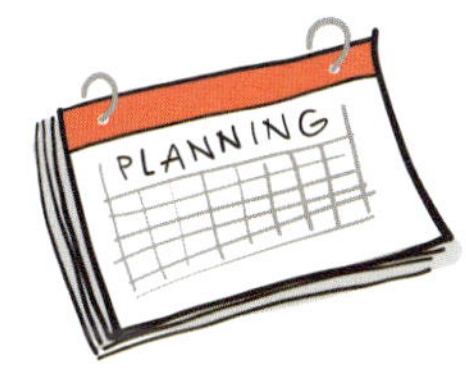

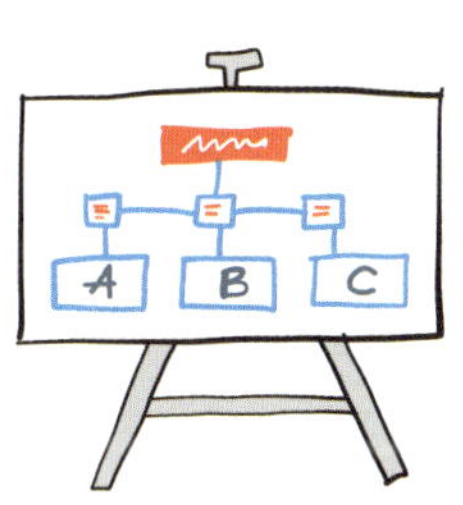

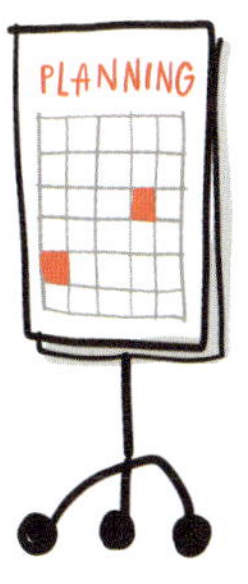

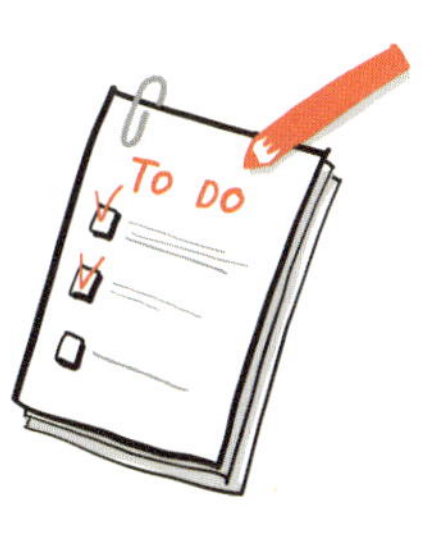

HOW TO DRAW

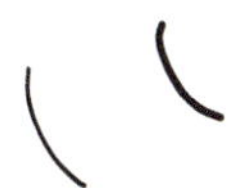
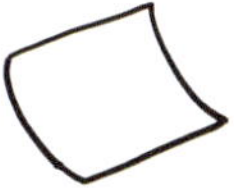

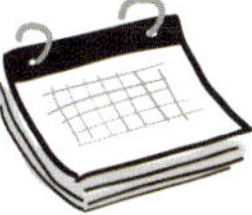

REMOTE WORKING

BASIC ICONS

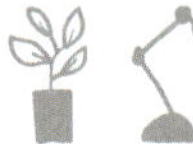
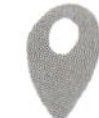
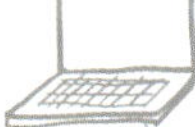
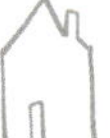
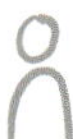
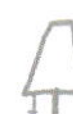
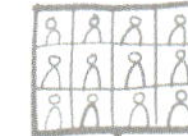

COMBINED ICONS

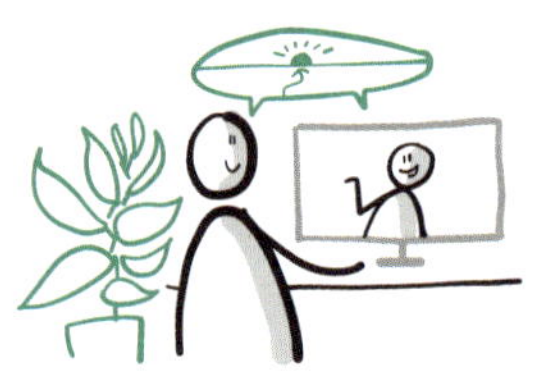
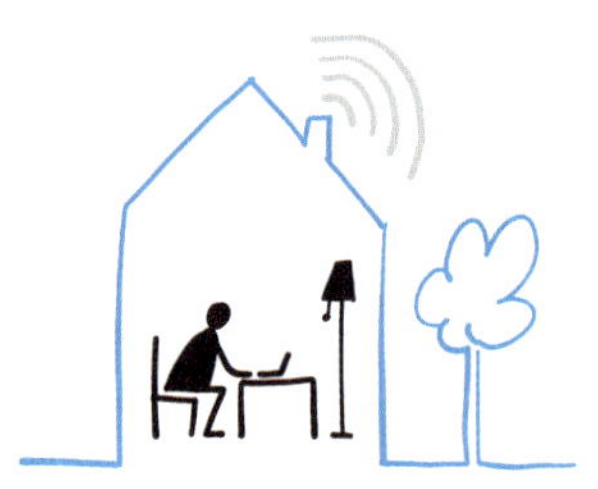
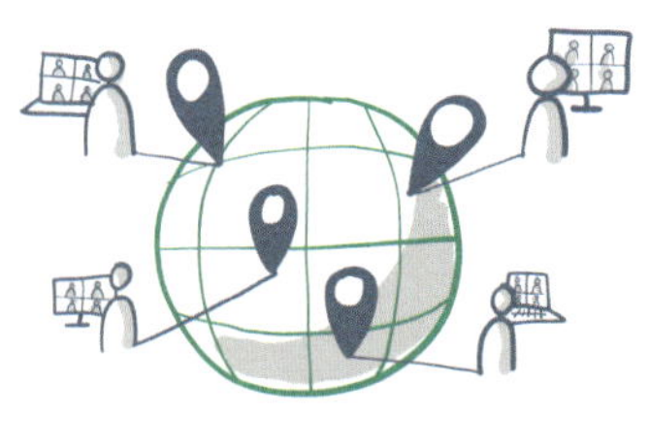
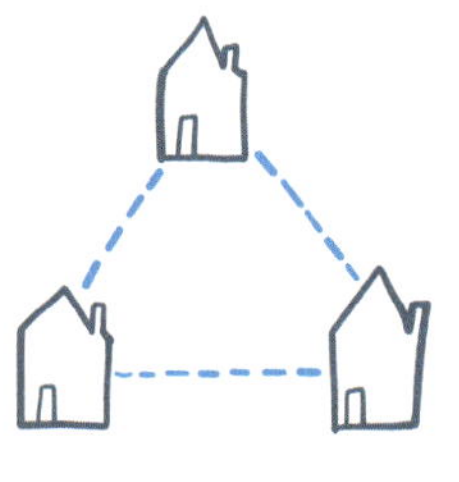

HOW TO DRAW

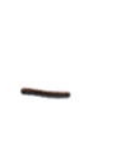
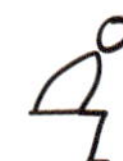
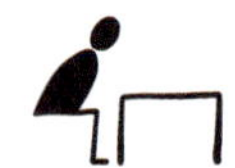
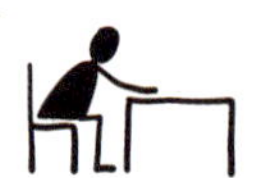

SOCIAL DISTANCING

BASIC ICONS

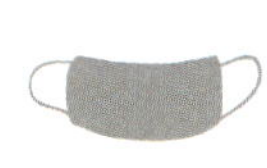
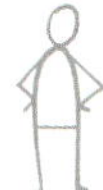
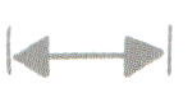
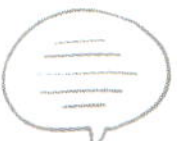
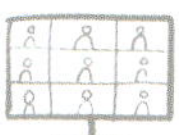
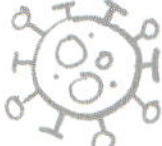

COMBINED ICONS

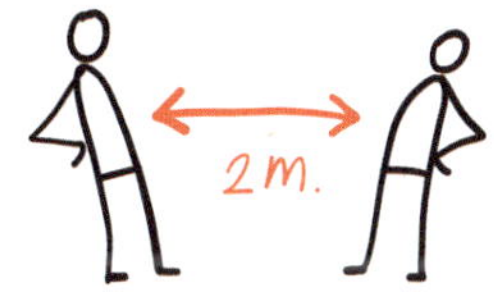

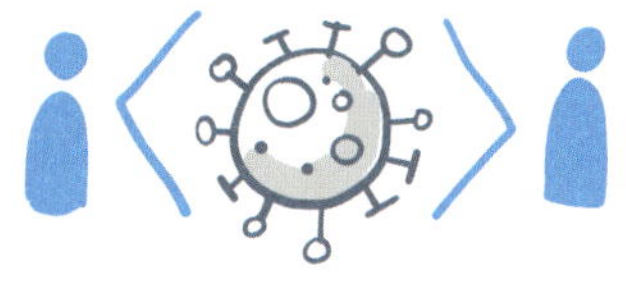

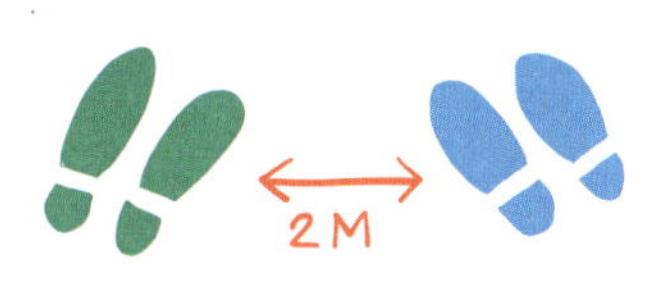

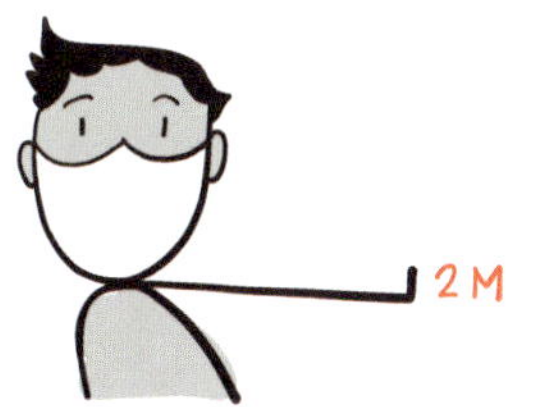

HOW TO DRAW

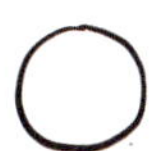

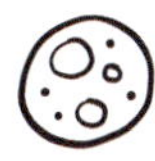
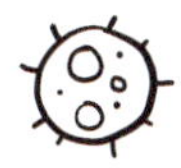
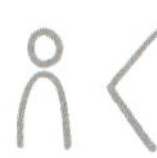
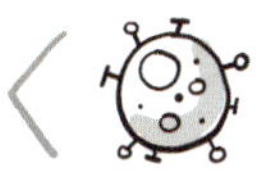
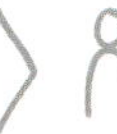

STAND-UP

BASIC ICONS

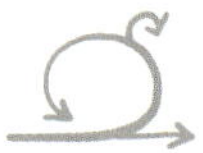 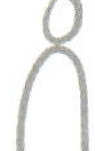 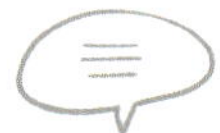 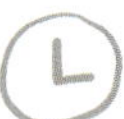 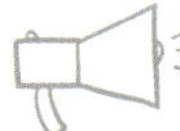 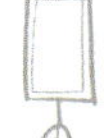 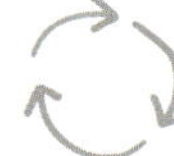

COMBINED ICONS

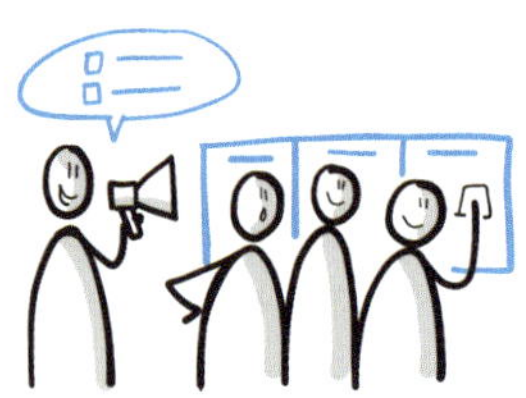

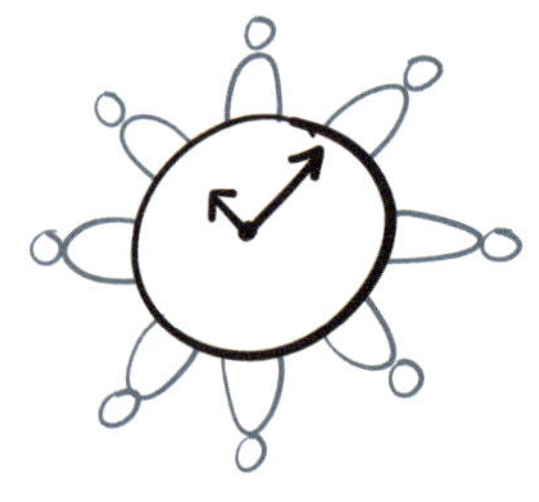

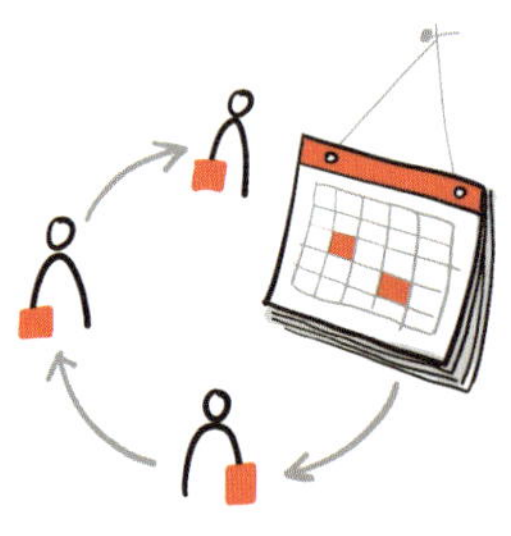

HOW TO DRAW

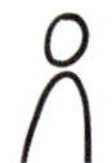 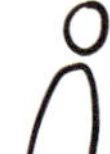 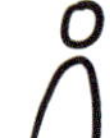 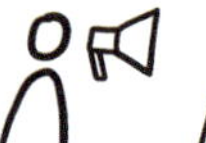 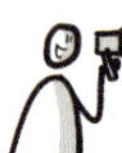

 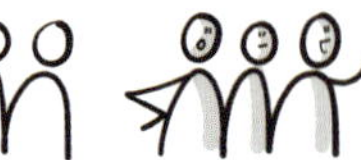

TASKS

BASIC ICONS

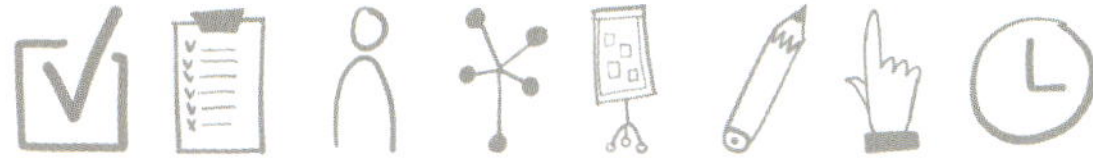

COMBINED ICONS

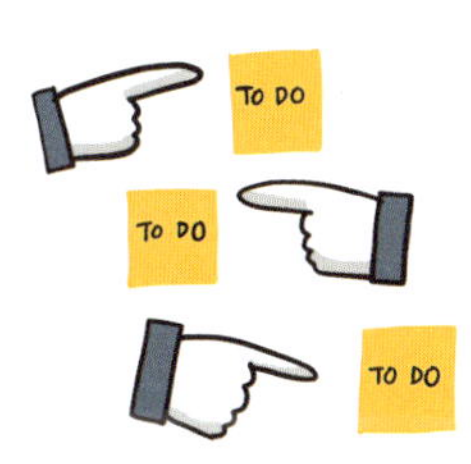

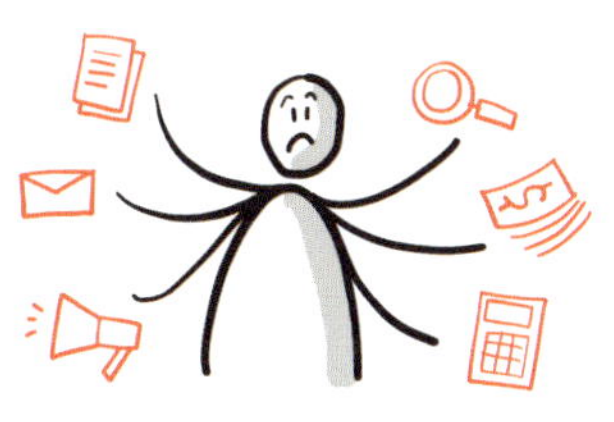

HOW TO DRAW

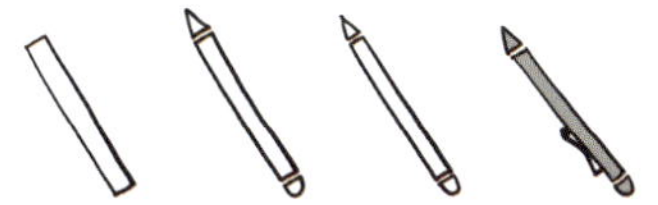

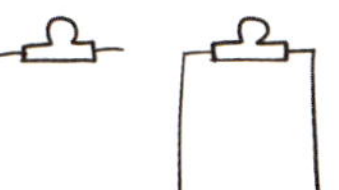

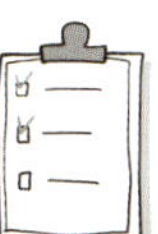

URGENCY

BASIC ICONS

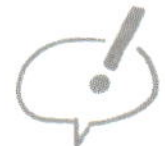

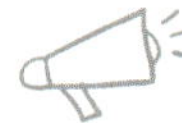
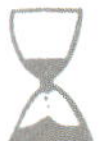
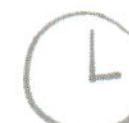

COMBINED ICONS

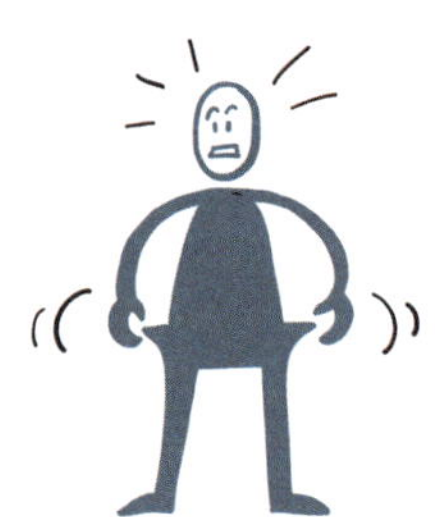

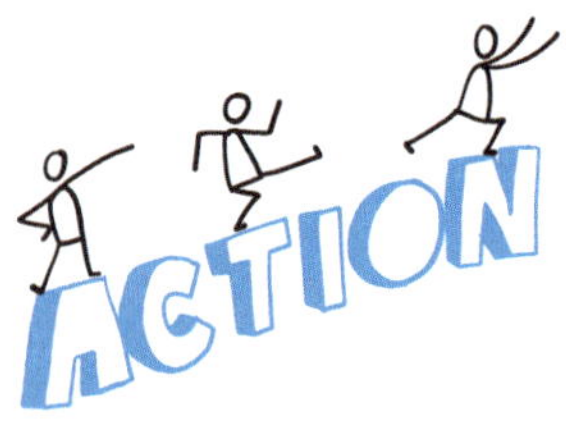

HOW TO DRAW

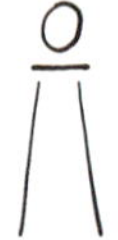
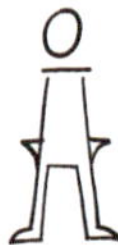
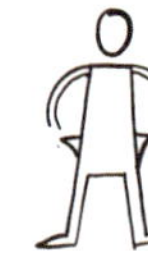
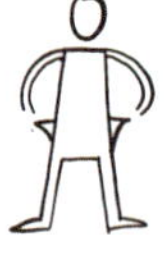
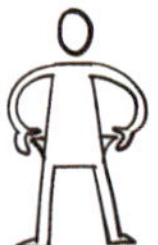
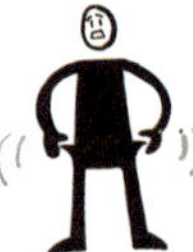

WORK OVERLOAD

BASIC ICONS

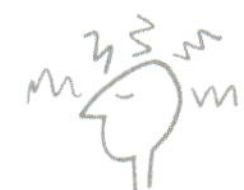

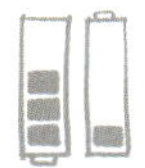
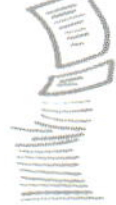

COMBINED ICONS

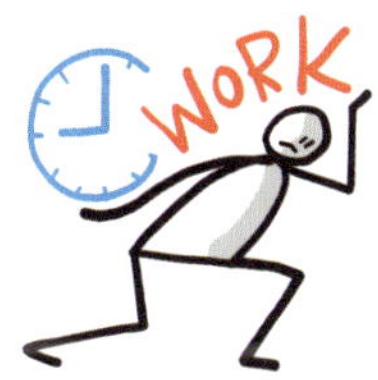

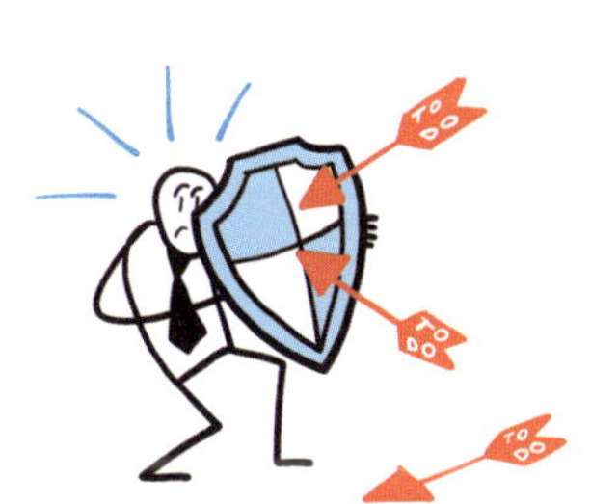

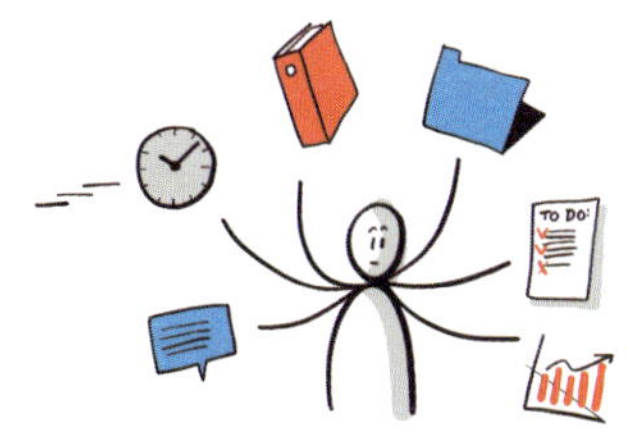

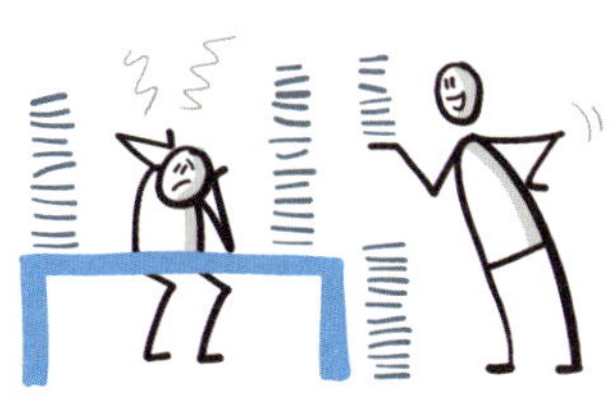

HOW TO DRAW

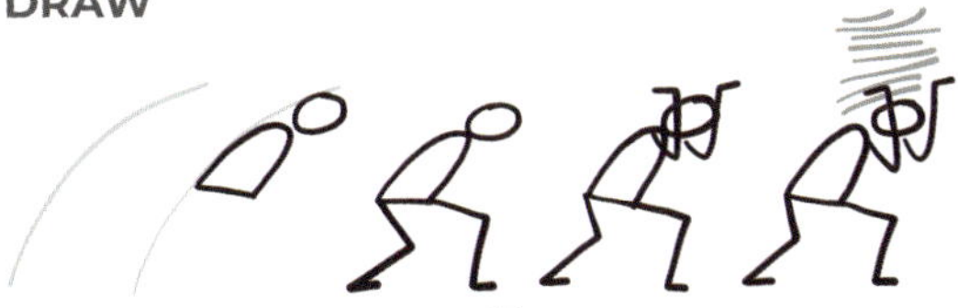

Daily work

FINANCE

SHOW ME THE MONEY

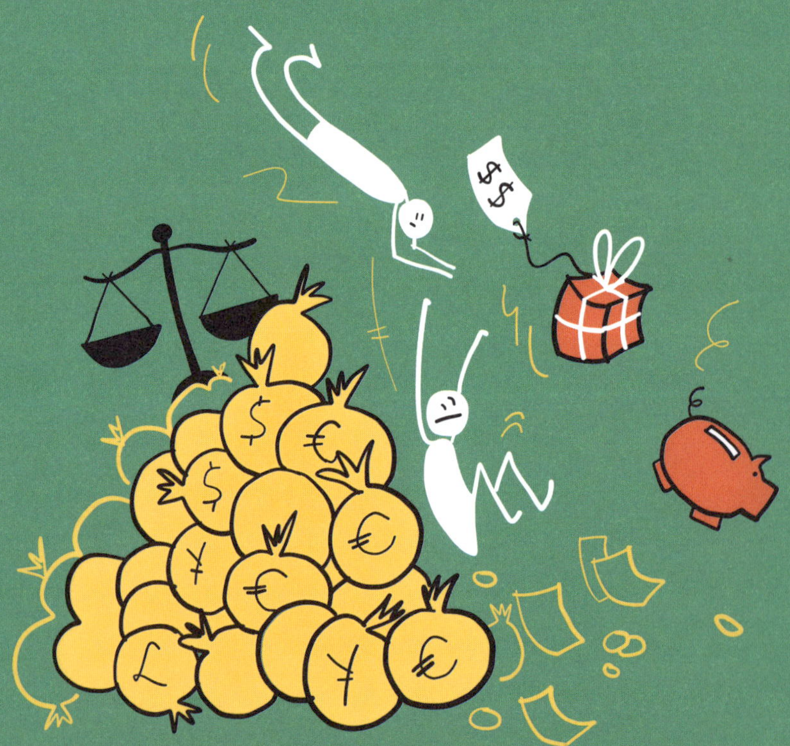

ACCOUNTING

BASIC ICONS

 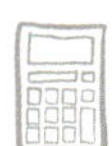 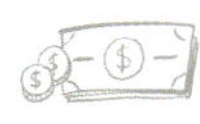 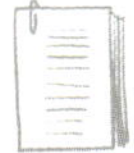 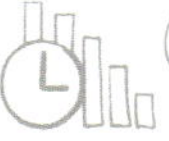 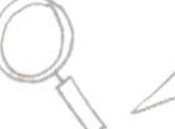 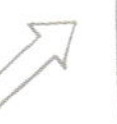 

COMBINED ICONS

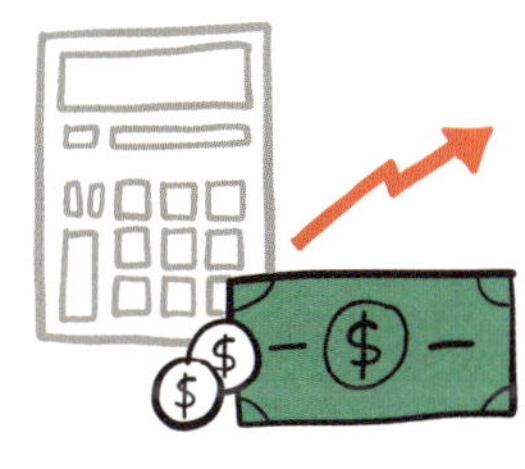

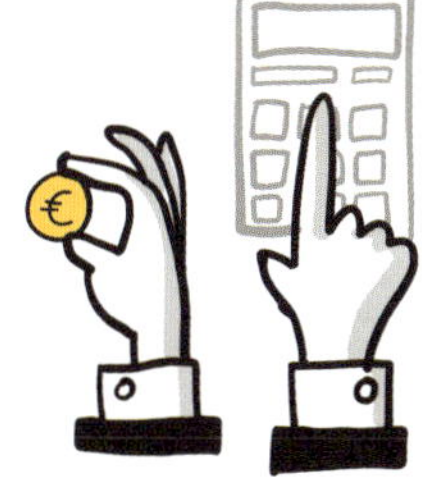

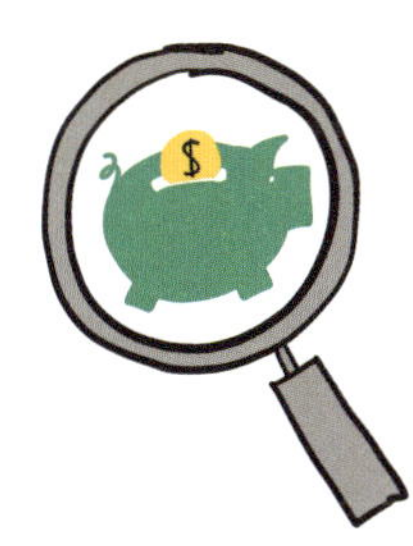

Finance

HOW TO DRAW

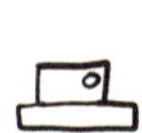 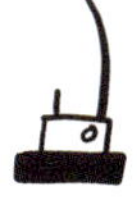 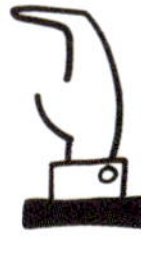 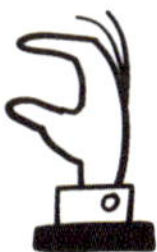 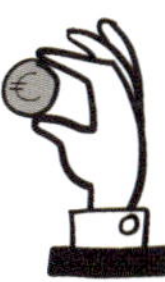

ACCURACY

BASIC ICONS

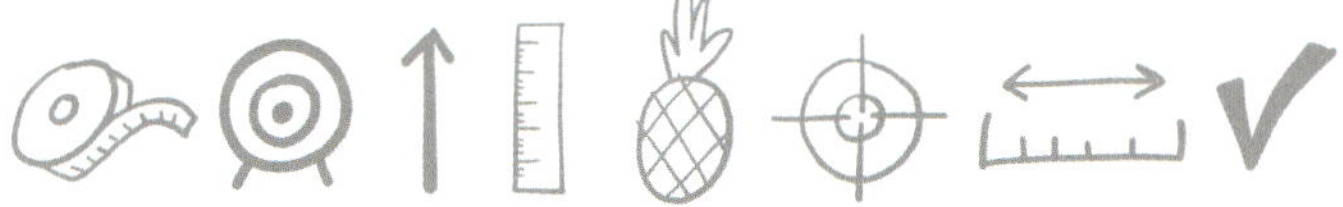

COMBINED ICONS

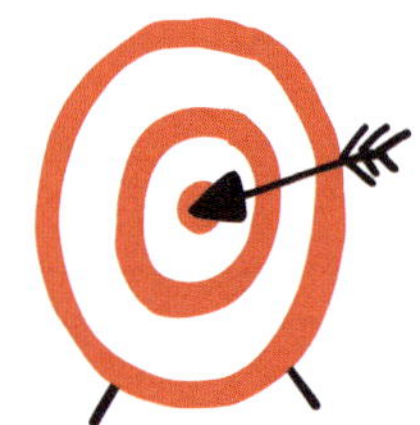

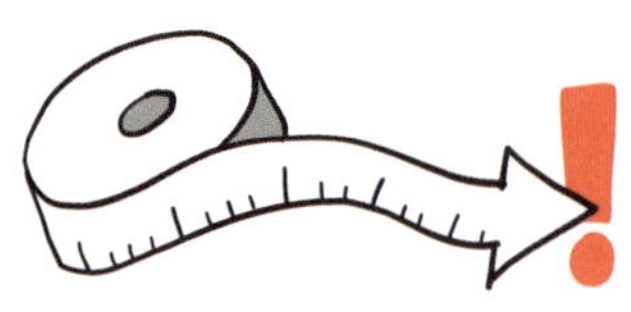

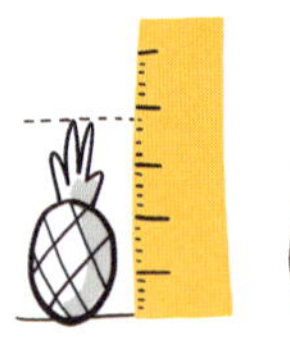

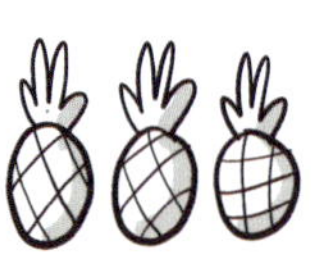

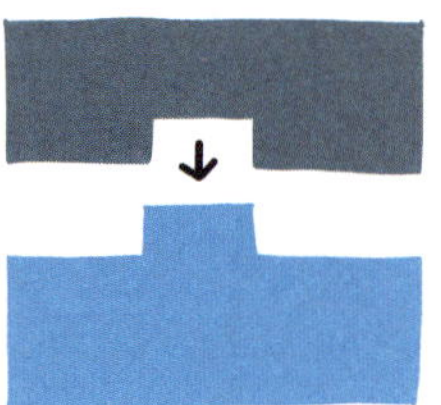

HOW TO DRAW

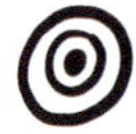

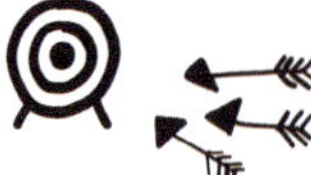

ANALYSIS

BASIC ICONS

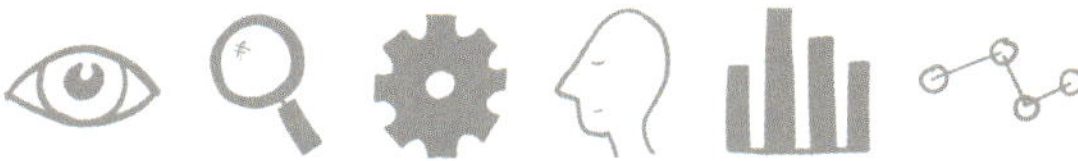

COMBINED ICONS

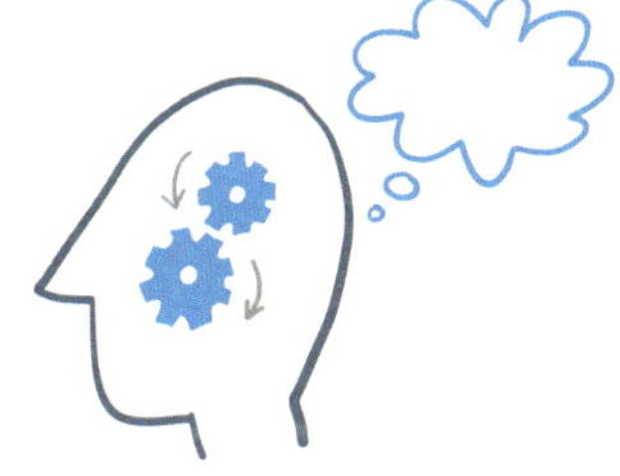

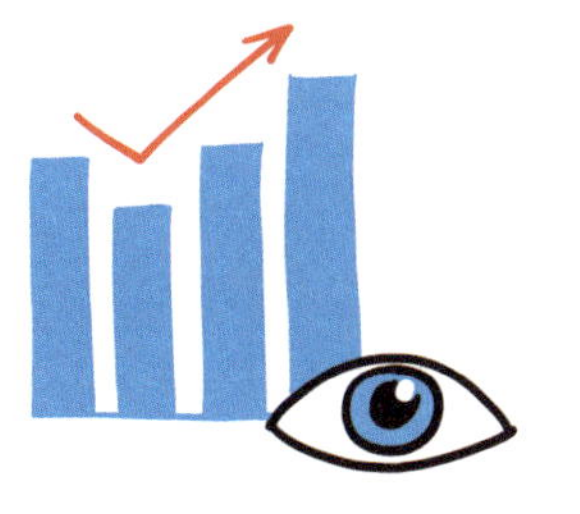

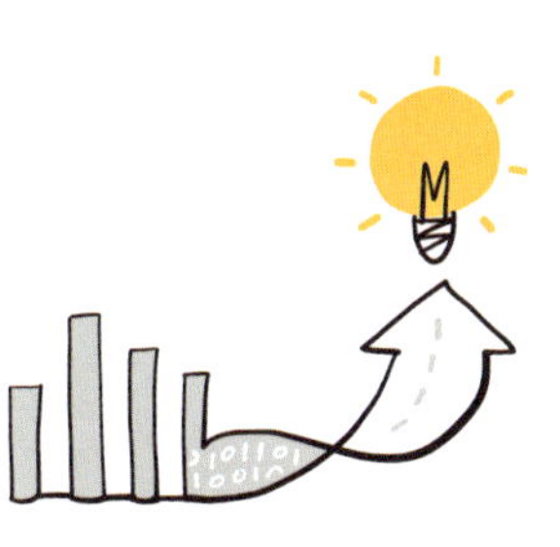

HOW TO DRAW

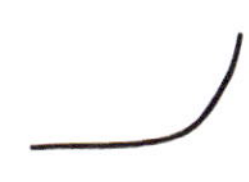

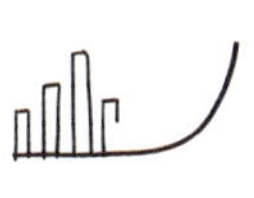

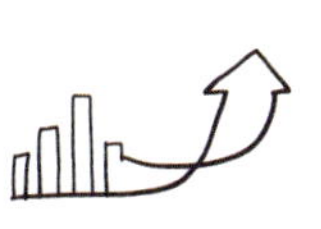

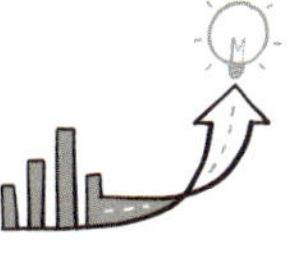

BANKING

BASIC ICONS

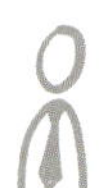
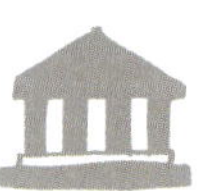
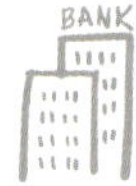

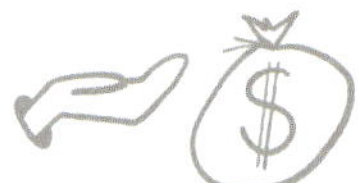
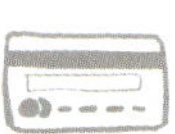
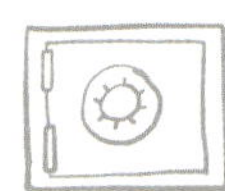
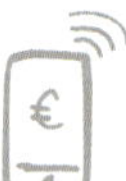

COMBINED ICONS

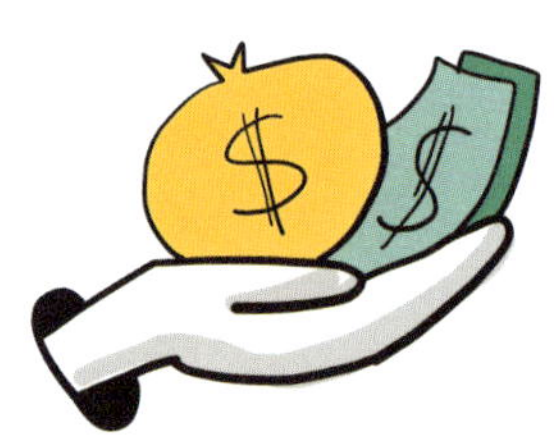
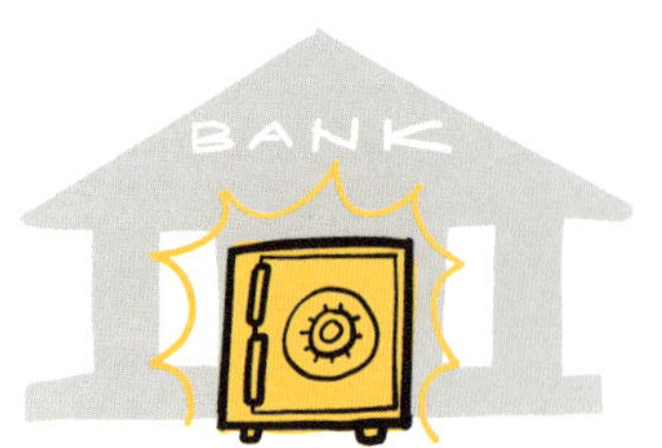

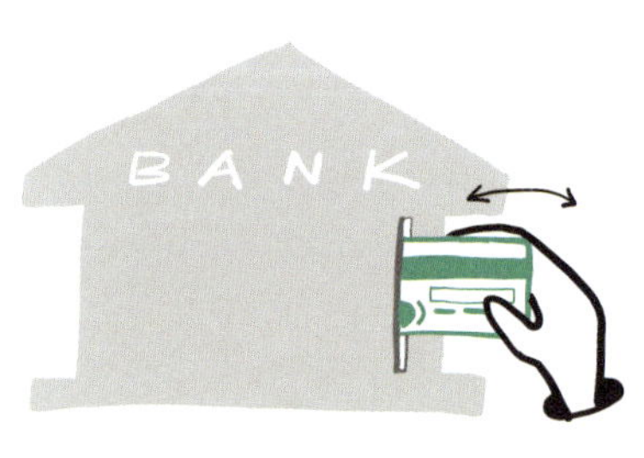

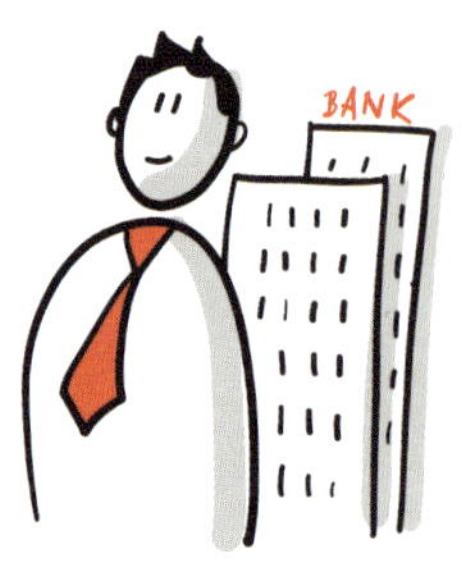

HOW TO DRAW

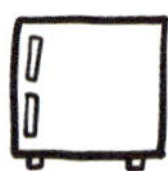
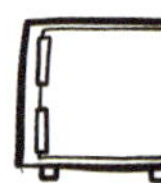
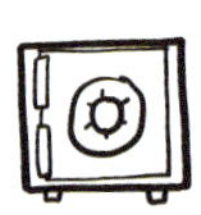
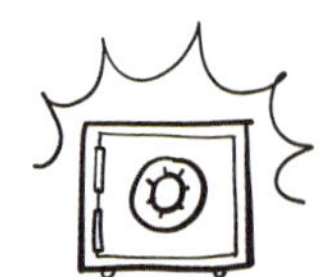

BUDGET

BASIC ICONS

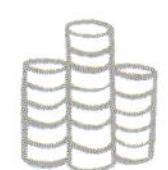
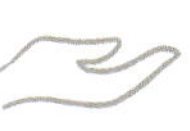
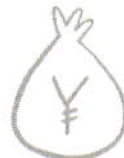
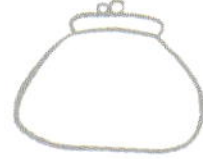
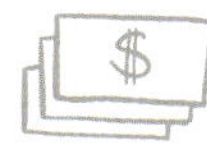
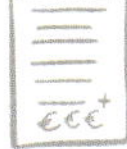
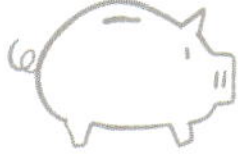

COMBINED ICONS

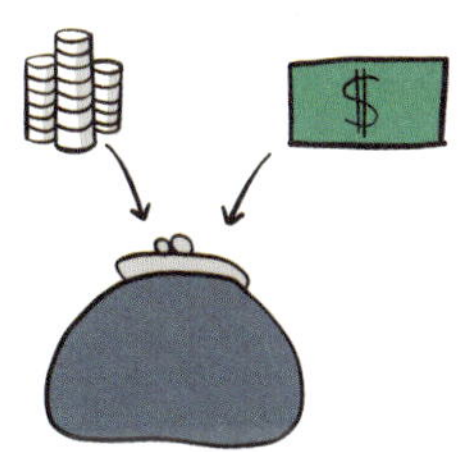
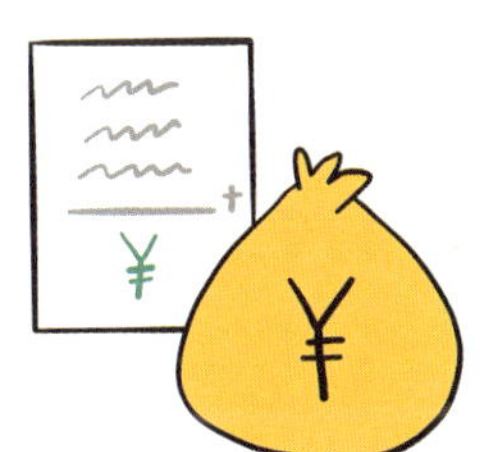
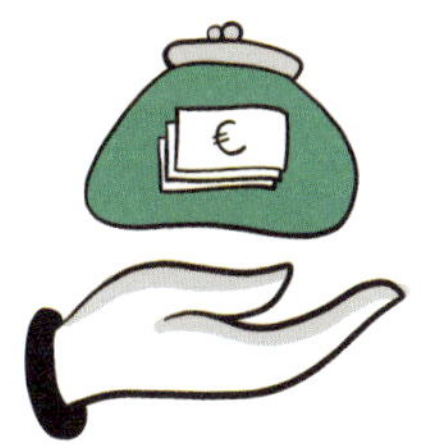
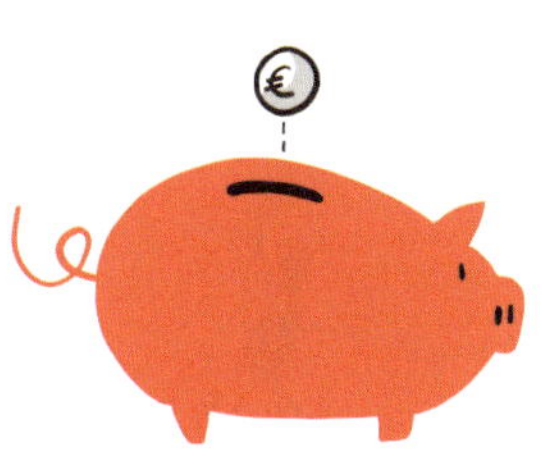

HOW TO DRAW

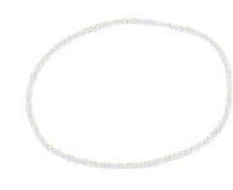
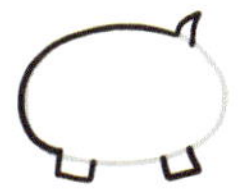
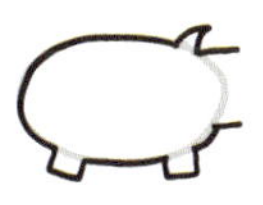
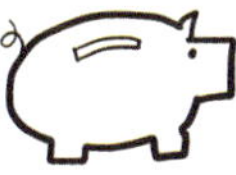

CHANCE (OPPOSITE OF RISK)

BASIC ICONS

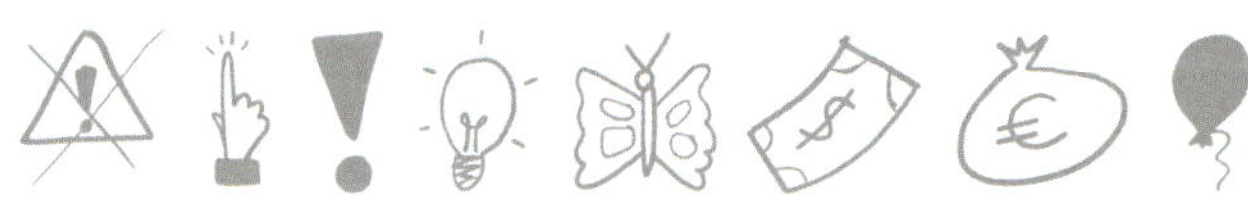

COMBINED ICONS

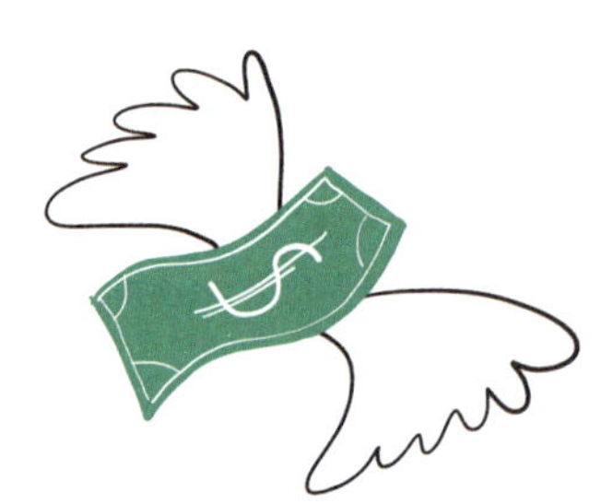

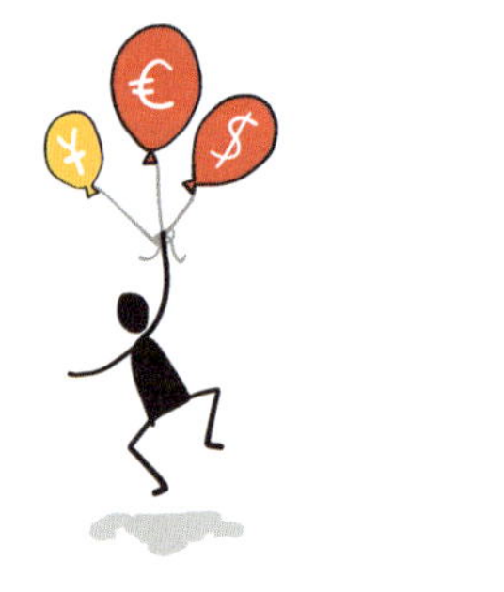

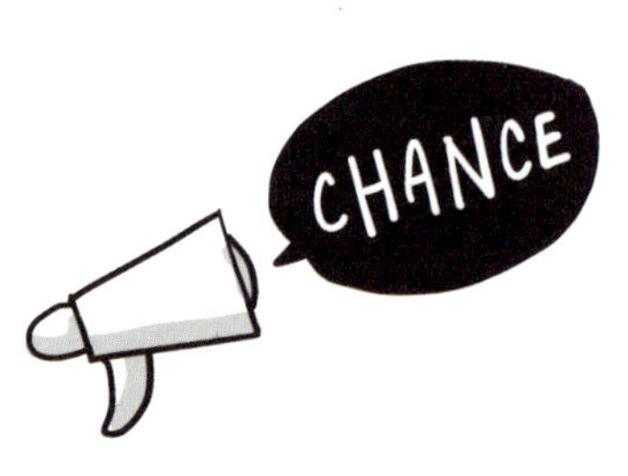

HOW TO DRAW

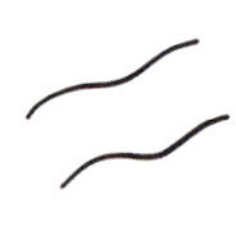

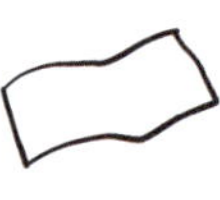

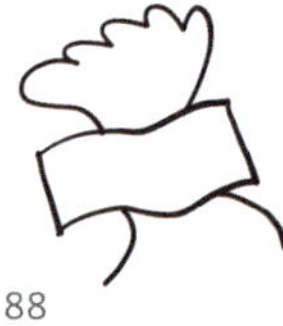

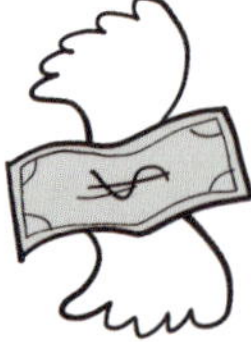

COST CUTTING

BASIC ICONS

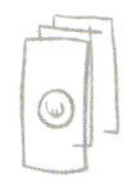
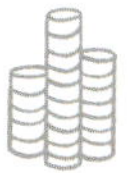
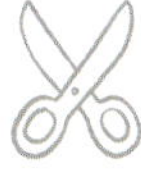
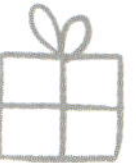
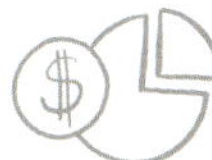

COMBINED ICONS

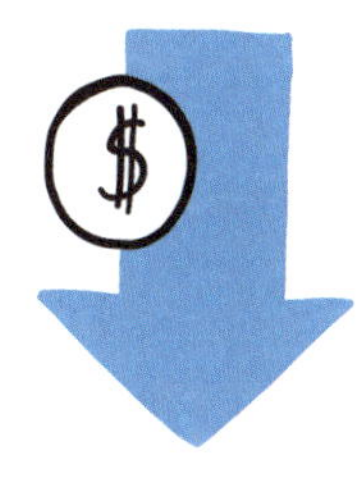
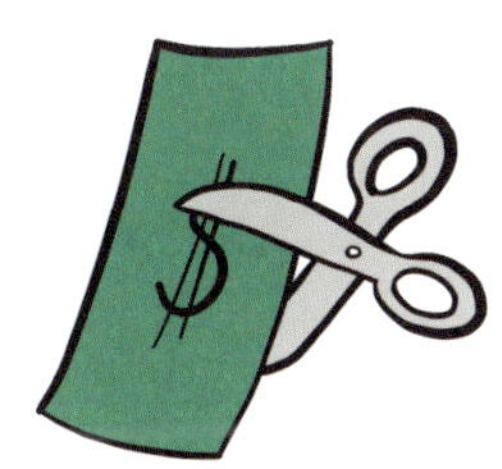
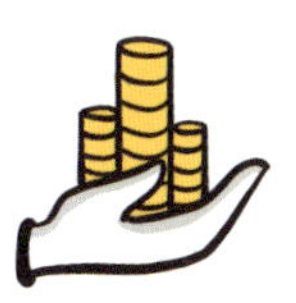
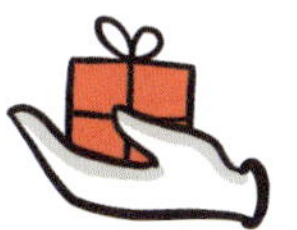
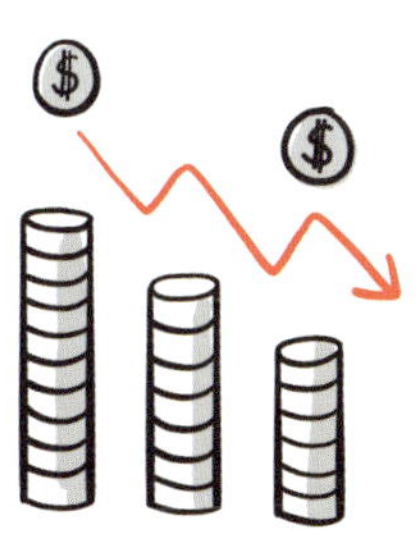

HOW TO DRAW

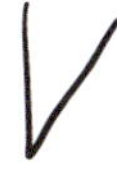
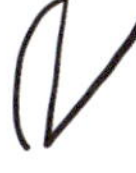
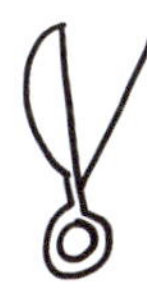
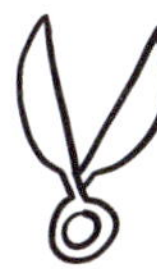
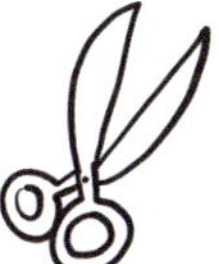

Finance

DECLINE, GROWTH

BASIC ICONS

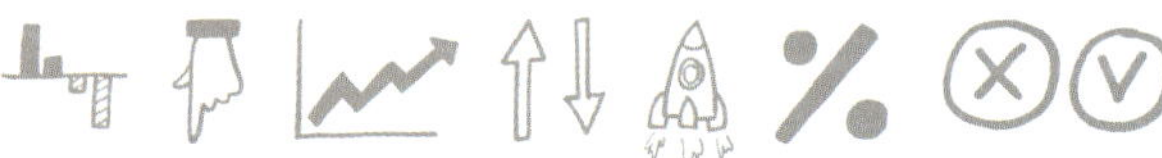

COMBINED ICONS

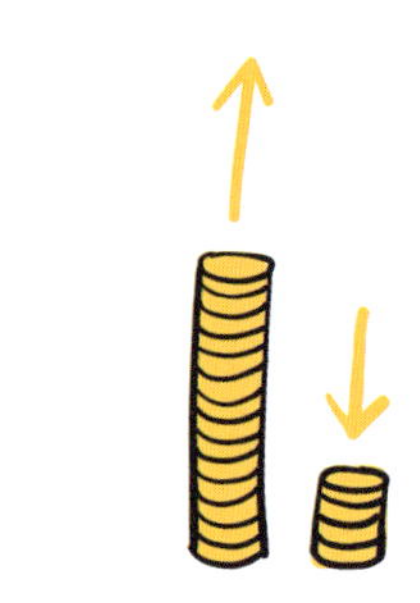

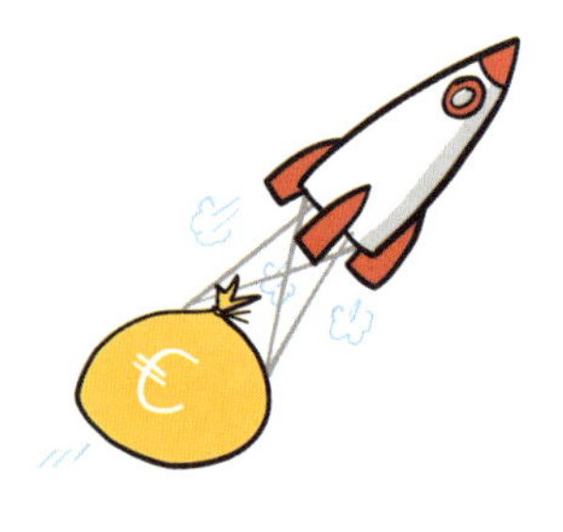

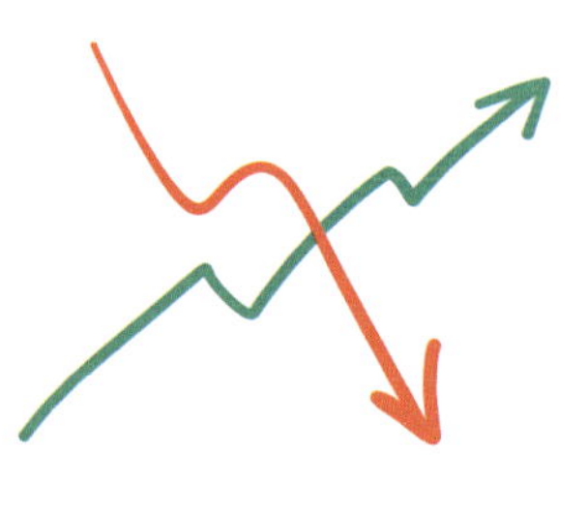

HOW TO DRAW

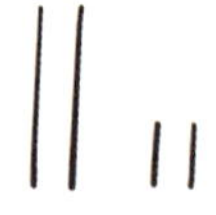

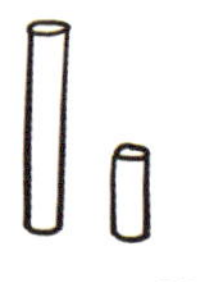

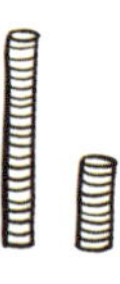

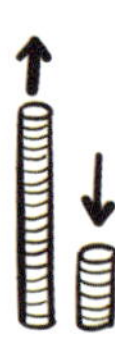

ECONOMICS

BASIC ICONS

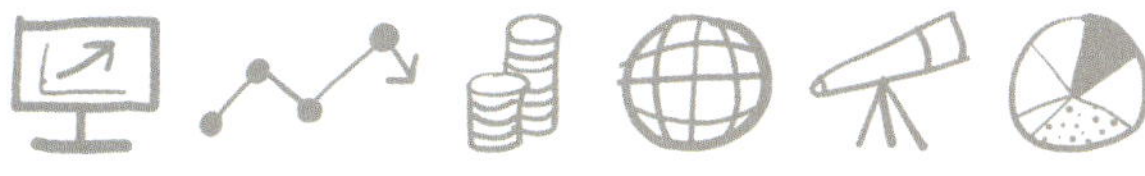

COMBINED ICONS

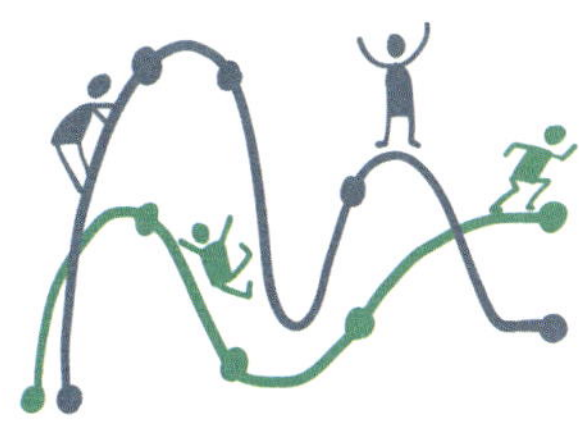

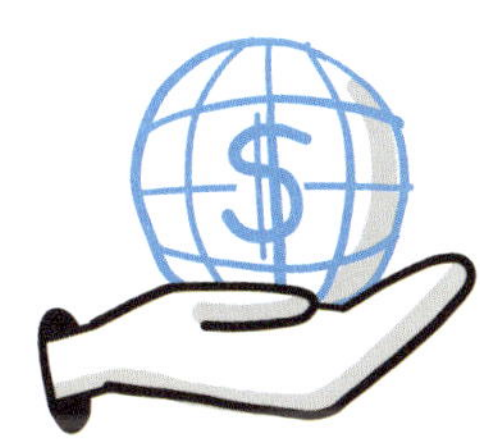

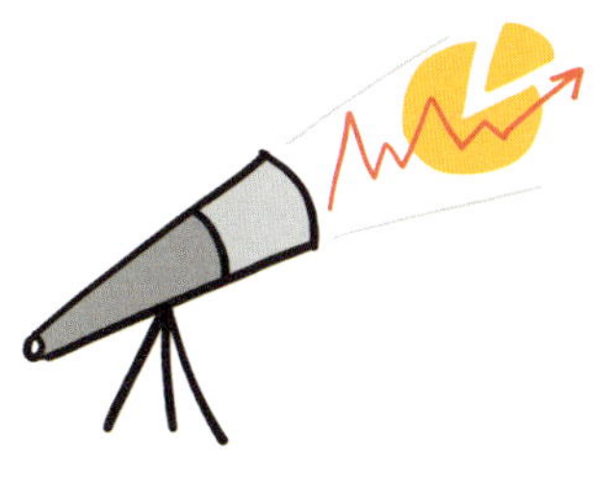

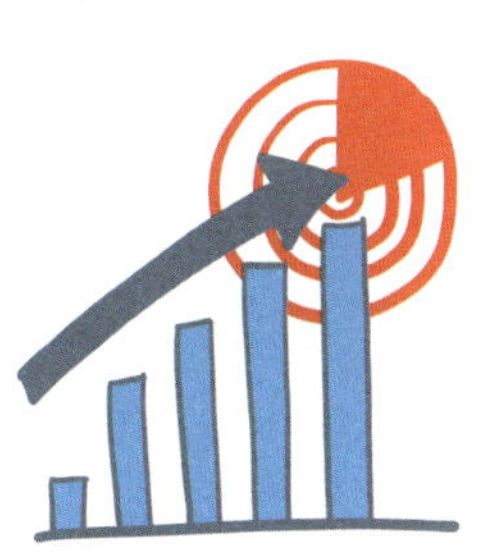

HOW TO DRAW

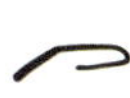

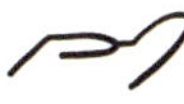

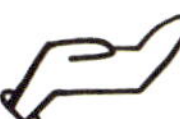

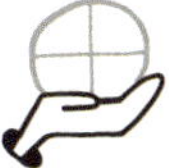

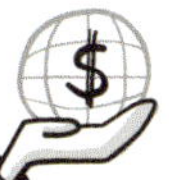

FINANCE

BASIC ICONS

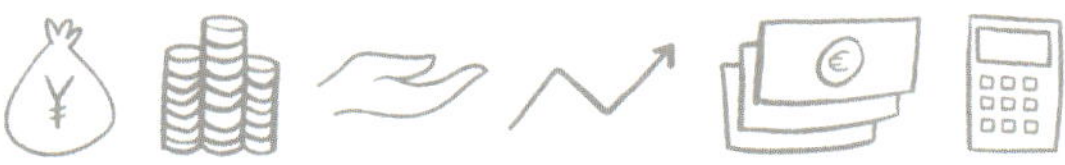

COMBINED ICONS

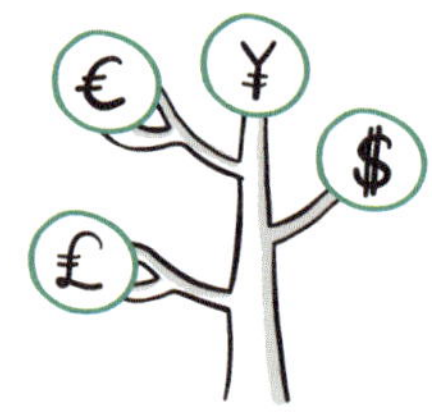

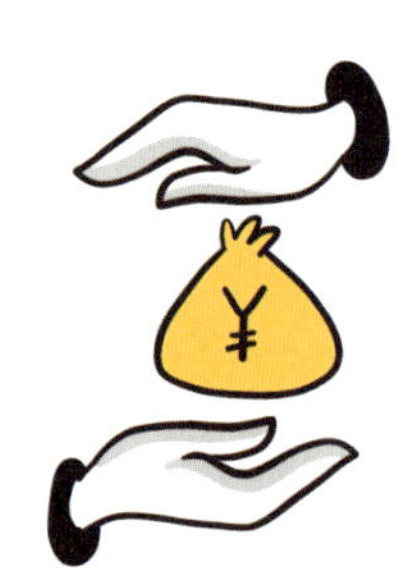

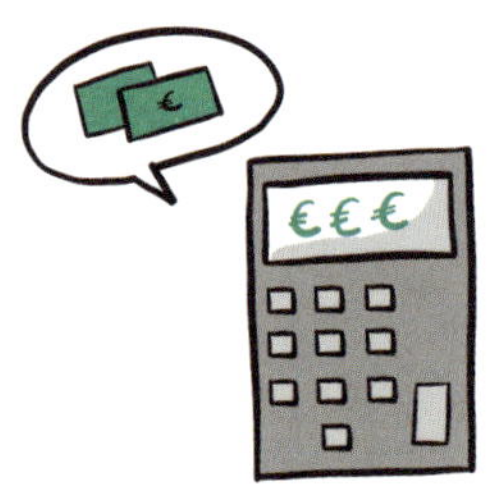

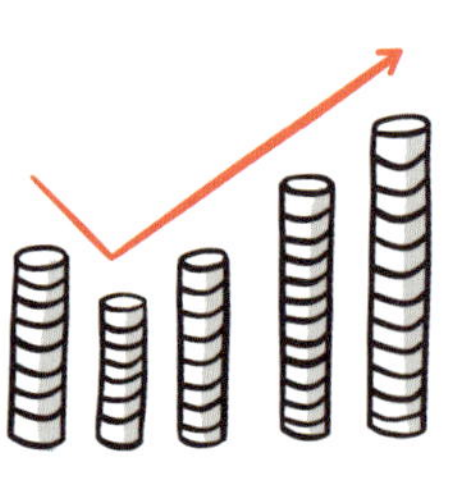

HOW TO DRAW

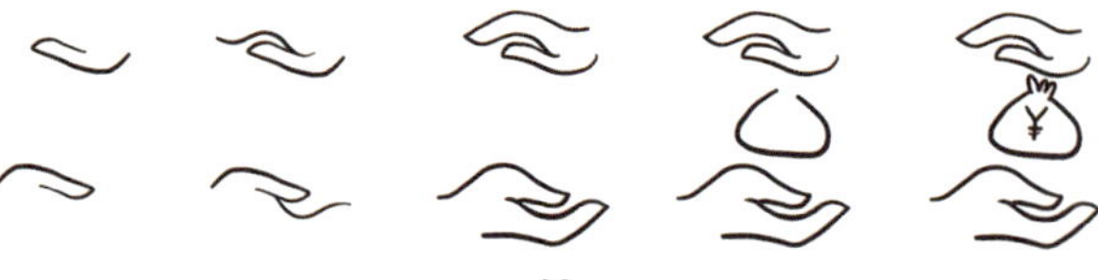

FORECASTING

BASIC ICONS

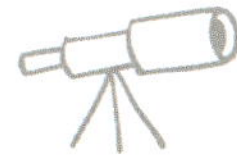
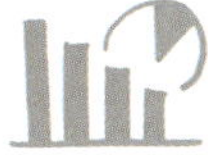
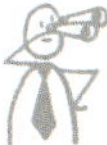
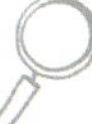
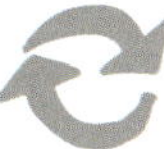

COMBINED ICONS

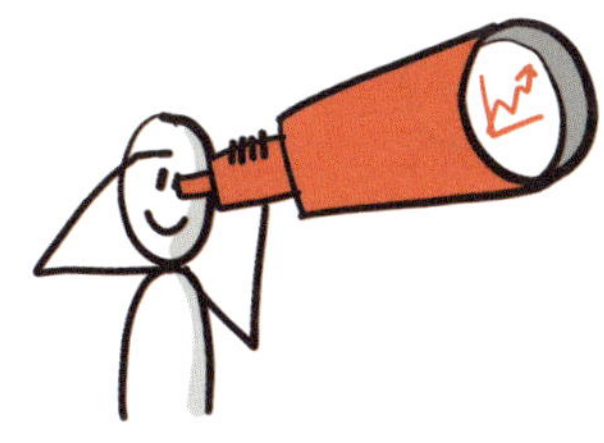
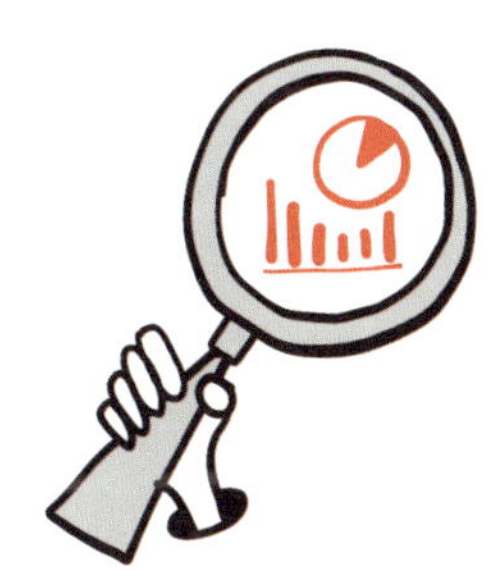
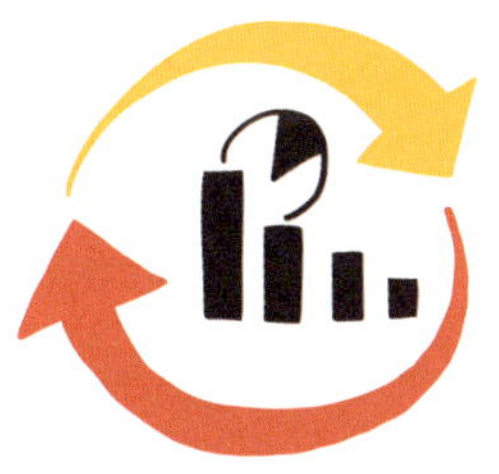

Finance

HOW TO DRAW

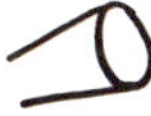
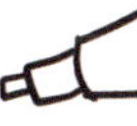
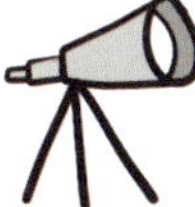

INVESTMENT

BASIC ICONS

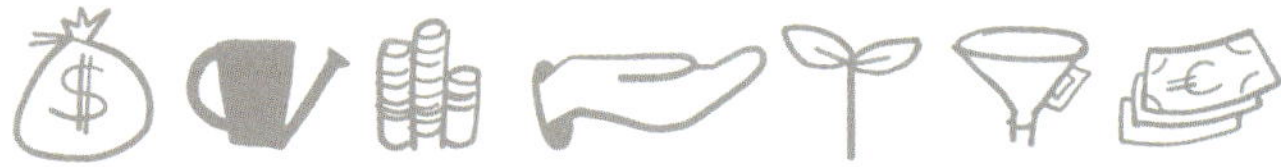

COMBINED ICONS

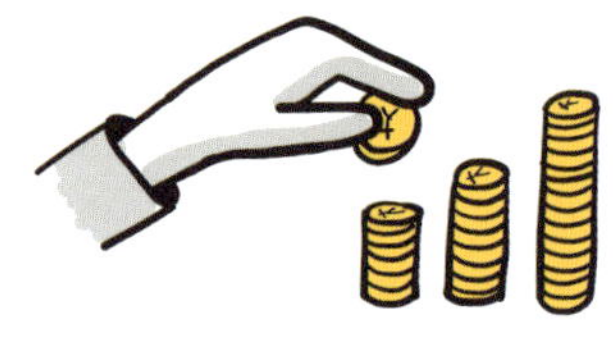

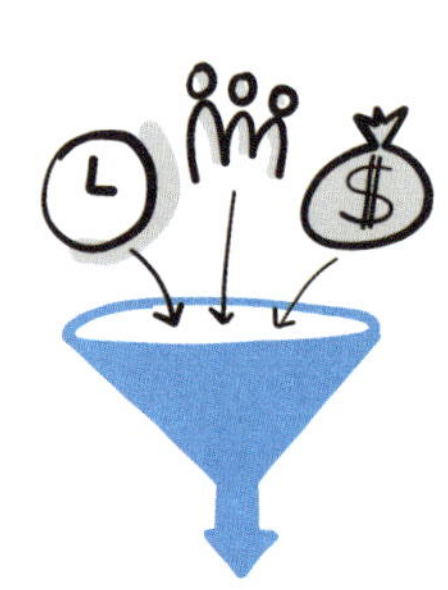

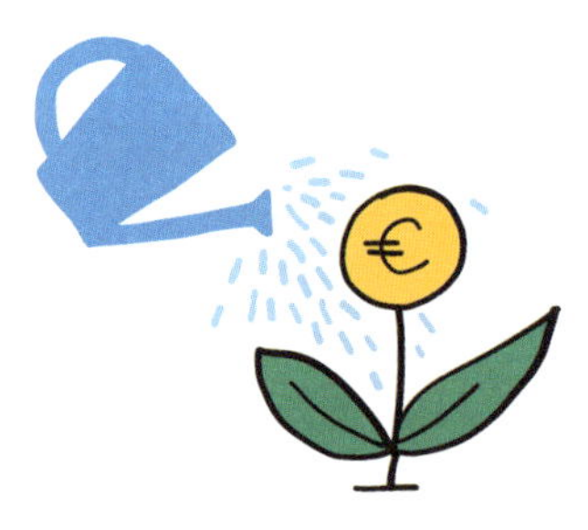

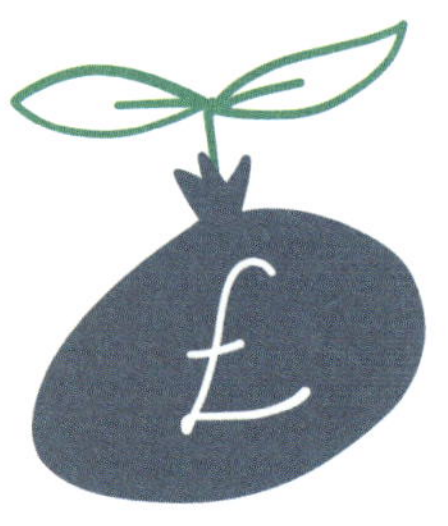

HOW TO DRAW

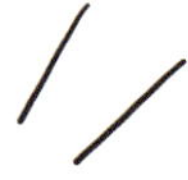

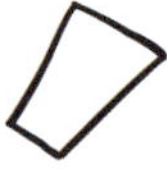

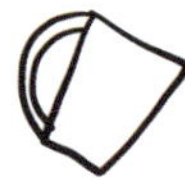

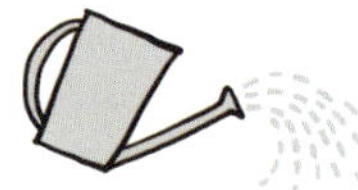

LEGAL

BASIC ICONS

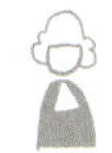
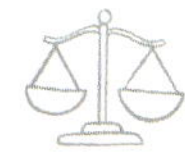
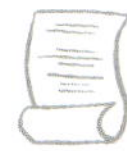
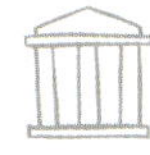
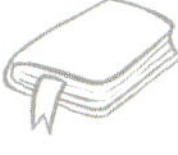
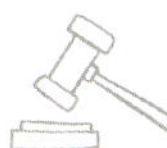

COMBINED ICONS

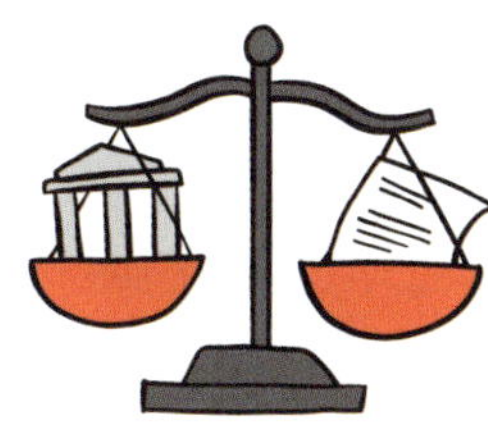

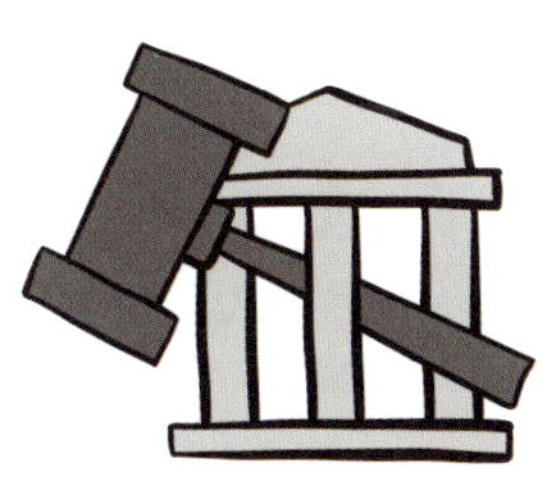

Finance

HOW TO DRAW

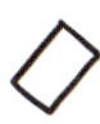
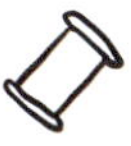

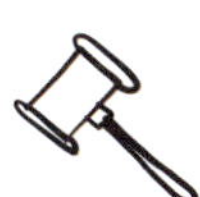

PRICING

BASIC ICONS

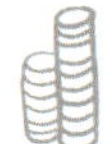
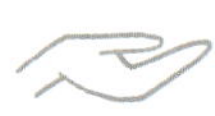
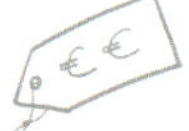

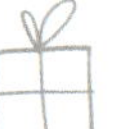
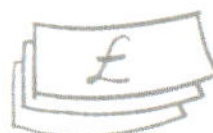

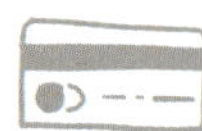

COMBINED ICONS

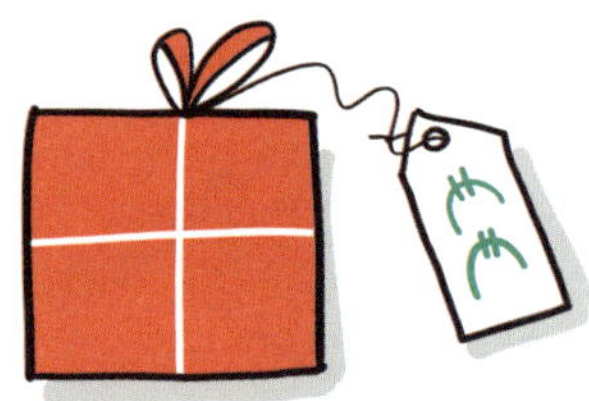
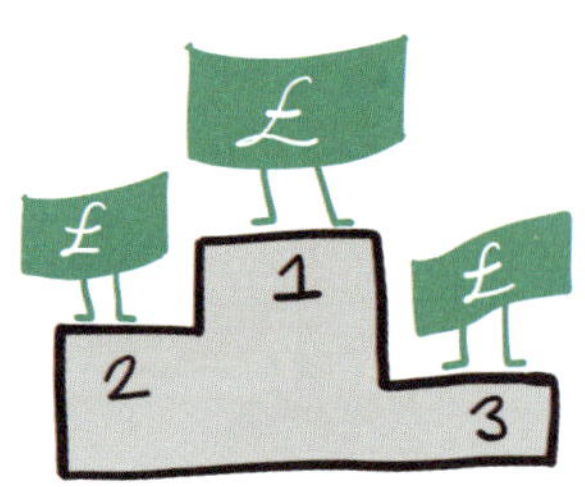

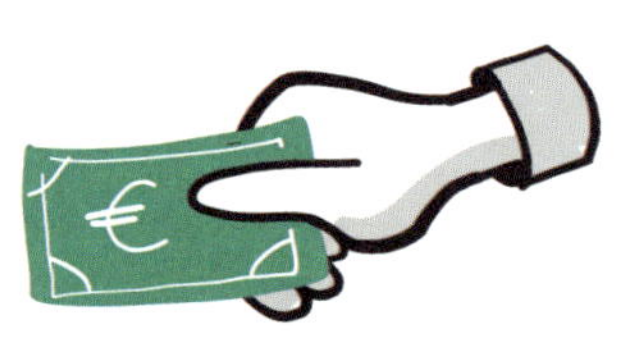

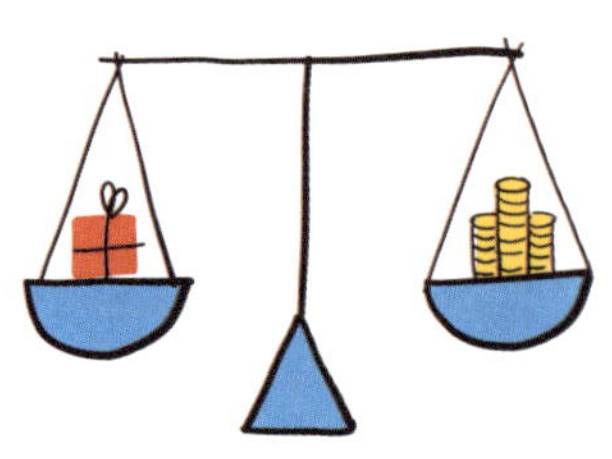

HOW TO DRAW

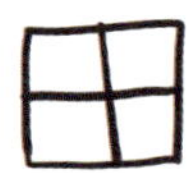
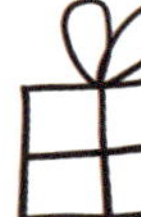
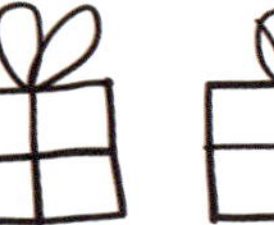
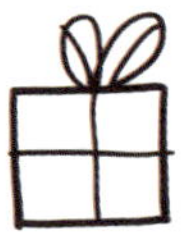
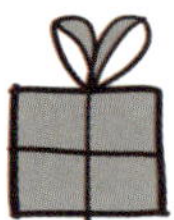

PURCHASE

BASIC ICONS

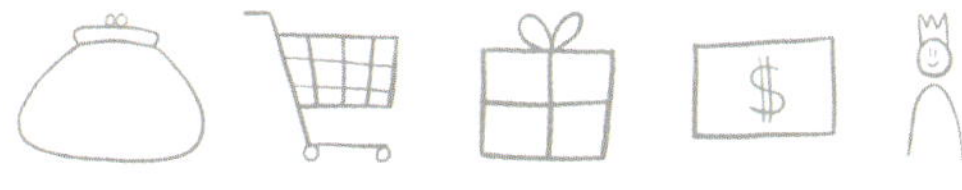

COMBINED ICONS

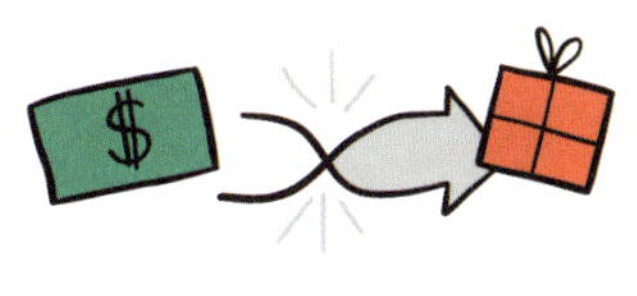

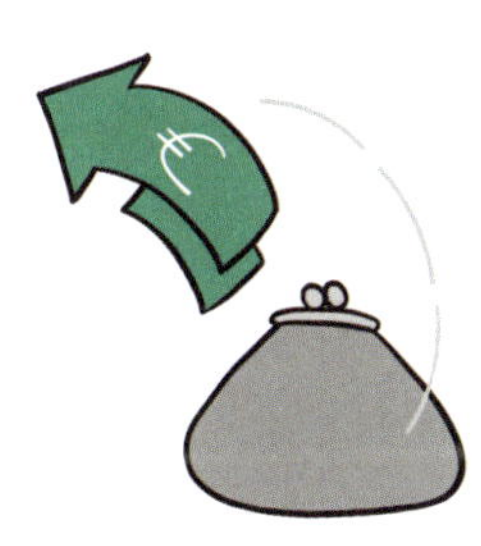

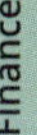

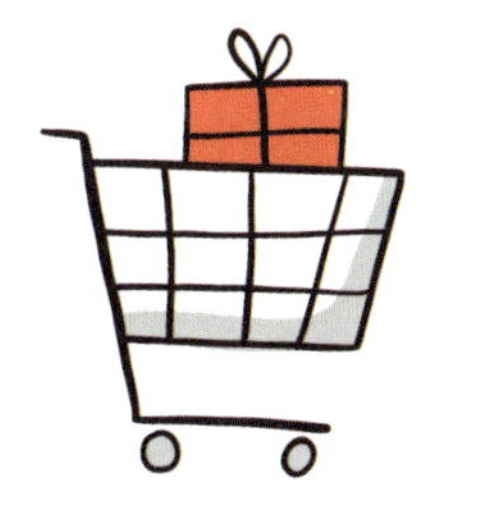

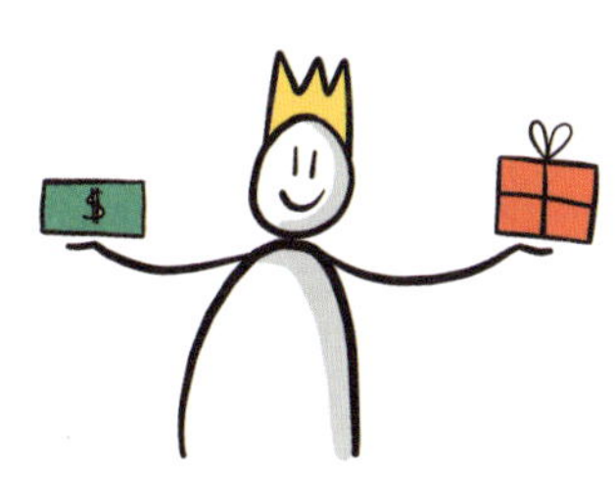

HOW TO DRAW

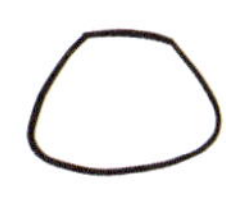

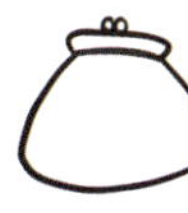

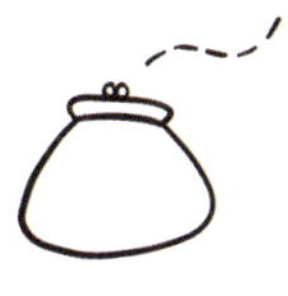

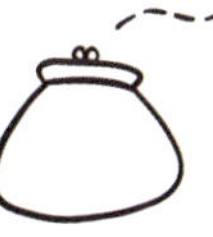

RELIABILITY

BASIC ICONS

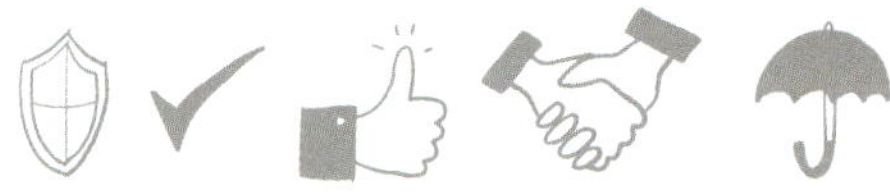

COMBINED ICONS

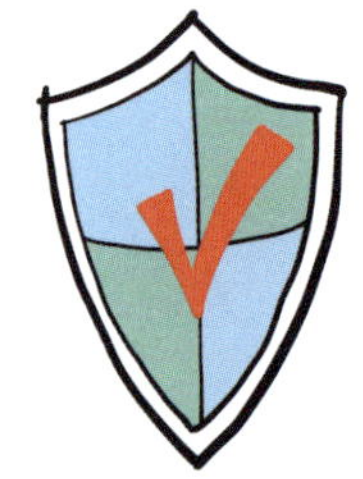

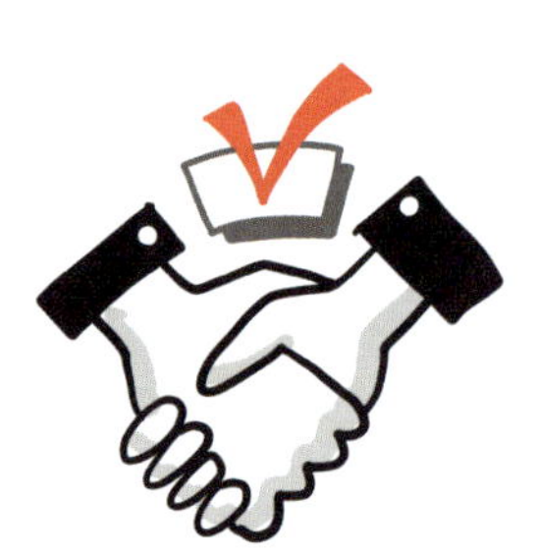

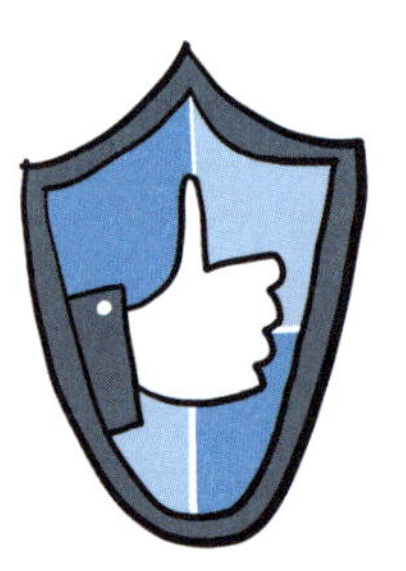

HOW TO DRAW

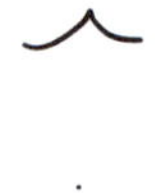
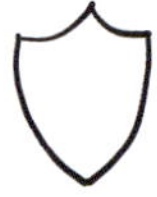

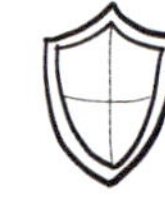
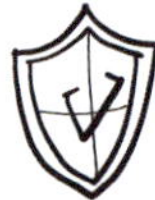
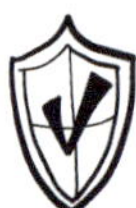

REVENUE

BASIC ICONS

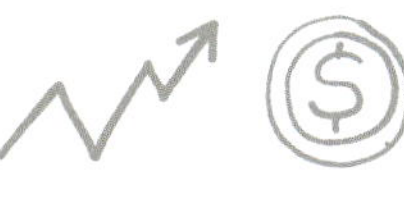
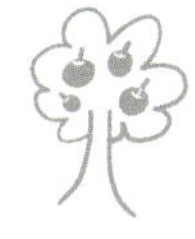
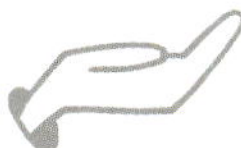

COMBINED ICONS

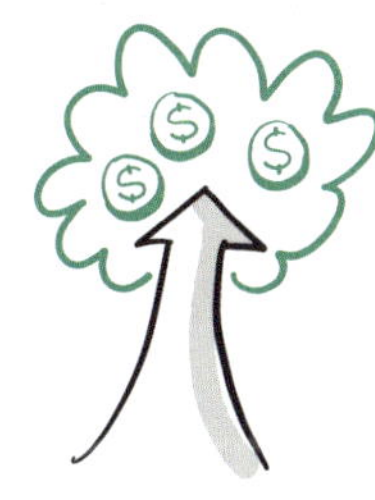
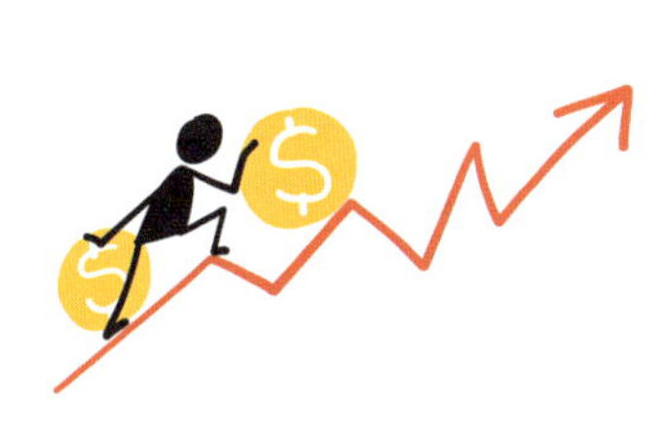
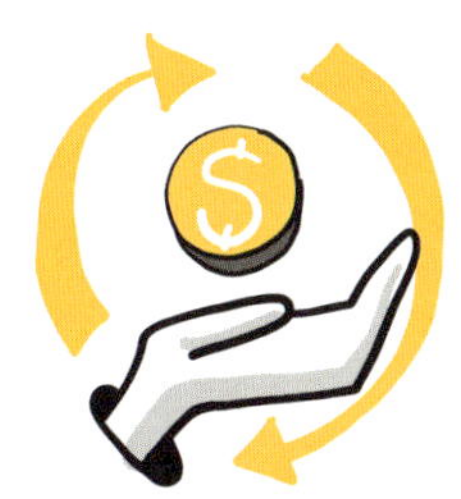
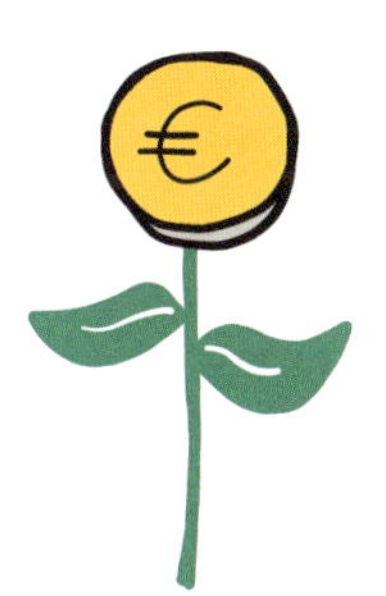

HOW TO DRAW

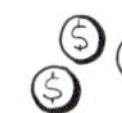
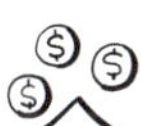
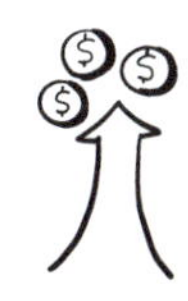
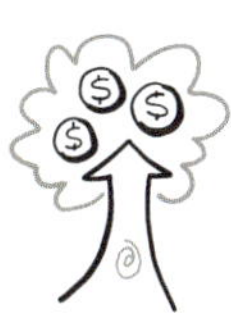

RISK

BASIC ICONS

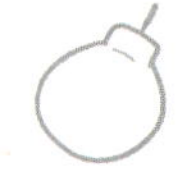 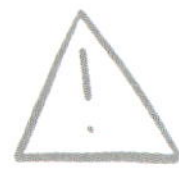 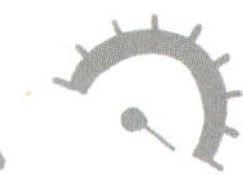 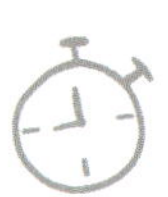 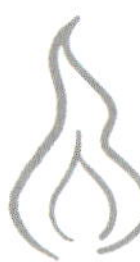

COMBINED ICONS

HOW TO DRAW

 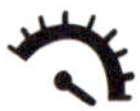  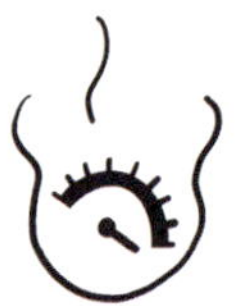 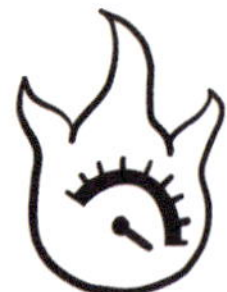

TARGETS

BASIC ICONS

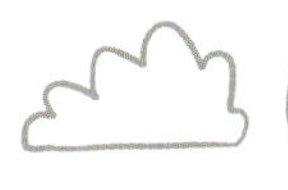 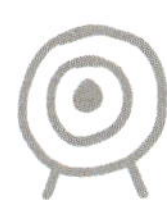 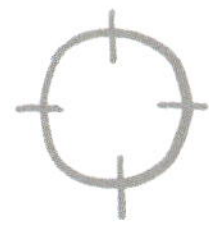 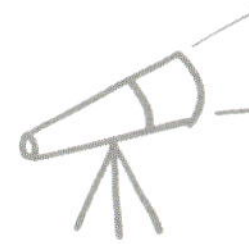 

COMBINED ICONS

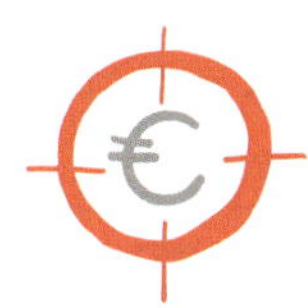

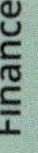

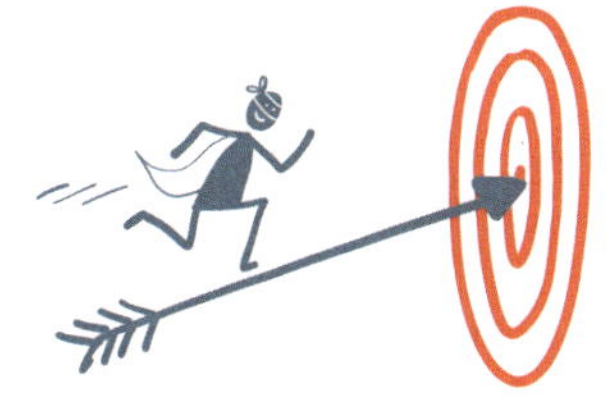

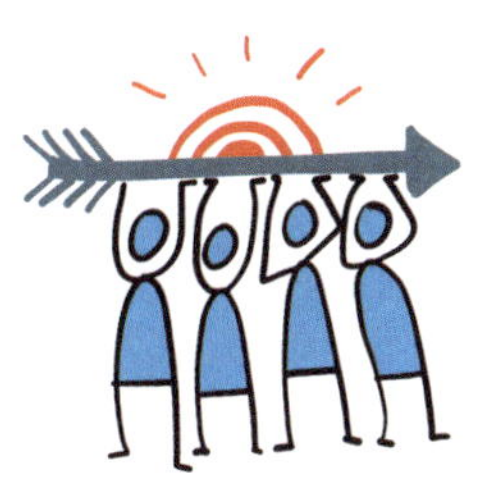

HOW TO DRAW

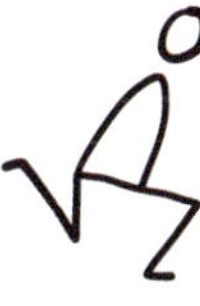 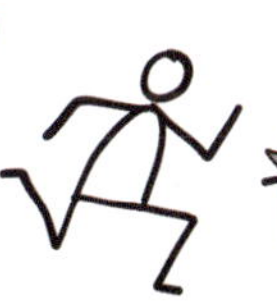 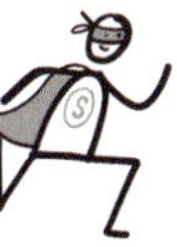

TAXES

BASIC ICONS

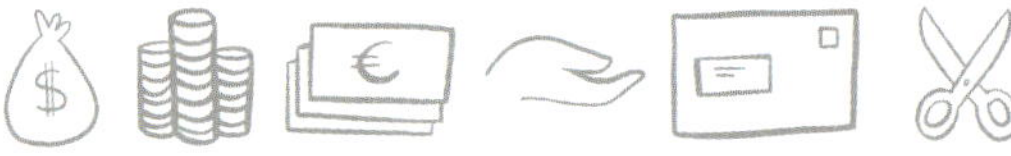

COMBINED ICONS

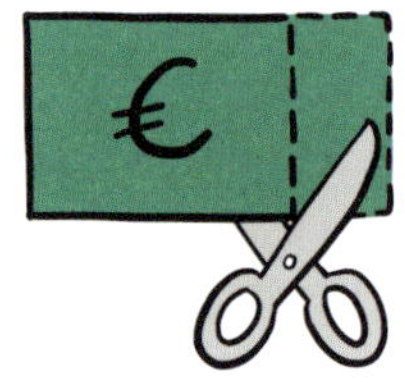

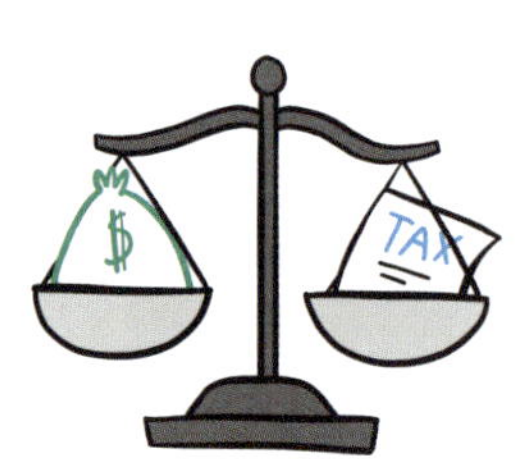

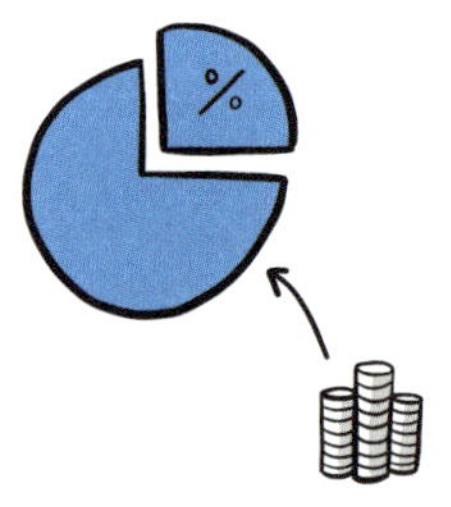

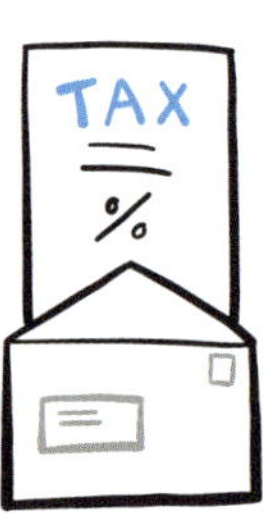

HOW TO DRAW

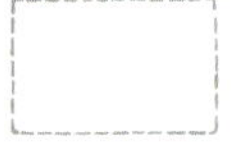

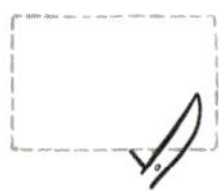

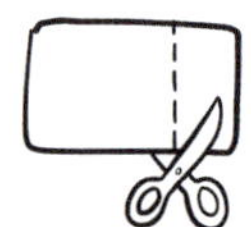

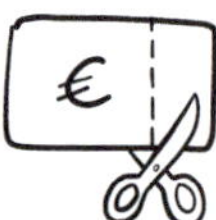

TRANSACTION

BASIC ICONS

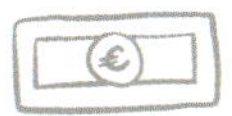
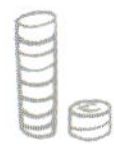
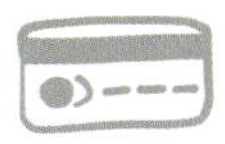
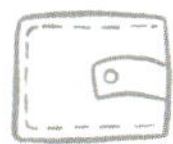
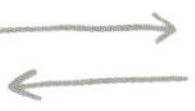

COMBINED ICONS

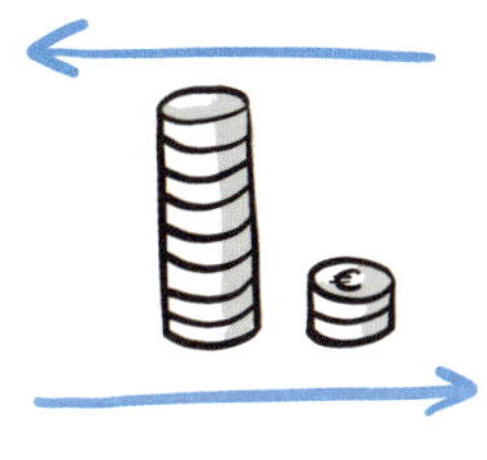
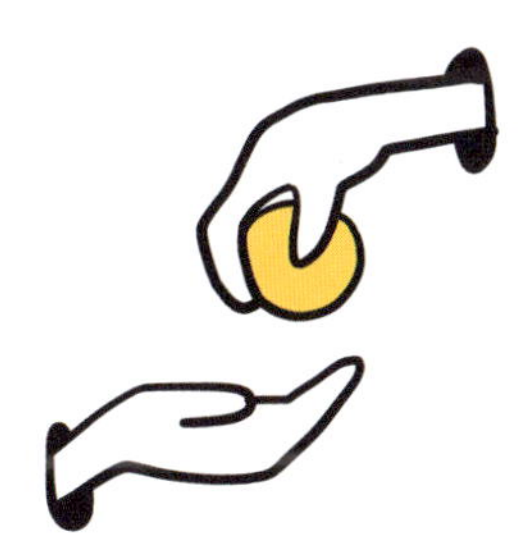
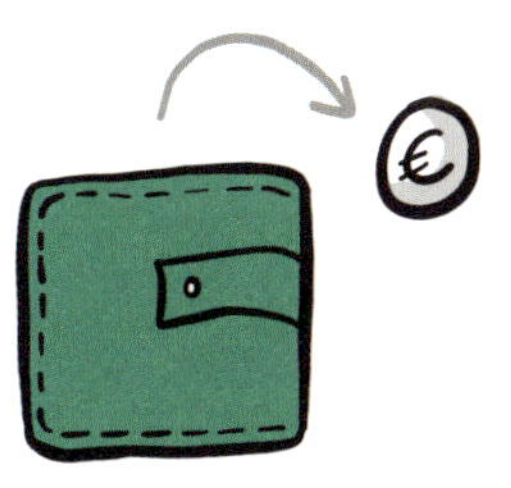
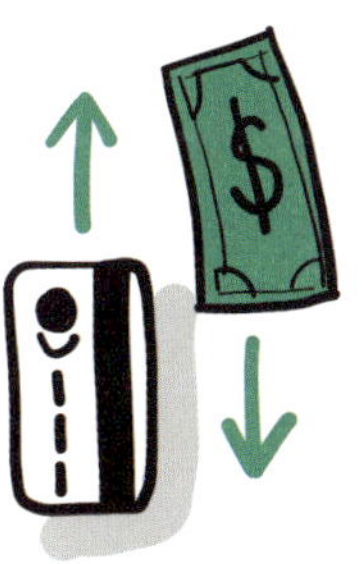

Finance

HOW TO DRAW

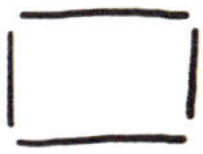

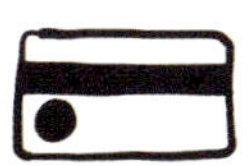
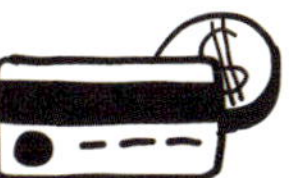

HR

OUR WORKING ENVIRONMENT

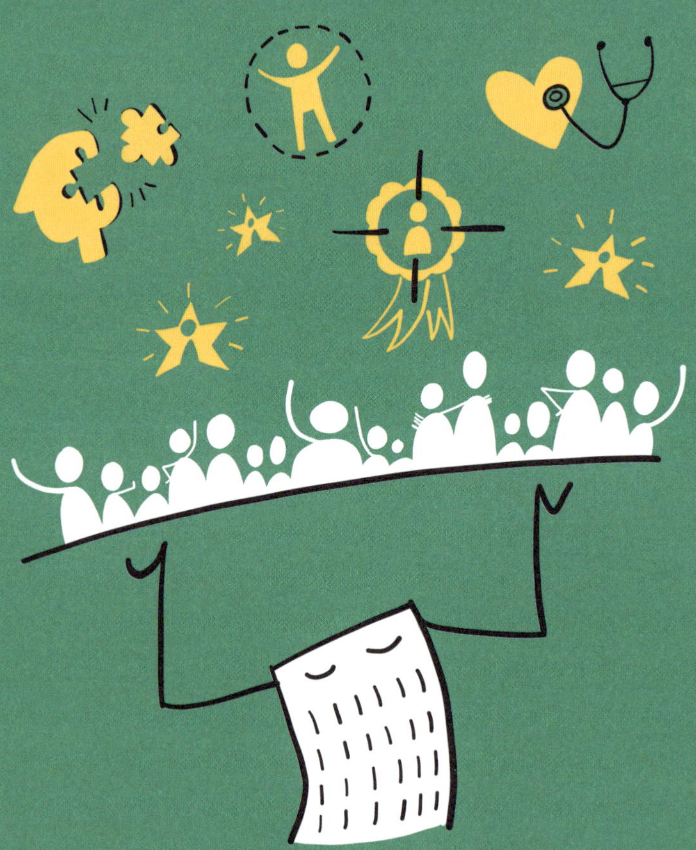

COMMUNICATION

BASIC ICONS

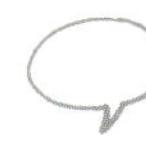
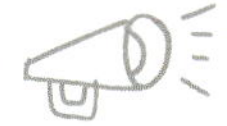
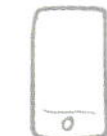
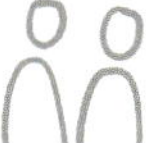
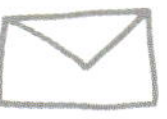
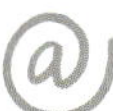

COMBINED ICONS

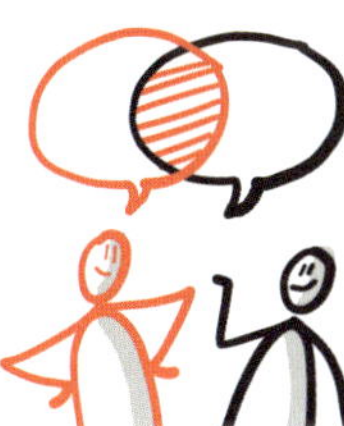

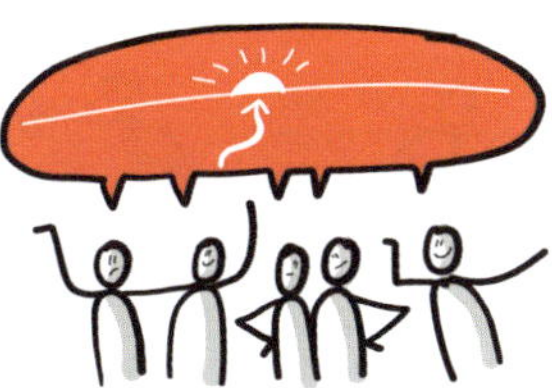

HR

HOW TO DRAW

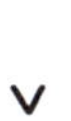
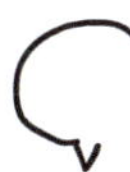
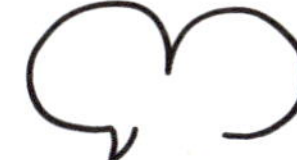
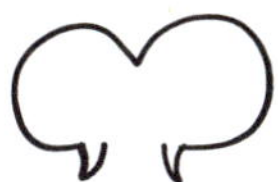

CONFLICT

BASIC ICONS

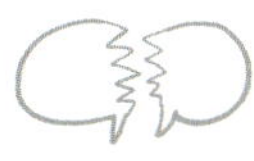

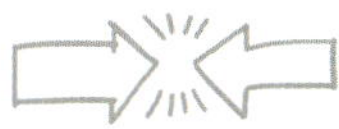
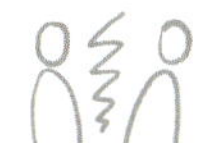

COMBINED ICONS

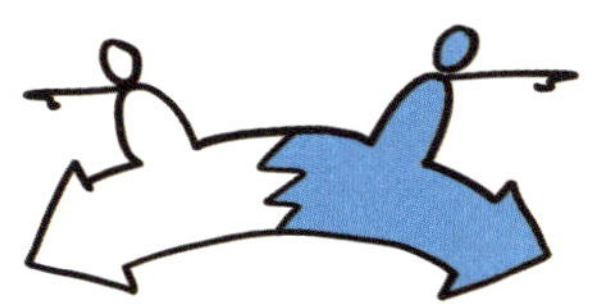
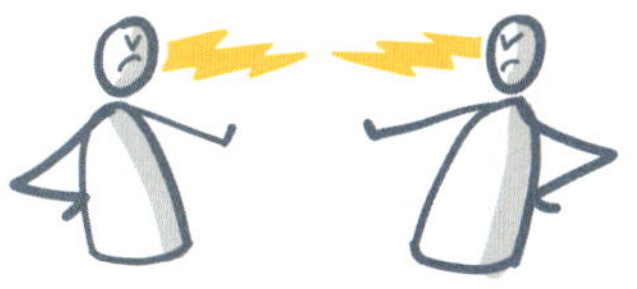

HOW TO DRAW

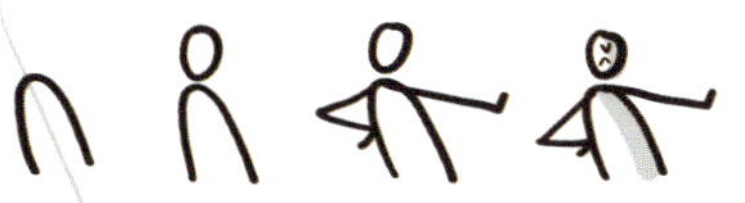

CULTURE

BASIC ICONS

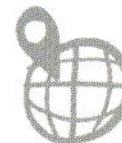
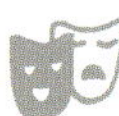
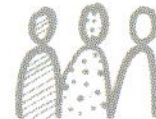
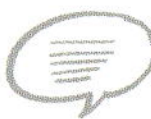
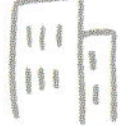
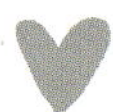

COMBINED ICONS

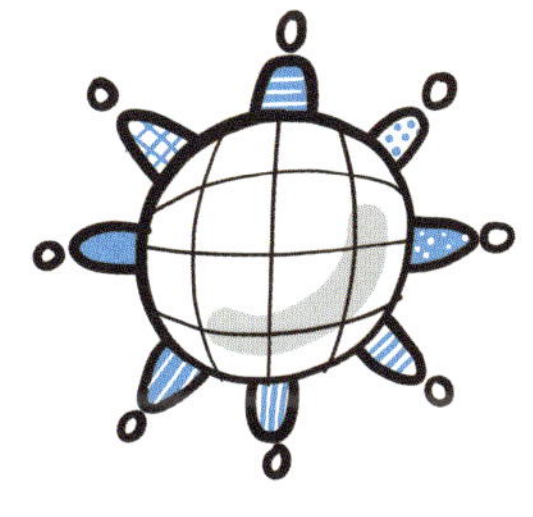
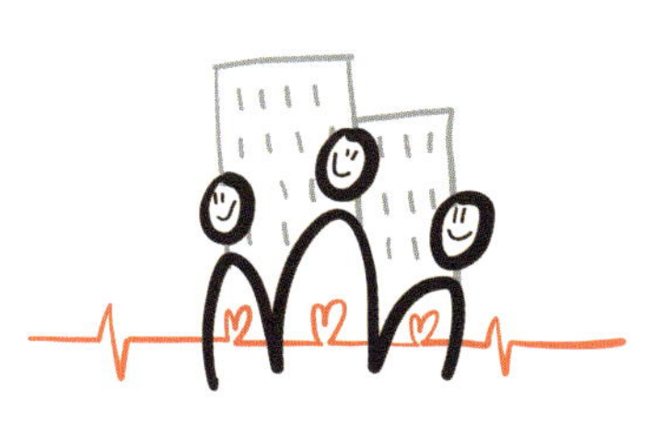
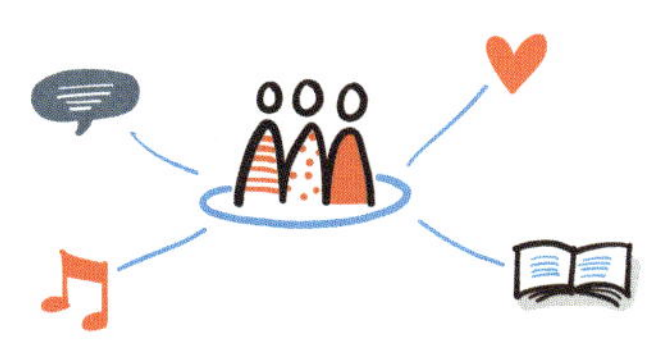
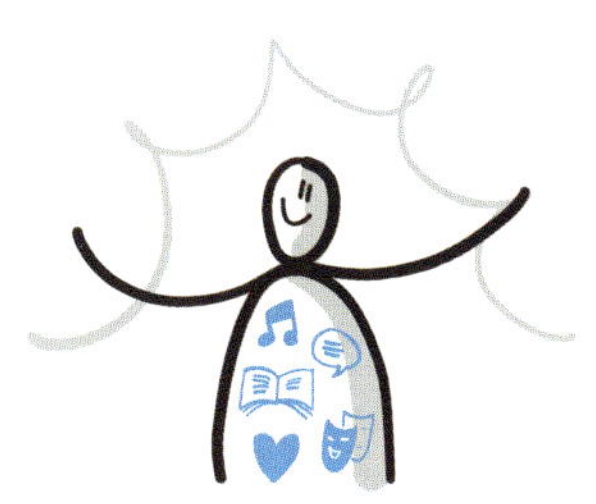

HOW TO DRAW

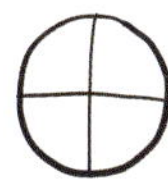
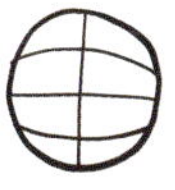
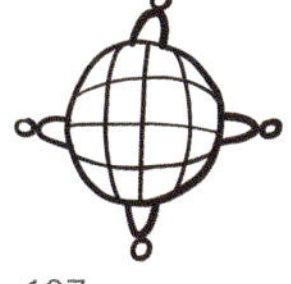
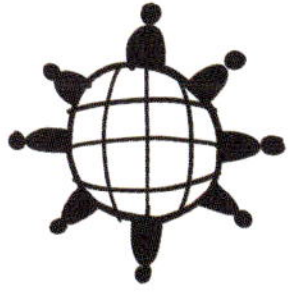

DEPLOYMENT

BASIC ICONS

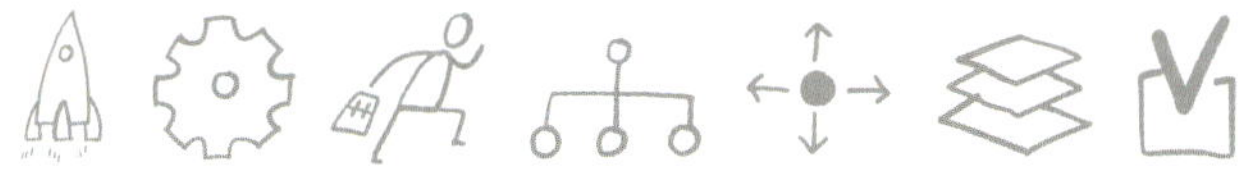

COMBINED ICONS

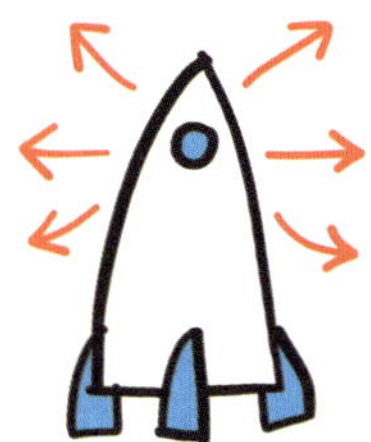

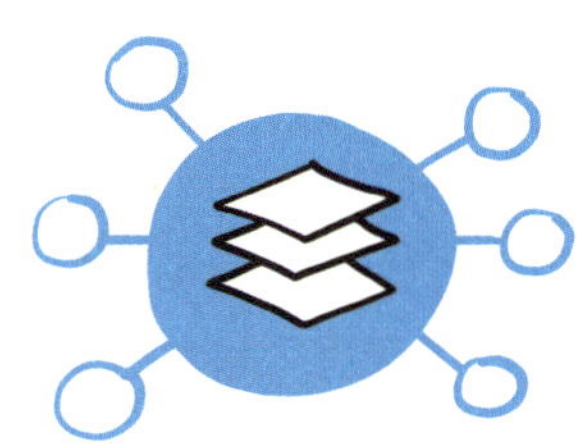

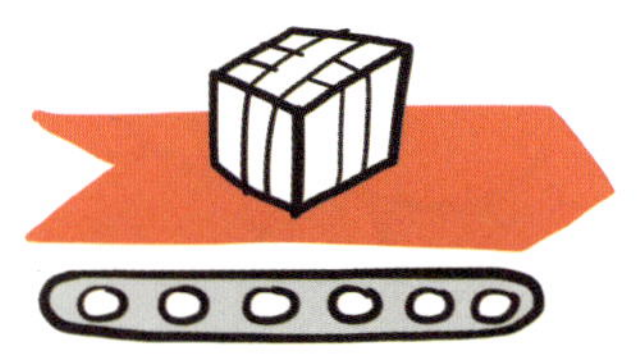

HOW TO DRAW

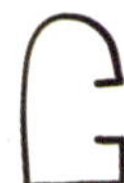

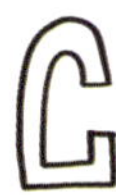

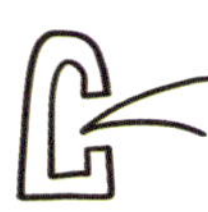

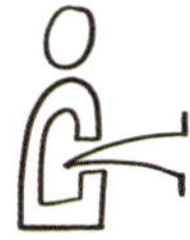

DISCRIMINATION

BASIC ICONS

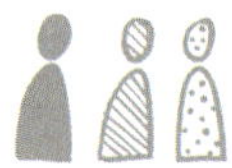
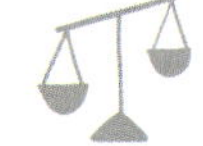

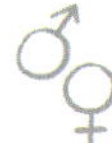

COMBINED ICONS

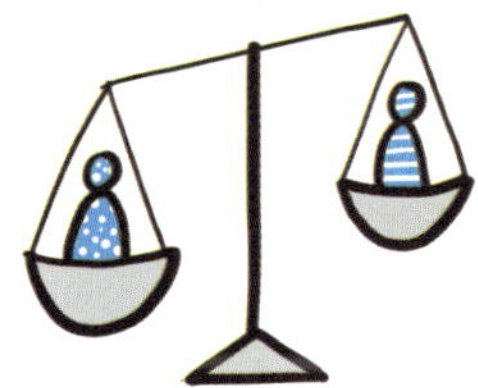

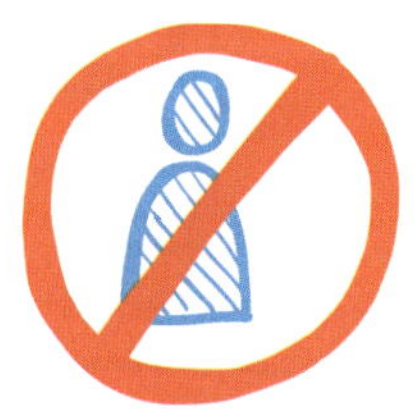
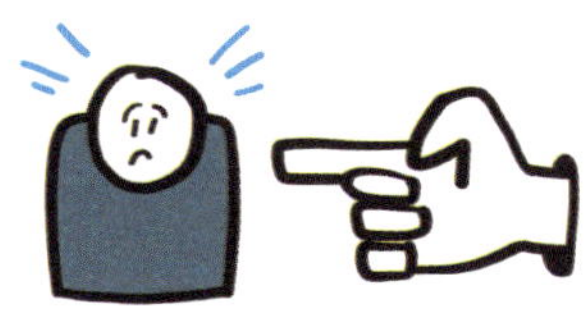

HOW TO DRAW

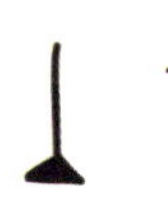
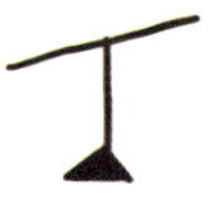
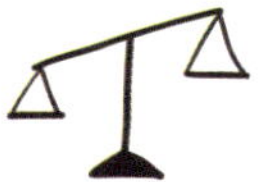
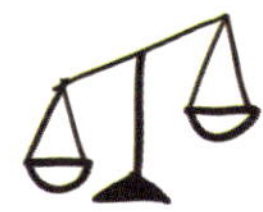
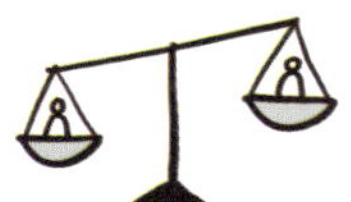

HR

EDUCATION

BASIC ICONS

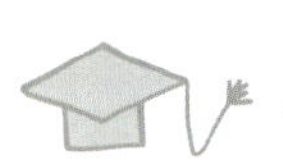

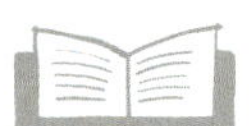

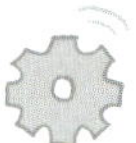
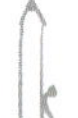
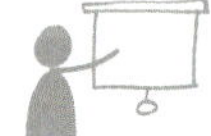

COMBINED ICONS

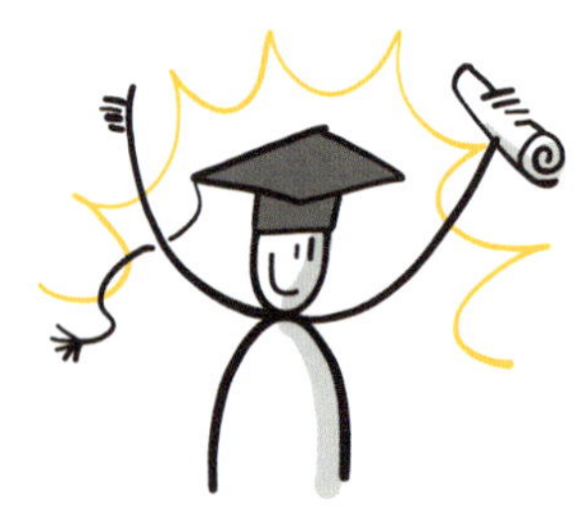
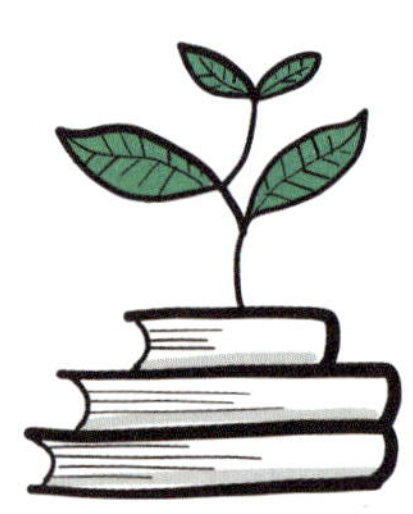

HOW TO DRAW

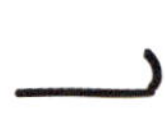
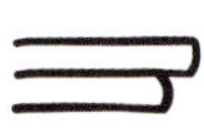
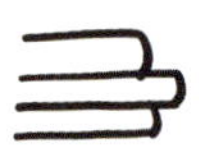
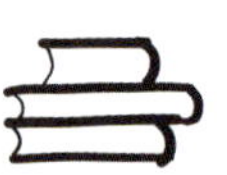

EMPLOYEE BRANDING

BASIC ICONS

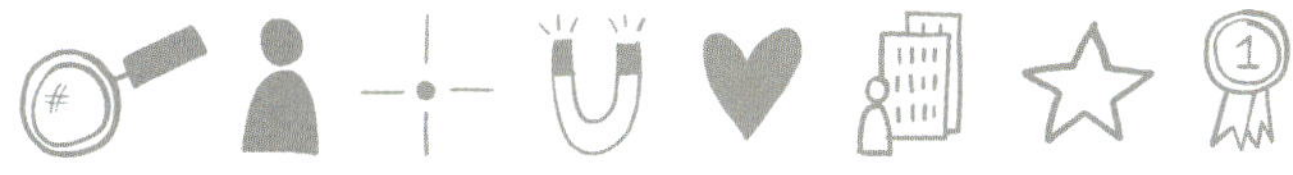

COMBINED ICONS

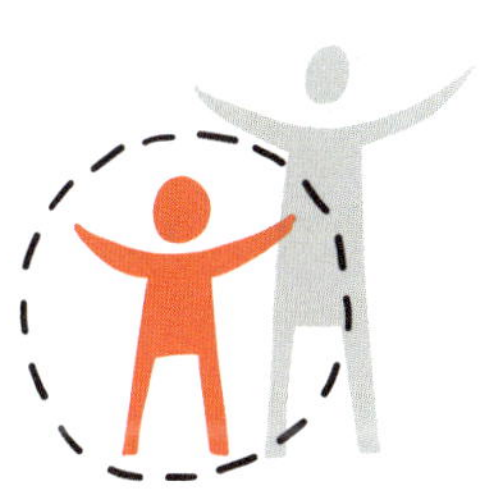

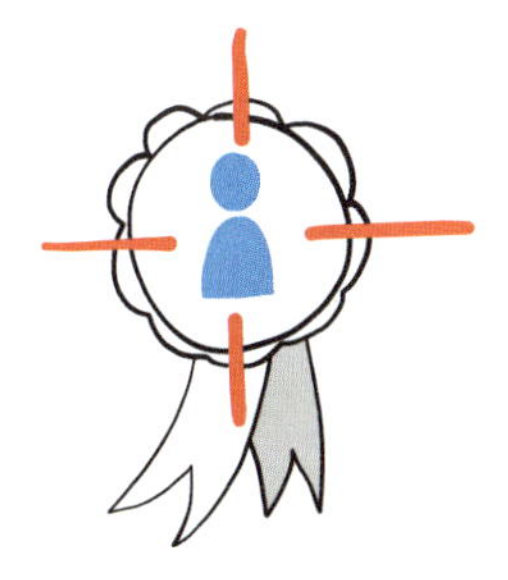

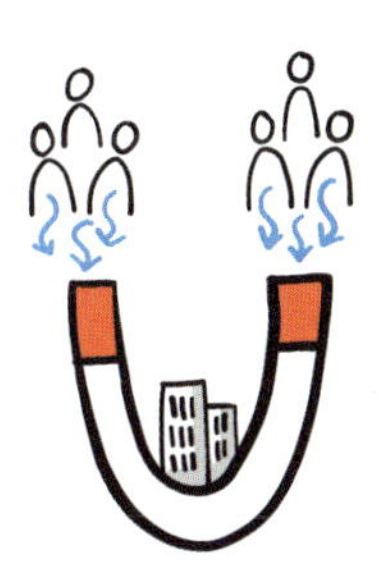

HOW TO DRAW

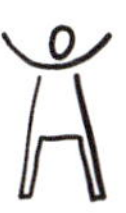

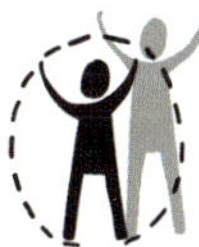

HR

HEALTH CARE

BASIC ICONS

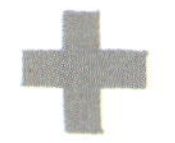 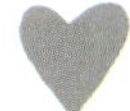 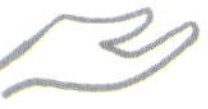 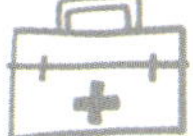 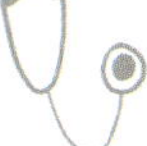 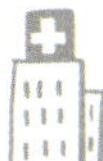 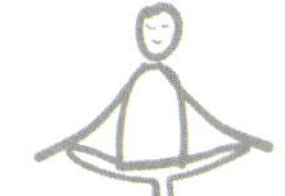

COMBINED ICONS

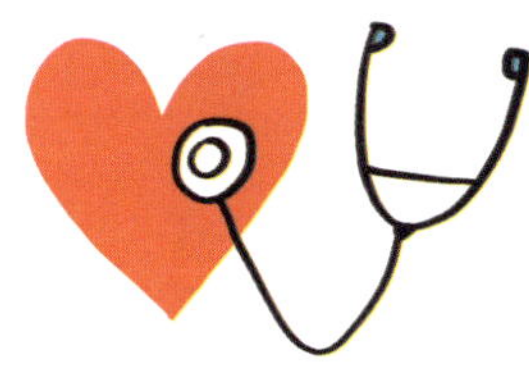

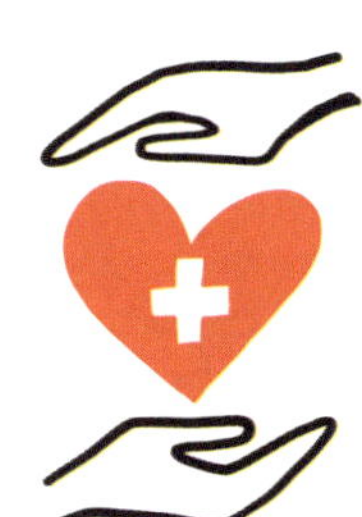

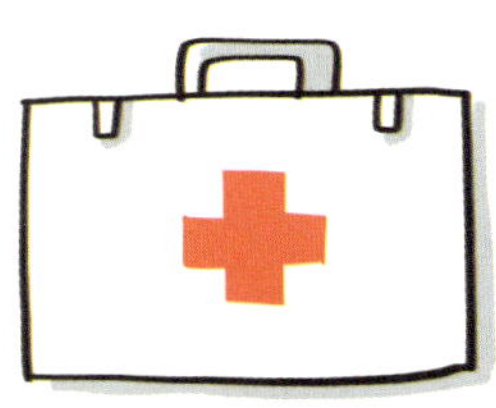

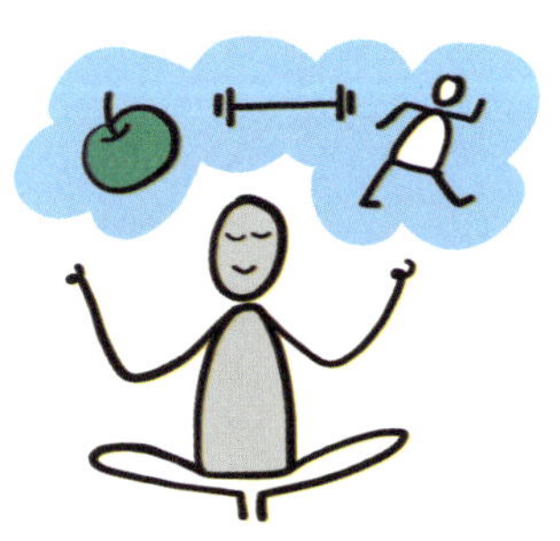

HOW TO DRAW

  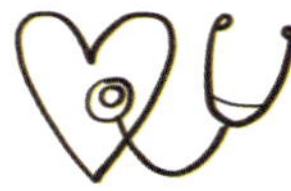

HUMAN CAPITAL

BASIC ICONS

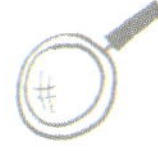
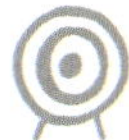
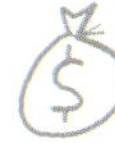
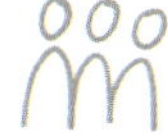
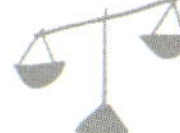
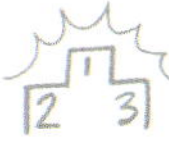
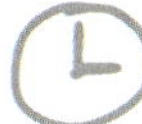

COMBINED ICONS

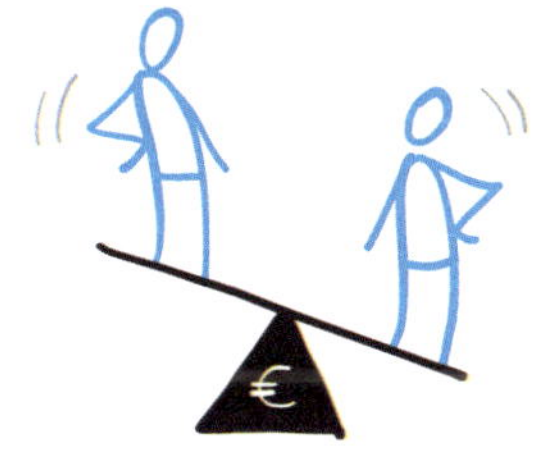
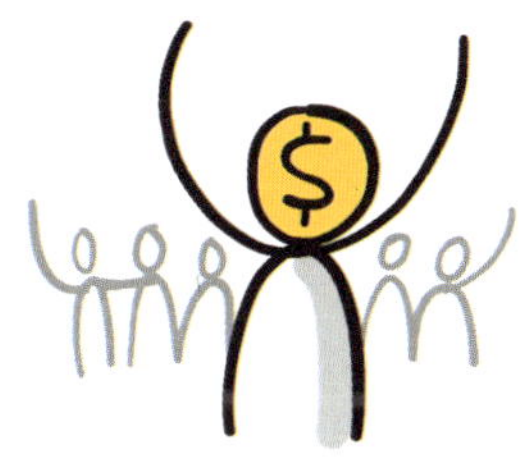
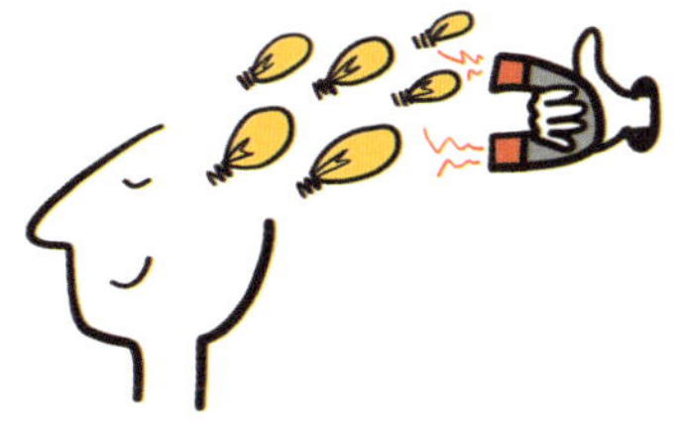
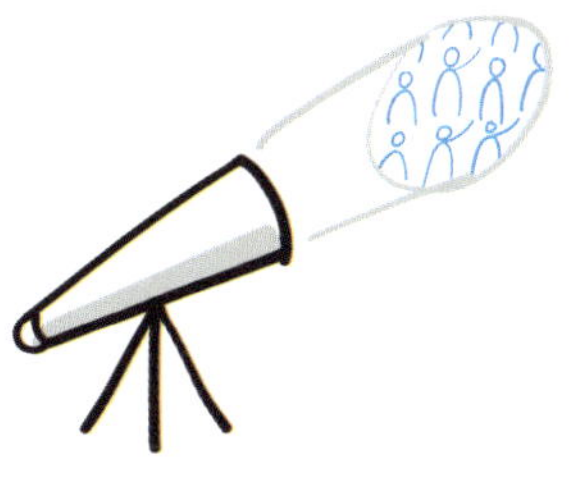

HOW TO DRAW

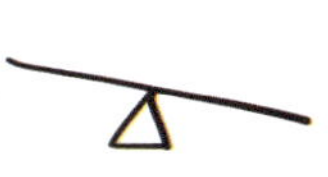
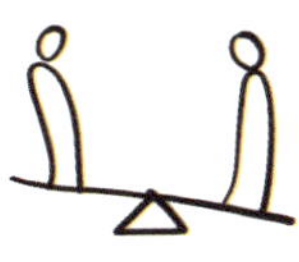
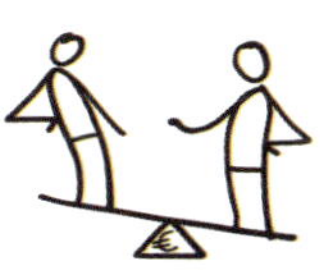

HUMAN RESOURCES (HR)

BASIC ICONS

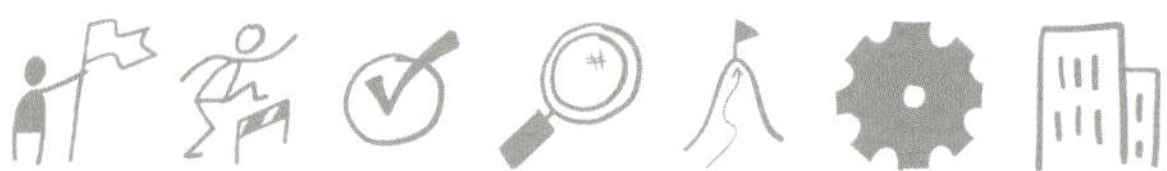

COMBINED ICONS

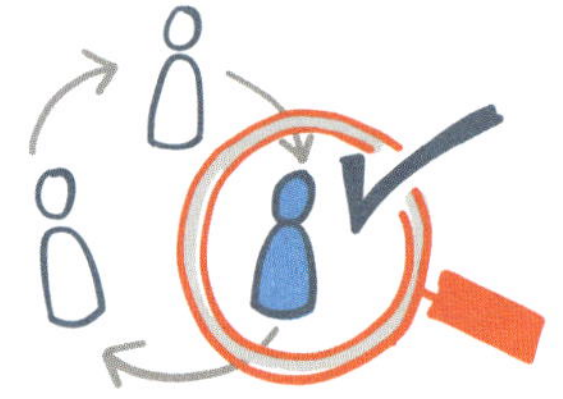

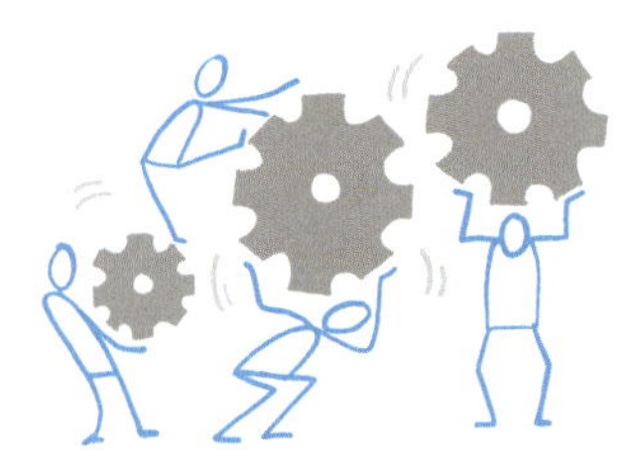

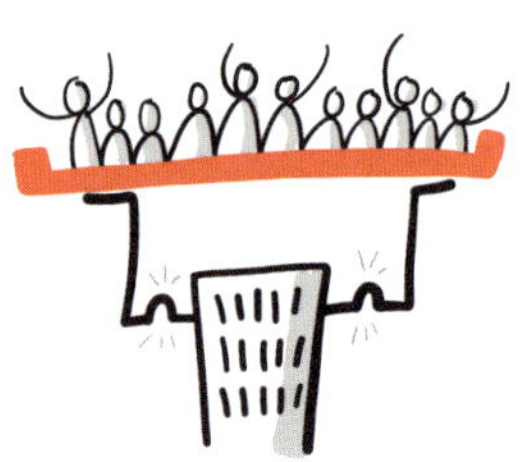

HOW TO DRAW

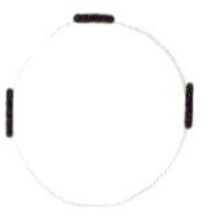

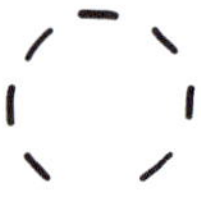

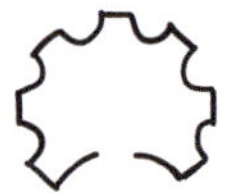

JOB SEARCH

BASIC ICONS

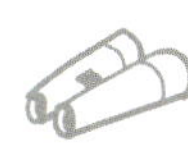
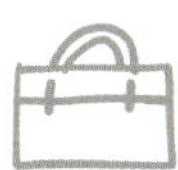
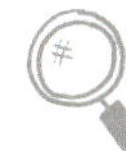
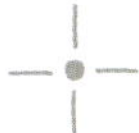
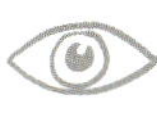
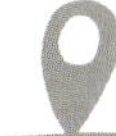
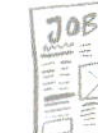

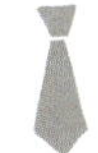

COMBINED ICONS

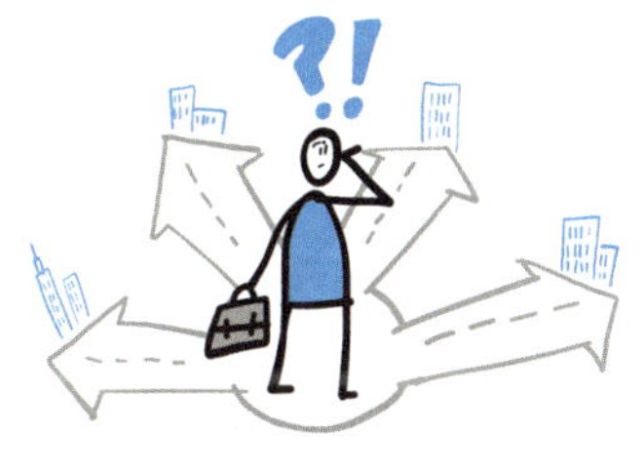

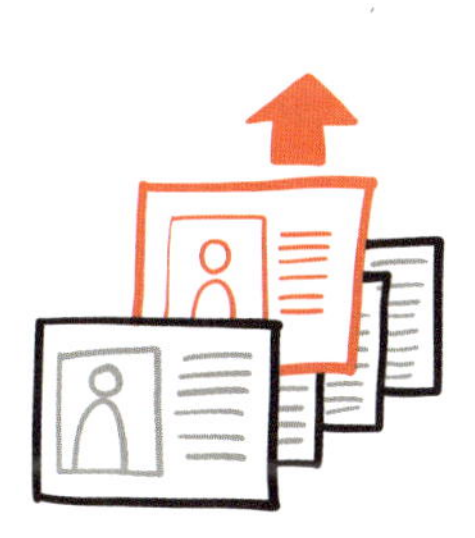
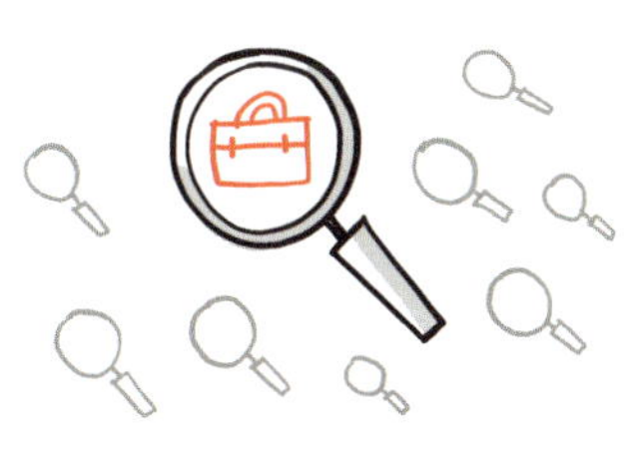
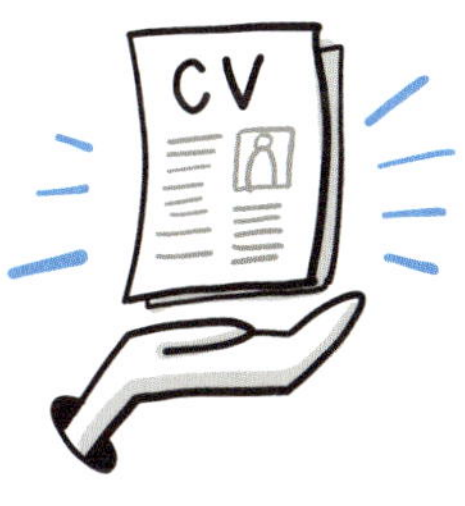

HOW TO DRAW

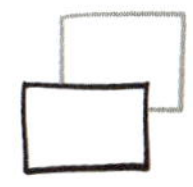
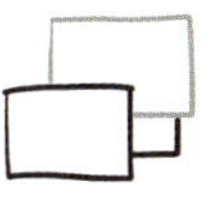
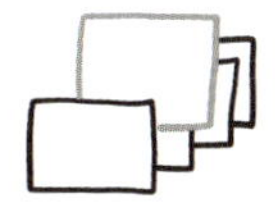
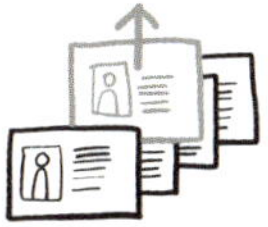

HR

LEARNING

BASIC ICONS

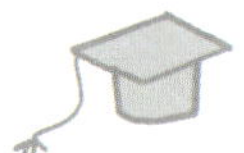

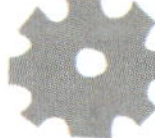
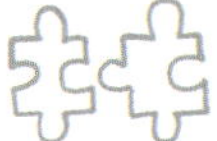

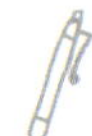

COMBINED ICONS

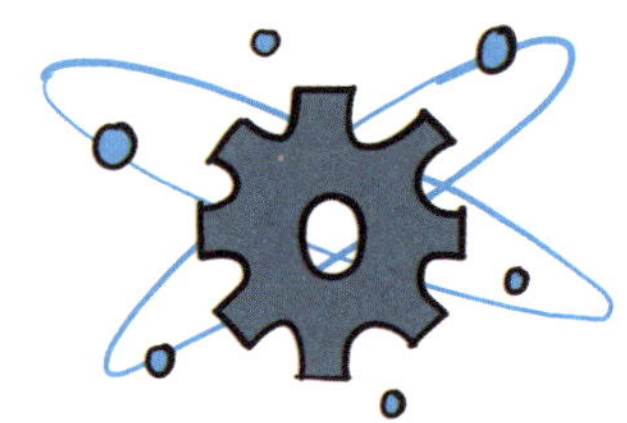

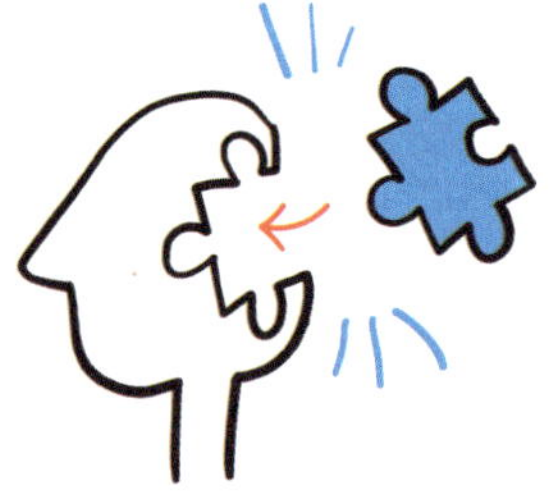
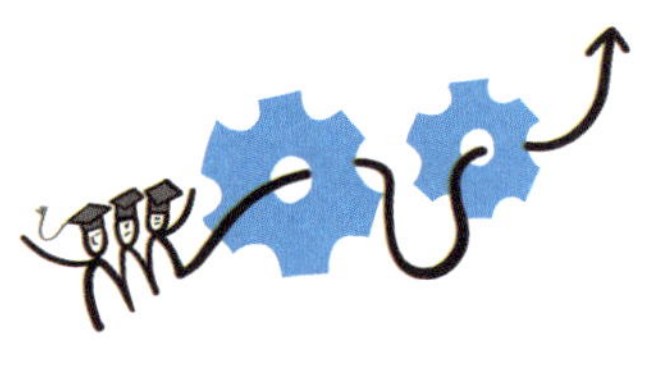

HOW TO DRAW

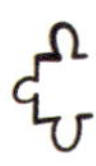
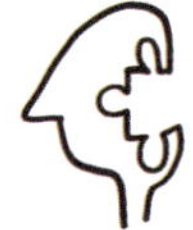
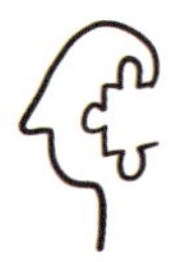
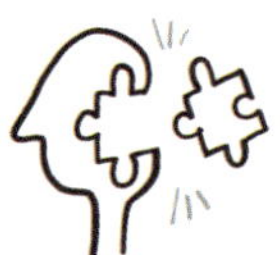

MOBILITY

BASIC ICONS

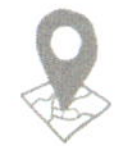 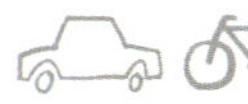 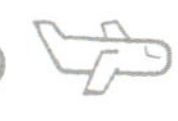 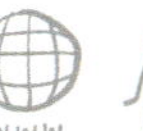 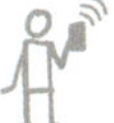

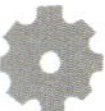 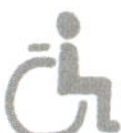

COMBINED ICONS

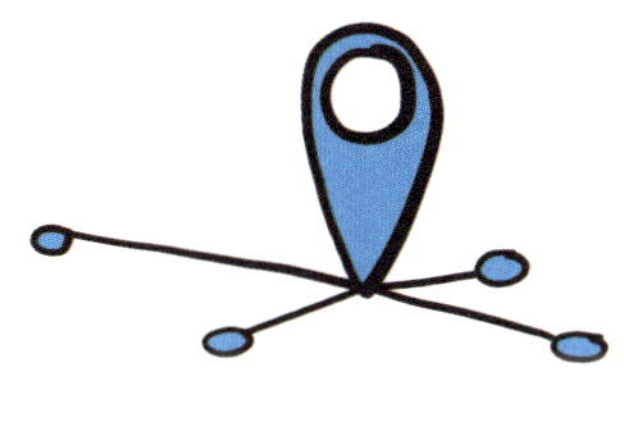

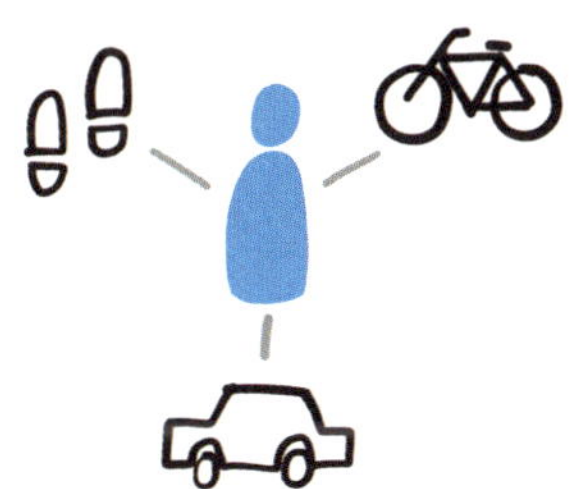

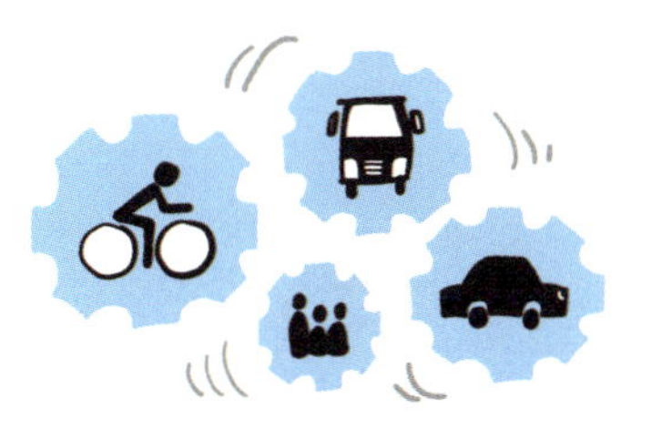

HOW TO DRAW

 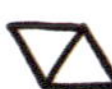 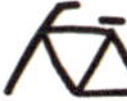 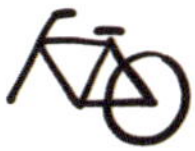 

PENSION FUNDS

BASIC ICONS

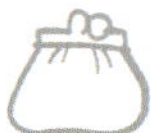
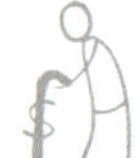
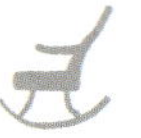
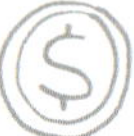
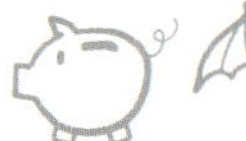

COMBINED ICONS

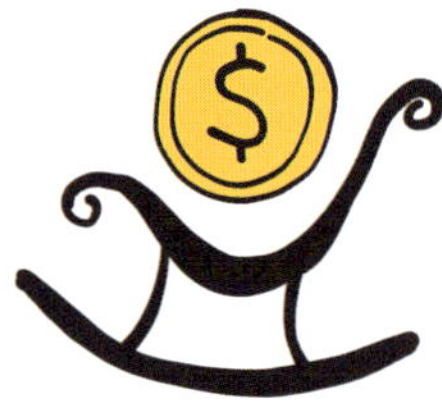
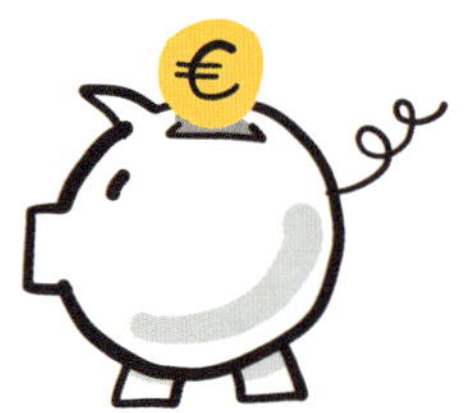
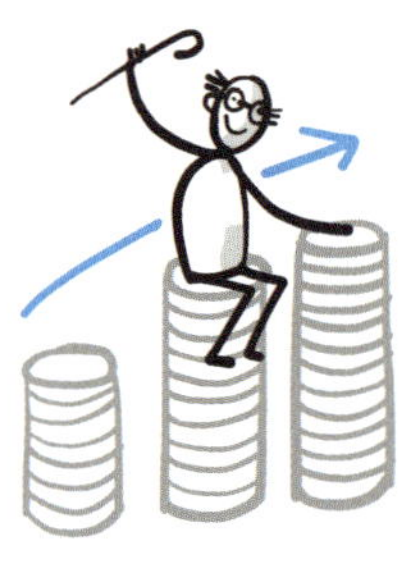
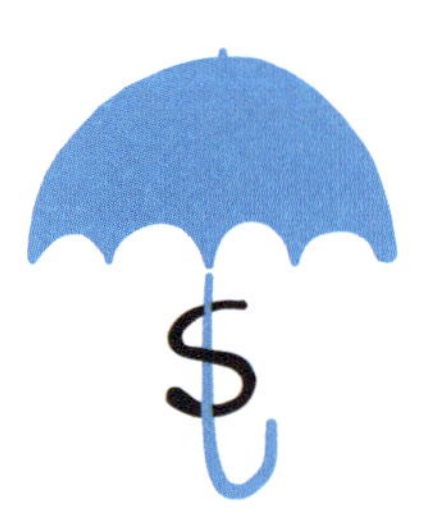

HOW TO DRAW

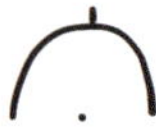
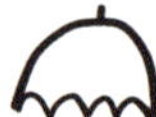

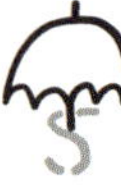
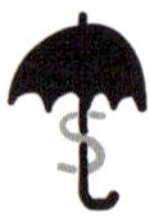

PERFORMANCE

BASIC ICONS

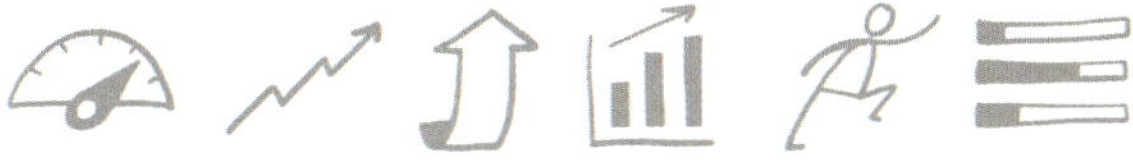

COMBINED ICONS

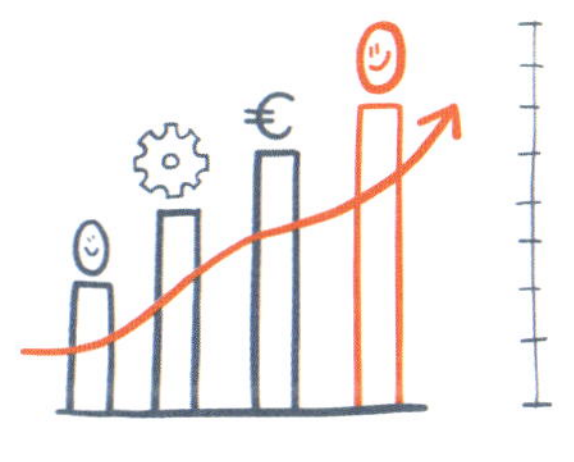

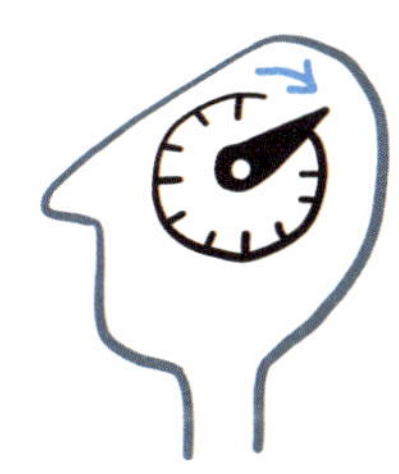

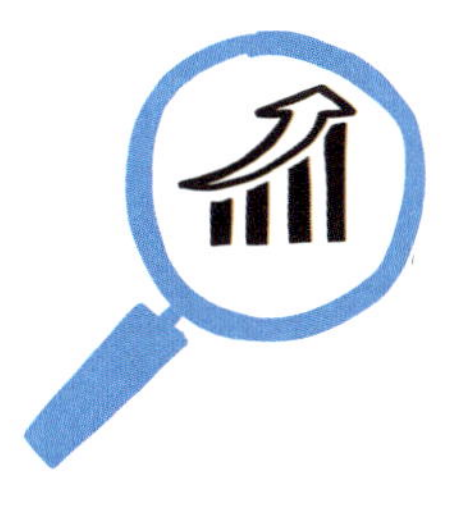

HOW TO DRAW

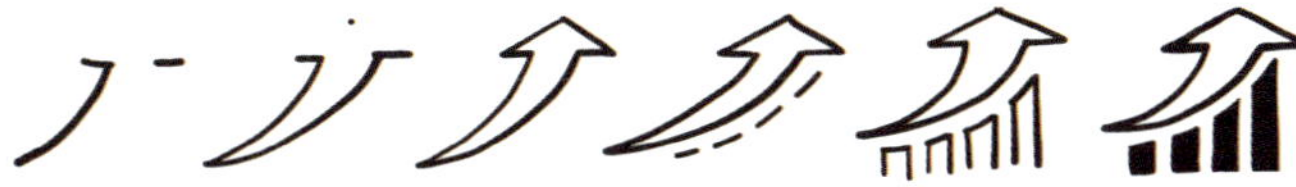

PERSONAL DEVELOPMENT

BASIC ICONS

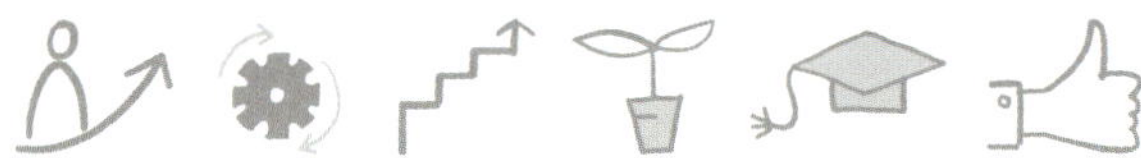

COMBINED ICONS

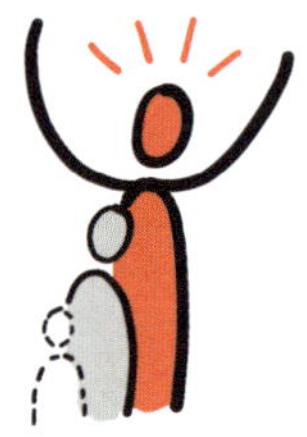

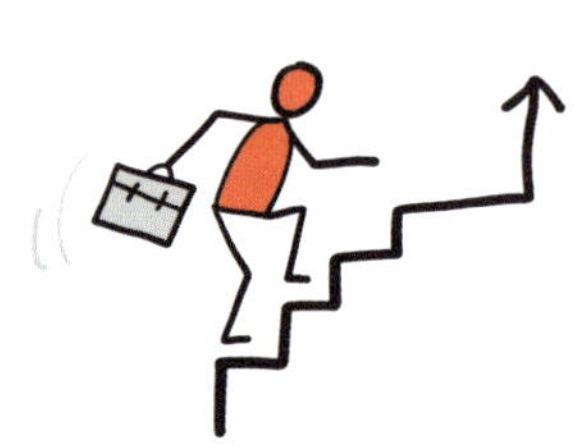

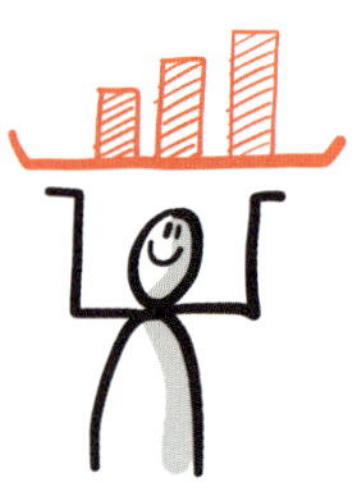

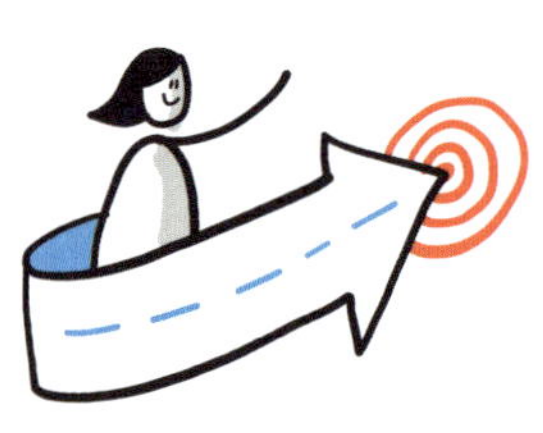

HOW TO DRAW

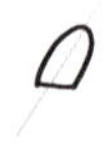

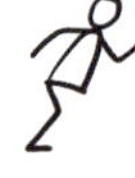

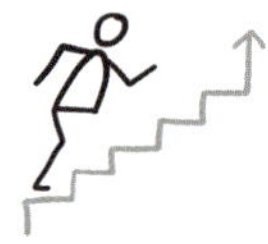

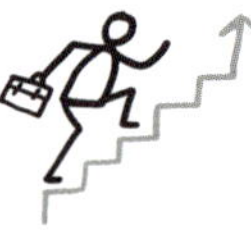

PROJECT MANAGEMENT

BASIC ICONS

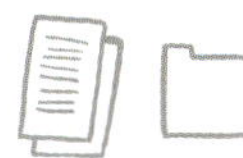
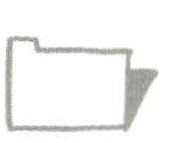

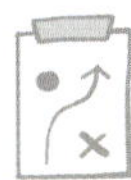
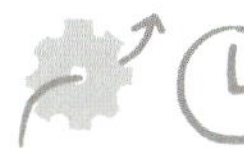

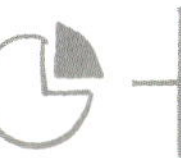

COMBINED ICONS

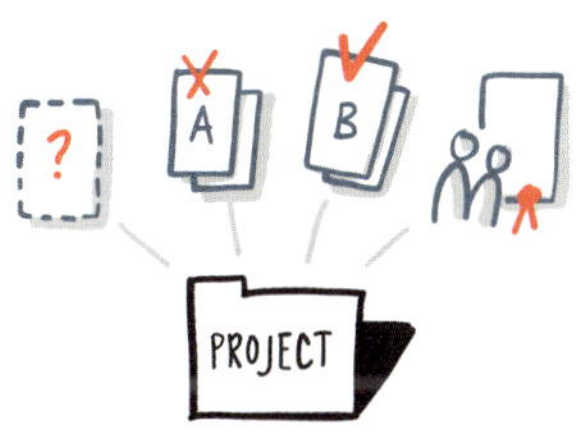

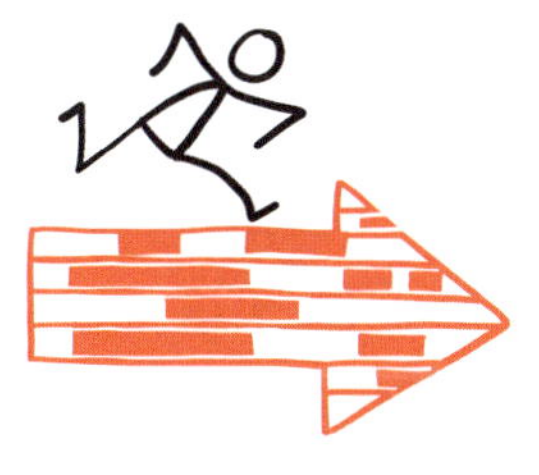

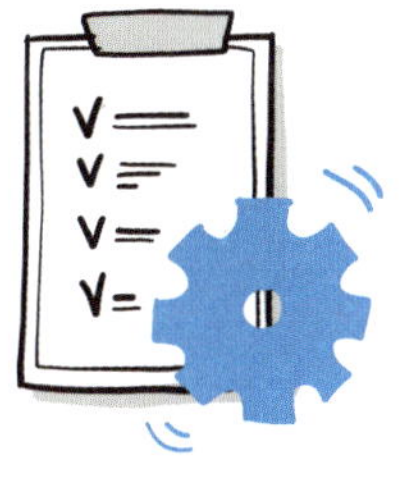

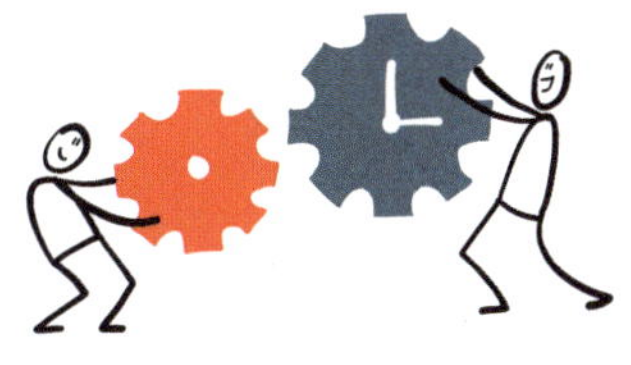

HOW TO DRAW

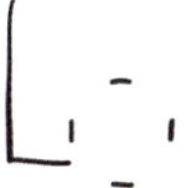
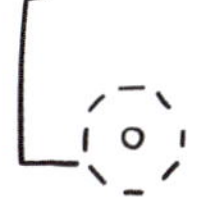
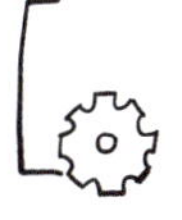
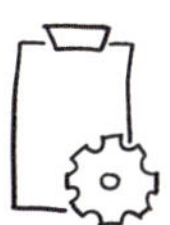
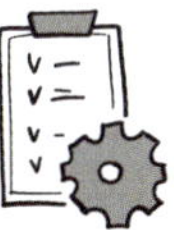

REWARD

BASIC ICONS

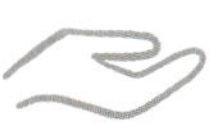
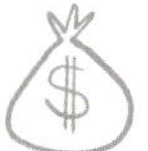

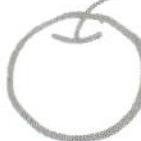
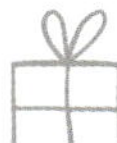
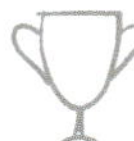

COMBINED ICONS

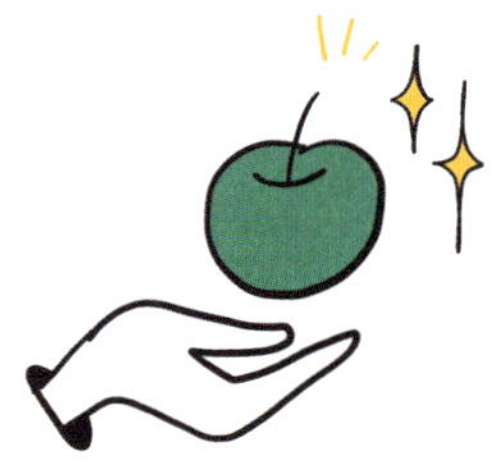
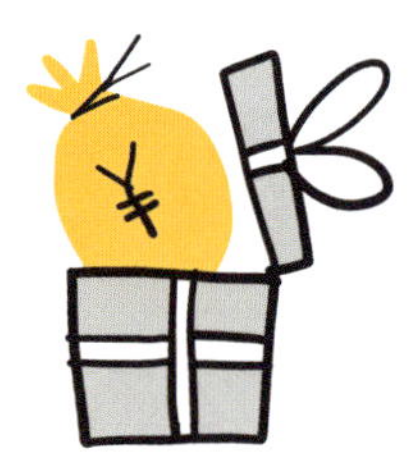

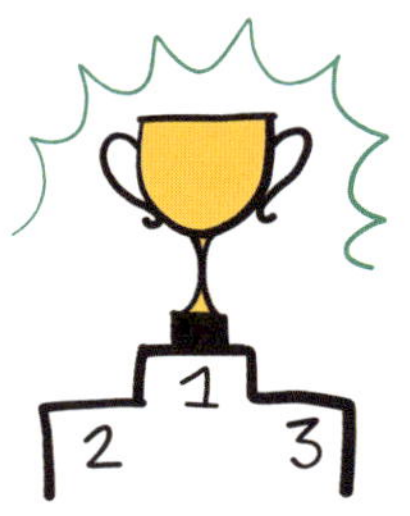

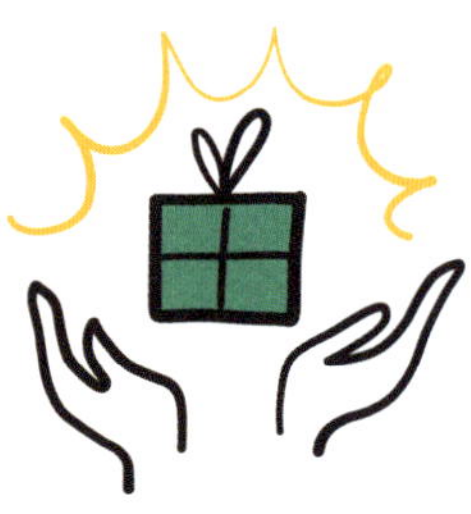

HOW TO DRAW

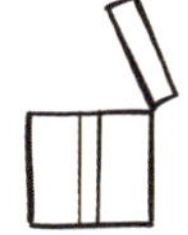
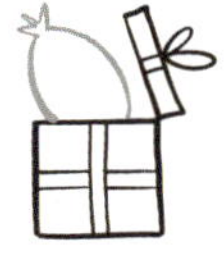
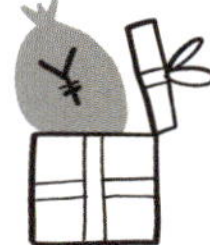

STRESS

BASIC ICONS

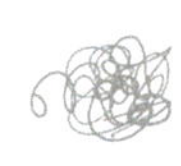
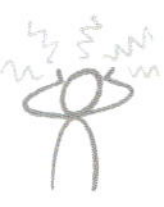

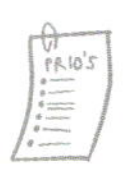

COMBINED ICONS

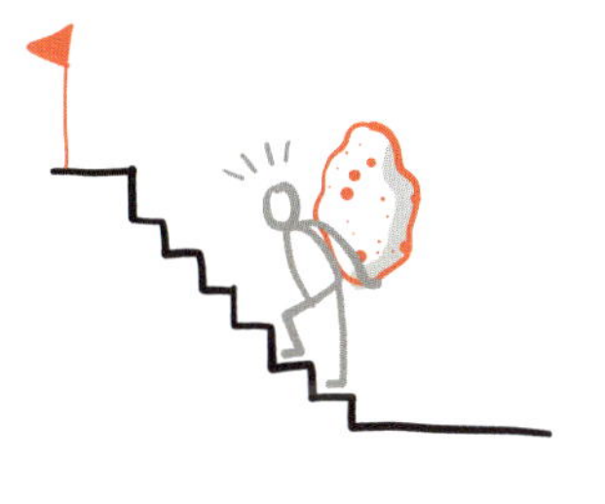
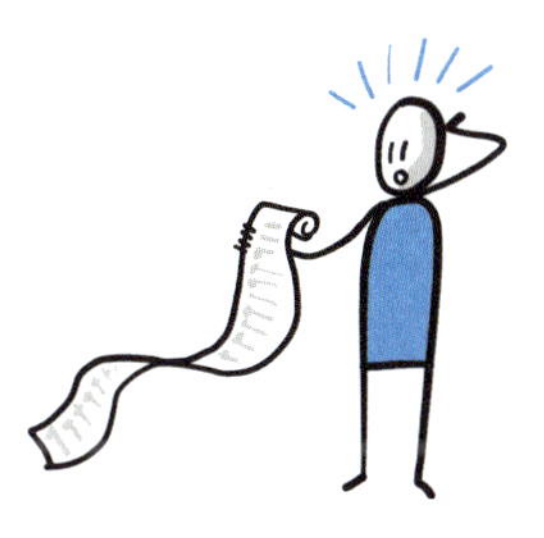
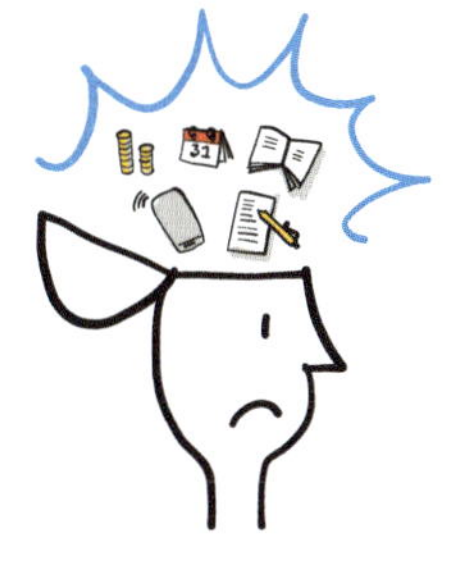

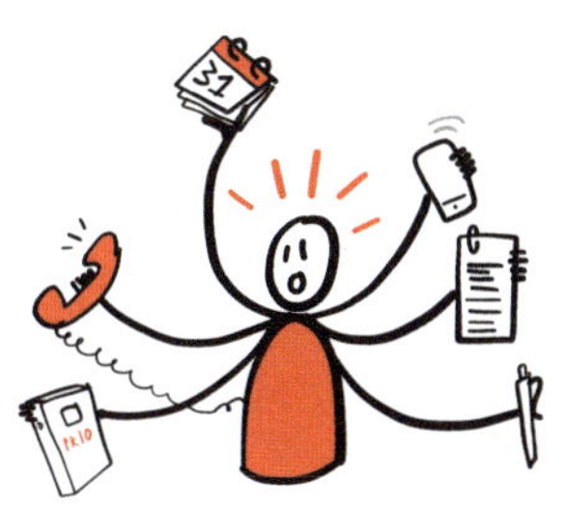

HOW TO DRAW

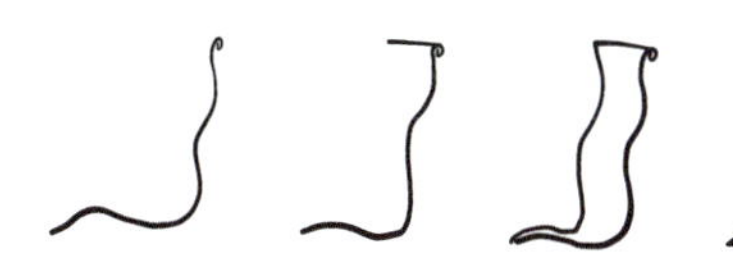
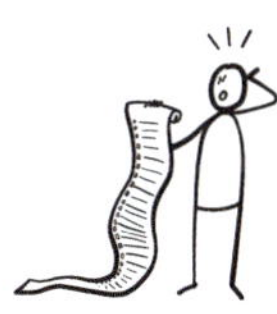

HR

TALENT

BASIC ICONS

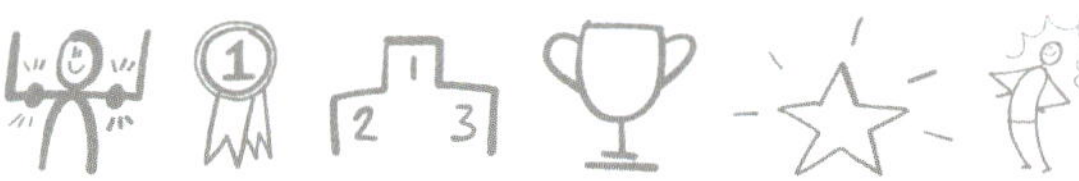

COMBINED ICONS

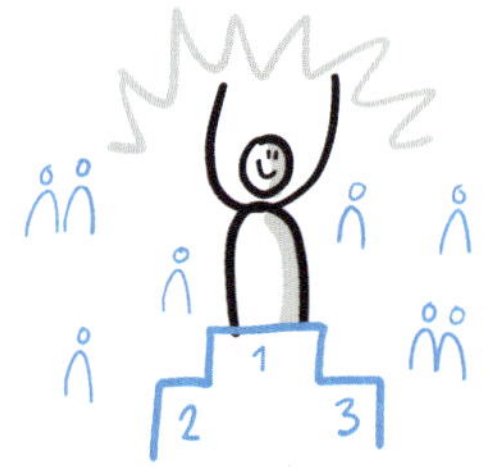

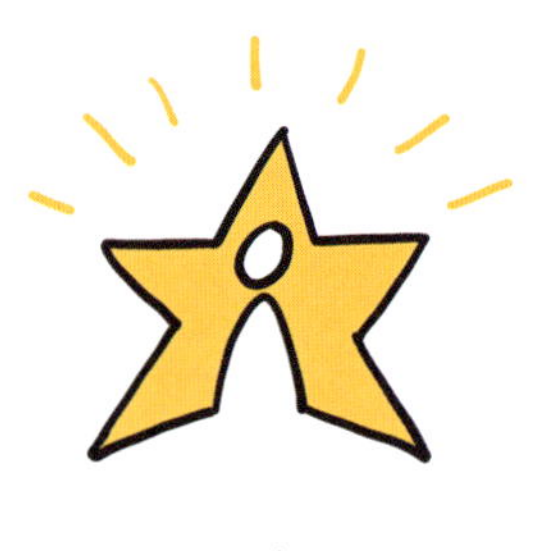

HOW TO DRAW

 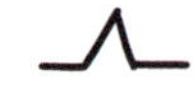   

WORKPLACE

BASIC ICONS

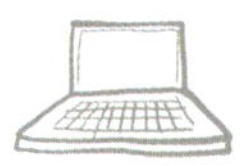
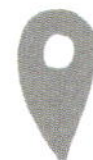
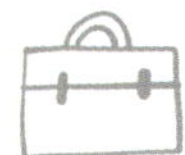
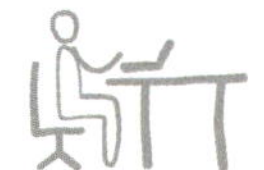
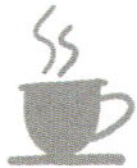

COMBINED ICONS

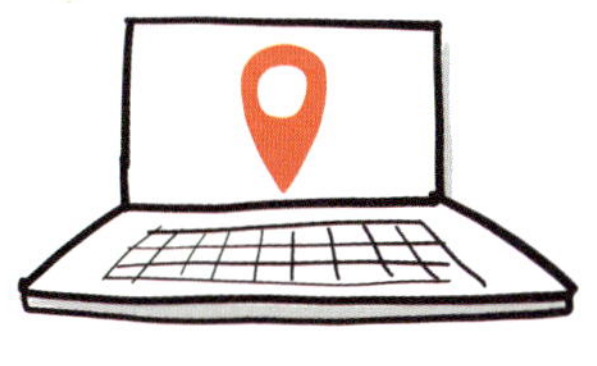

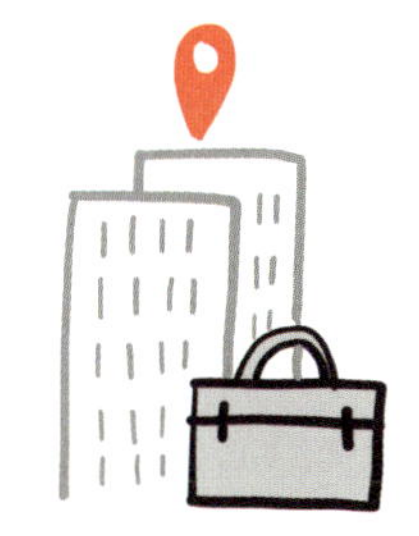
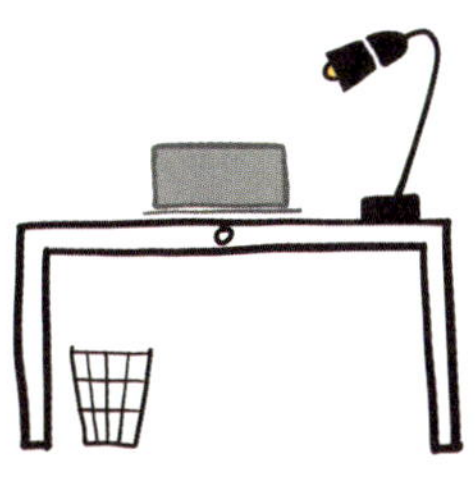

HOW TO DRAW

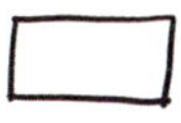

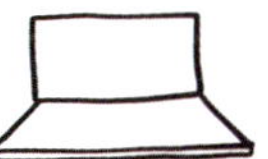
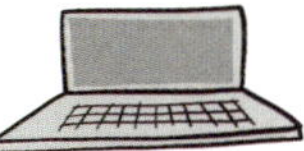

INNOVATION

HOW WE TRAILBLAZE

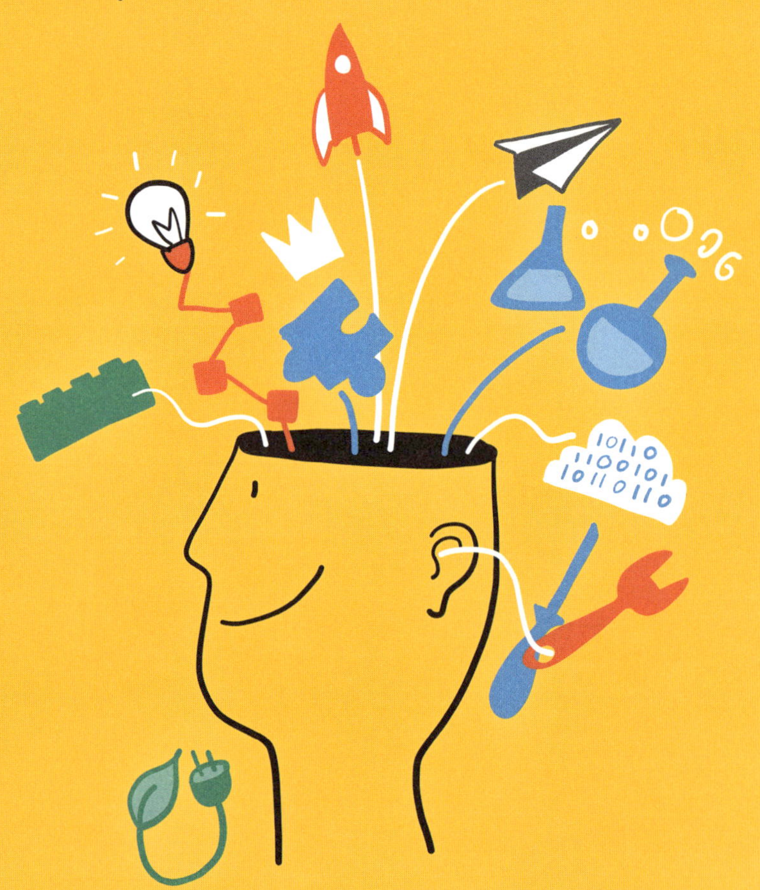

AGREEMENT

BASIC ICONS

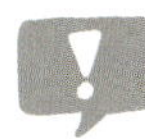
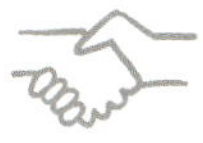

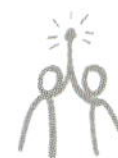

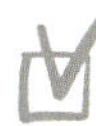
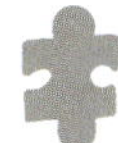

COMBINED ICONS

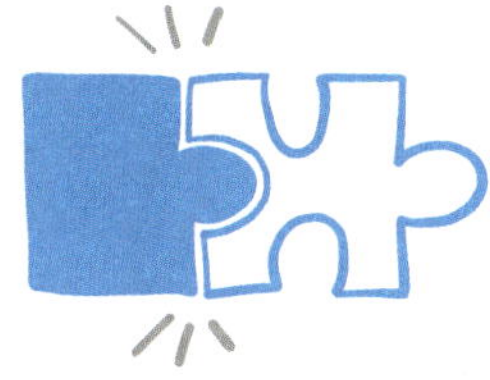
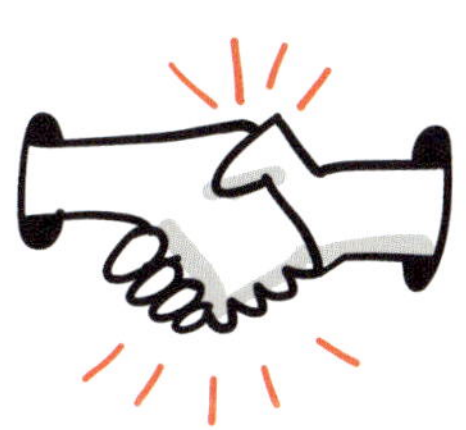
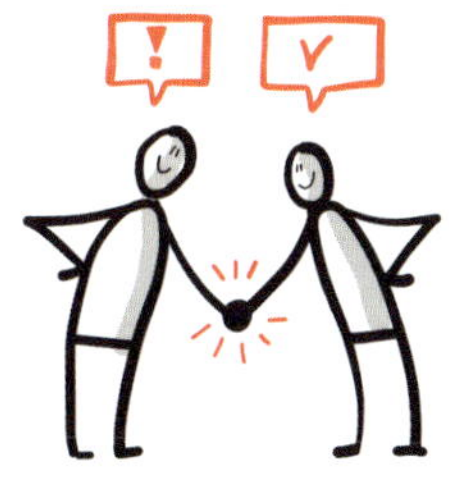

HOW TO DRAW

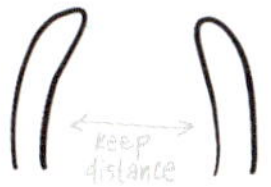

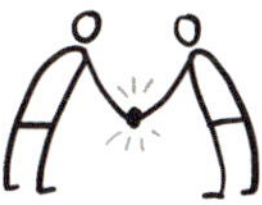

Innovation

BRAINSTORM

BASIC ICONS

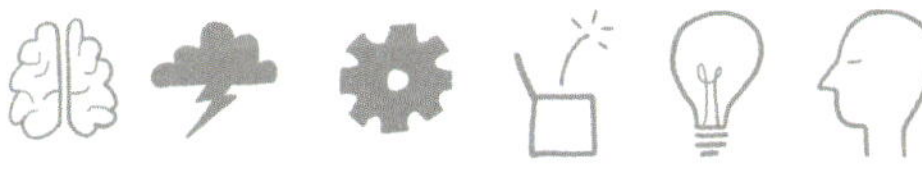

COMBINED ICONS

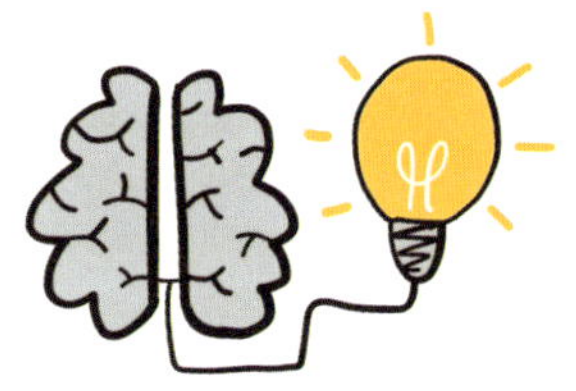

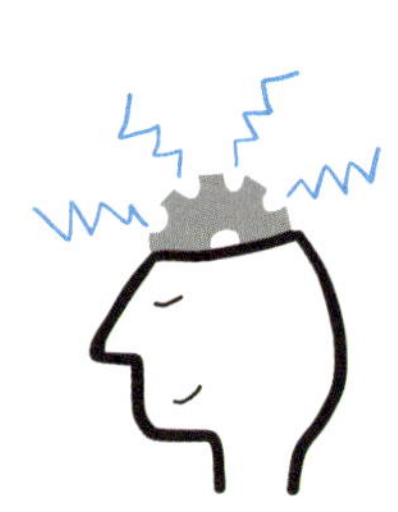

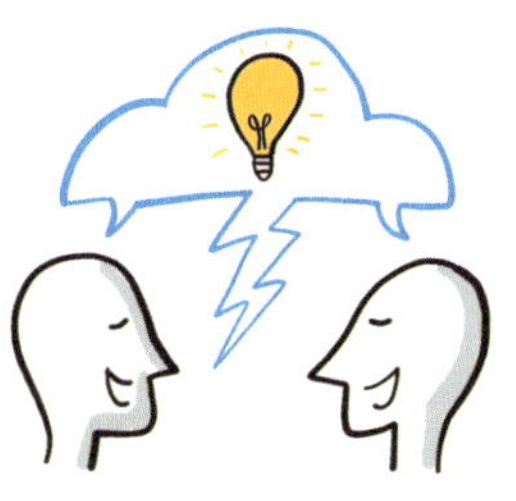

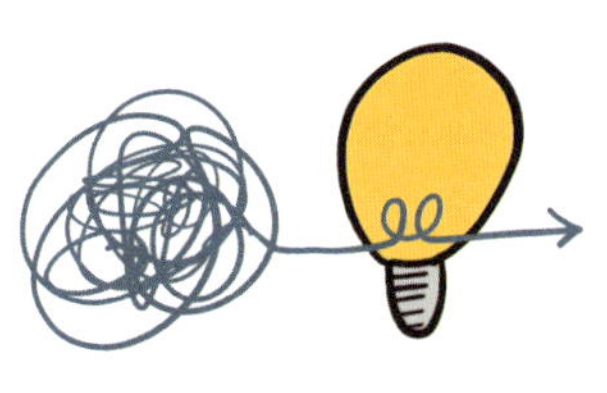

HOW TO DRAW

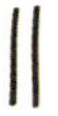

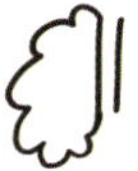

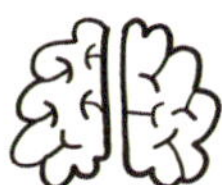

CHANGE

BASIC ICONS

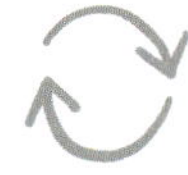
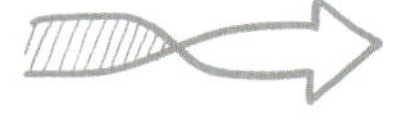
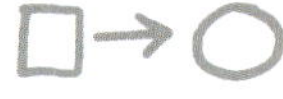

COMBINED ICONS

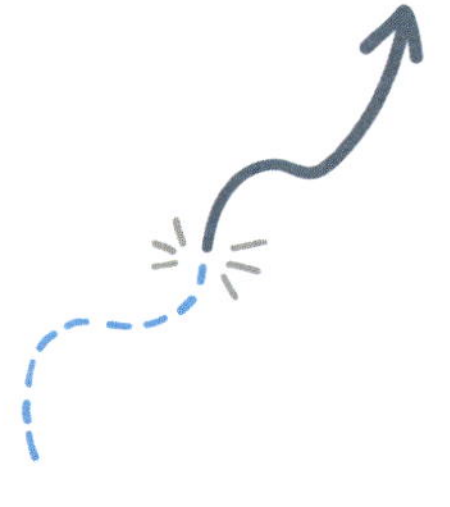
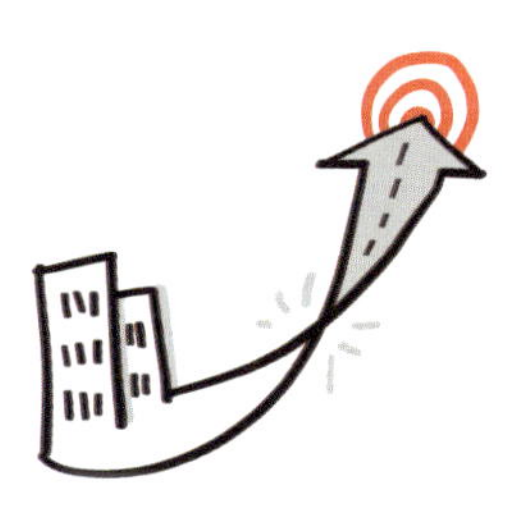

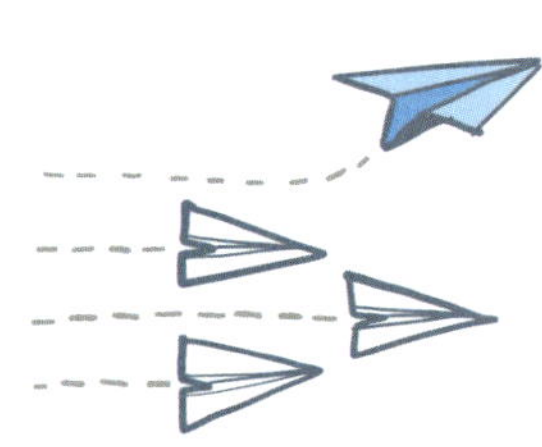

Innovation

HOW TO DRAW

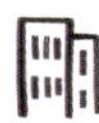
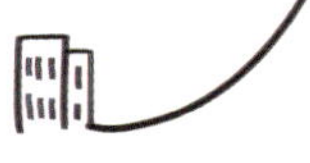
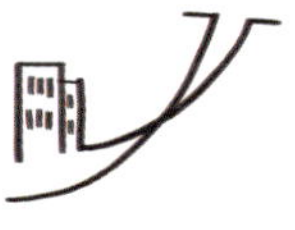
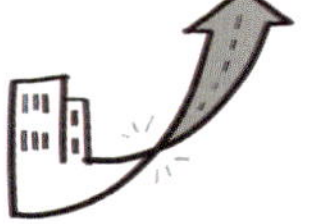

DISRUPTION

BASIC ICONS

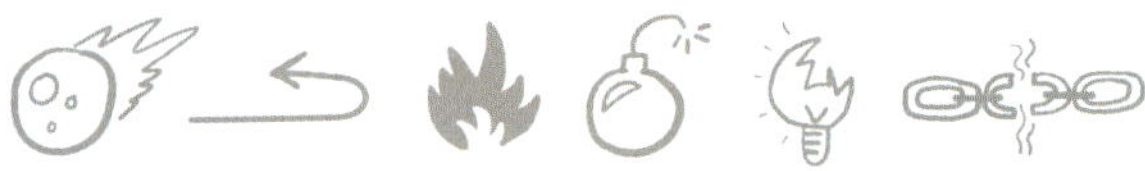

COMBINED ICONS

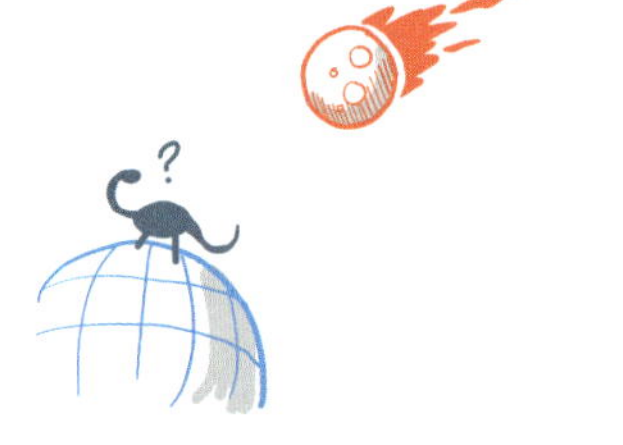

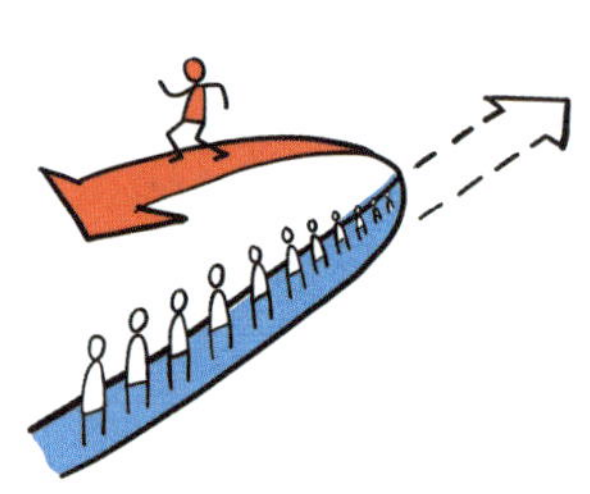

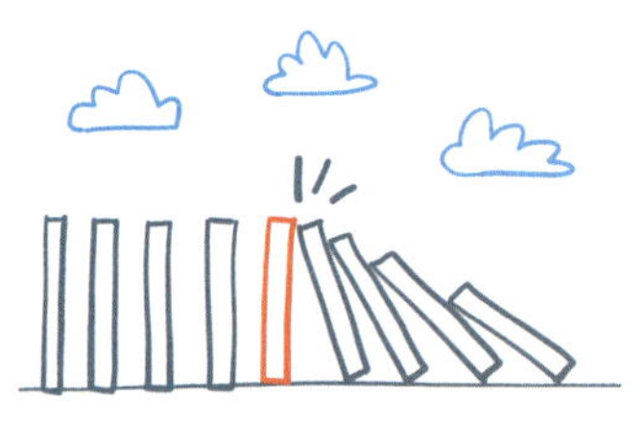

HOW TO DRAW

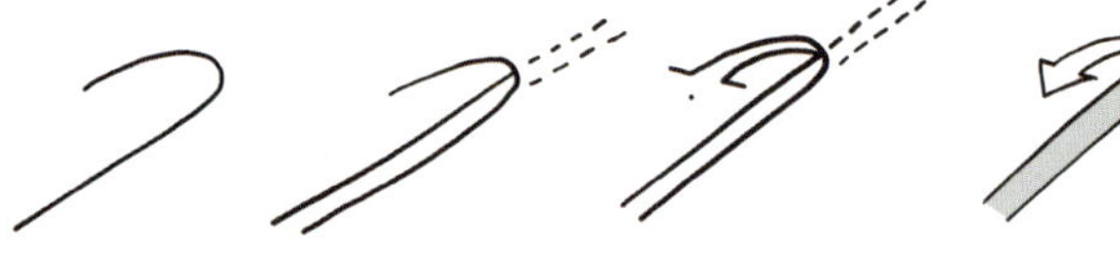

EXPERIMENT

BASIC ICONS

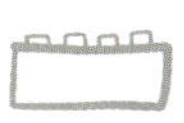
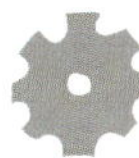
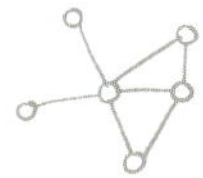
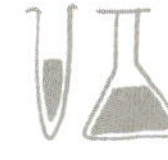

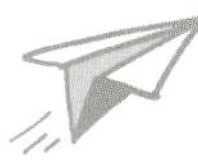

COMBINED ICONS

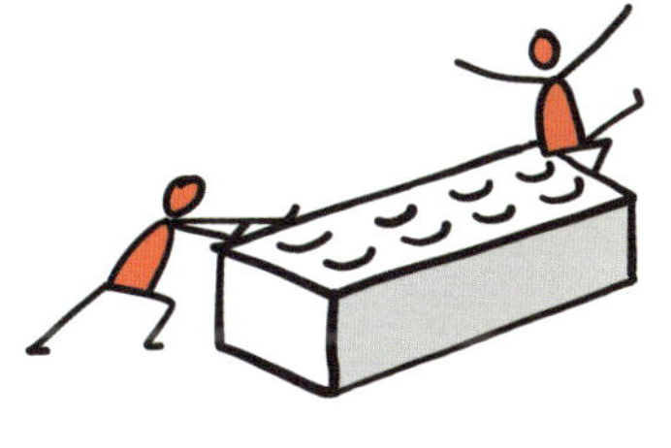
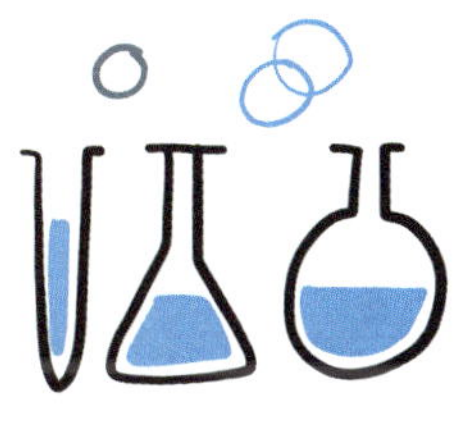
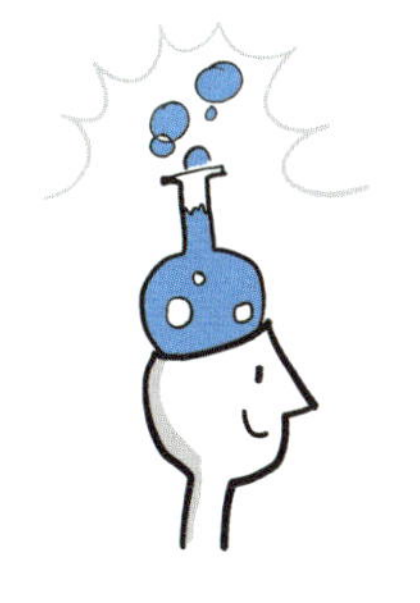
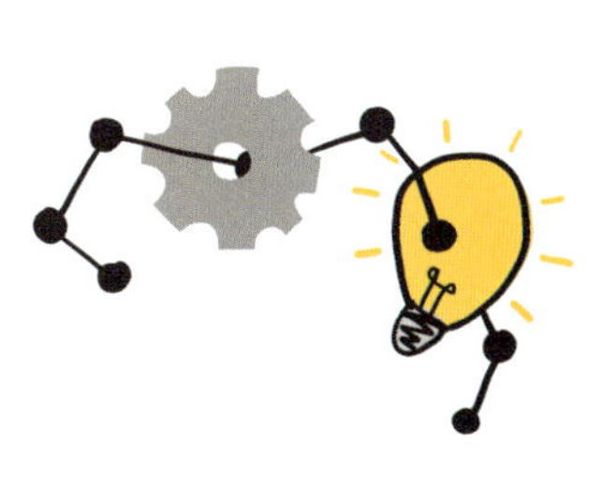

HOW TO DRAW

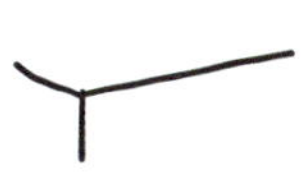
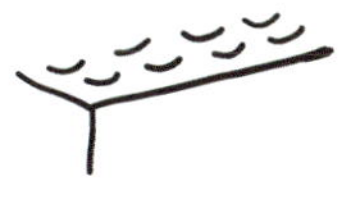
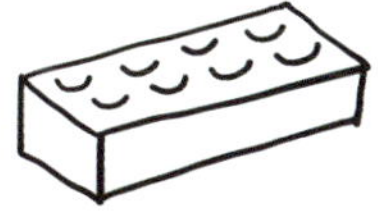

Innovation

FUTURE

BASIC ICONS

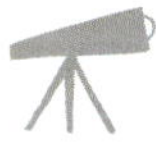  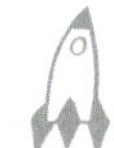 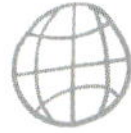  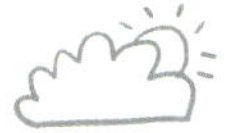 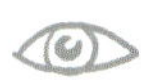

COMBINED ICONS

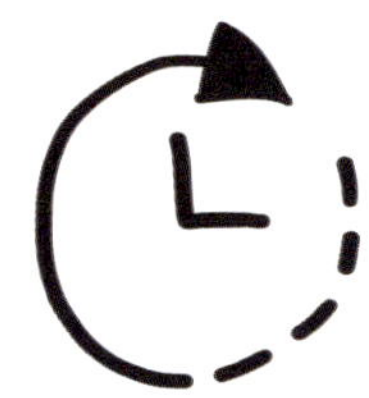

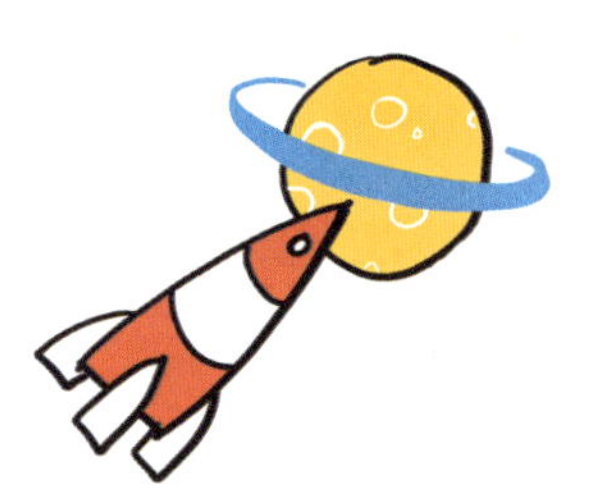

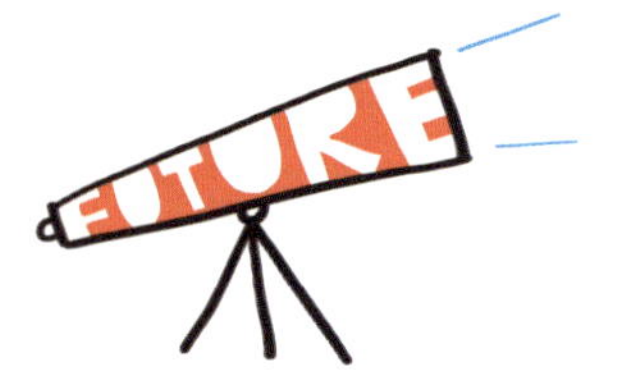

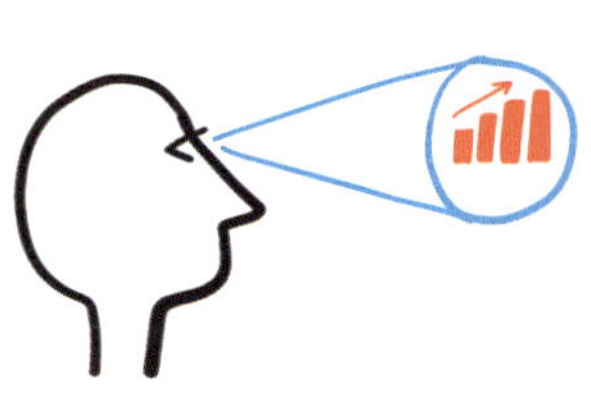

HOW TO DRAW

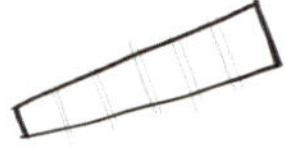 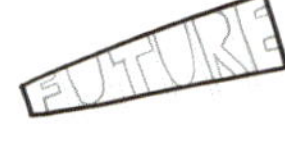

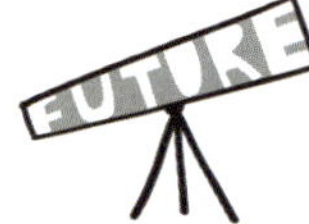

IDEA GENERATION

BASIC ICONS

 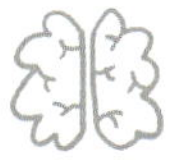 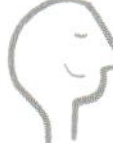  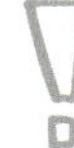 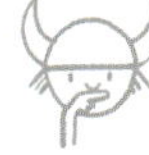 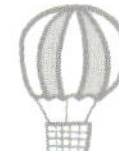

COMBINED ICONS

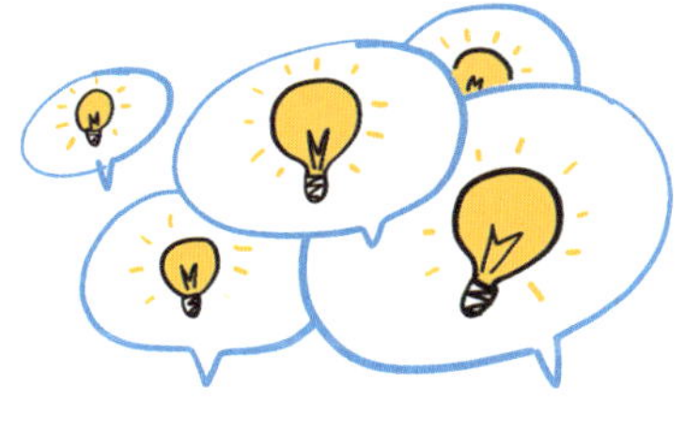

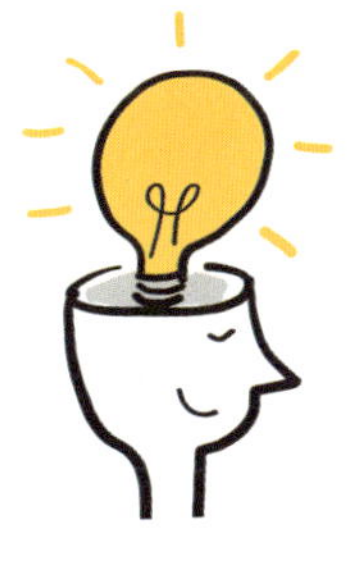

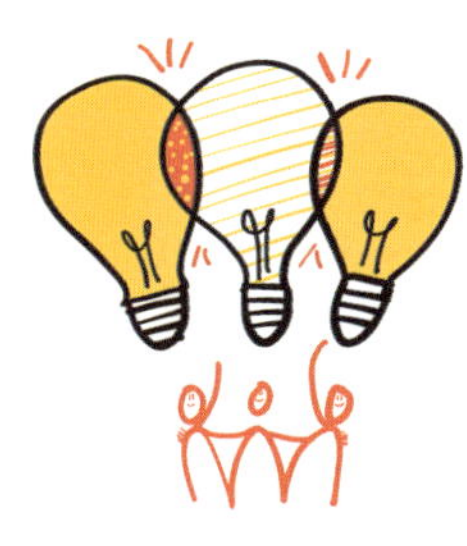

HOW TO DRAW

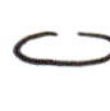 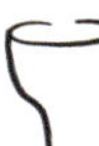 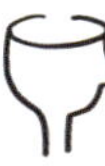 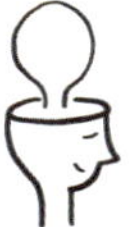 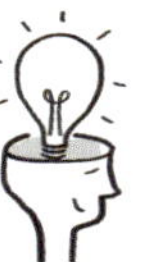

Innovation

INNOVATION

BASIC ICONS

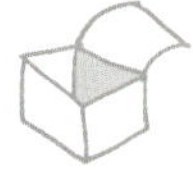
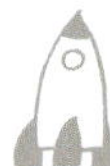
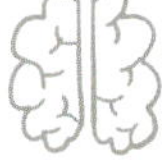
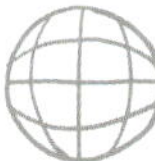
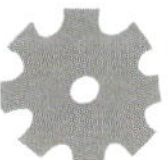

COMBINED ICONS

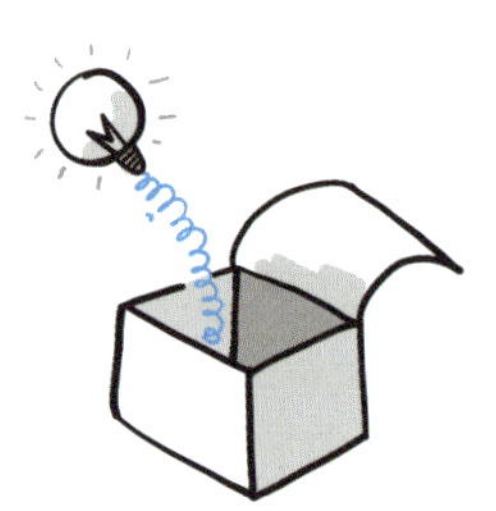
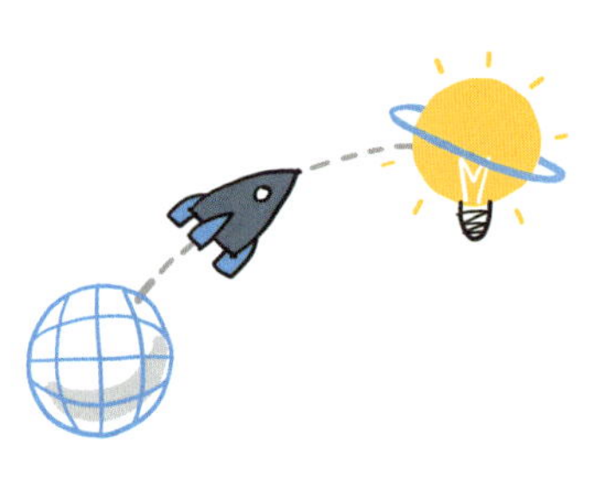
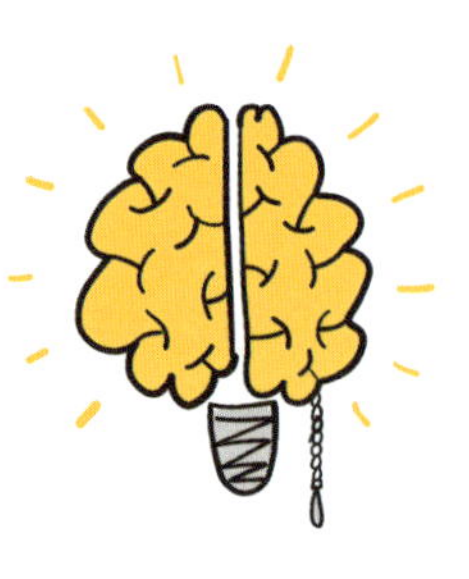

HOW TO DRAW

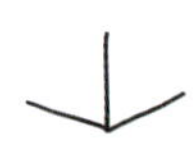
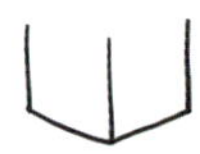
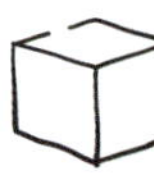
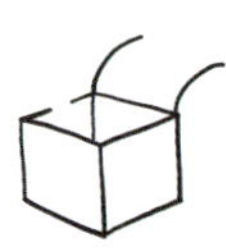
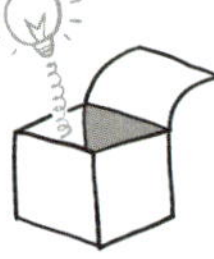

INSIGHTS

BASIC ICONS

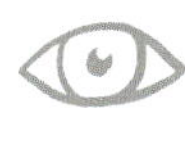

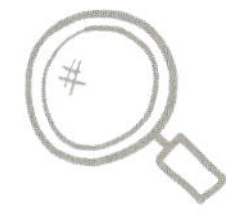
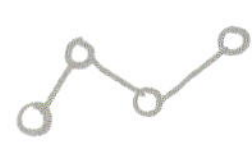
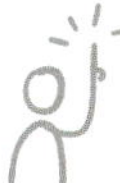

COMBINED ICONS

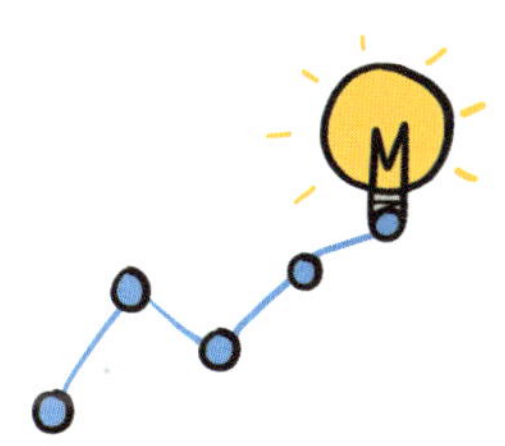
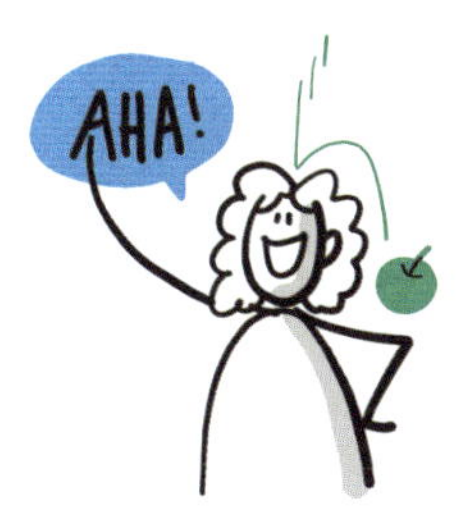

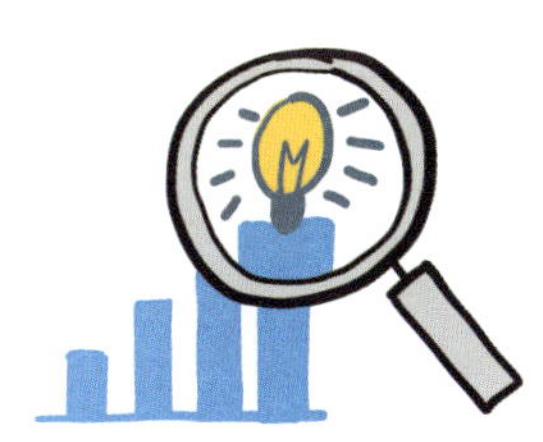

Innovation

HOW TO DRAW

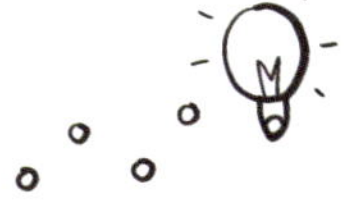
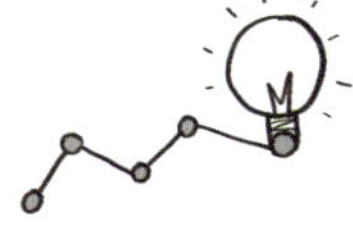

INSPIRATION

BASIC ICONS

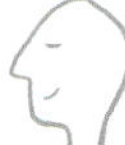
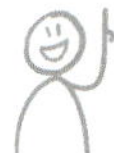

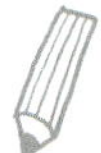

COMBINED ICONS

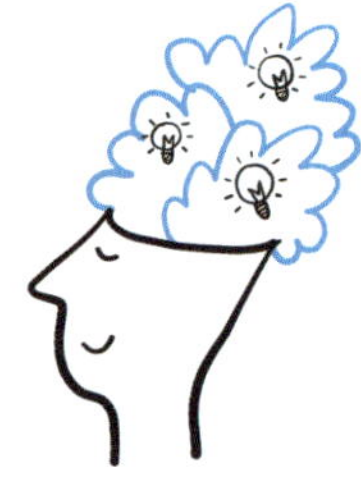
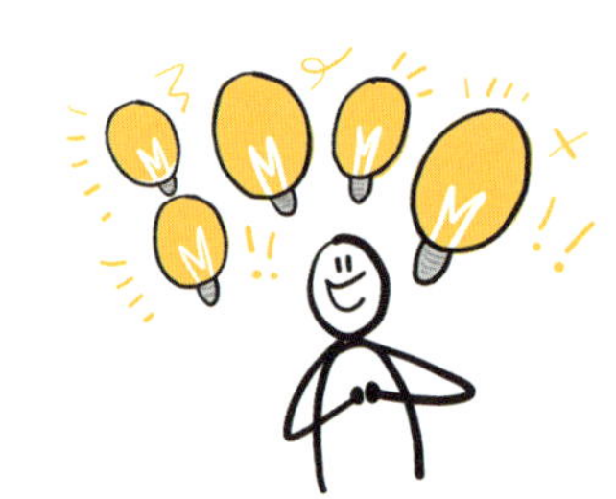
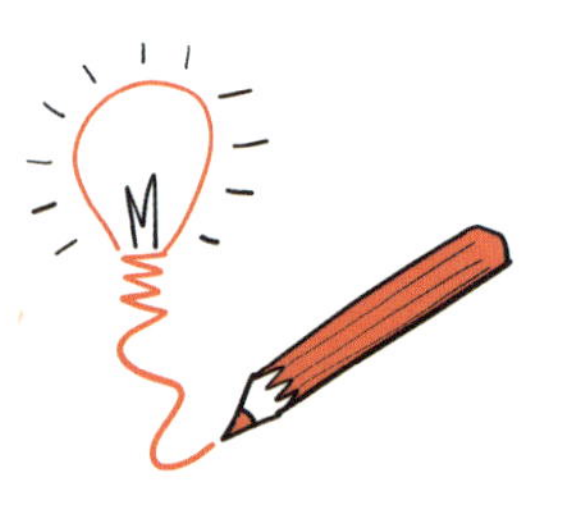
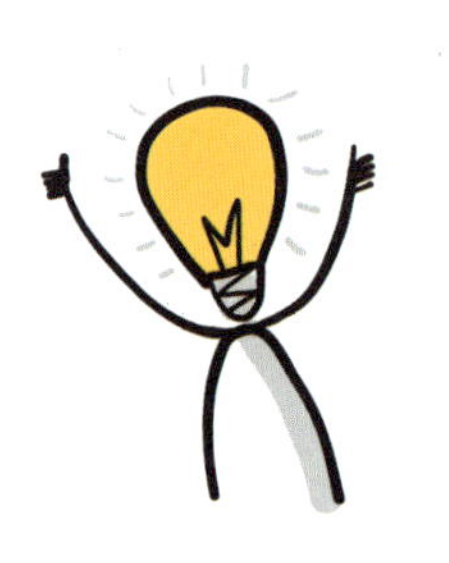

HOW TO DRAW

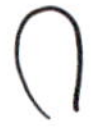
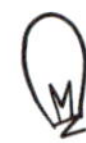

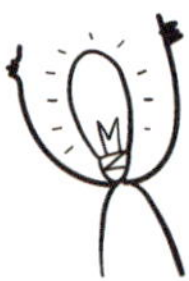

OPPORTUNITY

BASIC ICONS

COMBINED ICONS

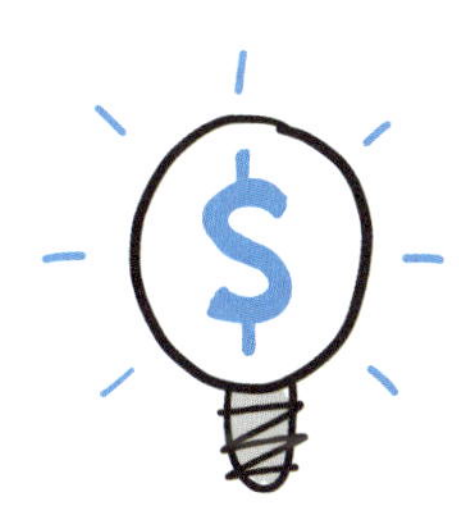

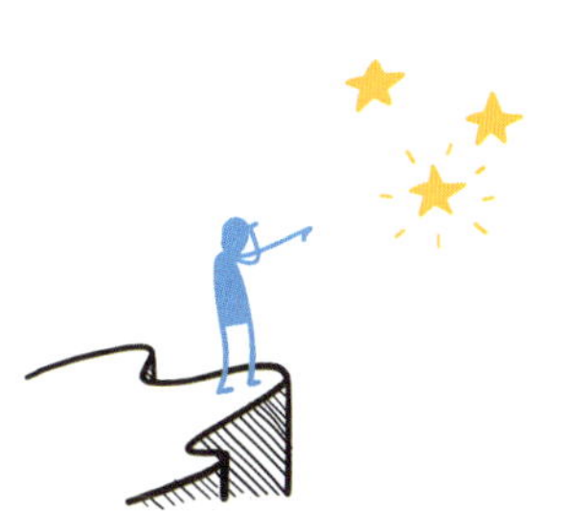

HOW TO DRAW

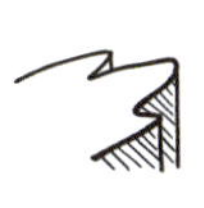

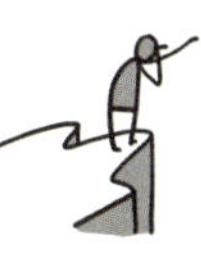

Innovation

PROBLEM FINDING

BASIC ICONS

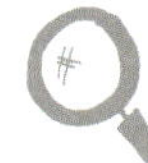

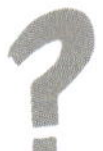

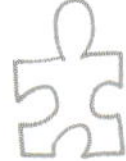

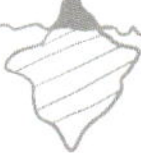

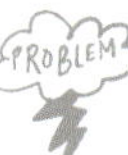

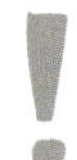

COMBINED ICONS

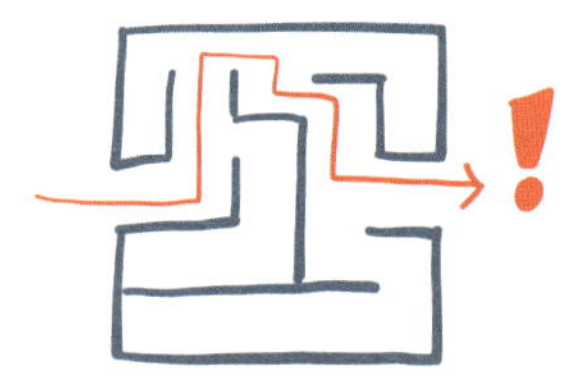

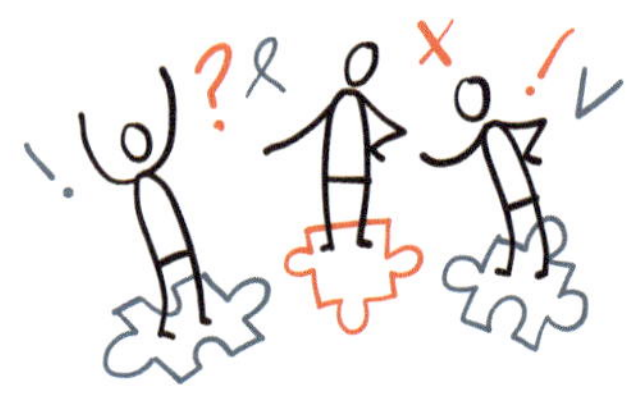

HOW TO DRAW

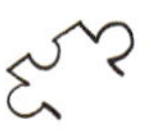

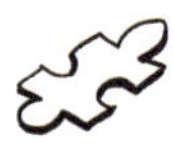

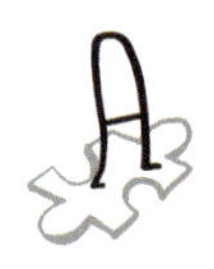

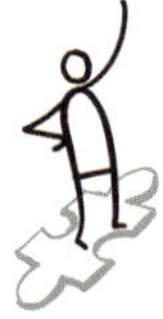

PRODUCT LAUNCH

BASIC ICONS

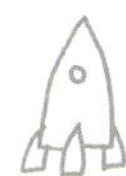
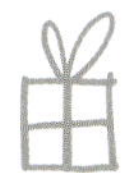

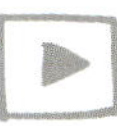
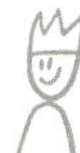

COMBINED ICONS

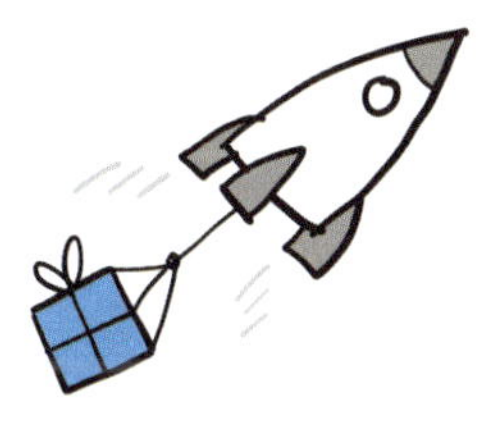
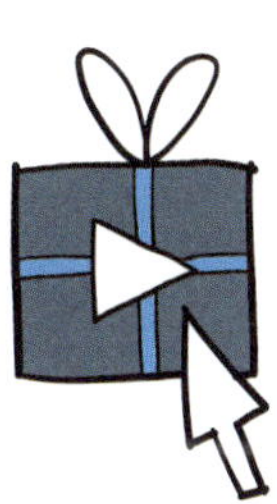
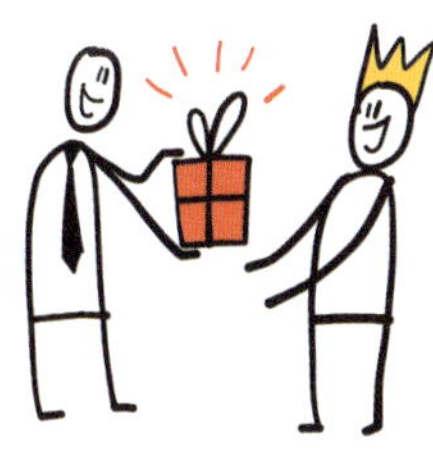

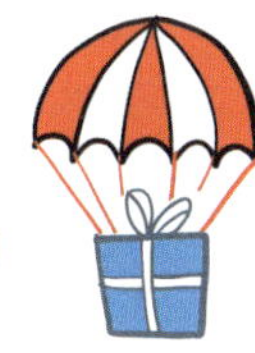

HOW TO DRAW

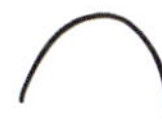
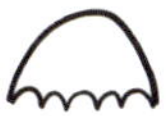

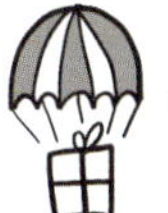

PROTOTYPE, TEST

BASIC ICONS

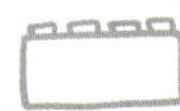
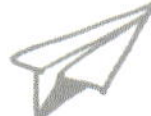
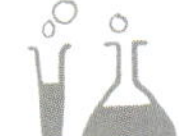
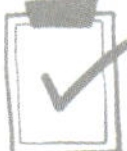
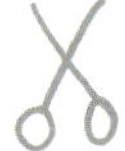
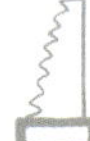
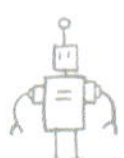

COMBINED ICONS

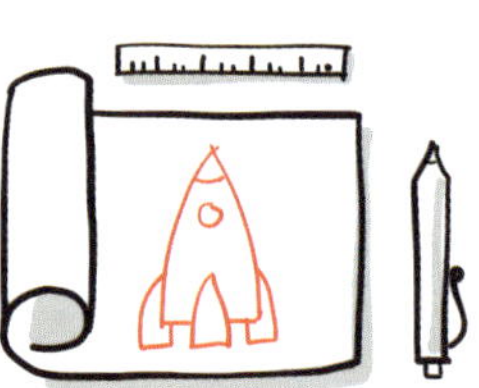
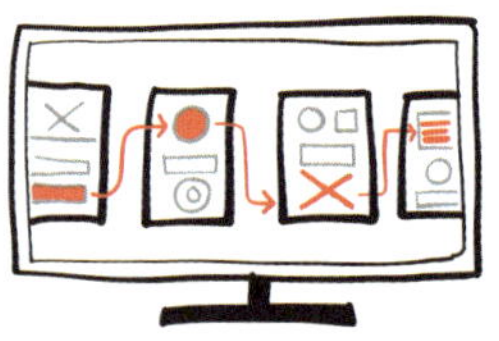
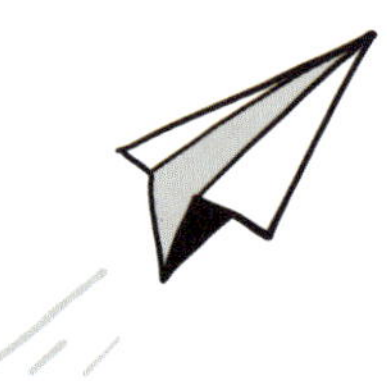

HOW TO DRAW

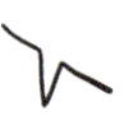
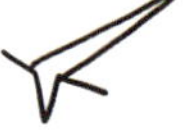
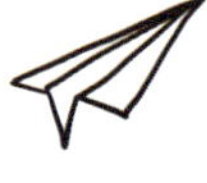
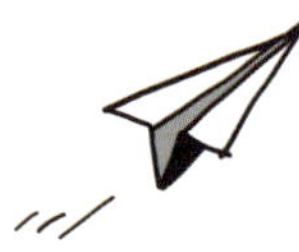

RECYCLE

BASIC ICONS

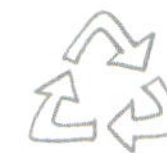 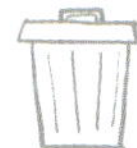 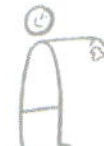 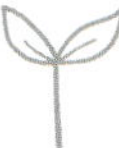 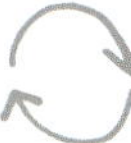

COMBINED ICONS

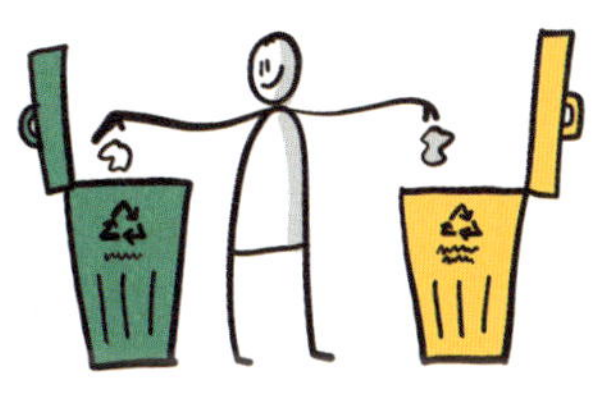

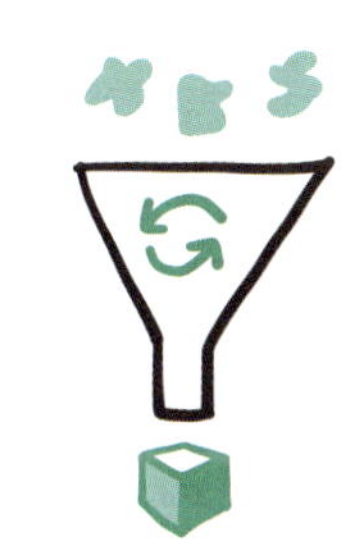

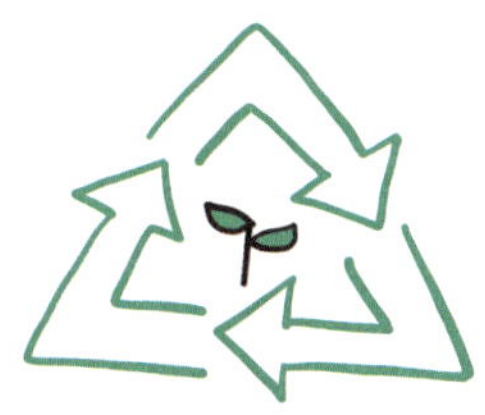

Innovation

HOW TO DRAW

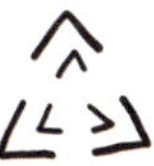 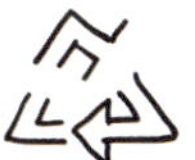 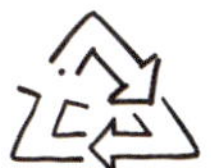 

REQUIREMENT

BASIC ICONS

COMBINED ICONS

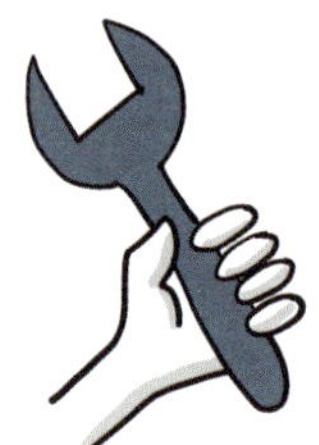

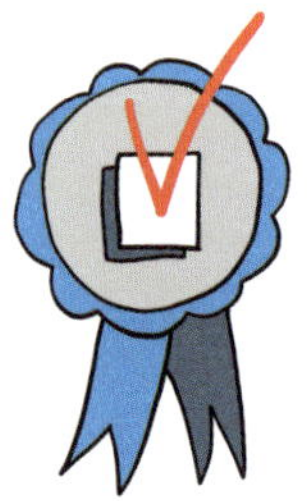

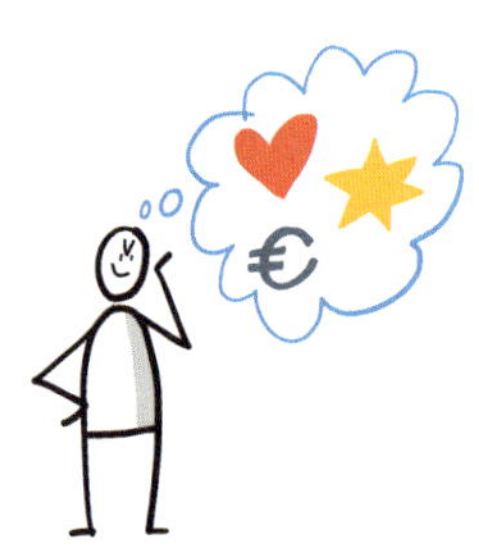

HOW TO DRAW

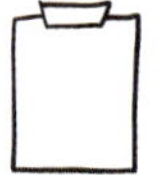
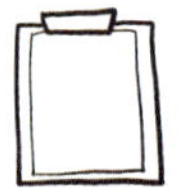
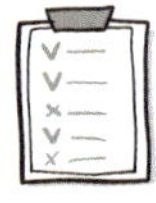
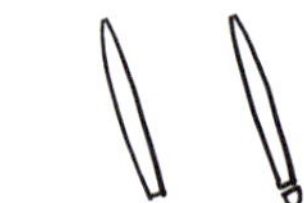
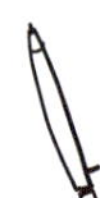
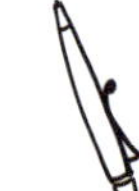

SIMPLIFICATION

BASIC ICONS

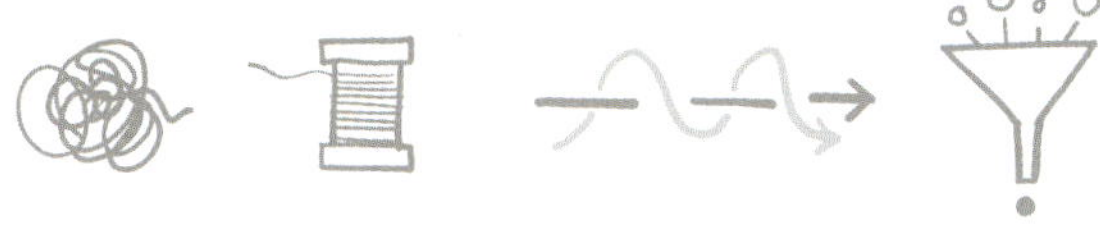

COMBINED ICONS

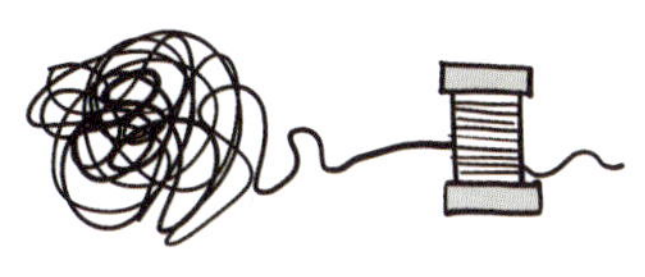

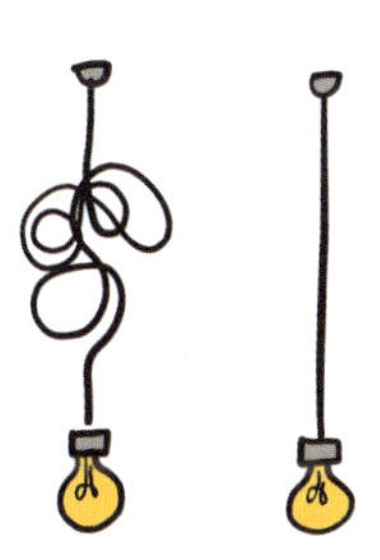

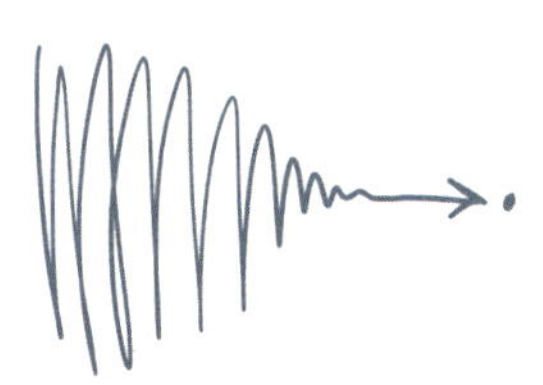

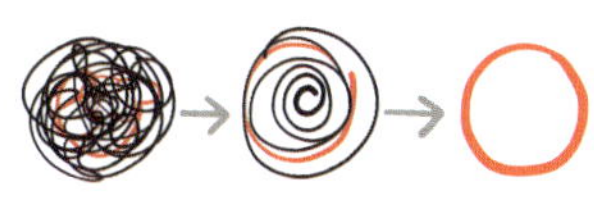

HOW TO DRAW

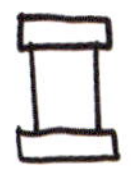

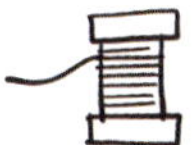

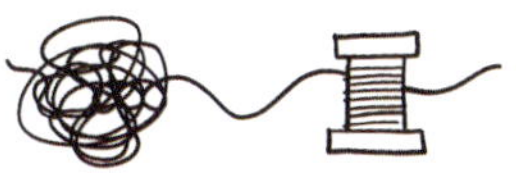

SOCIAL INNOVATION

BASIC ICONS

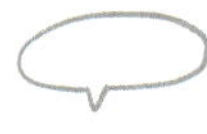

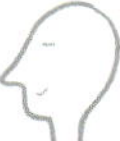
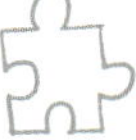
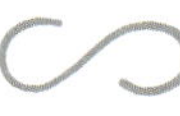

COMBINED ICONS

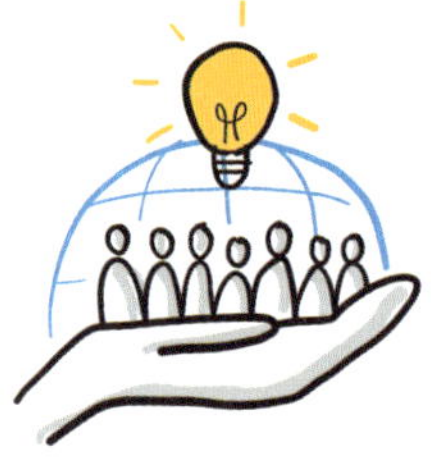

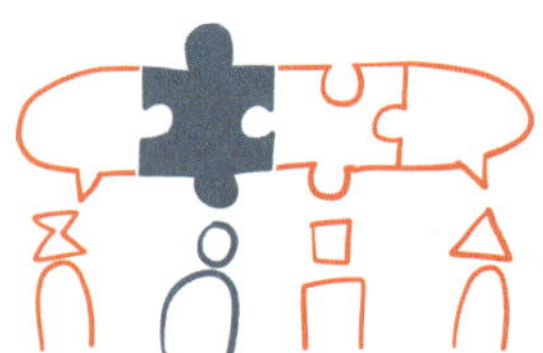
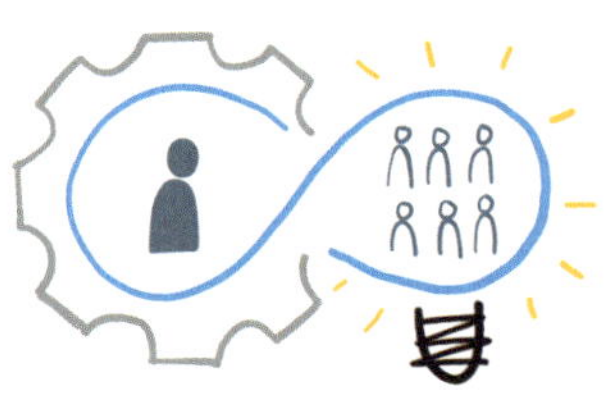

HOW TO DRAW

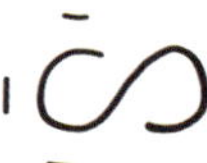
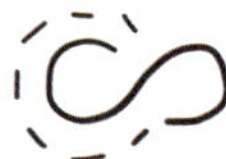

SOLUTIONS

BASIC ICONS

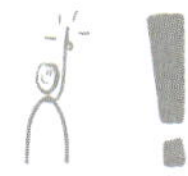
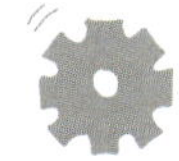
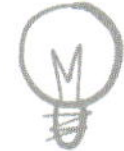
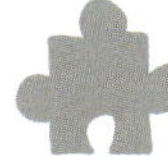
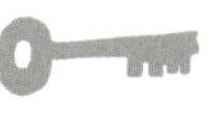
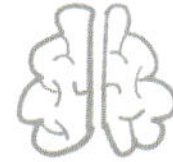

COMBINED ICONS

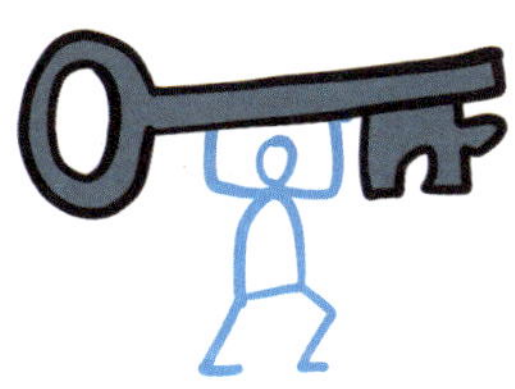
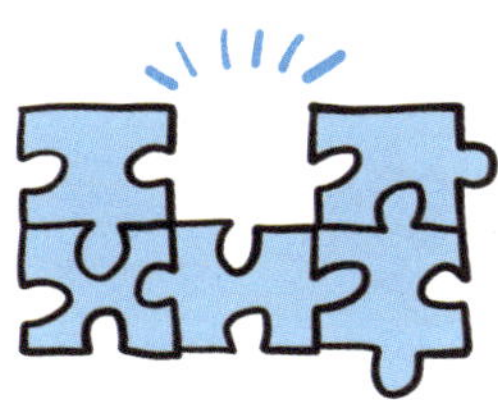
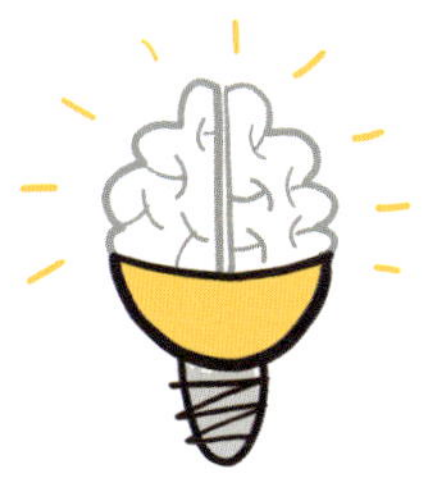

HOW TO DRAW

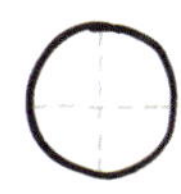
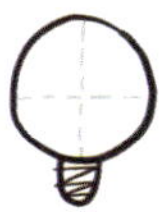

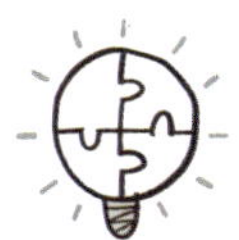

TEAM ALIGNMENT

BASIC ICONS

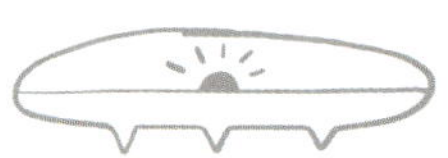 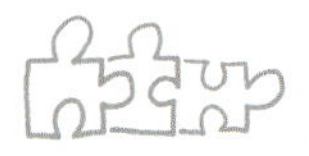 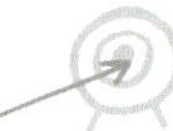 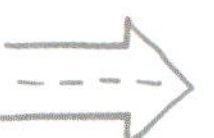 

COMBINED ICONS

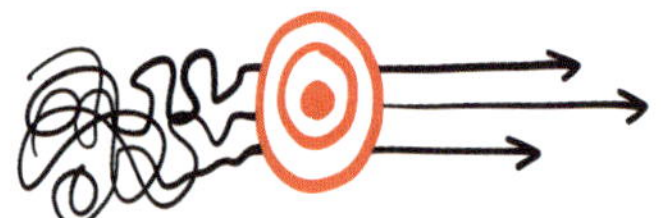

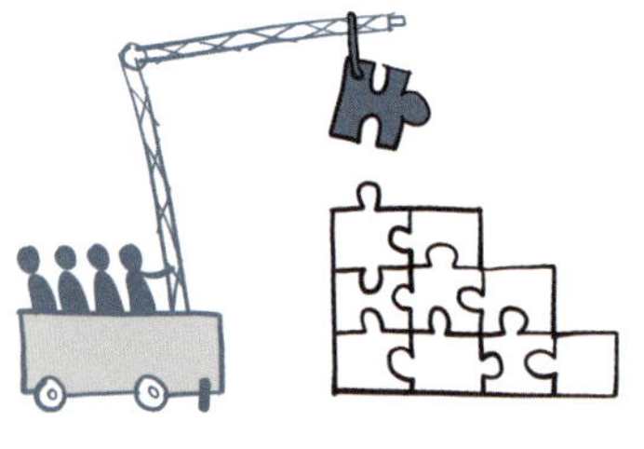

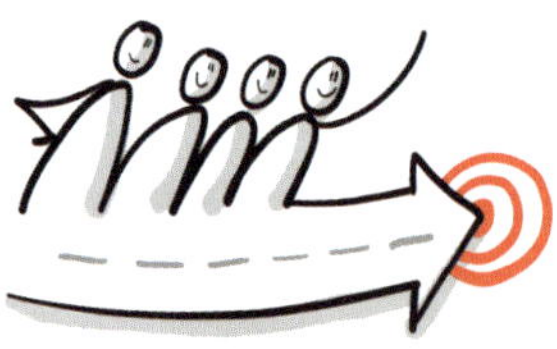

HOW TO DRAW

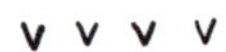 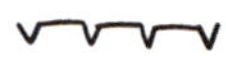 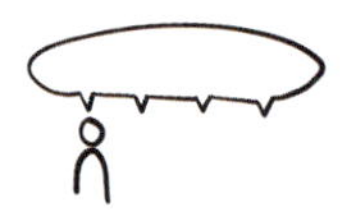 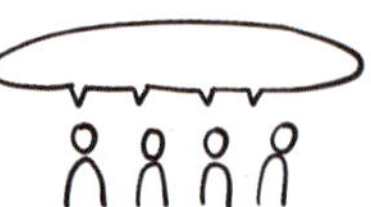

TOOLS

BASIC ICONS

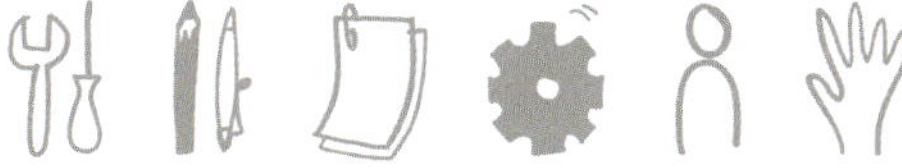

COMBINED ICONS

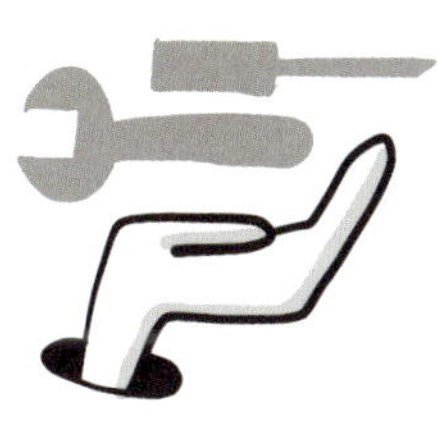

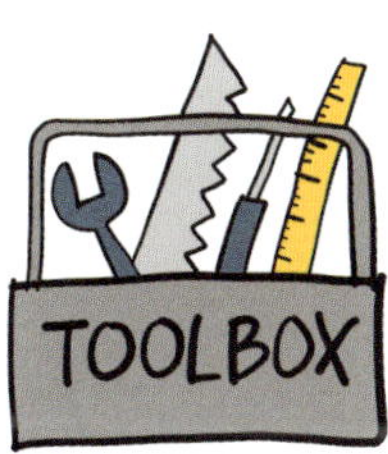

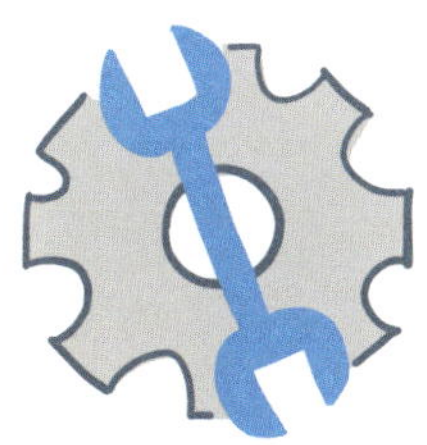

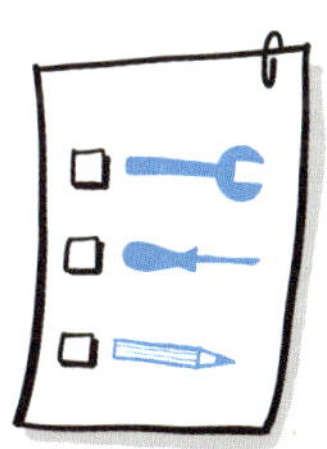

HOW TO DRAW

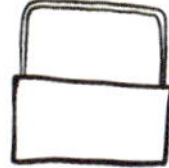

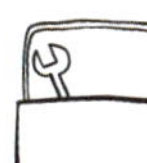

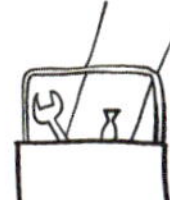

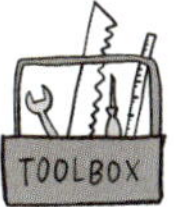

Innovation

TREND

BASIC ICONS

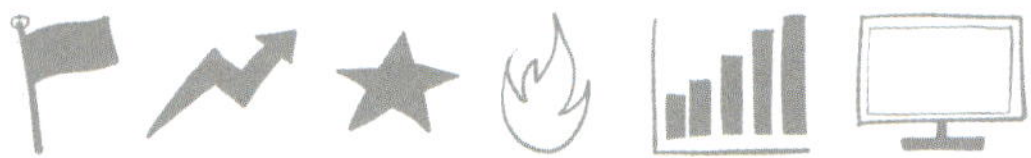

COMBINED ICONS

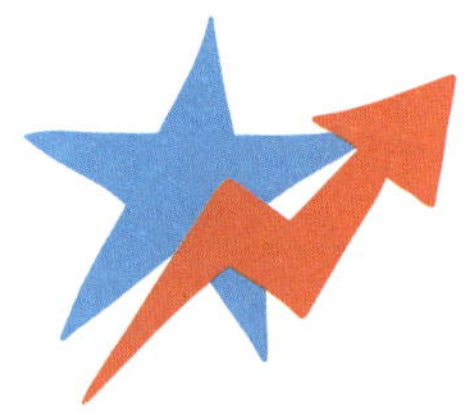

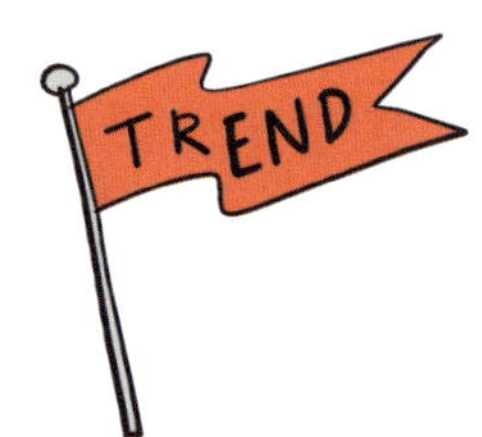

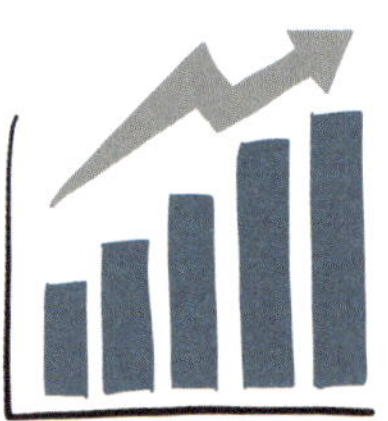

HOW TO DRAW

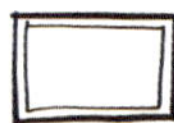

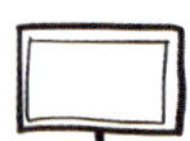

WHY?

BASIC ICONS

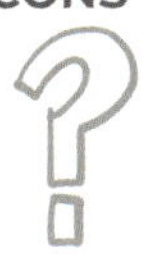

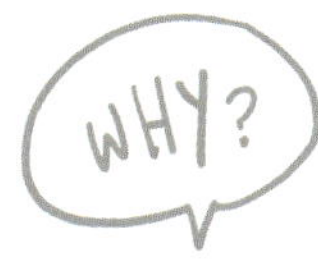

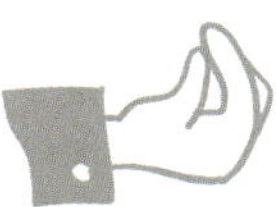

COMBINED ICONS

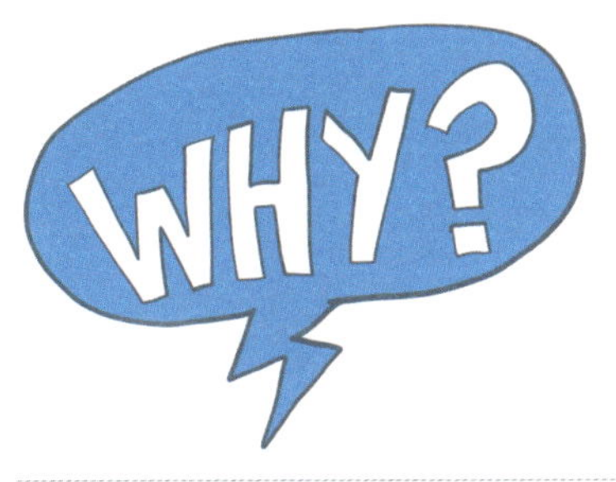

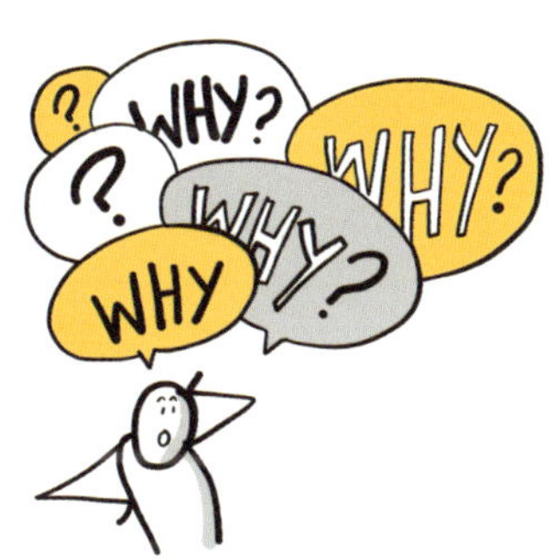

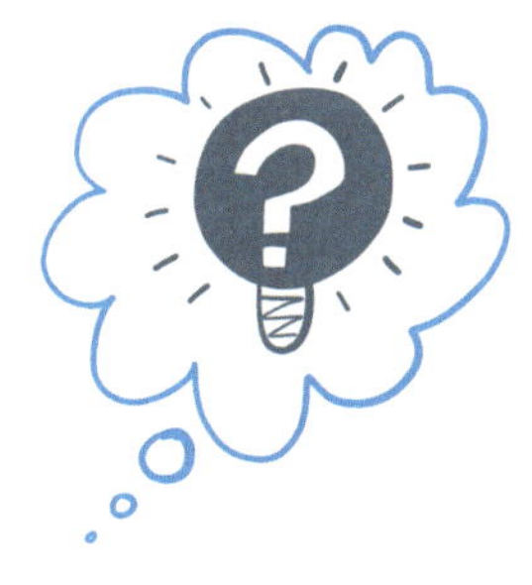

HOW TO DRAW

Innovation

SALES / MARKETING

HOW WE ADD VALUE

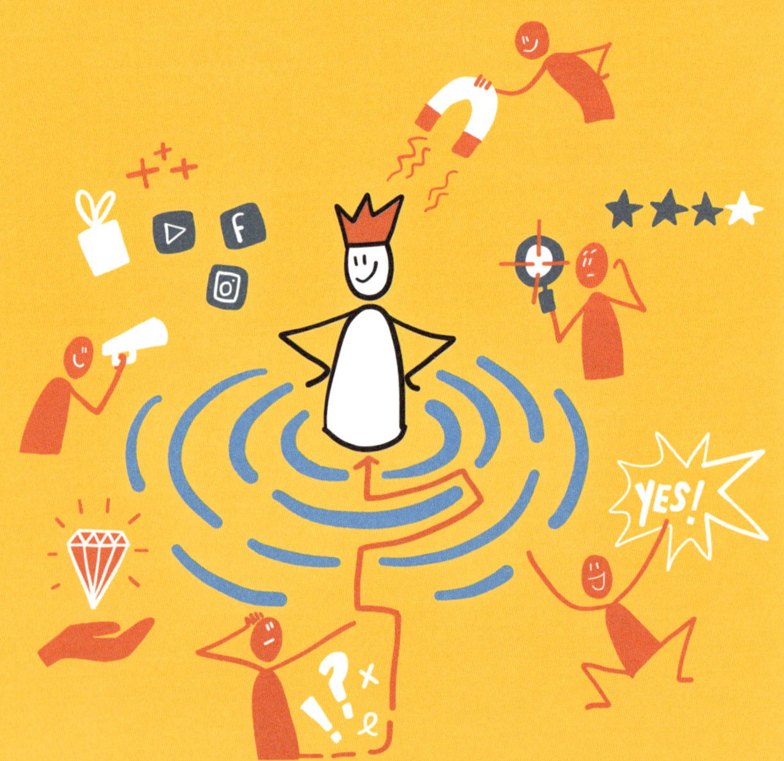

CLIENT CENTRICITY

BASIC ICONS

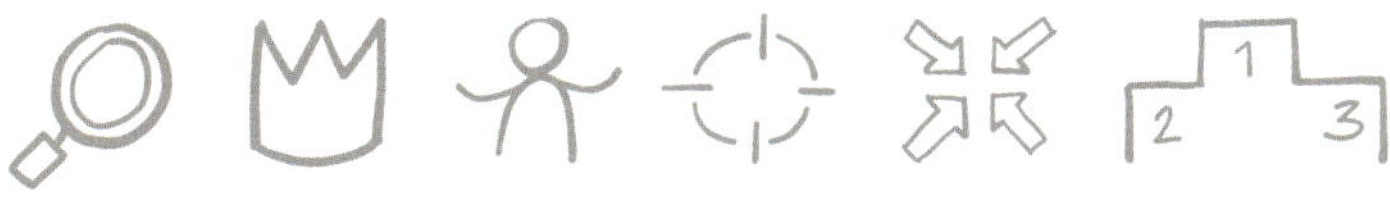

COMBINED ICONS

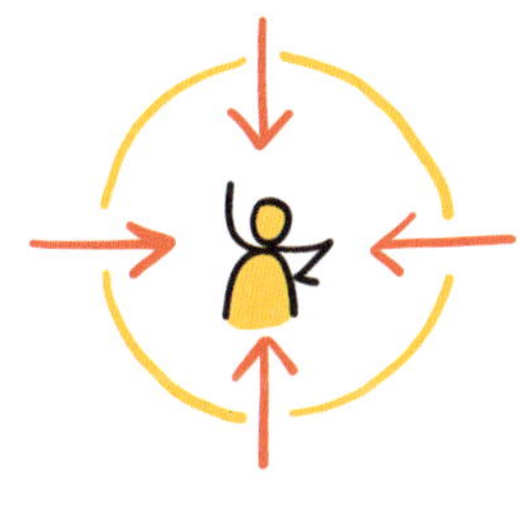

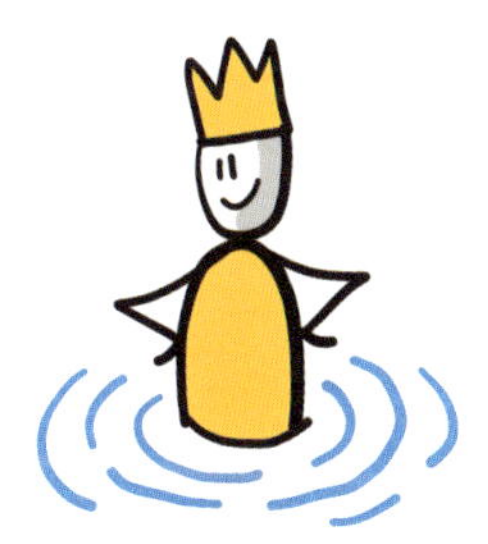

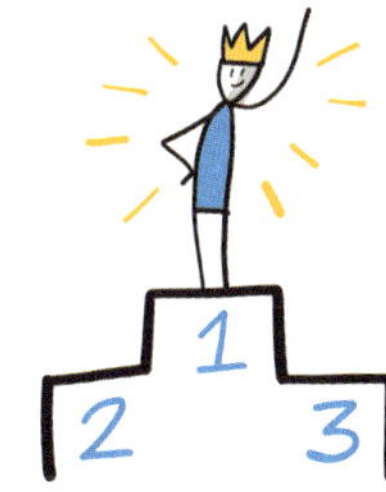

HOW TO DRAW

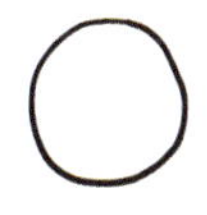

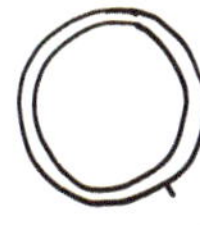

CUSTOMER

BASIC ICONS

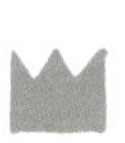
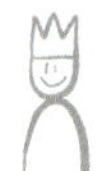
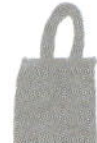

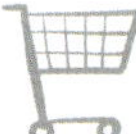
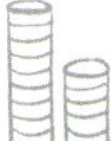
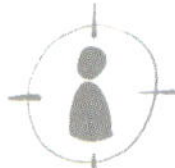

COMBINED ICONS

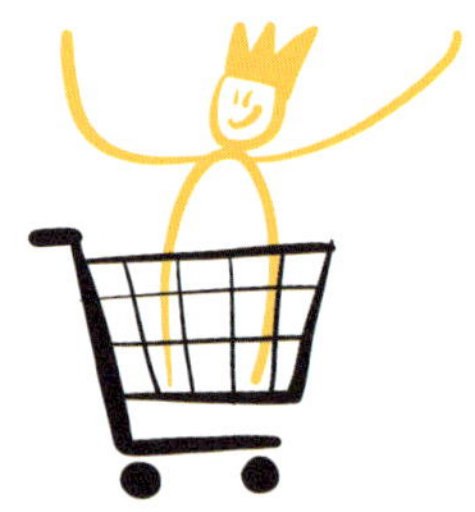
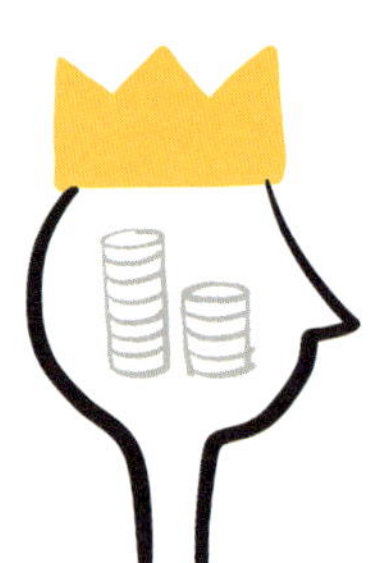
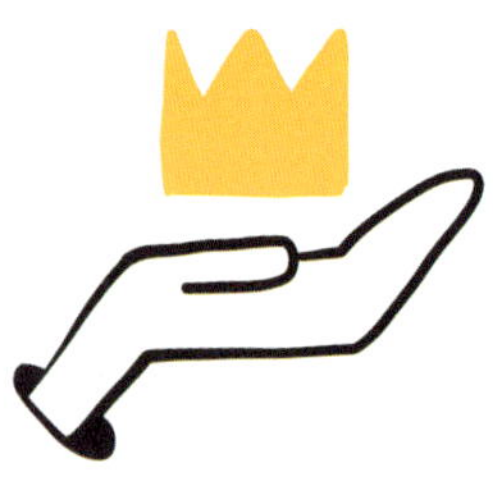

HOW TO DRAW

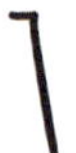
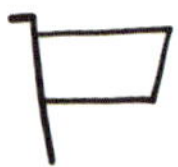
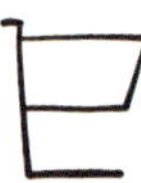
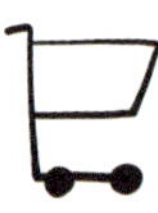
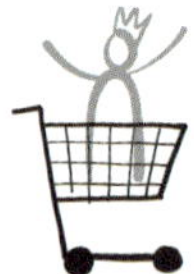

CUSTOMER NEEDS

BASIC ICONS

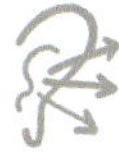
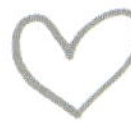
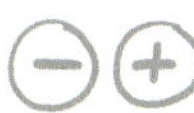
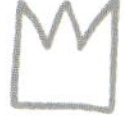
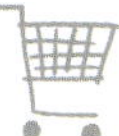

COMBINED ICONS

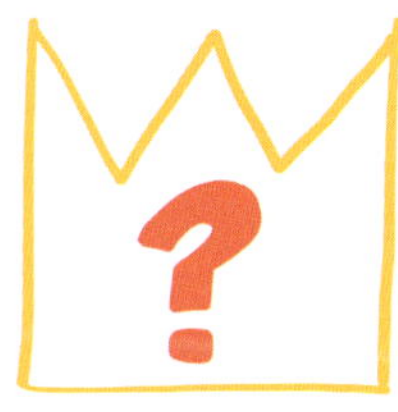
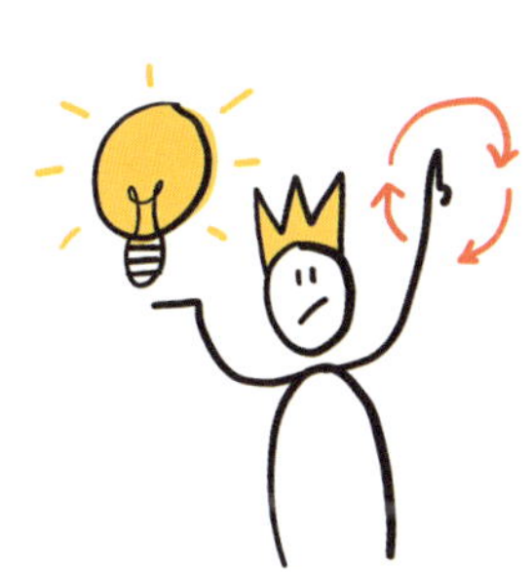
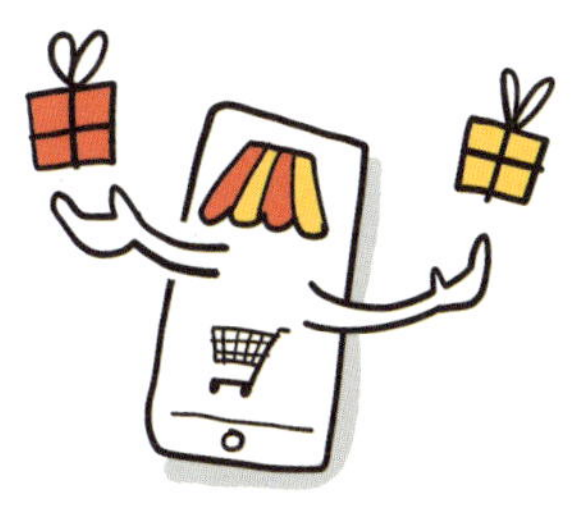
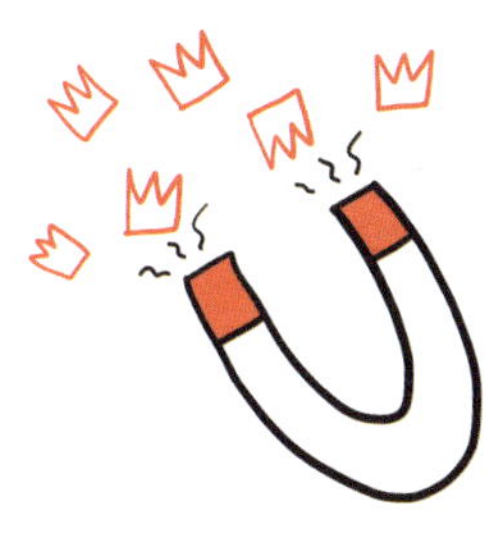

HOW TO DRAW

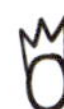
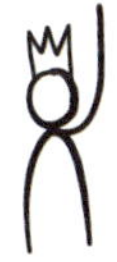
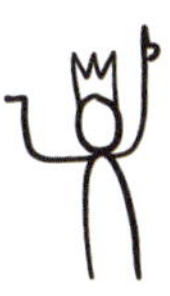
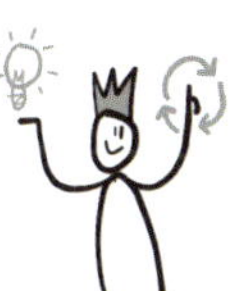

CUSTOMER SEGMENTATION

BASIC ICONS

 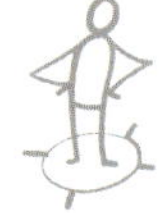 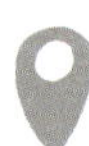 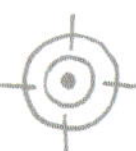 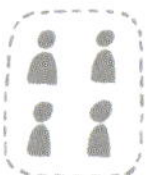

COMBINED ICONS

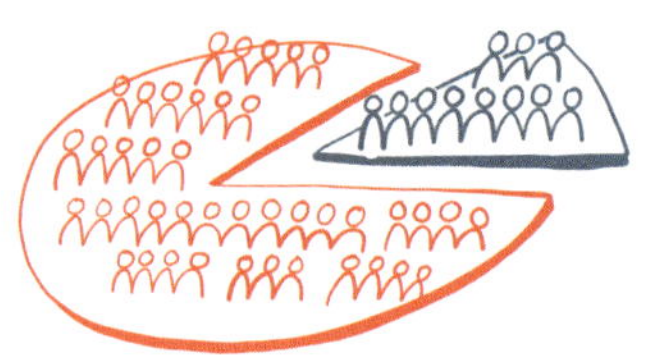

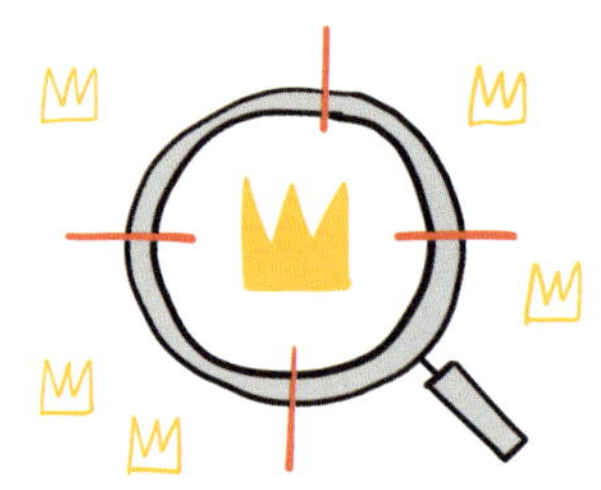

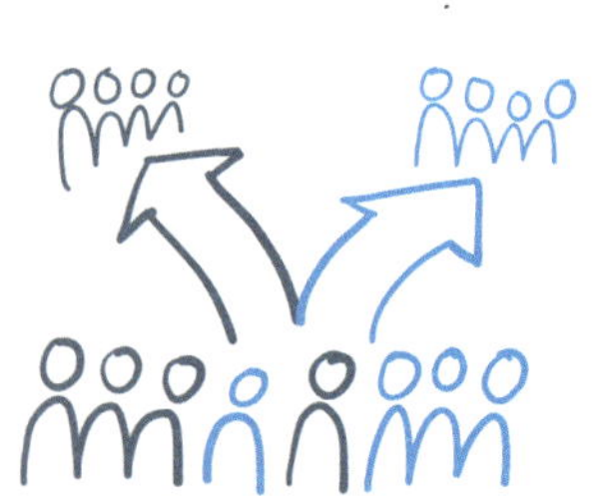

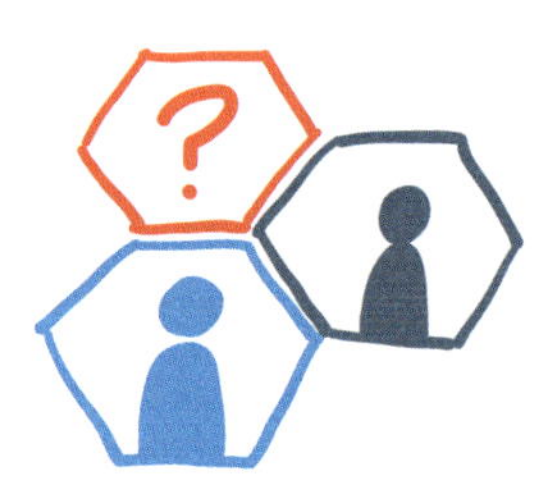

HOW TO DRAW

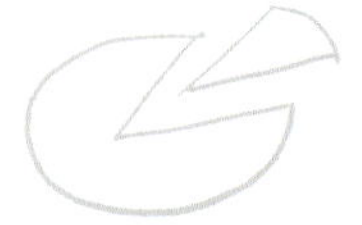 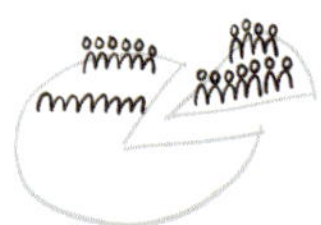 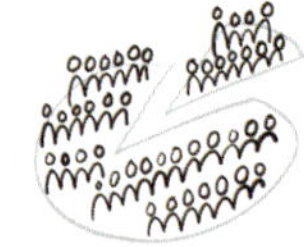 

CUSTOMER TOUCH POINTS

BASIC ICONS

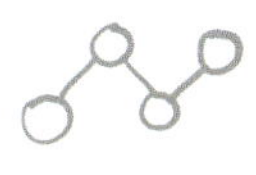
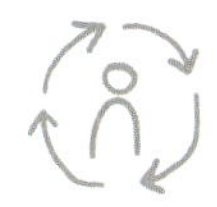
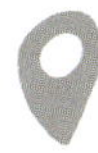
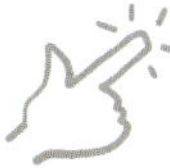
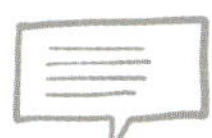

COMBINED ICONS

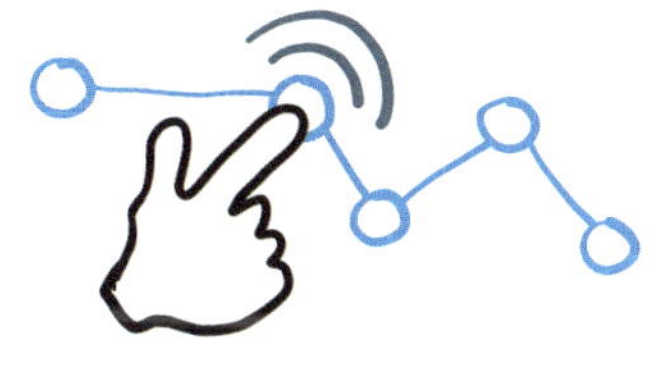
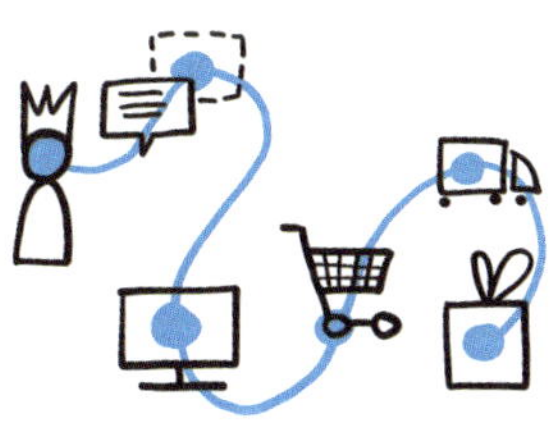
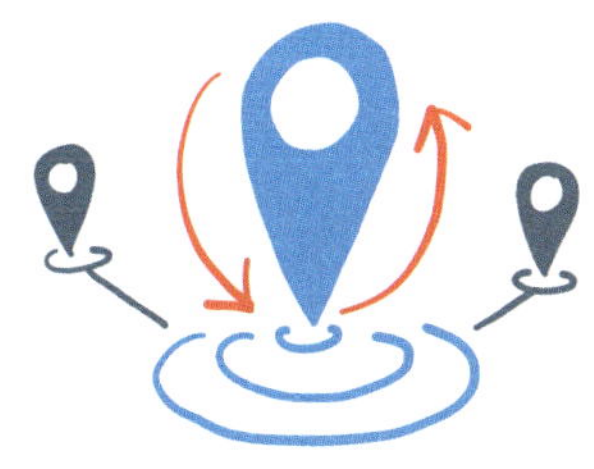
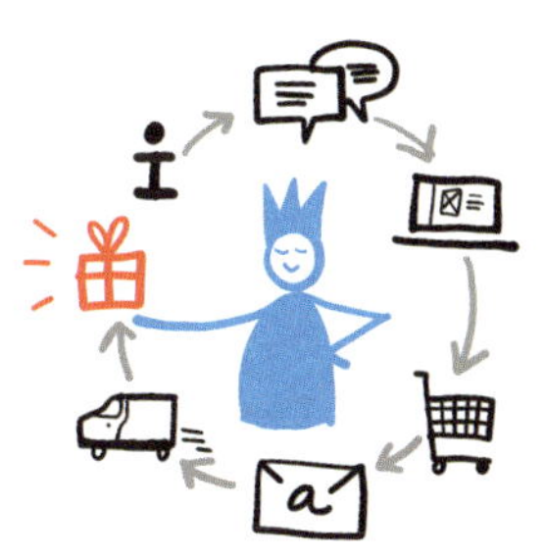

HOW TO DRAW

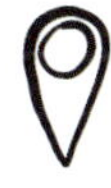
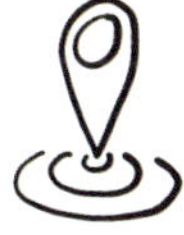
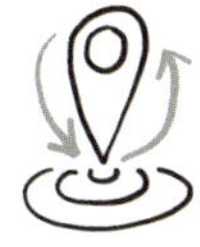
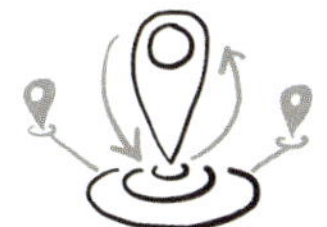

DELIVERY

BASIC ICONS

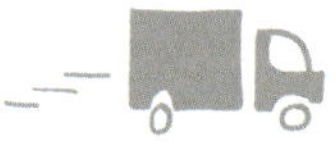
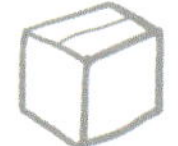
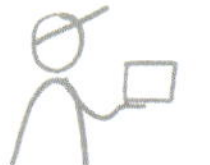
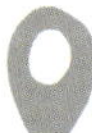
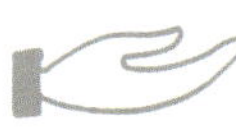
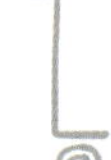

COMBINED ICONS

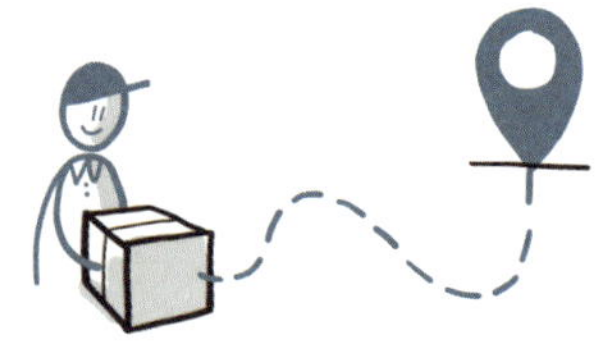
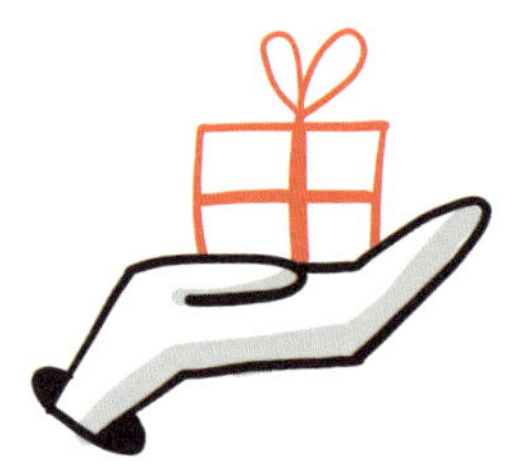
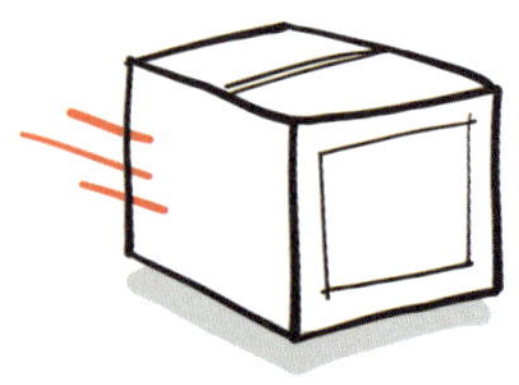
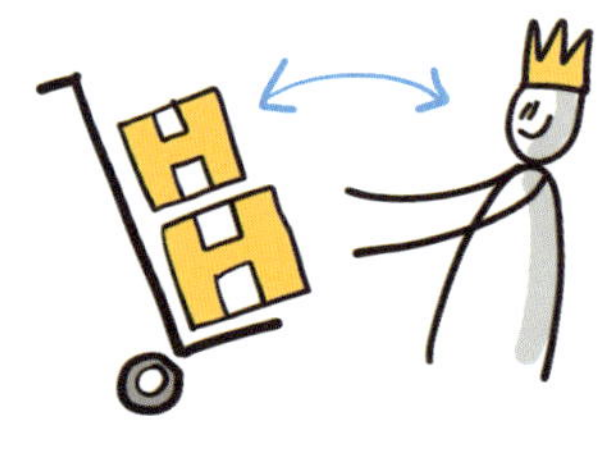

HOW TO DRAW

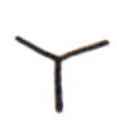
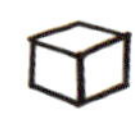
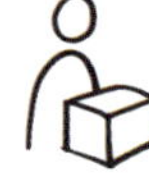
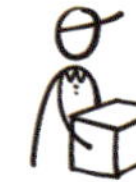
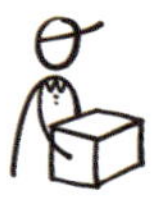
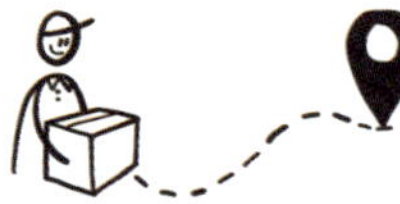

DEMAND (& SUPPLY)

BASIC ICONS

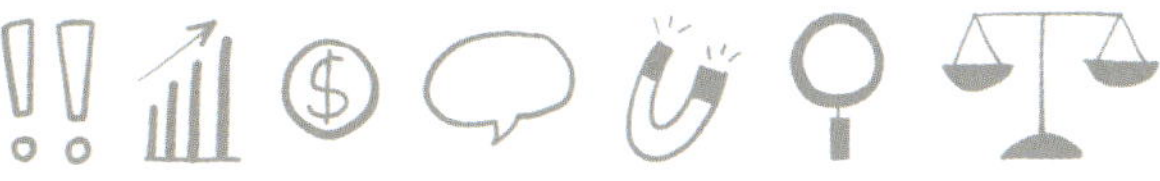

COMBINED ICONS

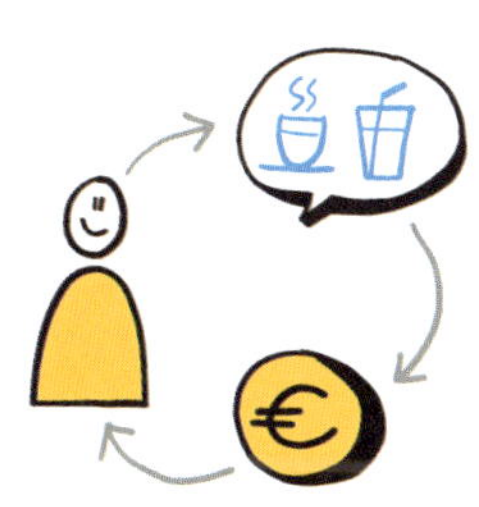

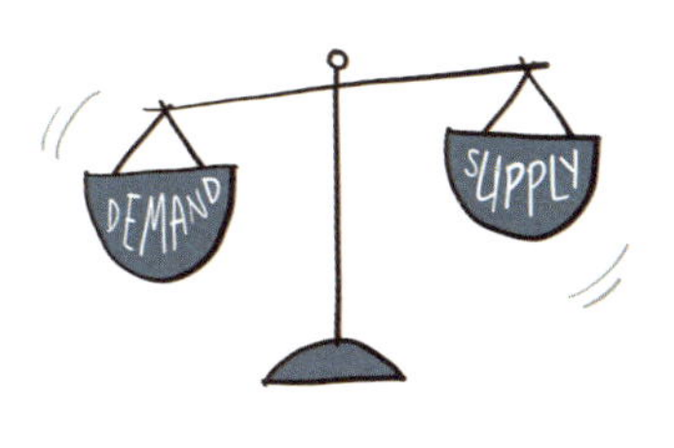

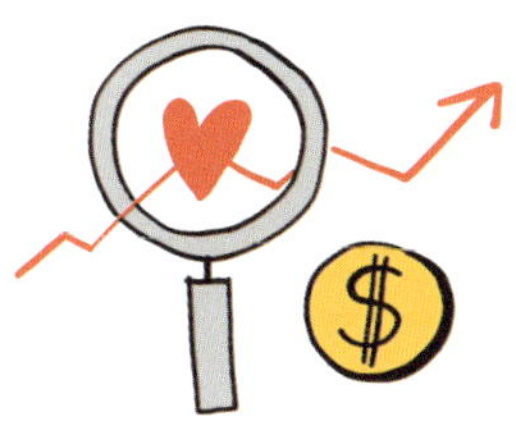

HOW TO DRAW

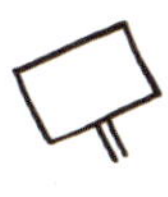

MAKING A DEAL

BASIC ICONS

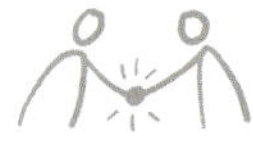

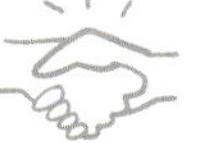
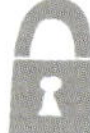

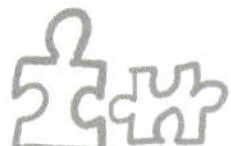

COMBINED ICONS

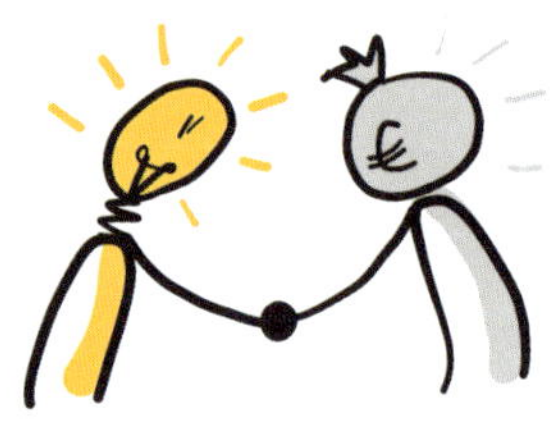
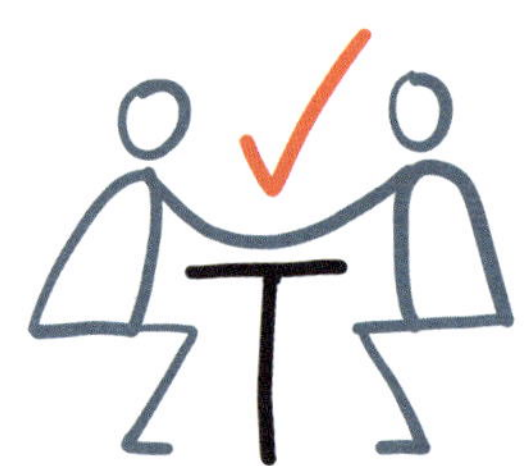
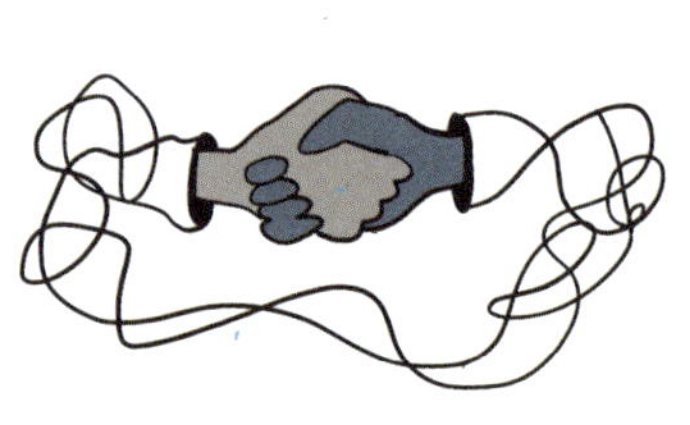
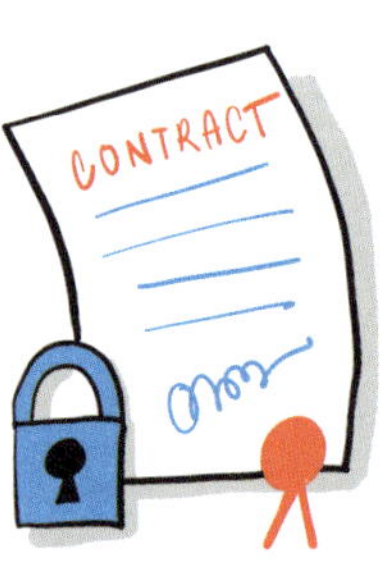

HOW TO DRAW

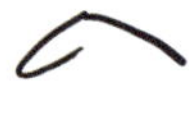
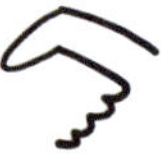

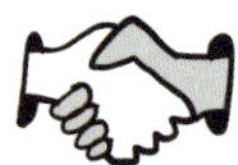

MARKET SURVEY

BASIC ICONS

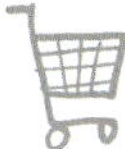
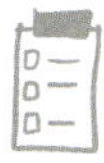
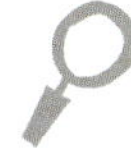

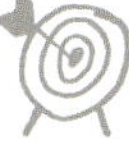
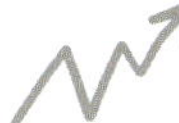

COMBINED ICONS

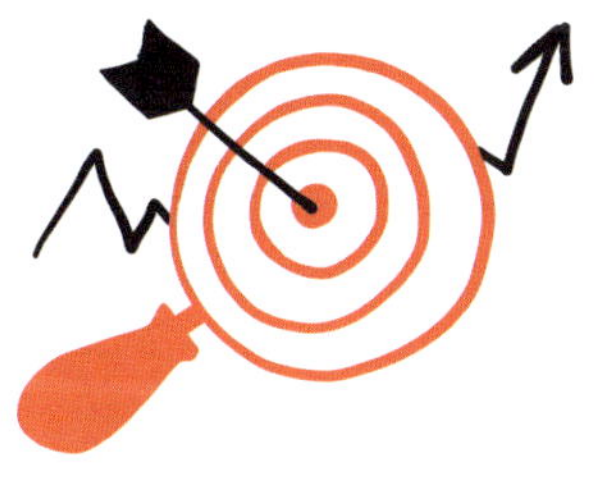

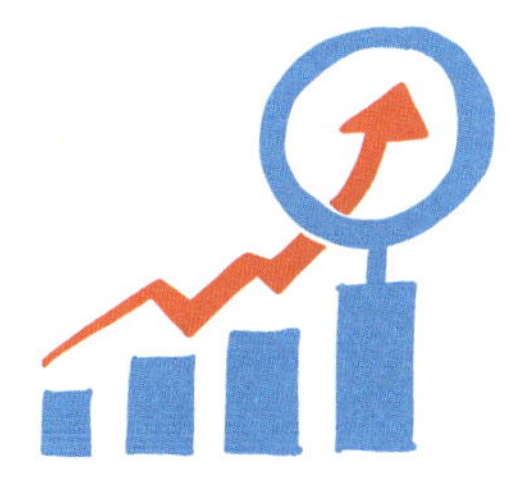
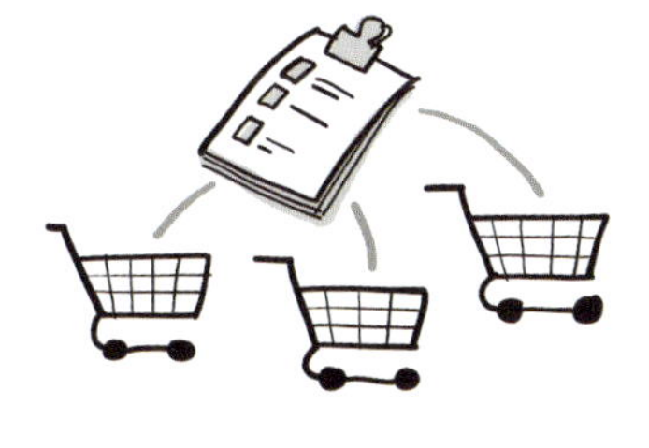

HOW TO DRAW

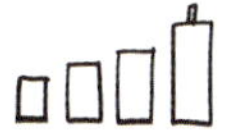
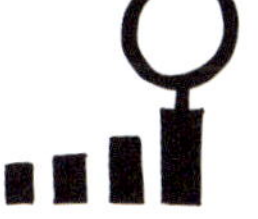
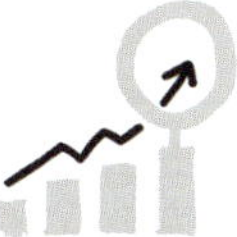

MARKETING

BASIC ICONS

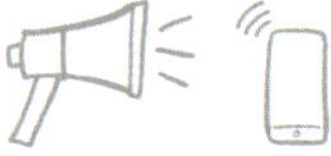

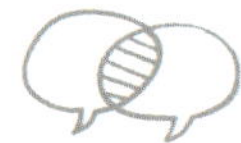
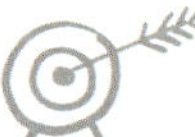
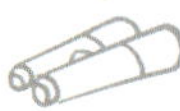

COMBINED ICONS

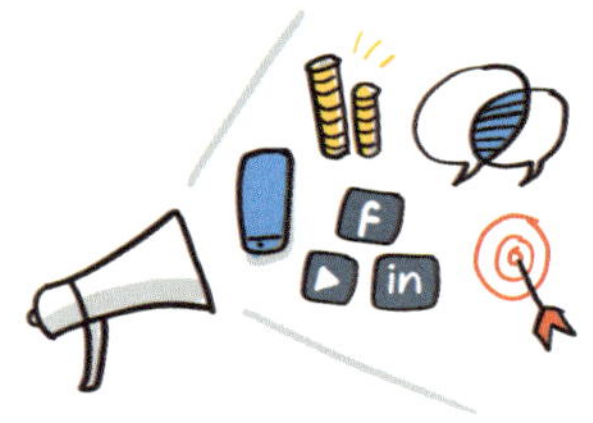
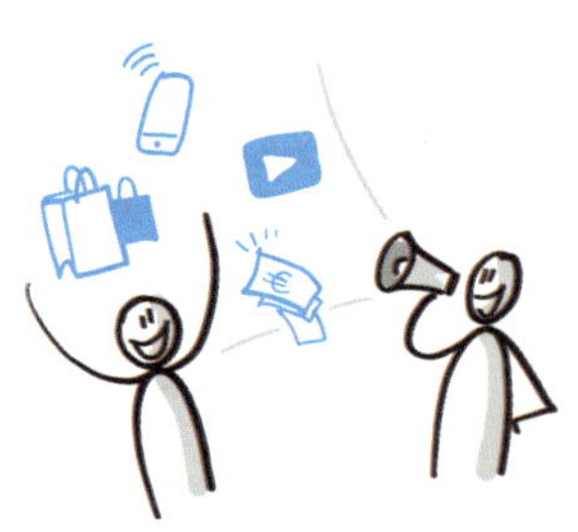
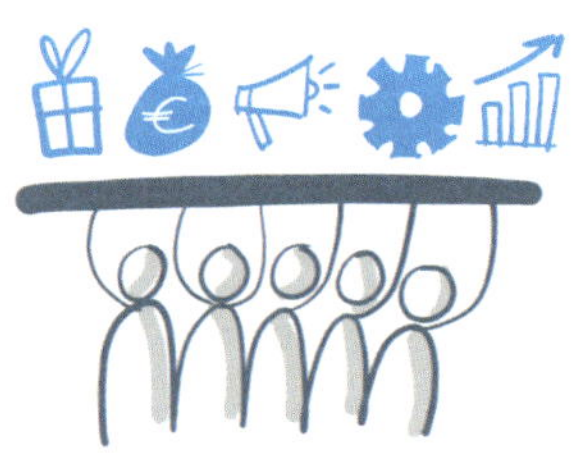
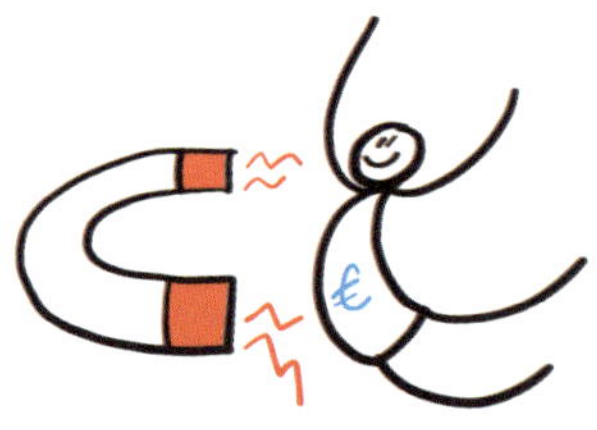

HOW TO DRAW

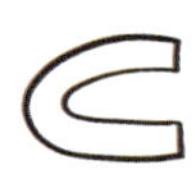
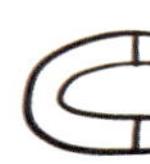
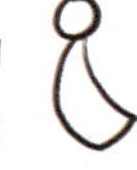
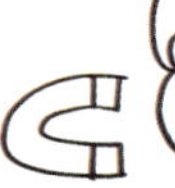
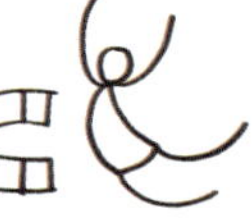
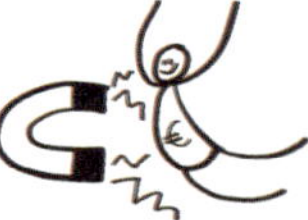

NEGOTIATION

BASIC ICONS

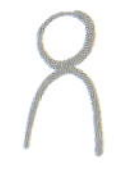
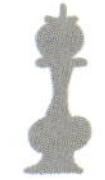

yes/no

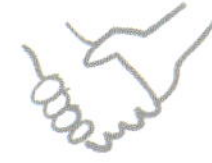
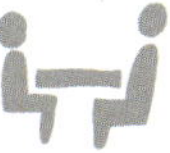
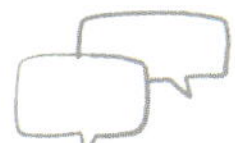

COMBINED ICONS

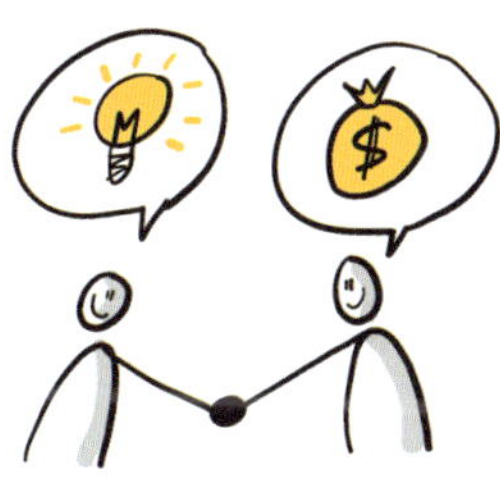
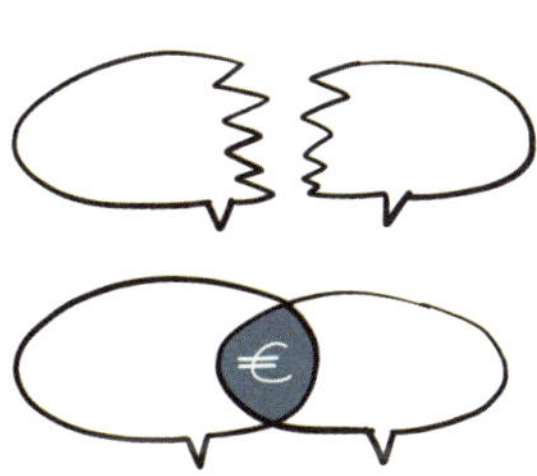
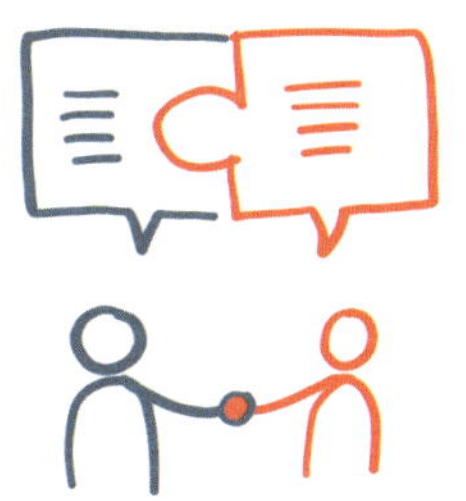
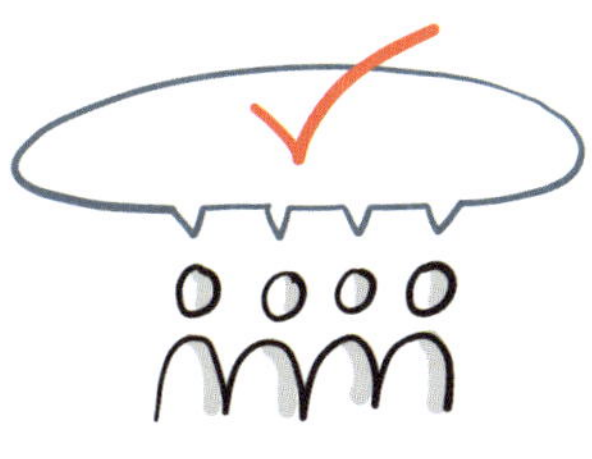

HOW TO DRAW

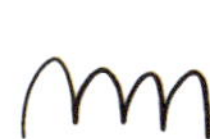
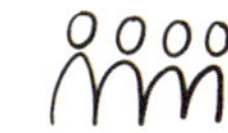
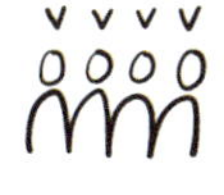
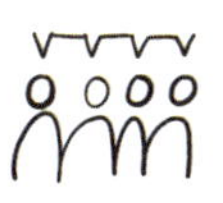
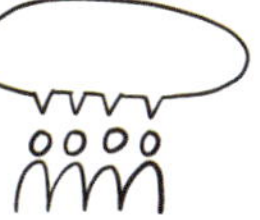

OMNI CHANNEL

BASIC ICONS

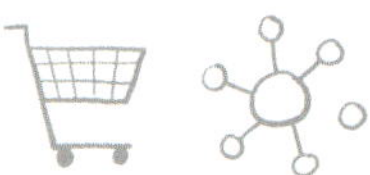
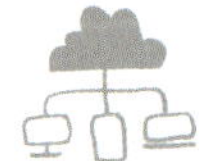
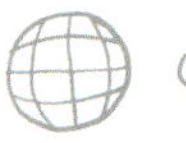
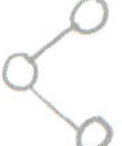
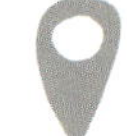
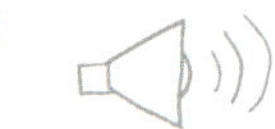

COMBINED ICONS

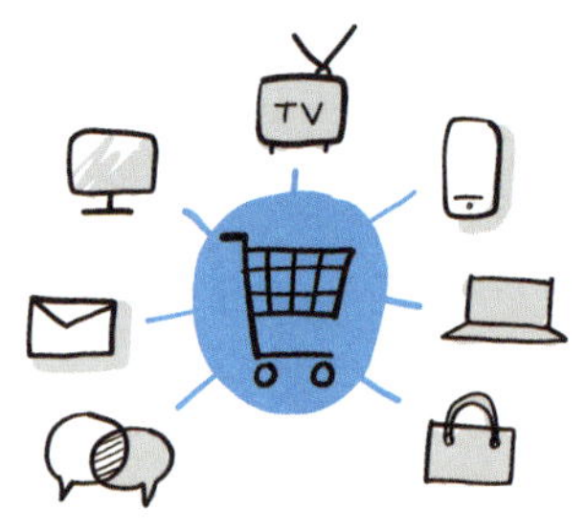

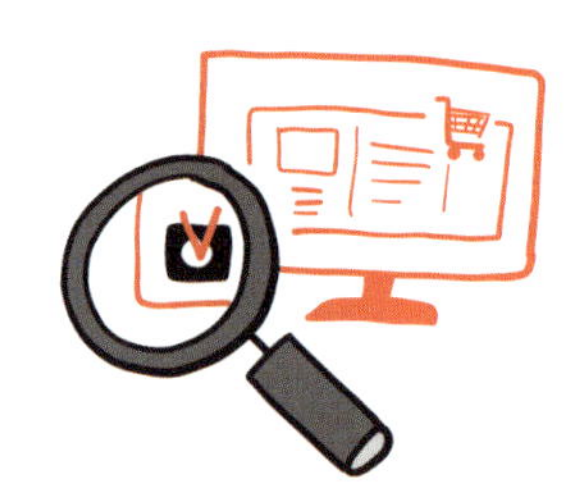

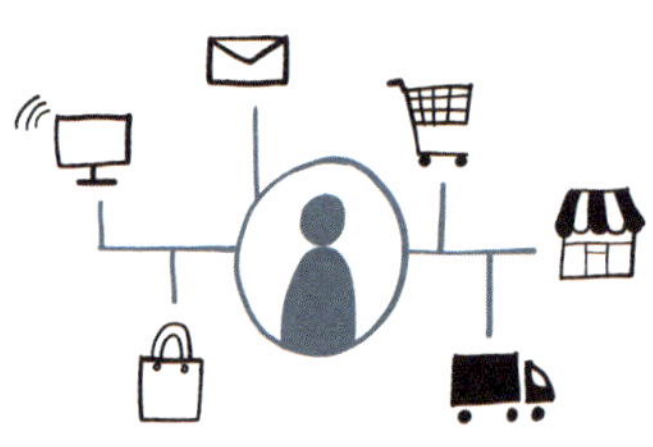

HOW TO DRAW

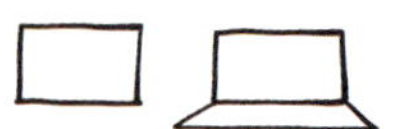
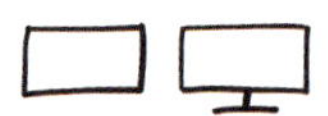
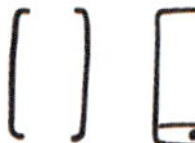

QUALITY

BASIC ICONS

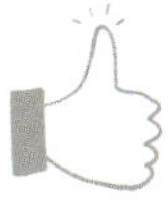
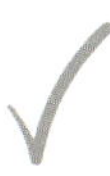
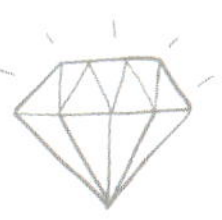
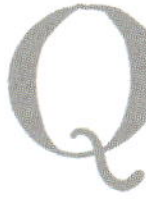

COMBINED ICONS

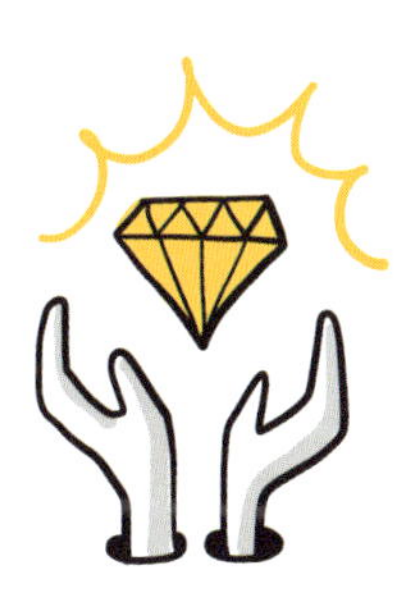

HOW TO DRAW

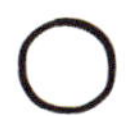
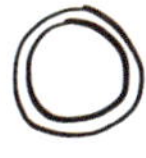
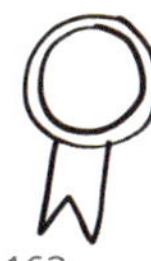

REPUTATION

BASIC ICONS

COMBINED ICONS

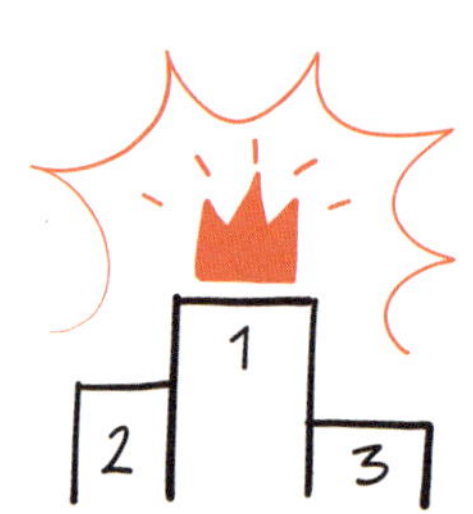

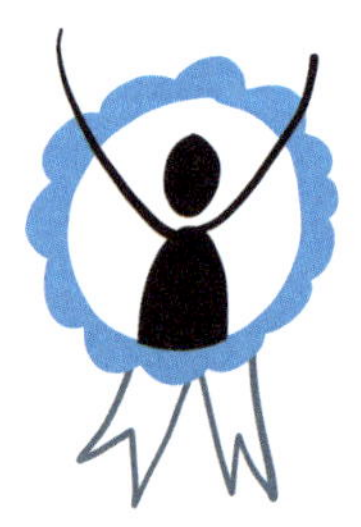

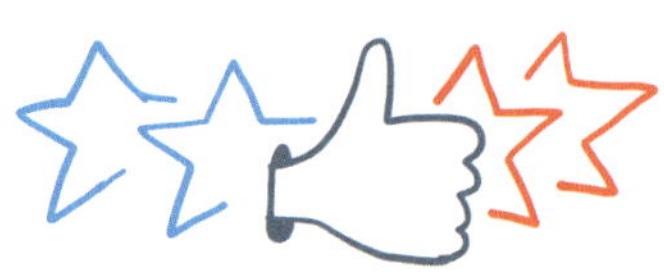

HOW TO DRAW

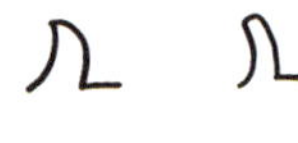

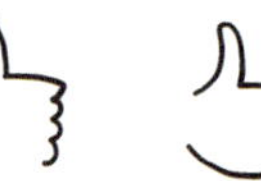

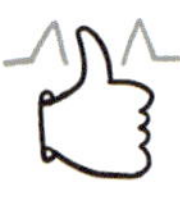

SALES

BASIC ICONS

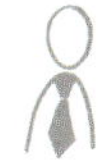
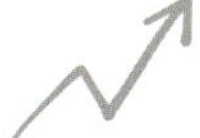
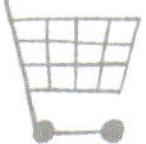
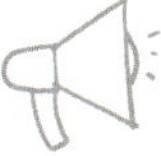
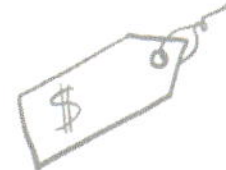

COMBINED ICONS

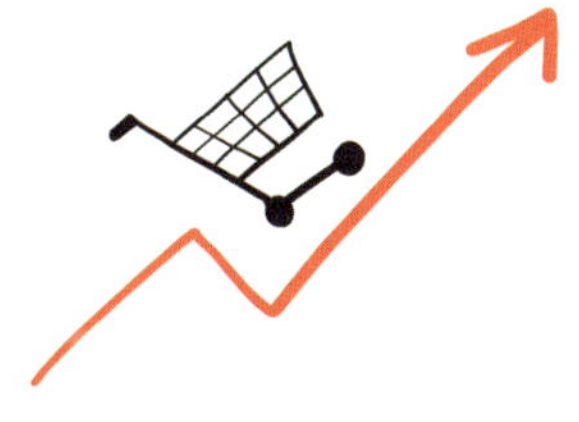
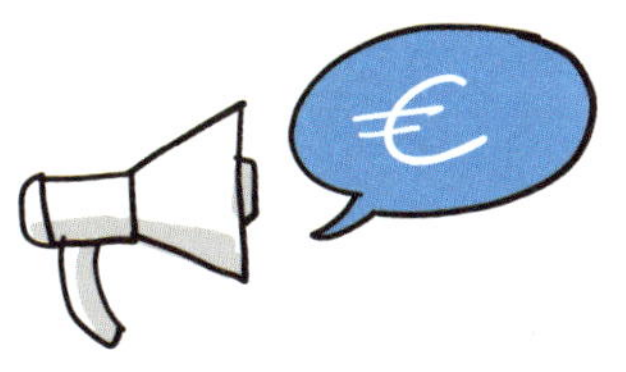
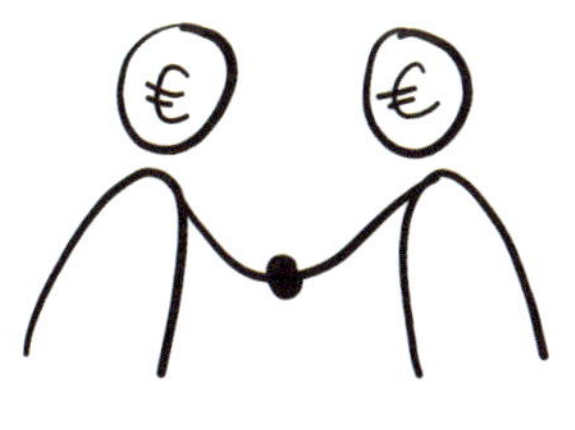
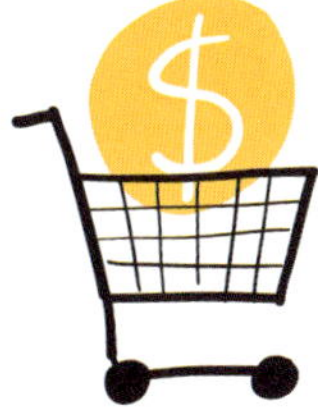

HOW TO DRAW

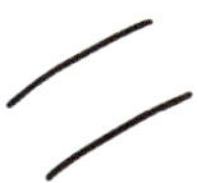
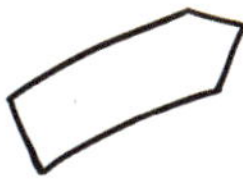
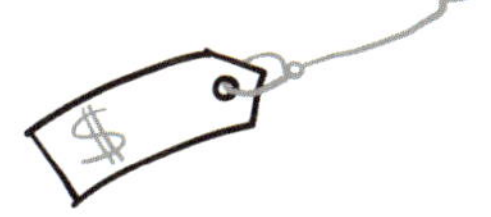

TARGET GROUP

BASIC ICONS

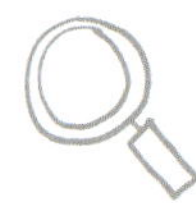
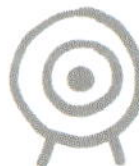
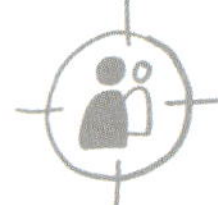
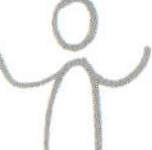
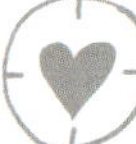

COMBINED ICONS

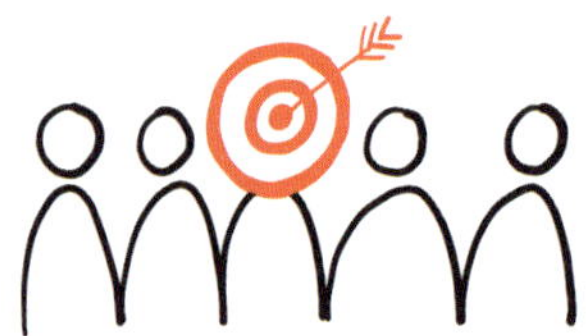
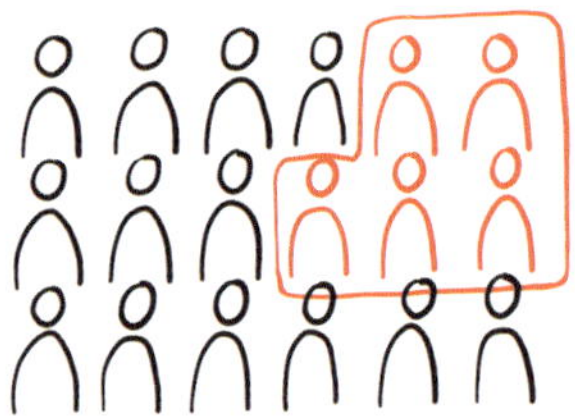

HOW TO DRAW

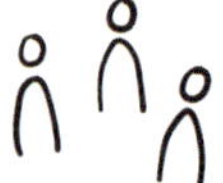
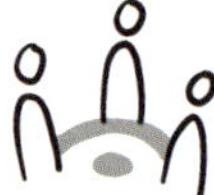

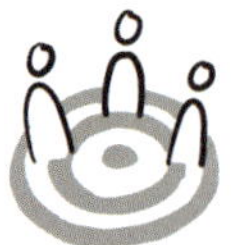

TERMS AND CONDITIONS

BASIC ICONS

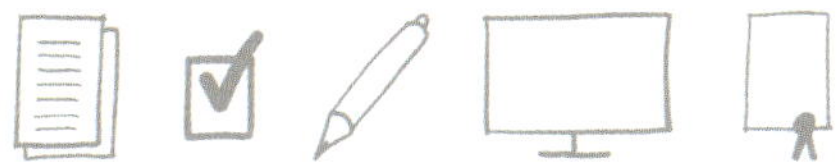

COMBINED ICONS

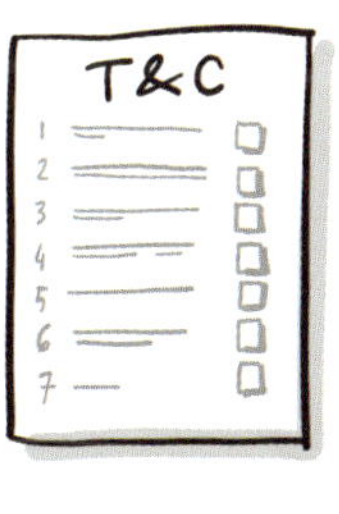

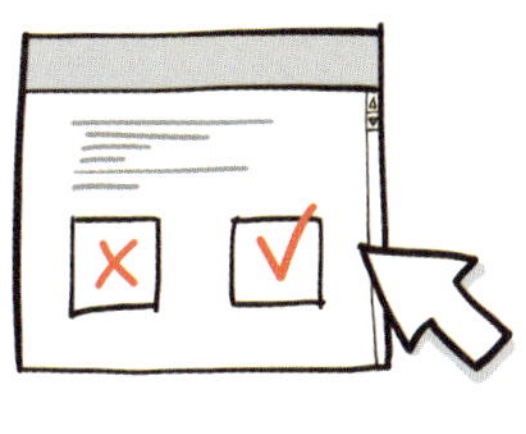

HOW TO DRAW

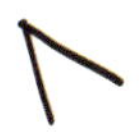
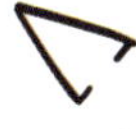

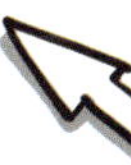

USP

BASIC ICONS

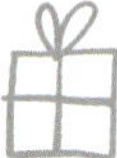  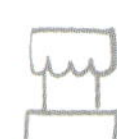 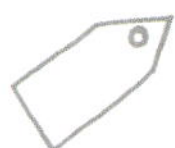 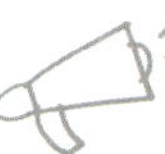 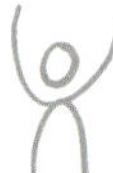

COMBINED ICONS

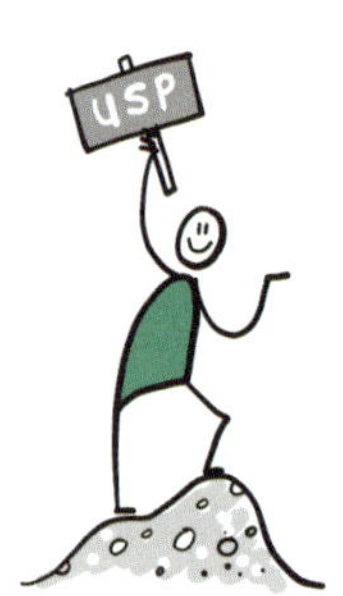

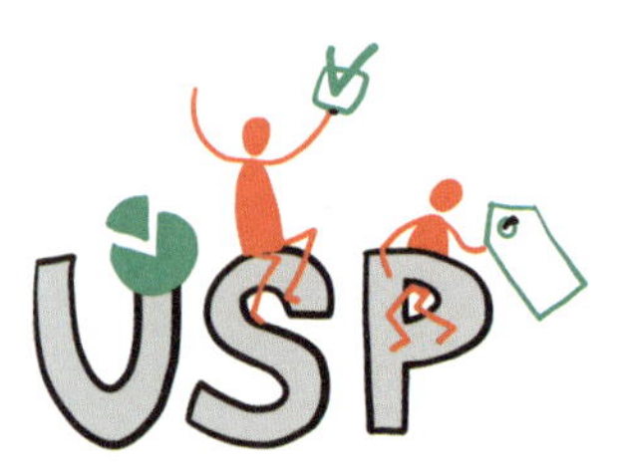

HOW TO DRAW

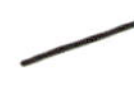 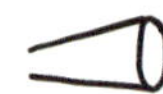 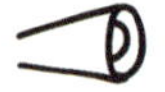 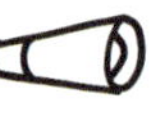 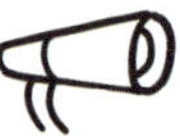 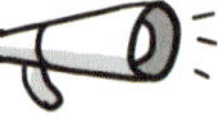

VALUE (ADDED VALUE)

BASIC ICONS

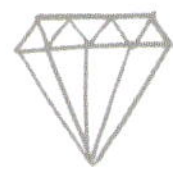
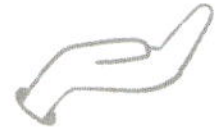
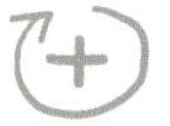
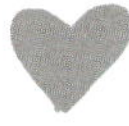
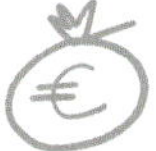
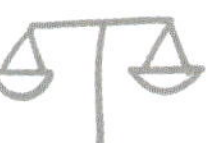

COMBINED ICONS

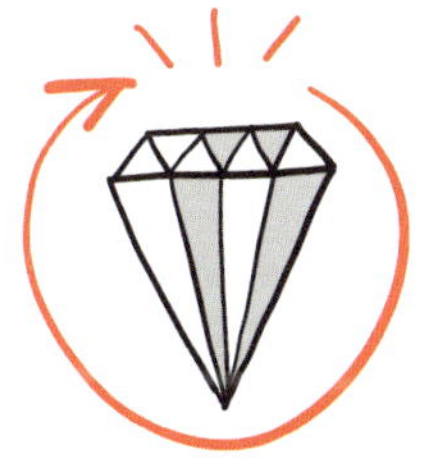
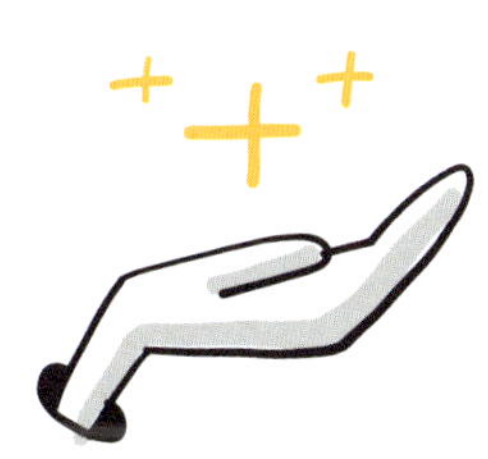
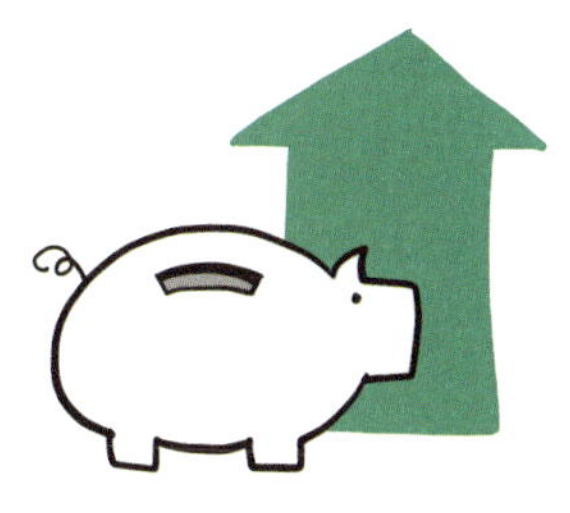
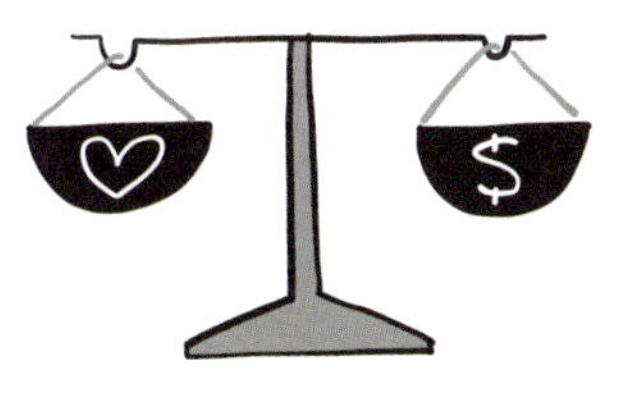

HOW TO DRAW

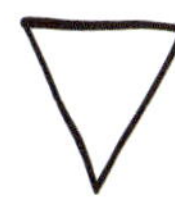
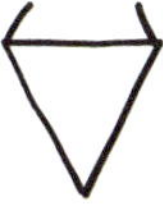
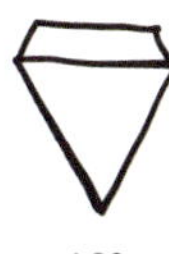
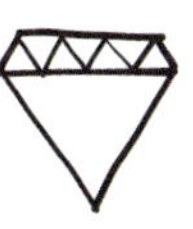
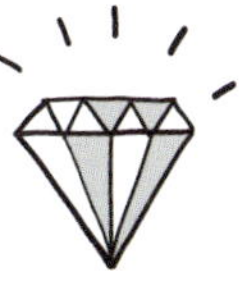

WHOLESALE

BASIC ICONS

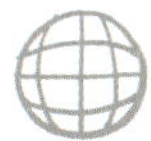
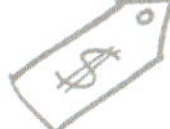
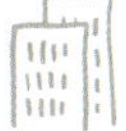
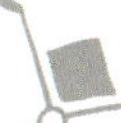
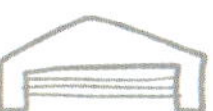

COMBINED ICONS

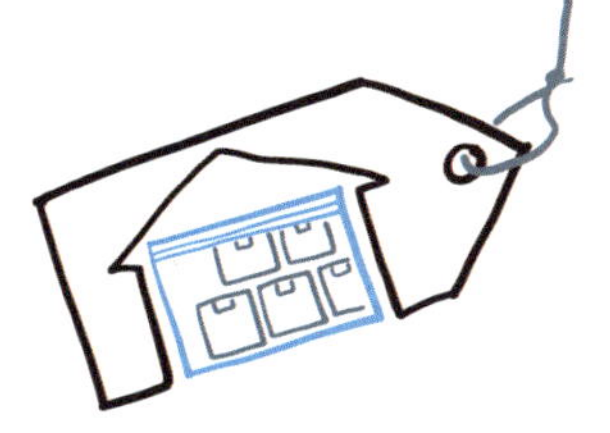
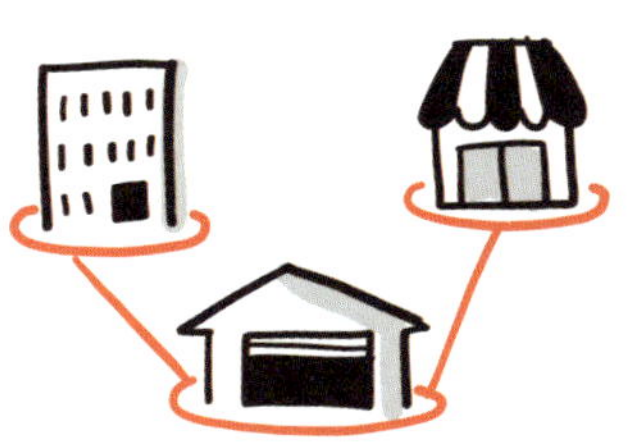
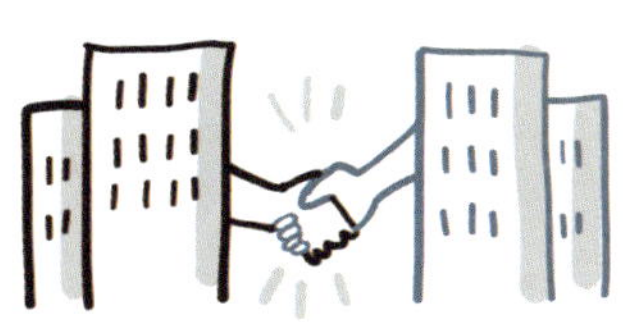
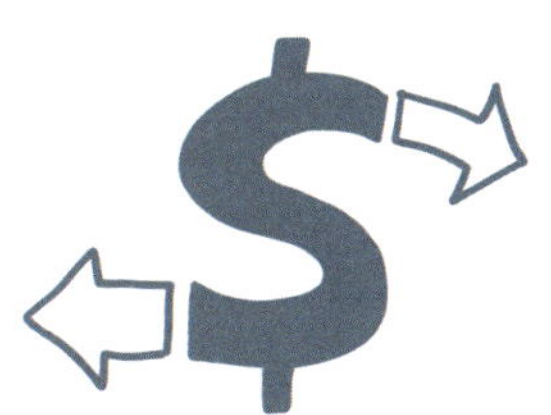

HOW TO DRAW

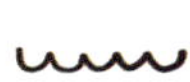
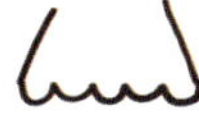
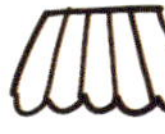
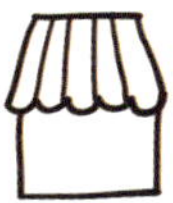
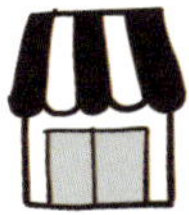

YES

BASIC ICONS

COMBINED ICONS

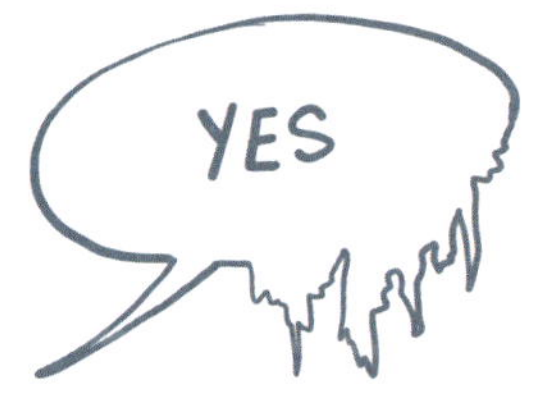

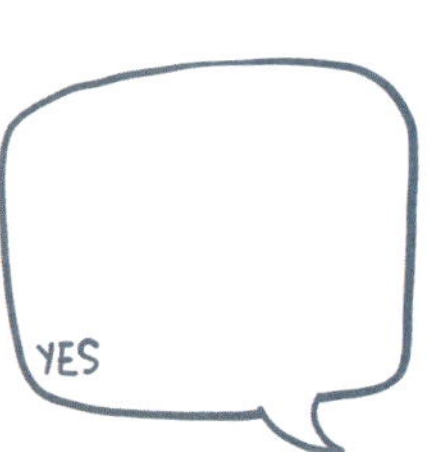

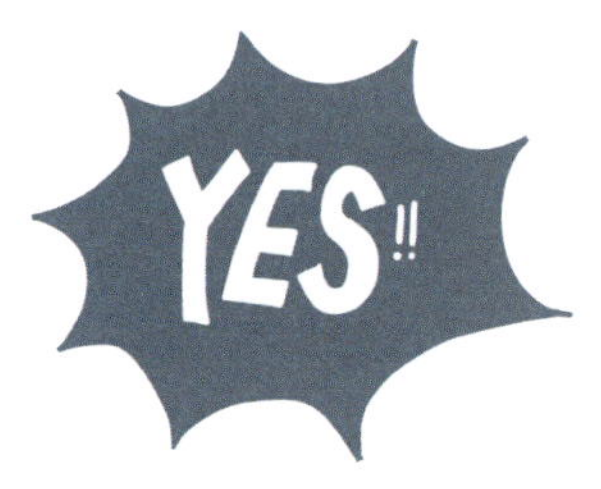

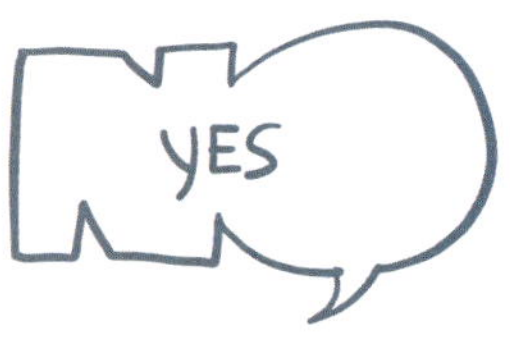

Inspired by David Mazzucchelli

HOW TO DRAW

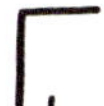

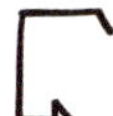

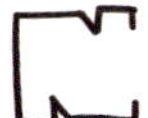

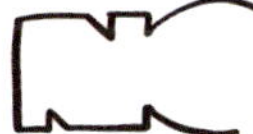

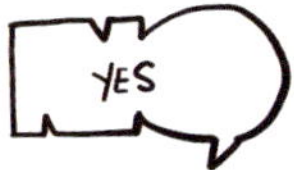

TECHNOLOGY

THE TECH WE USE

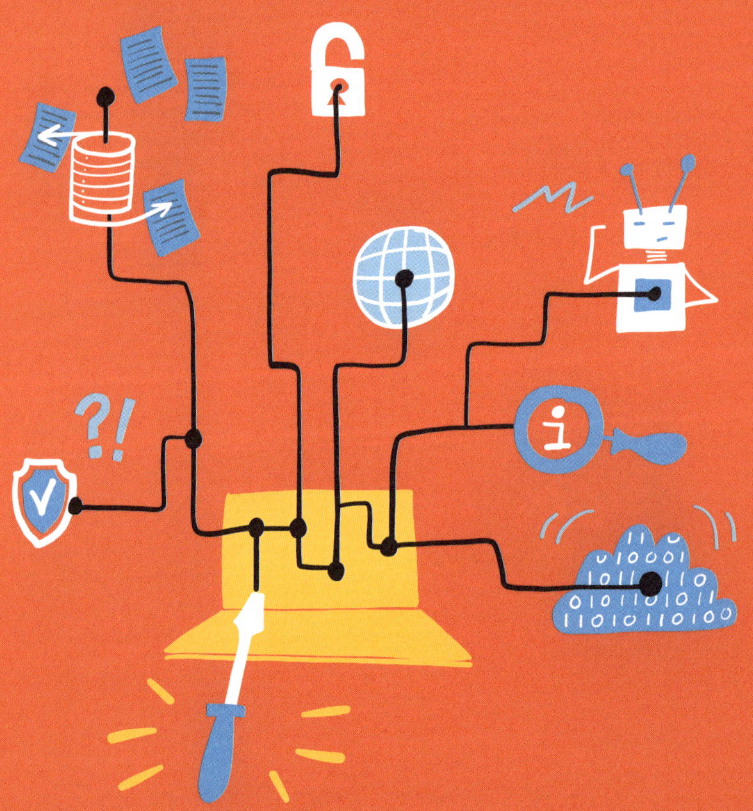

ARTIFICIAL INTELLIGENCE

BASIC ICONS

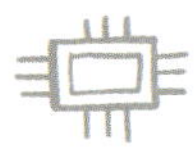
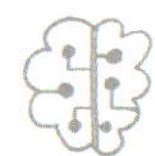
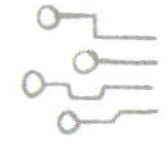
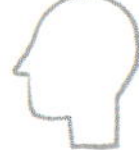
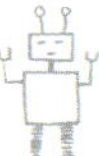
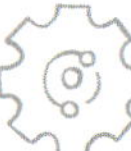

COMBINED ICONS

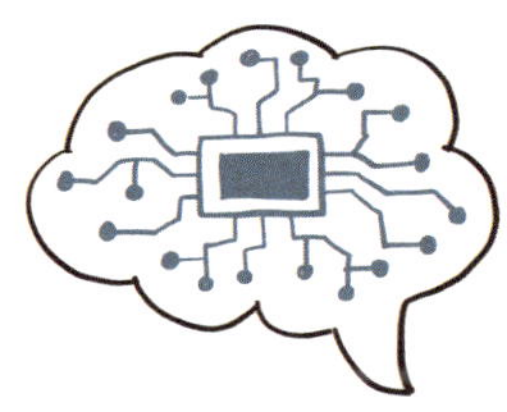
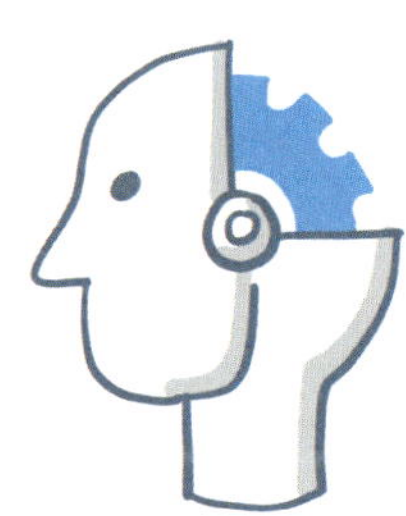
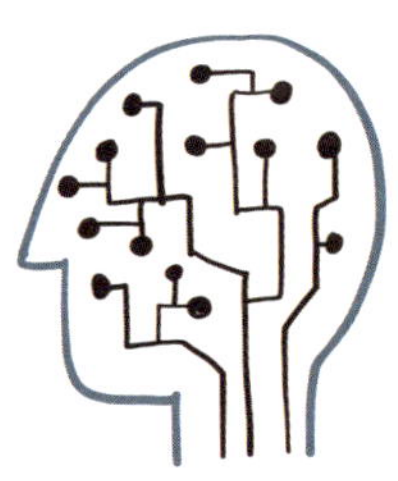
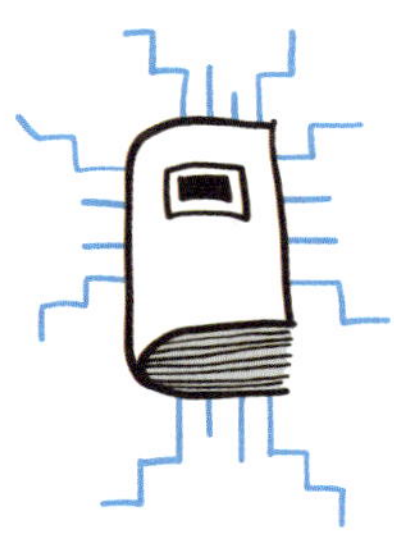

HOW TO DRAW

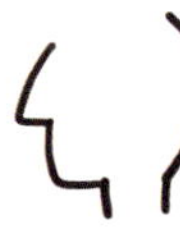

CONNECTIVITY

BASIC ICONS

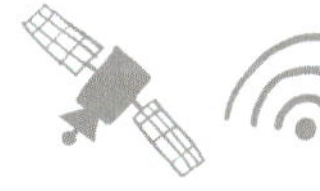
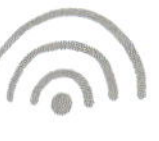
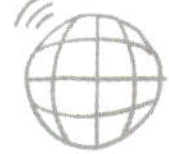
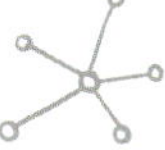
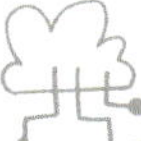
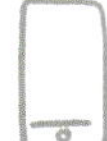

COMBINED ICONS

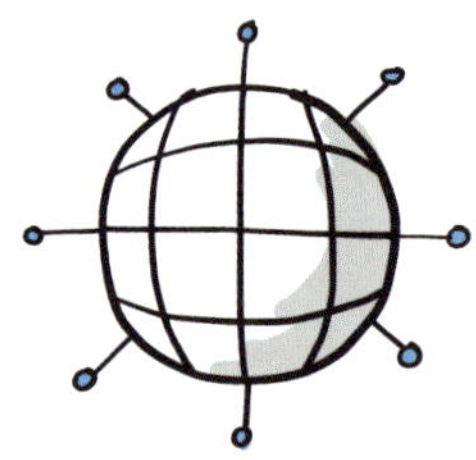
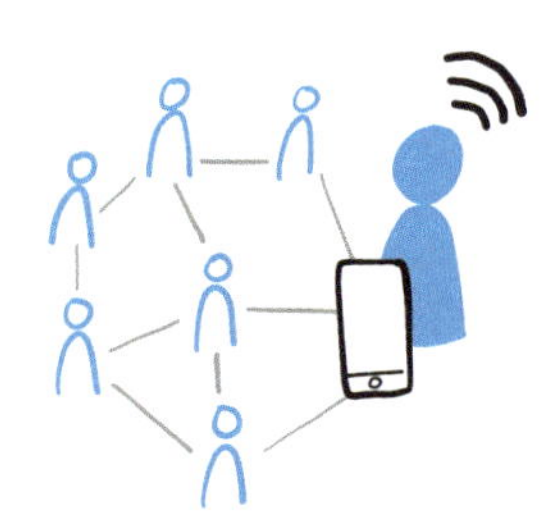
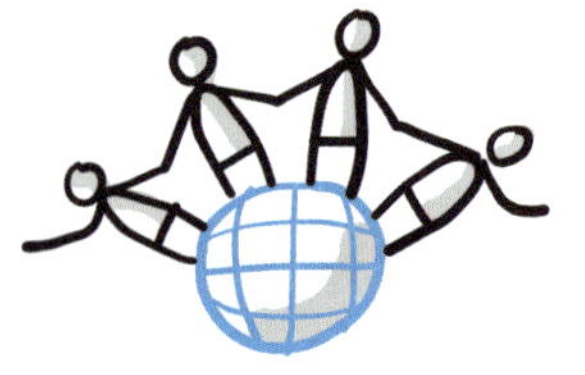
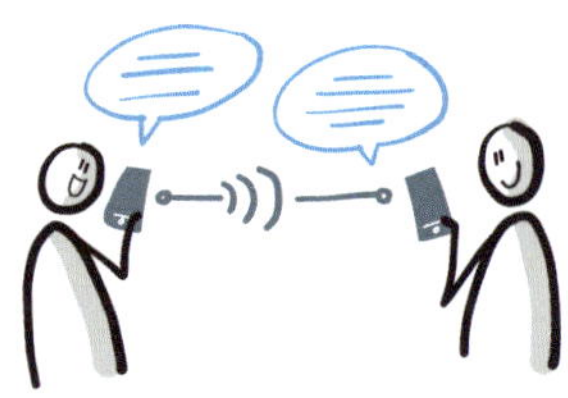

HOW TO DRAW

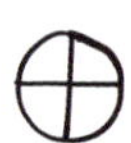
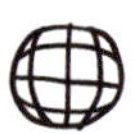
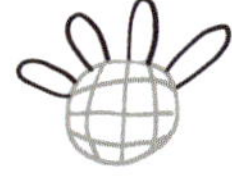
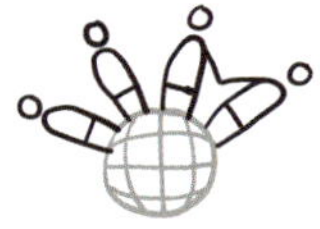
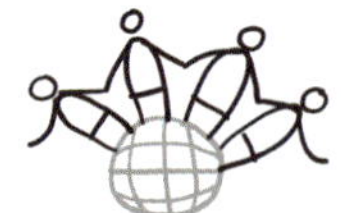

CRIMINAL ACTIVITY

BASIC ICONS

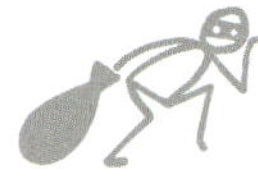
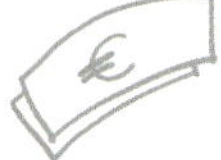
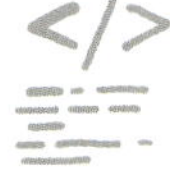
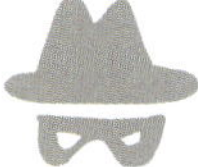
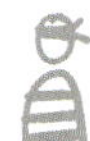
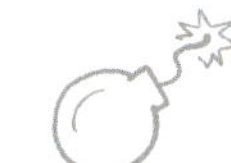

COMBINED ICONS

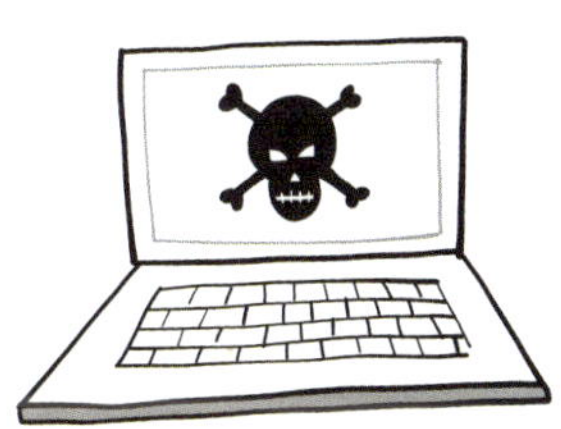
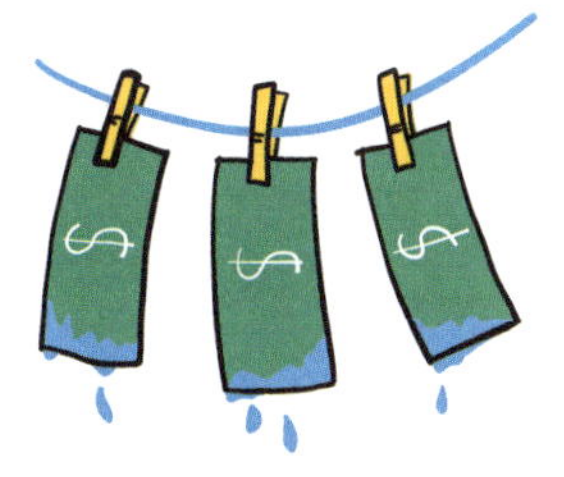

HOW TO DRAW

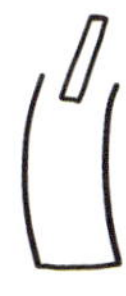
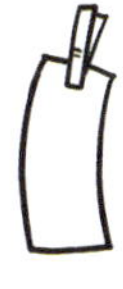
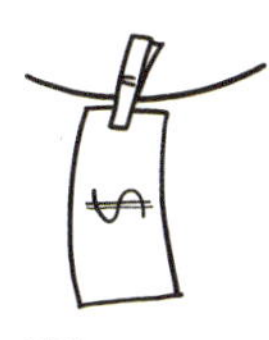
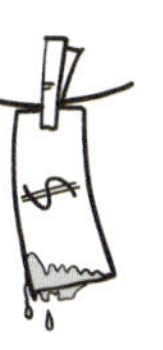

DATA

BASIC ICONS

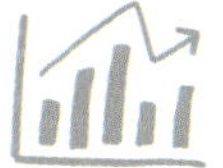
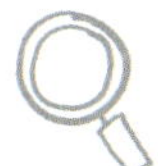
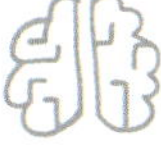
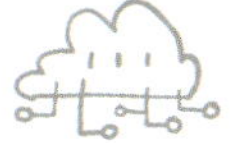
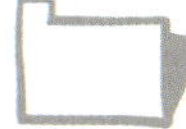
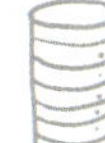

COMBINED ICONS

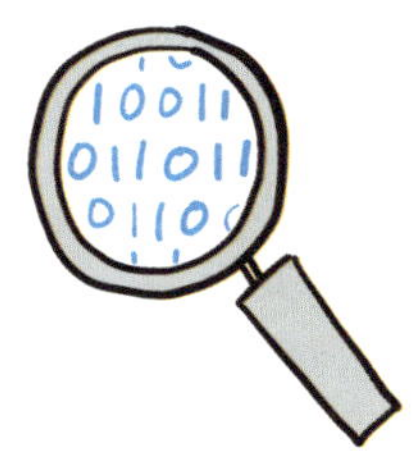

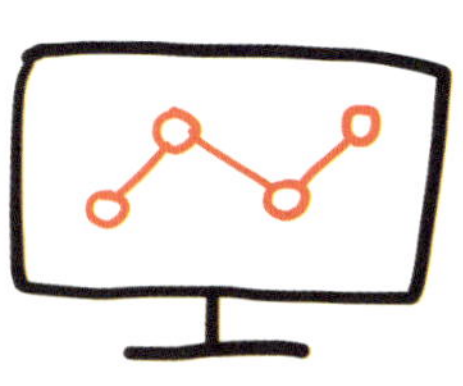

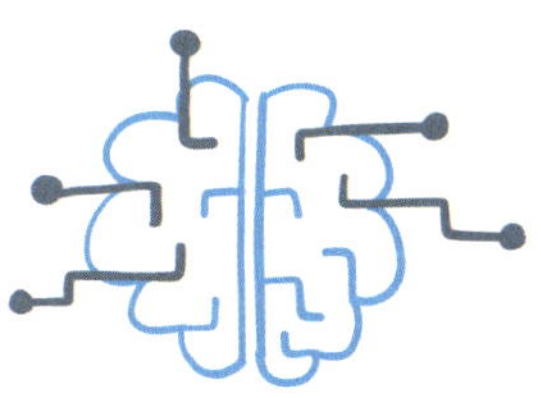

HOW TO DRAW

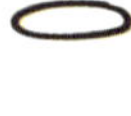
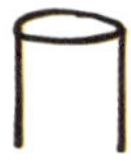
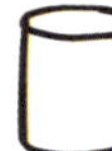
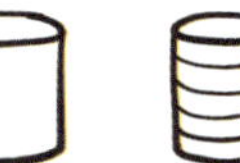
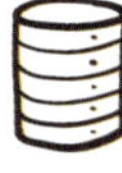
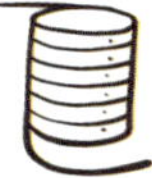
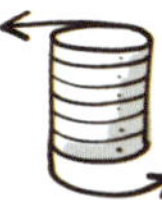

DEVELOPMENT

BASIC ICONS

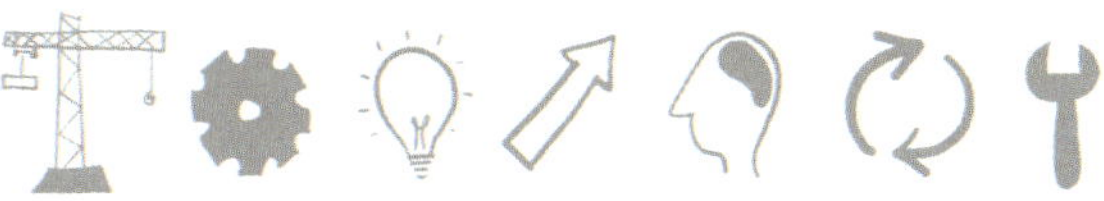

COMBINED ICONS

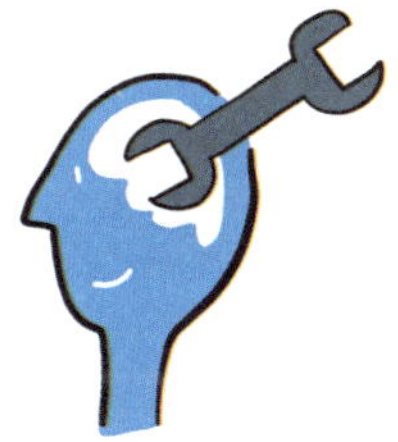

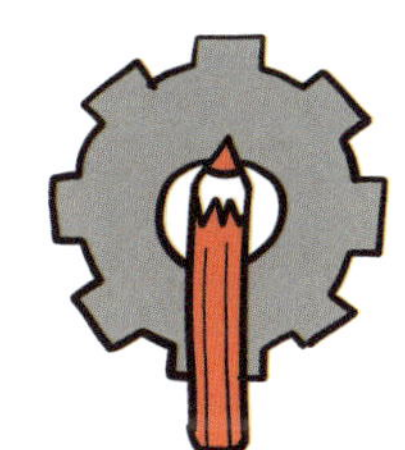

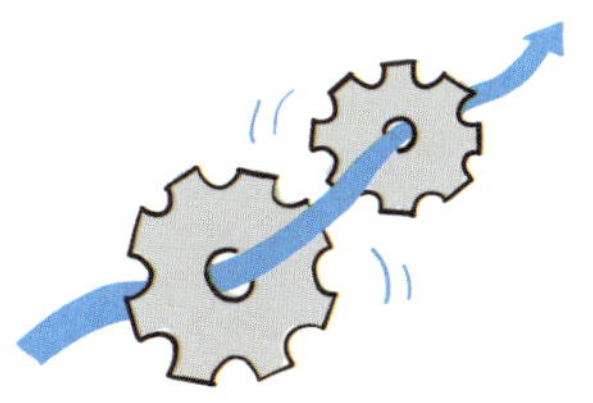

HOW TO DRAW

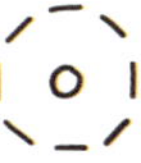

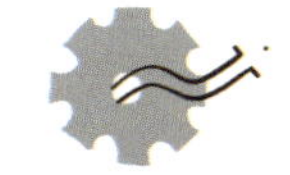

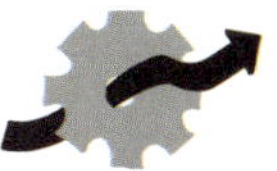

DIGITAL TOOLS

BASIC ICONS

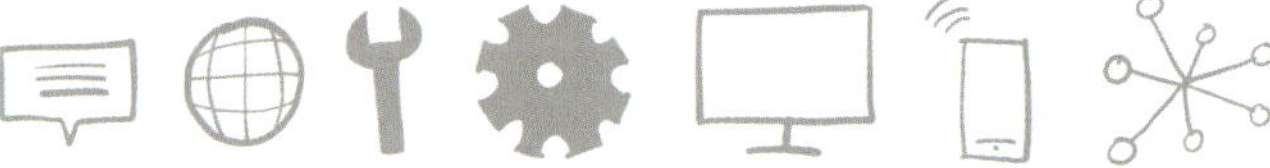

COMBINED ICONS

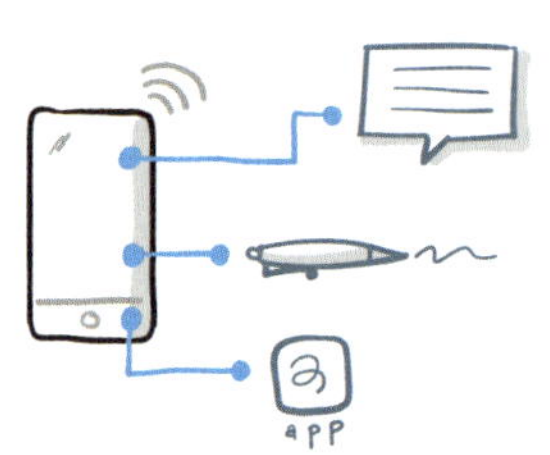

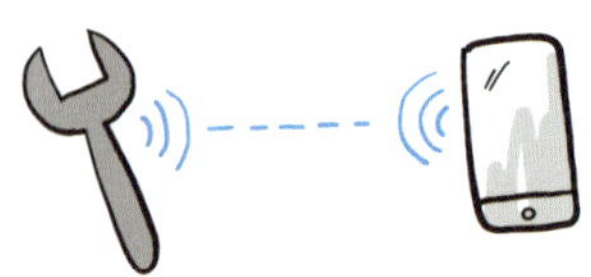

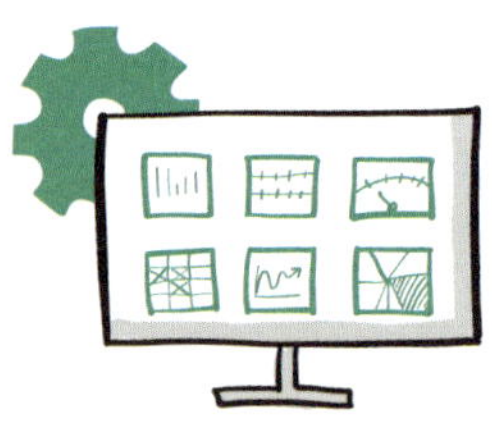

HOW TO DRAW

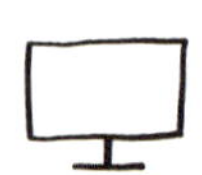
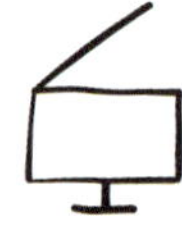
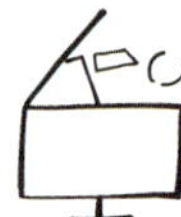

DIGITALLY

BASIC ICONS

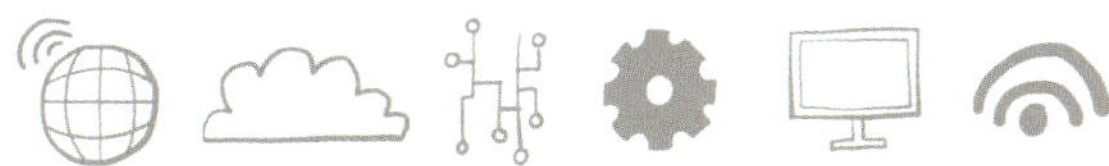

COMBINED ICONS

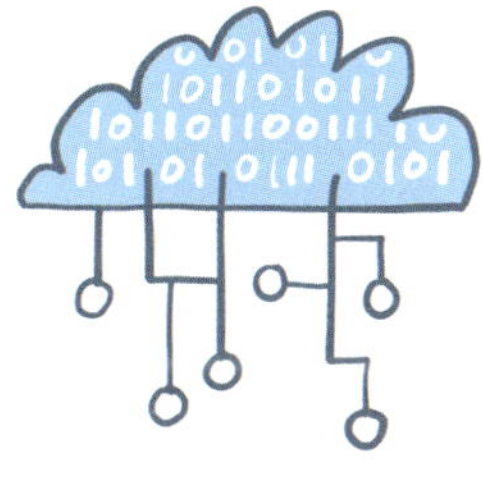

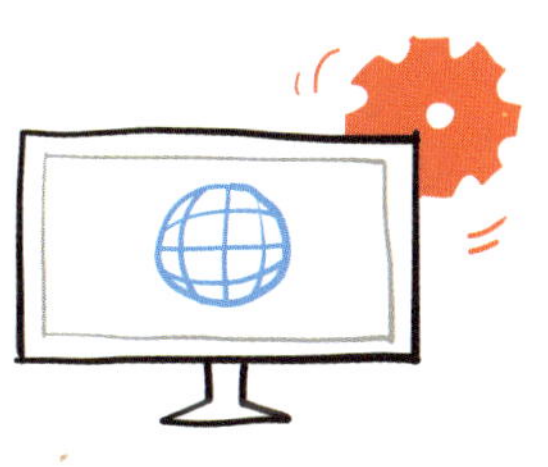

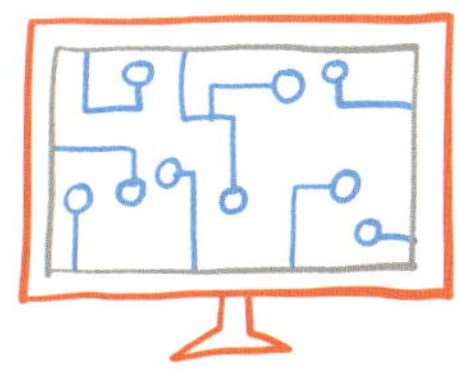

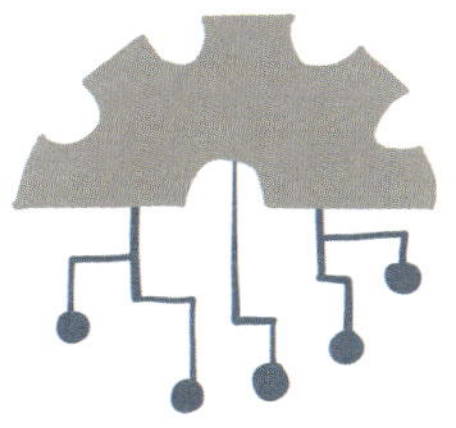

HOW TO DRAW

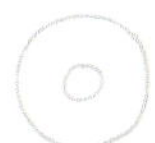

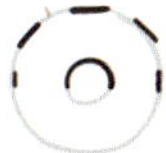

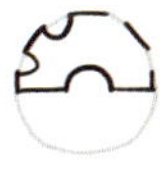

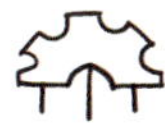

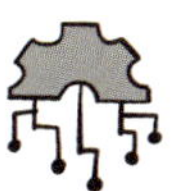

GAMIFICATION

BASIC ICONS

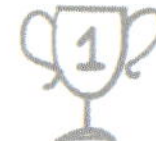

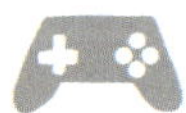
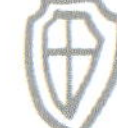
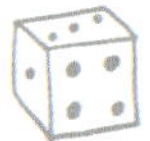
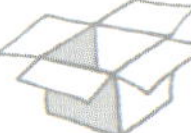
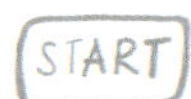

COMBINED ICONS

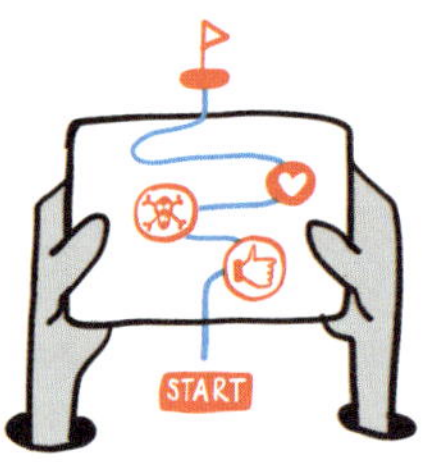

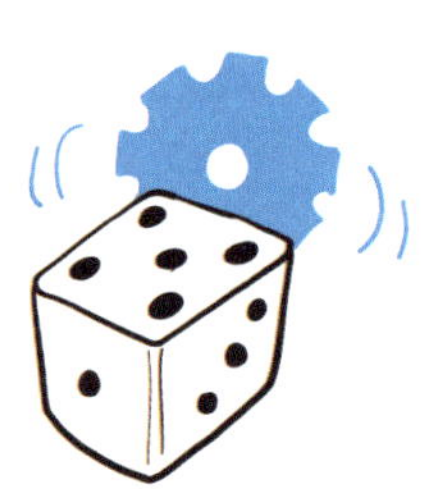

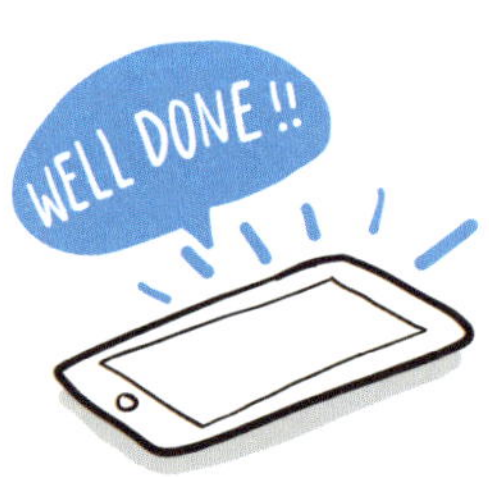

HOW TO DRAW

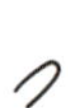
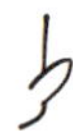
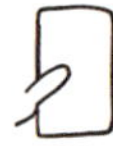
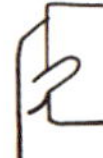
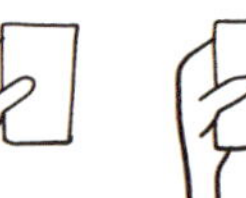
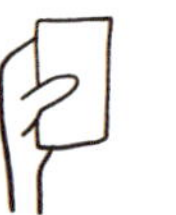
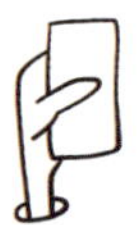
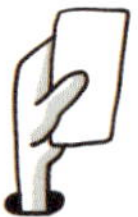

IMPACT

BASIC ICONS

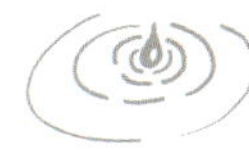

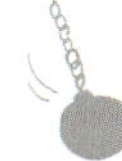
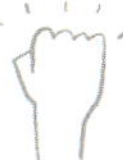
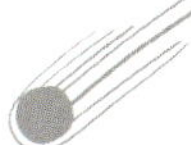

COMBINED ICONS

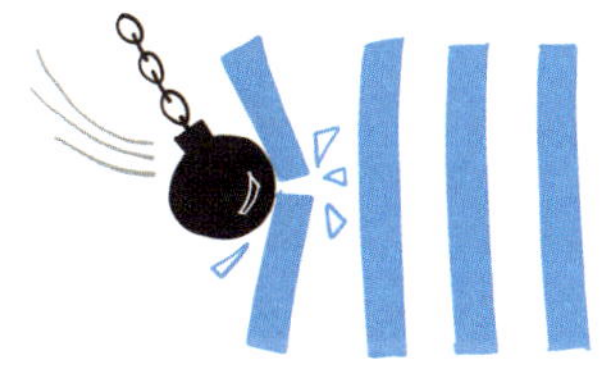
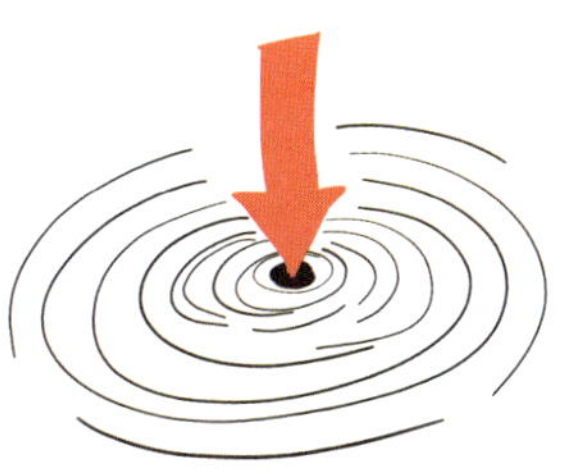
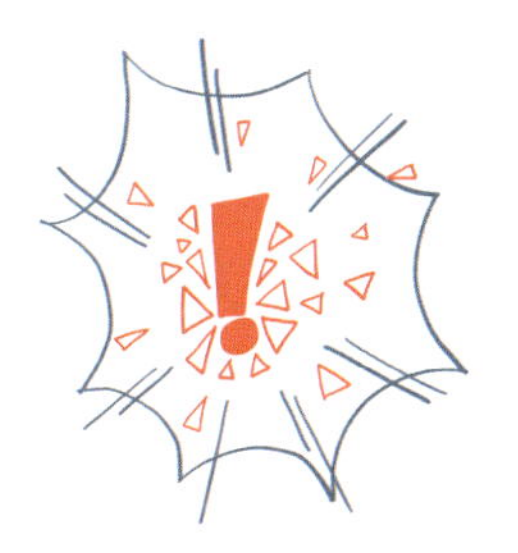
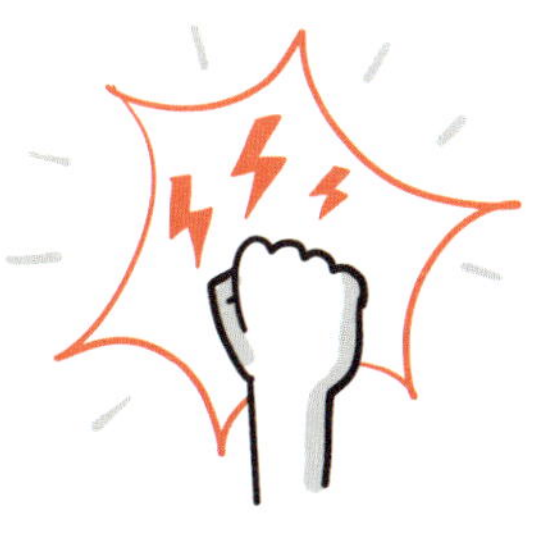

HOW TO DRAW

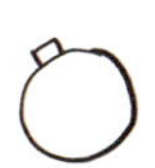
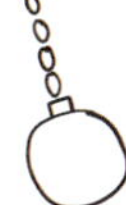
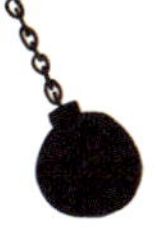
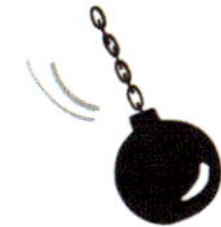

IMPLEMENTATION

BASIC ICONS

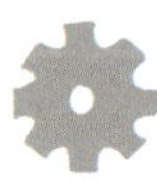
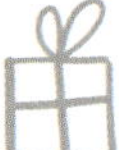

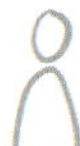

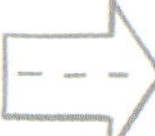
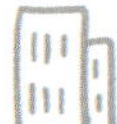

COMBINED ICONS

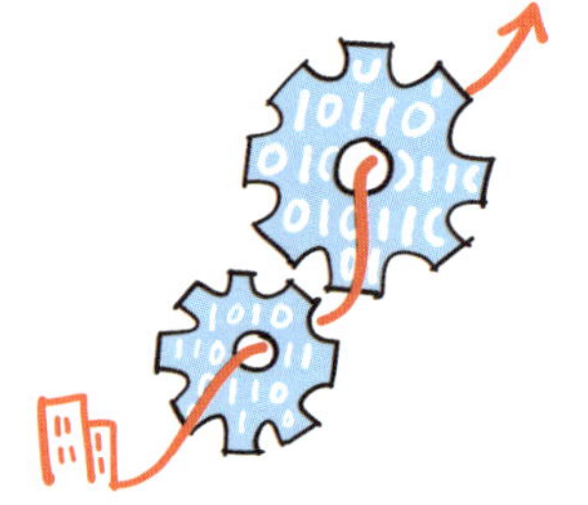
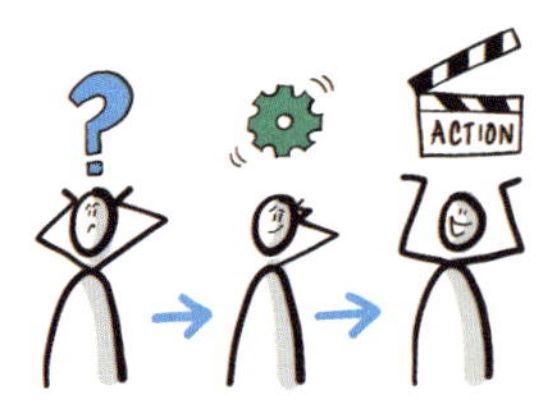

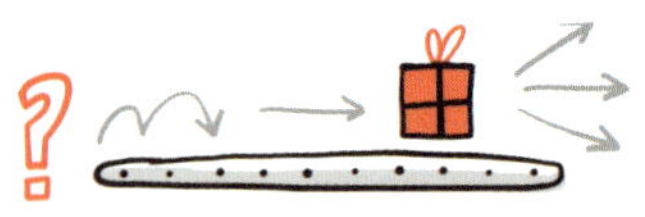
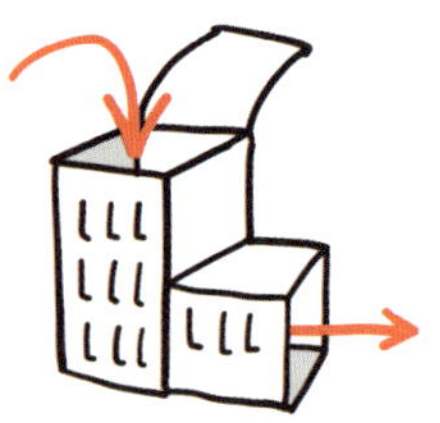

HOW TO DRAW

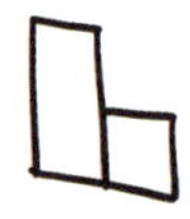
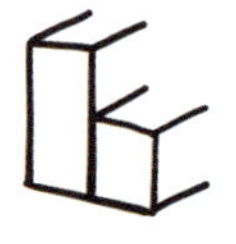
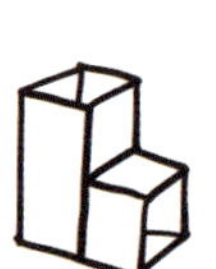
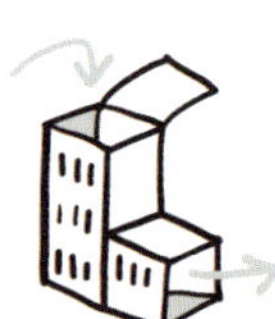

IMPROVEMENT

BASIC ICONS

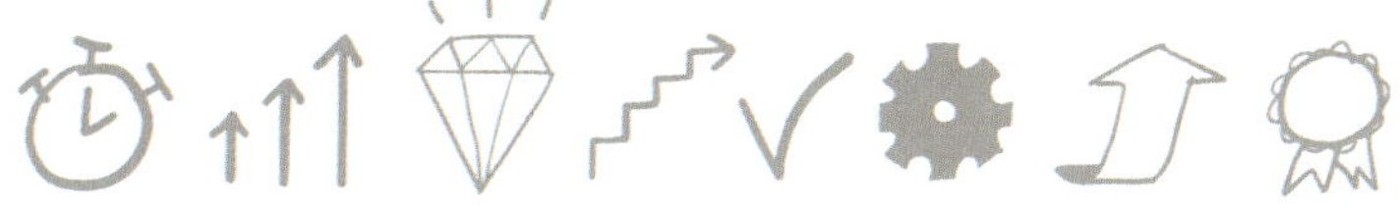

COMBINED ICONS

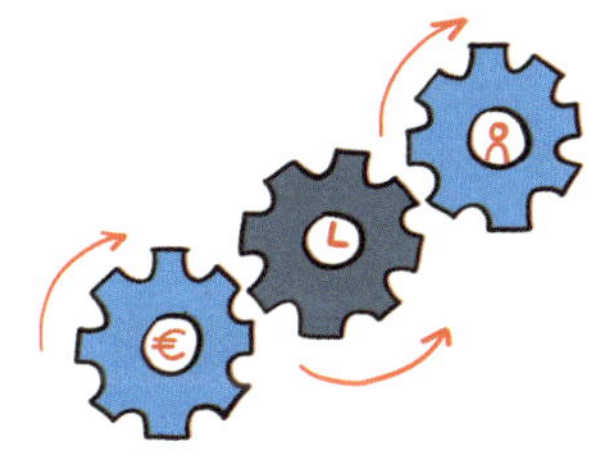

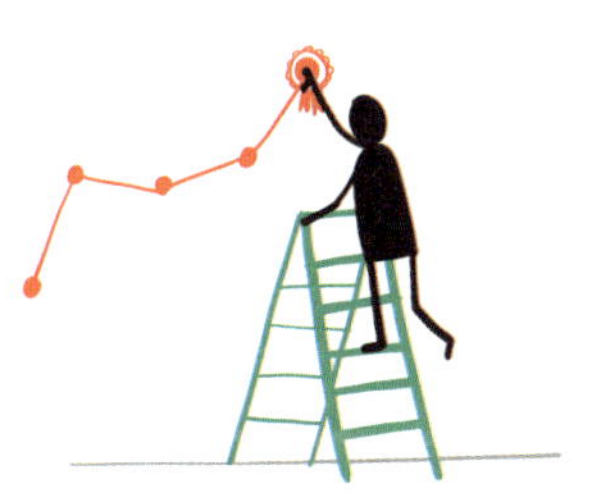

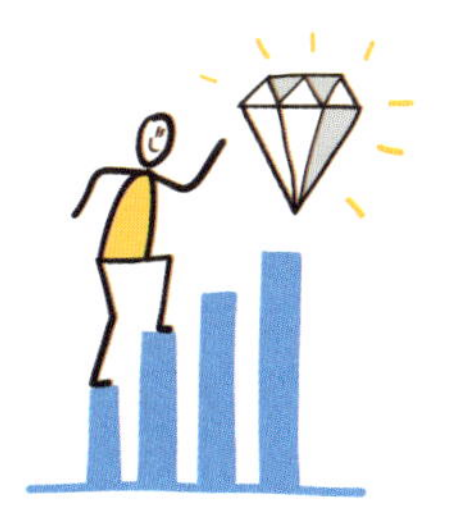

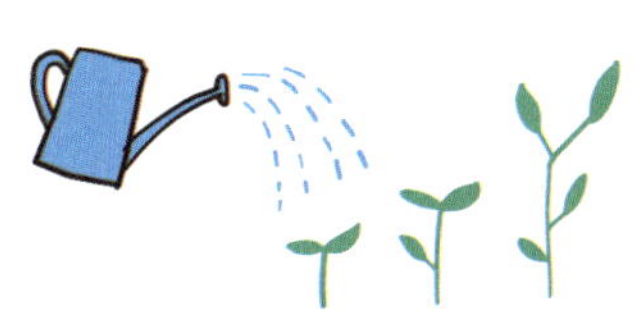

HOW TO DRAW

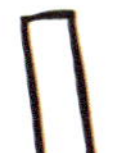

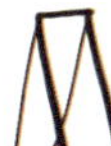

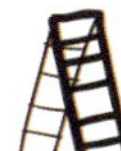

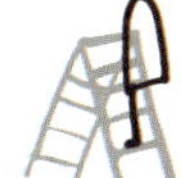

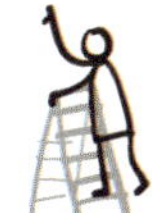

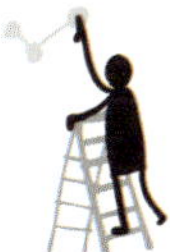

INFORMATION

BASIC ICONS

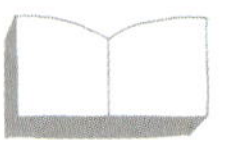 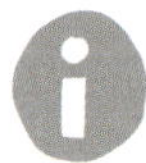 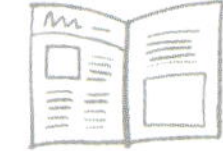 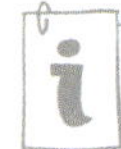 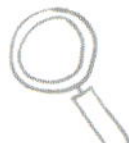 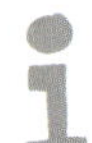 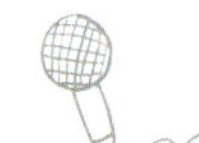

COMBINED ICONS

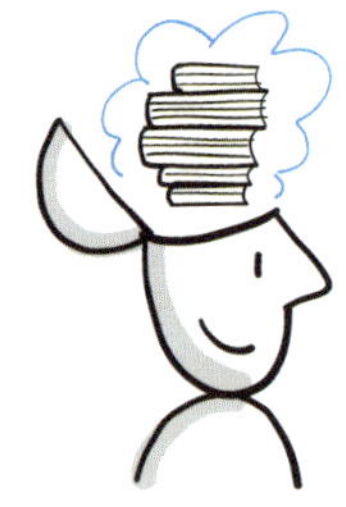

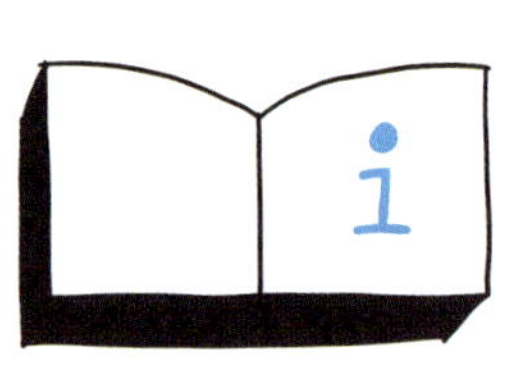

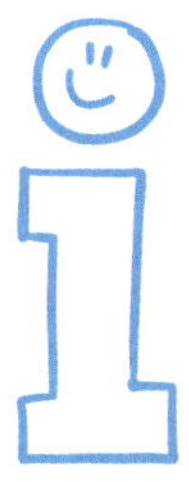

HOW TO DRAW

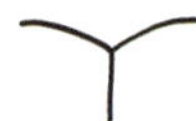 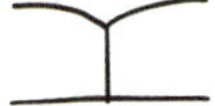 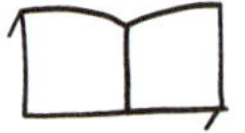 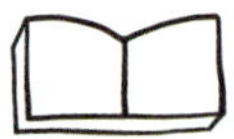 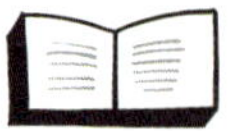

INTERNET OF THINGS

BASIC ICONS

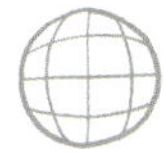 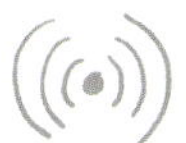 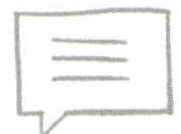 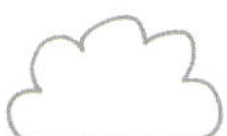 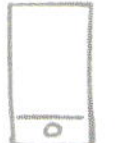 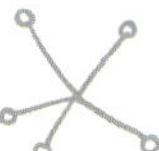

COMBINED ICONS

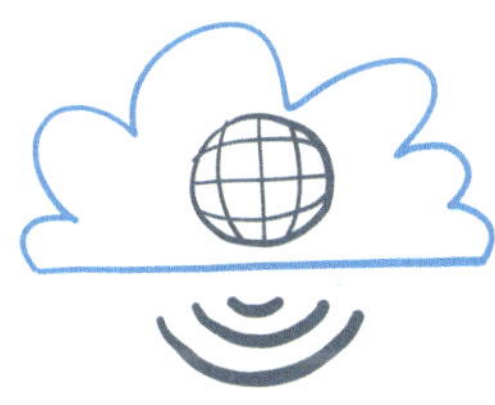

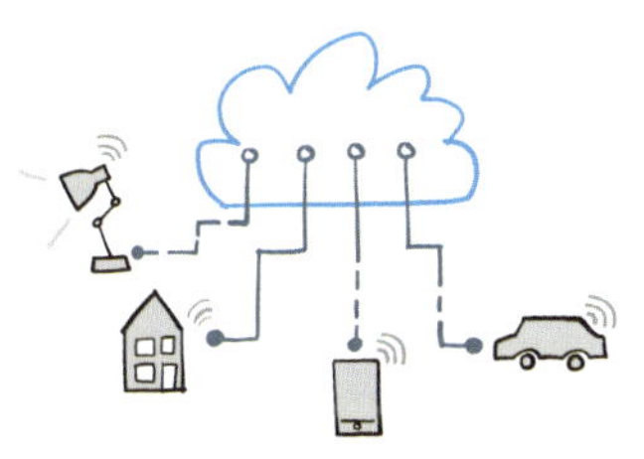

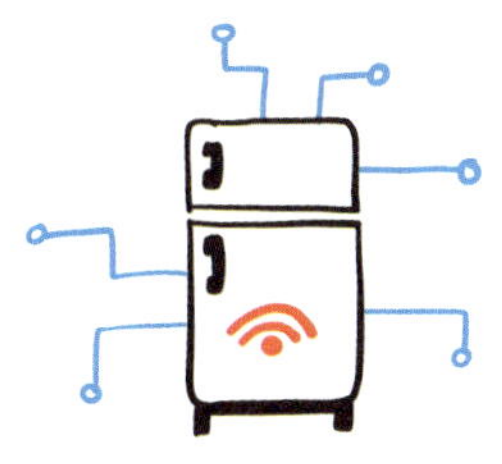

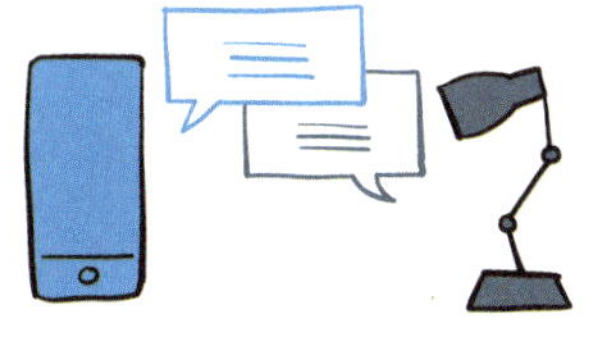

HOW TO DRAW

 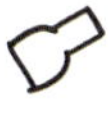 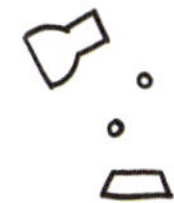 

MATHEMATICS

BASIC ICONS

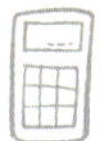
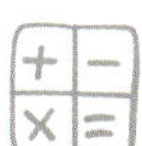

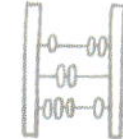
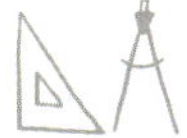
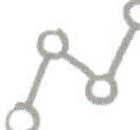
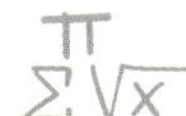

COMBINED ICONS

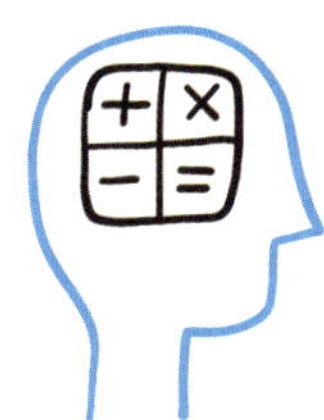

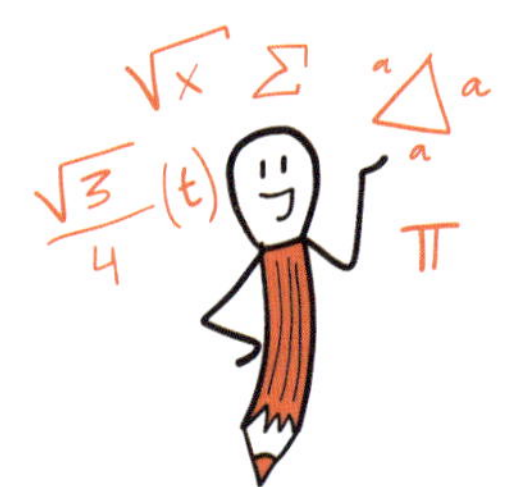

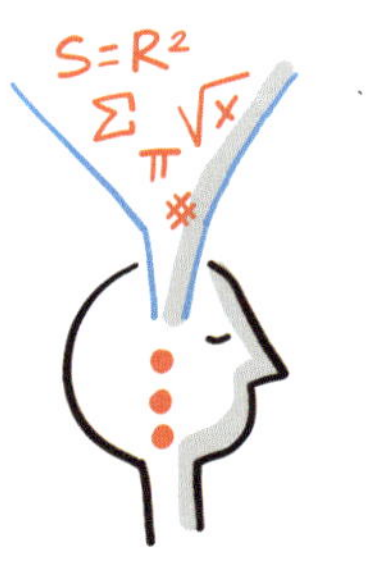

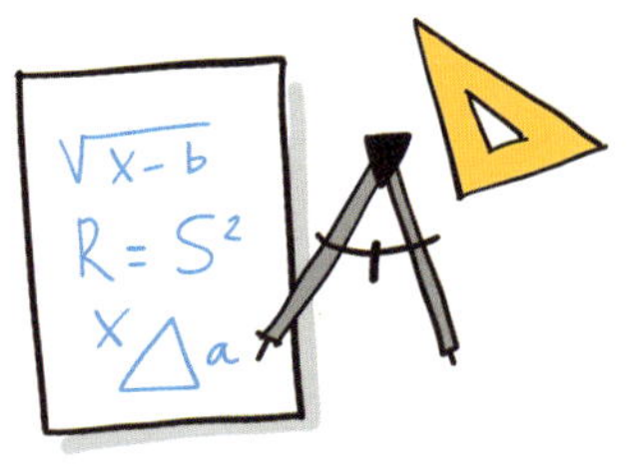

HOW TO DRAW

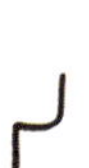
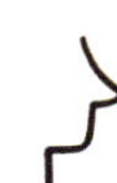
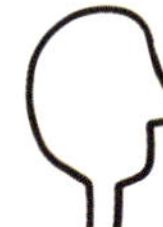
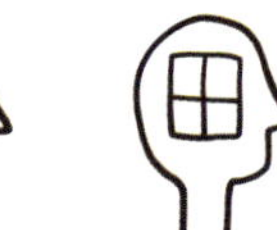
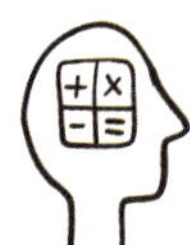

MEDIA

BASIC ICONS

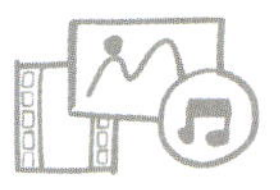 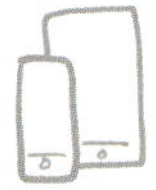 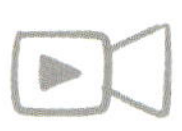 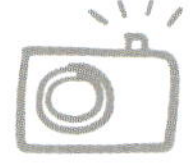 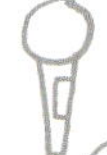 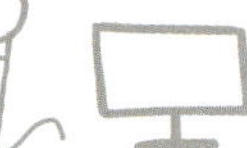

COMBINED ICONS

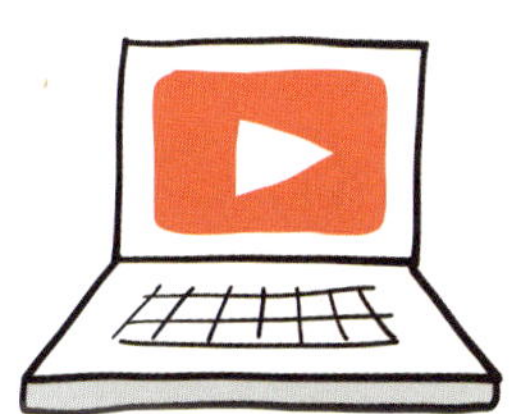

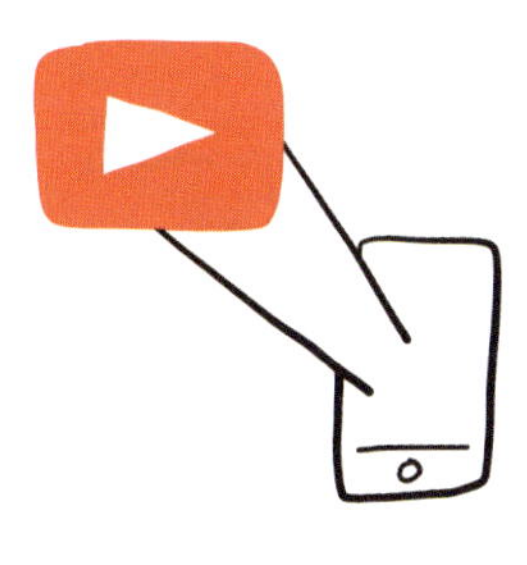

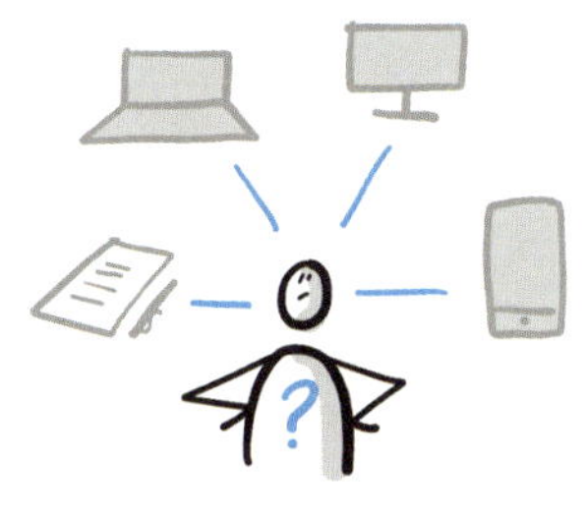

HOW TO DRAW

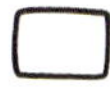 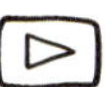 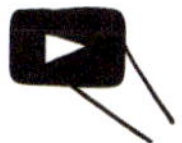 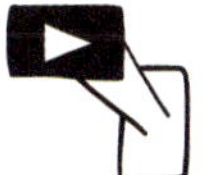 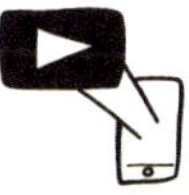

PRIVACY

BASIC ICONS

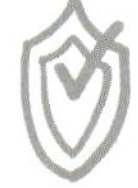
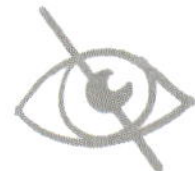

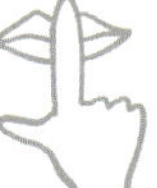

COMBINED ICONS

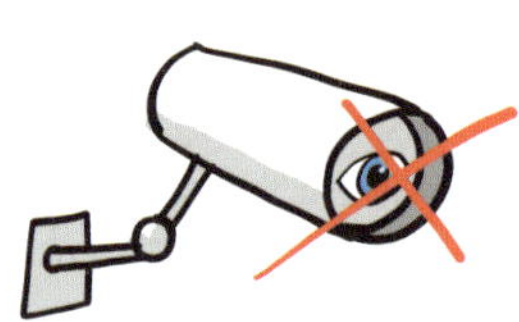
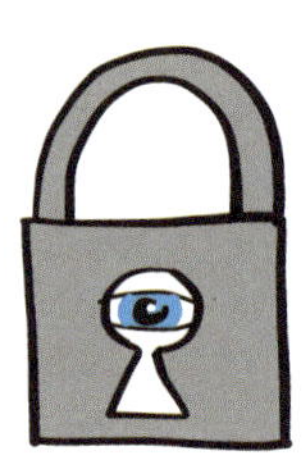

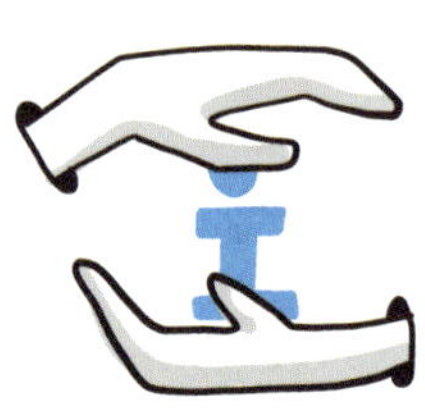

HOW TO DRAW

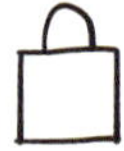
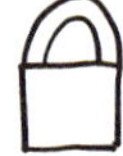

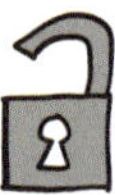

SECURITY

BASIC ICONS

 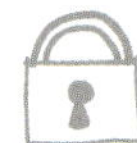 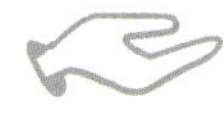  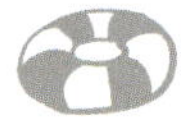 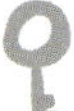

COMBINED ICONS

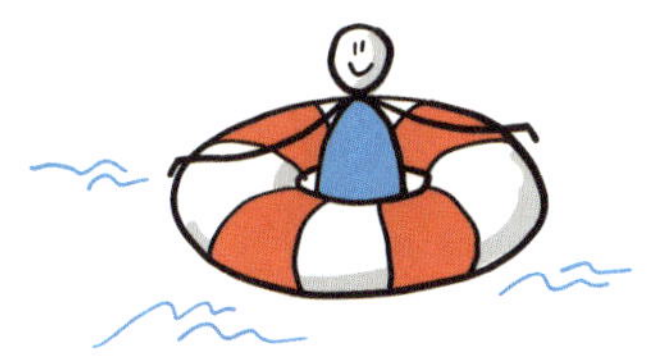

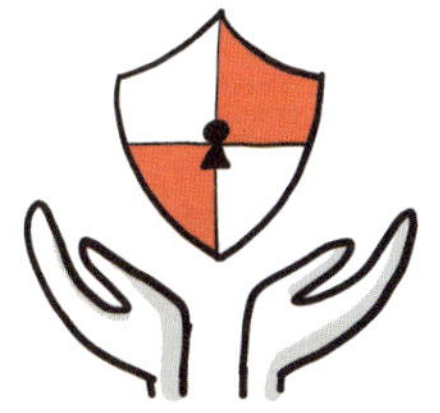

HOW TO DRAW

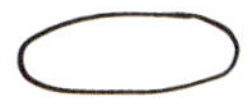 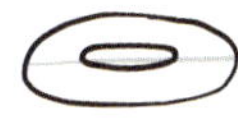 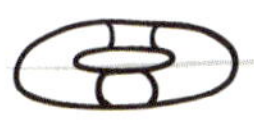 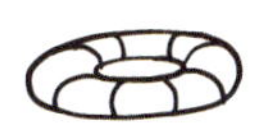 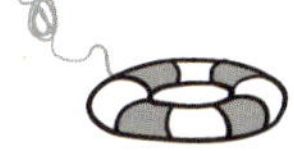

SYSTEM ARCHITECTURE

BASIC ICONS

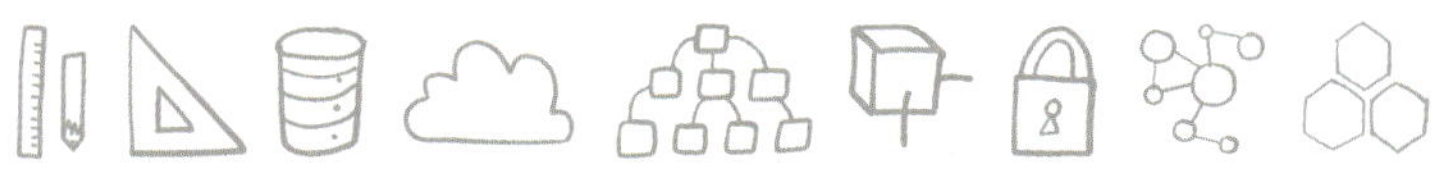

COMBINED ICONS

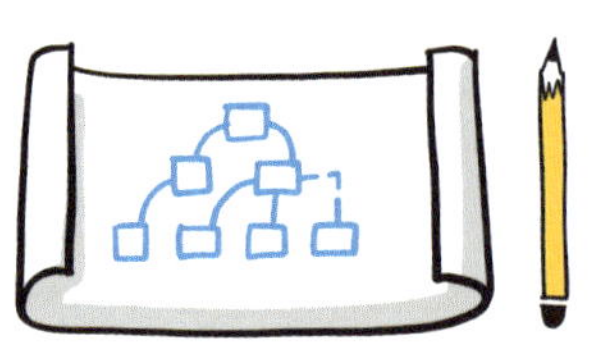

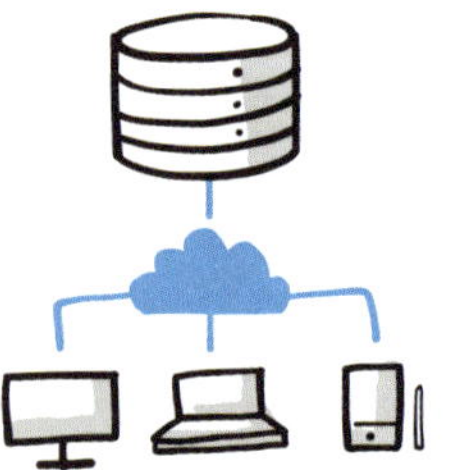

HOW TO DRAW

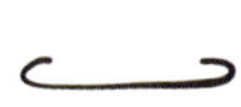

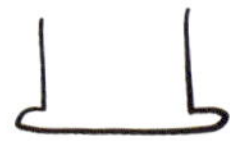

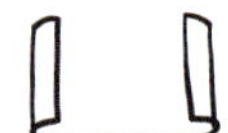

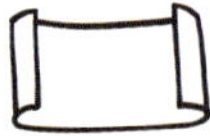

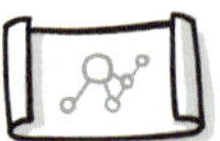

TECHNOLOGY

BASIC ICONS

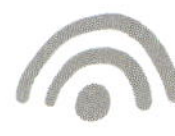
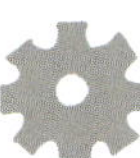
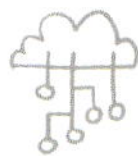
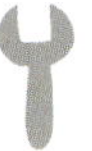
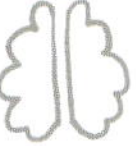
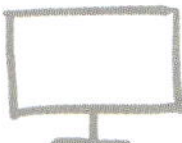

COMBINED ICONS

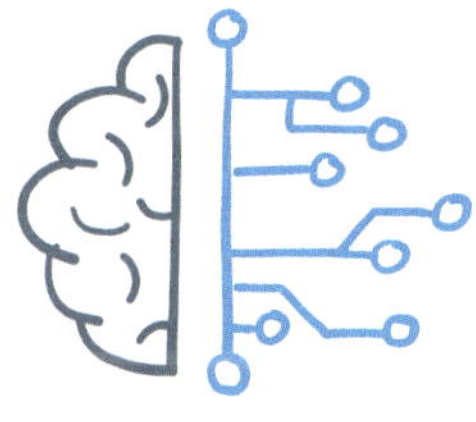

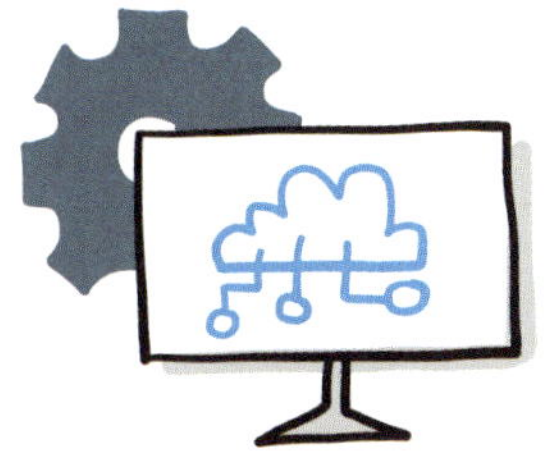

HOW TO DRAW

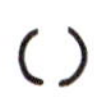
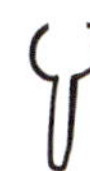
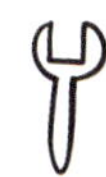
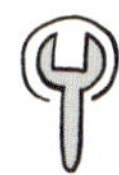
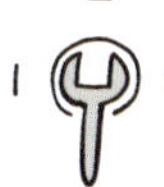

USABILITY

BASIC ICONS

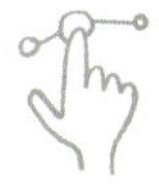
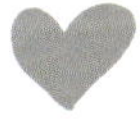

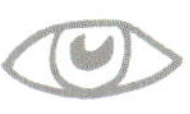
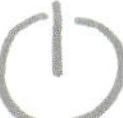
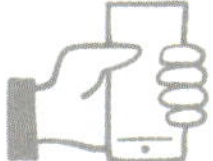
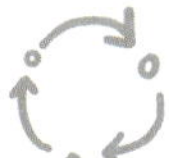

COMBINED ICONS

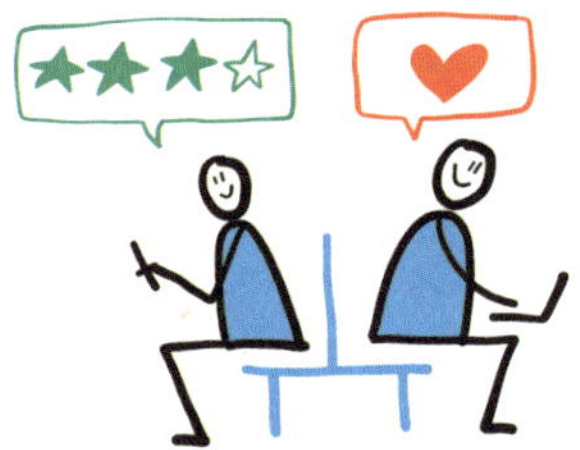
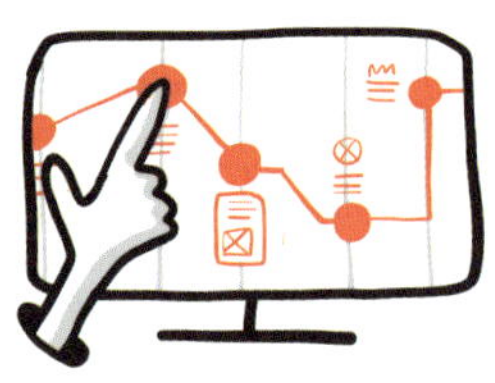

HOW TO DRAW

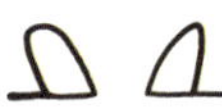
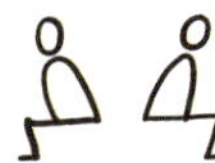
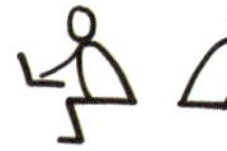
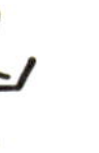
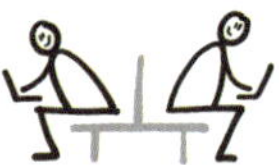

VIRTUAL ASSISTANT

BASIC ICONS

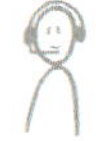
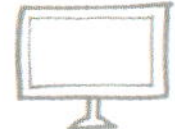
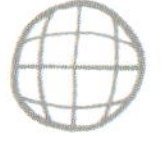
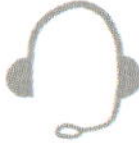
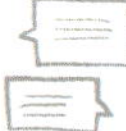

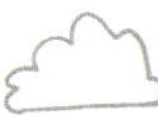

COMBINED ICONS

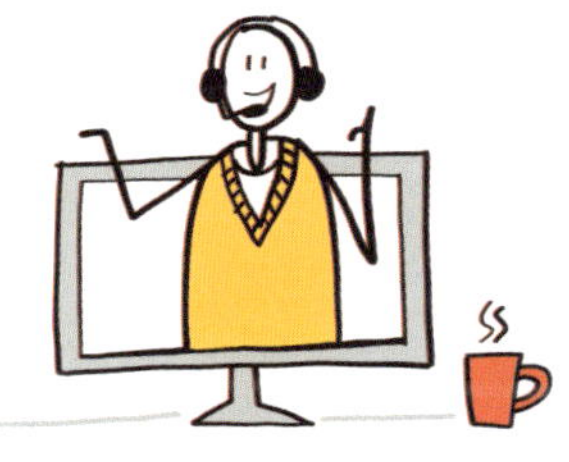
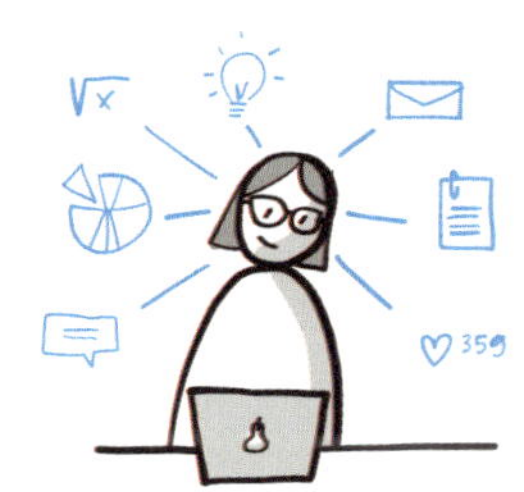
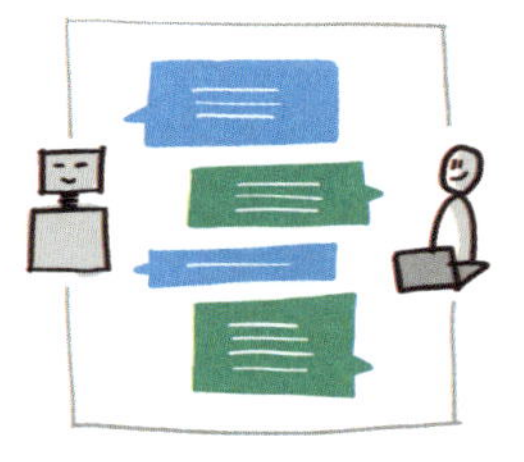
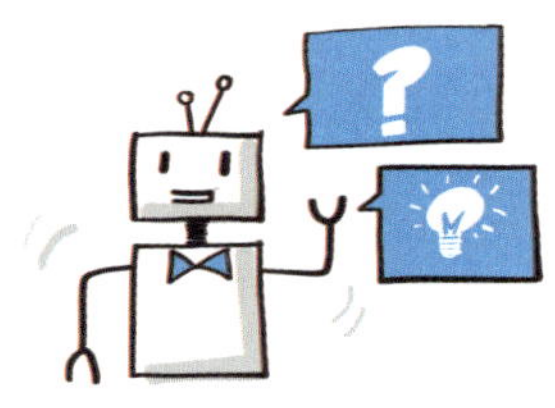

HOW TO DRAW

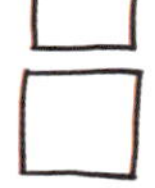
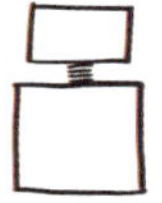
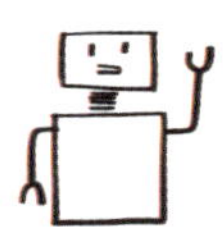

WAY OF WORKING

HOW WE COOPERATE

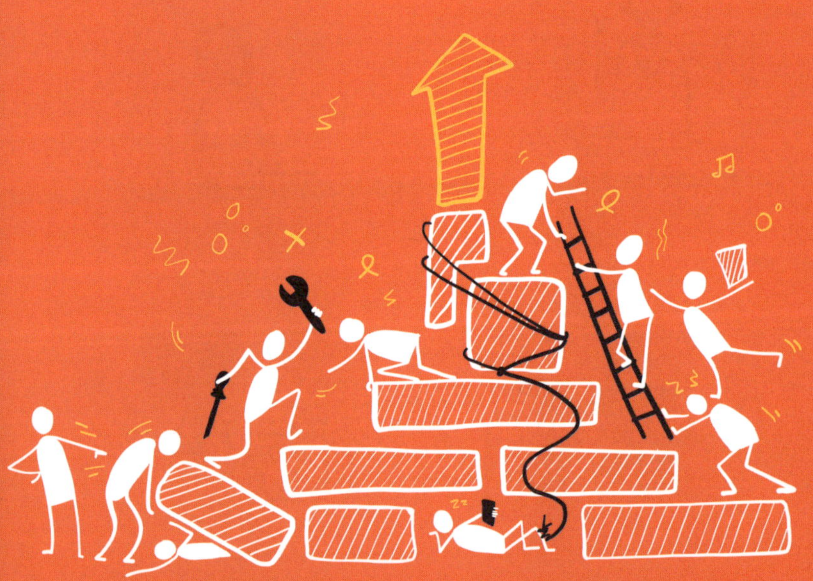

ACKNOWLEDGEMENT

BASIC ICONS

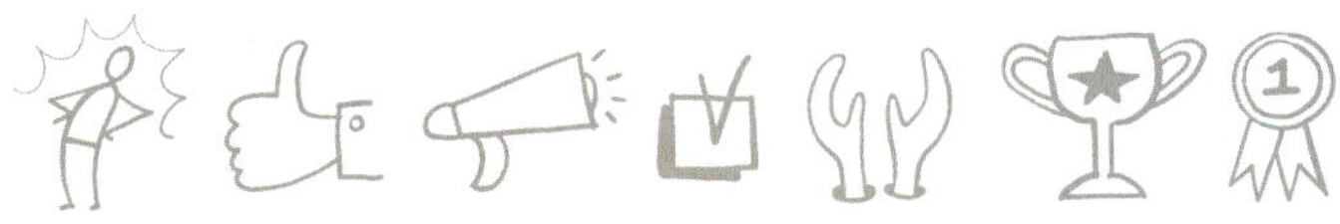

COMBINED ICONS

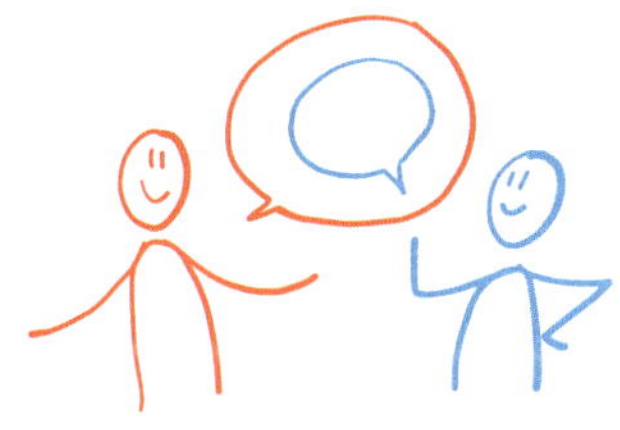

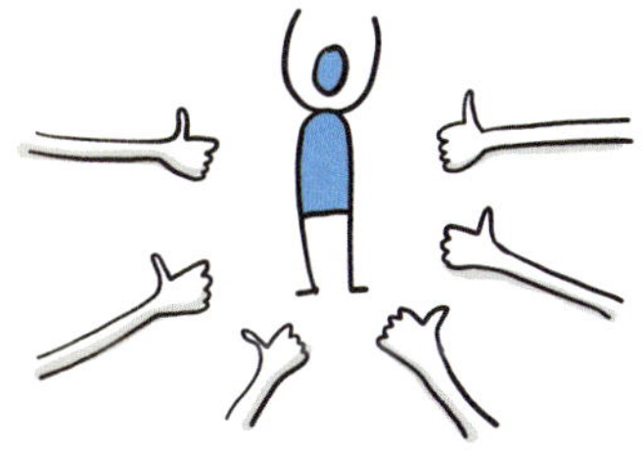

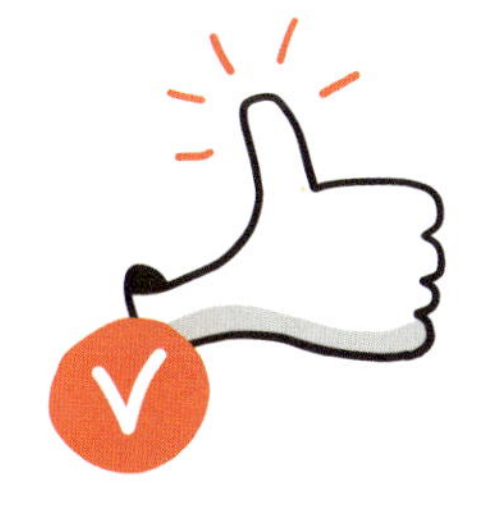

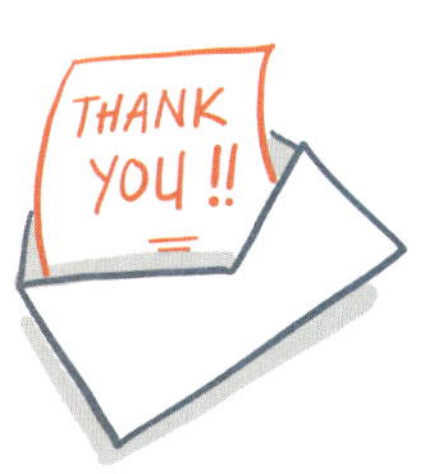

HOW TO DRAW

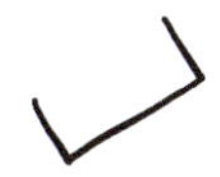

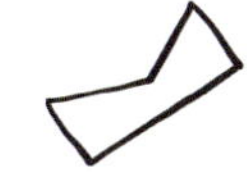

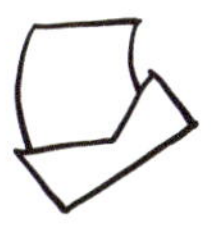

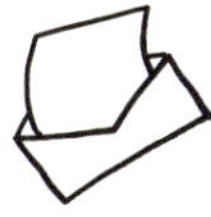

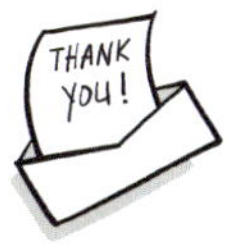

AGILITY

BASIC ICONS

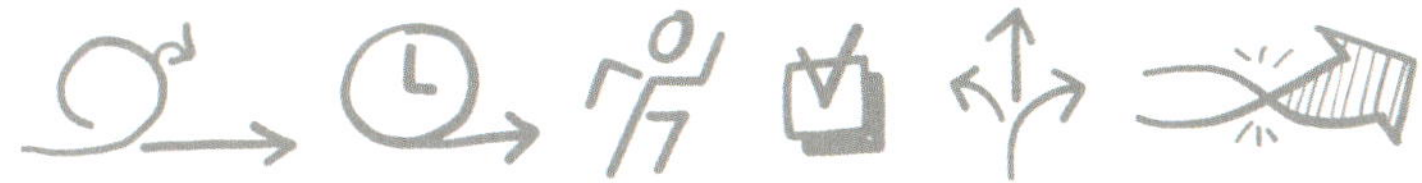

COMBINED ICONS

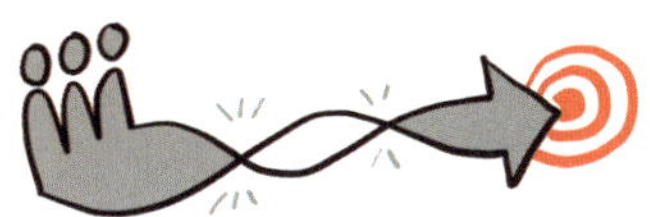

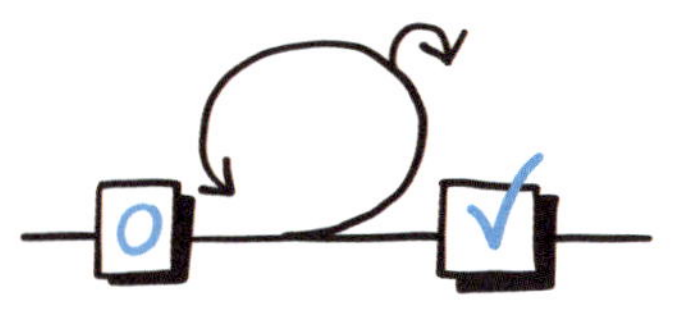

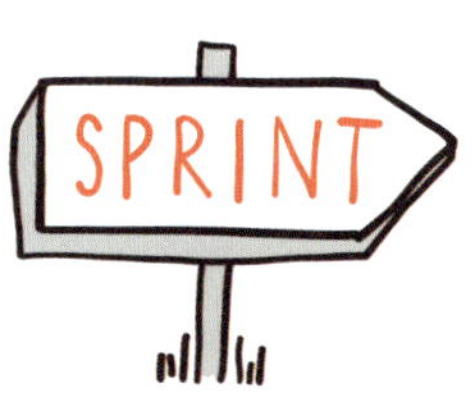

HOW TO DRAW

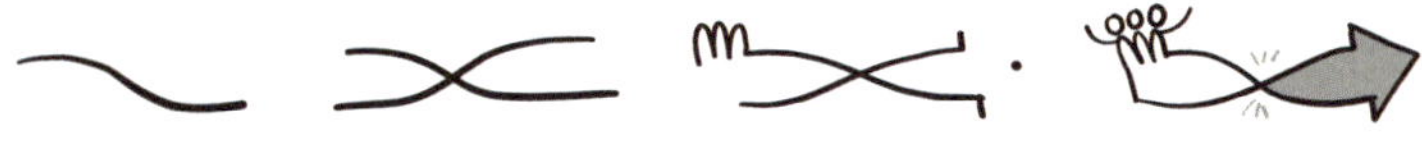

BUILDING TOGETHER

BASIC ICONS

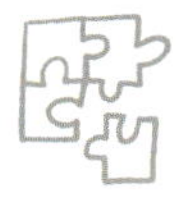
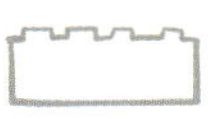

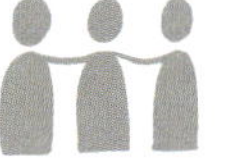
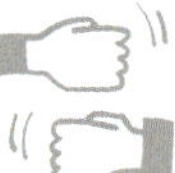

COMBINED ICONS

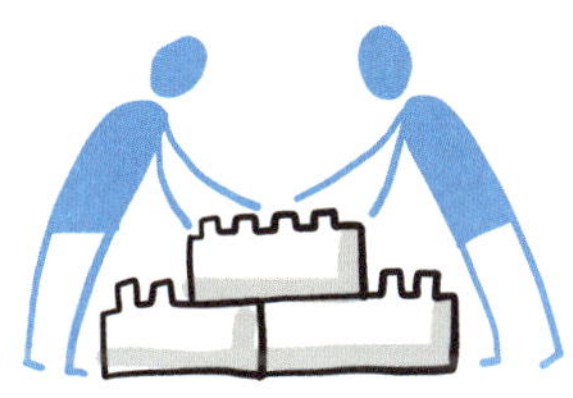
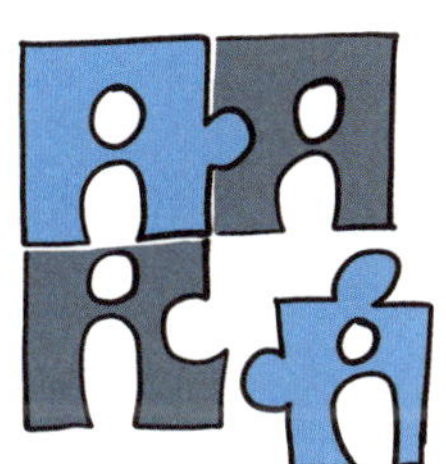
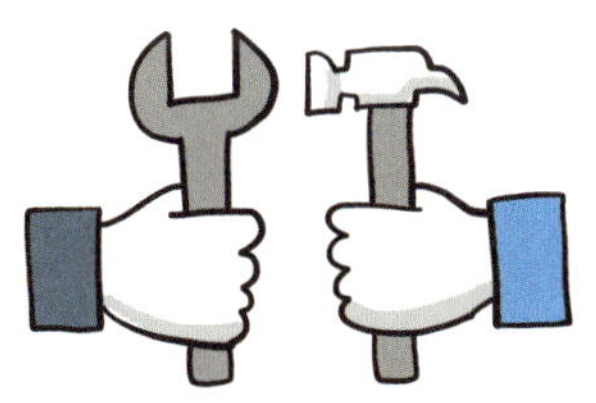
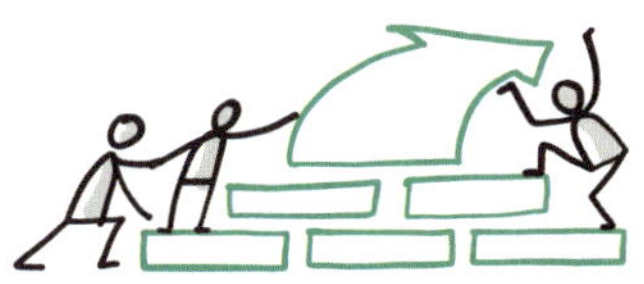

HOW TO DRAW

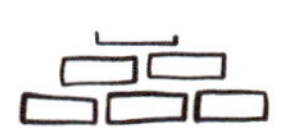
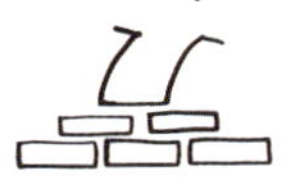
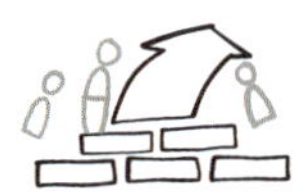
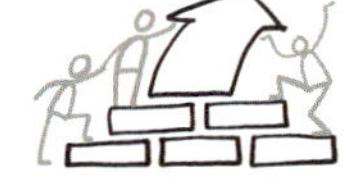

CREATIVE THINKING

BASIC ICONS

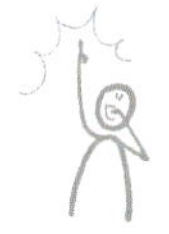
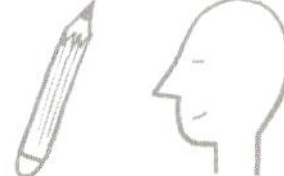

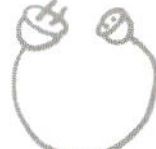
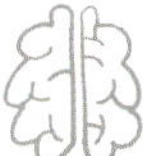

COMBINED ICONS

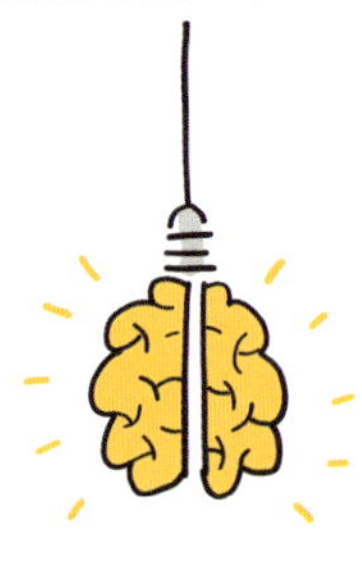
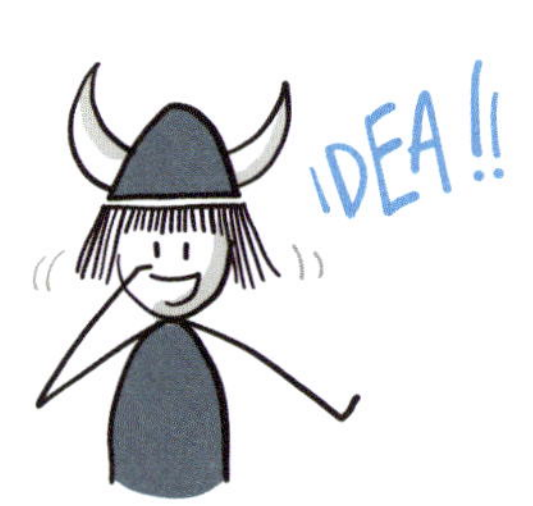

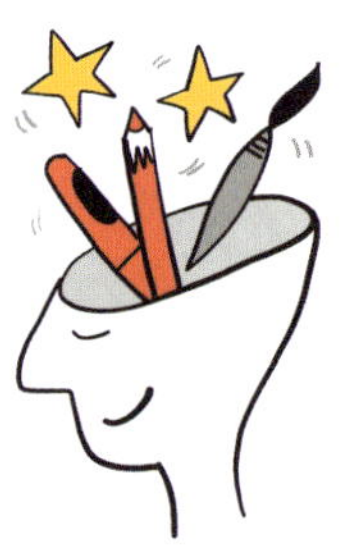
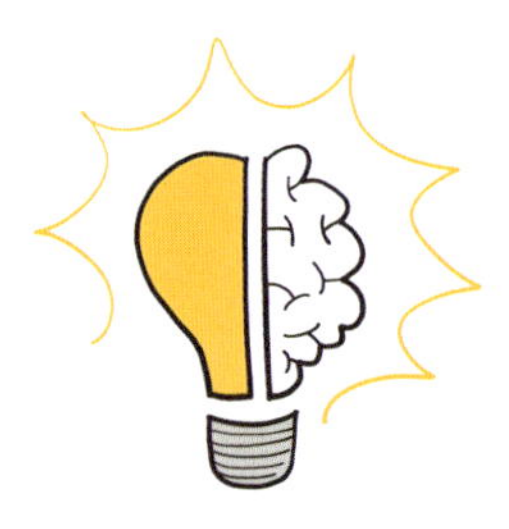

HOW TO DRAW

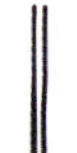
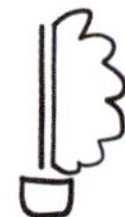

CREATIVITY

BASIC ICONS

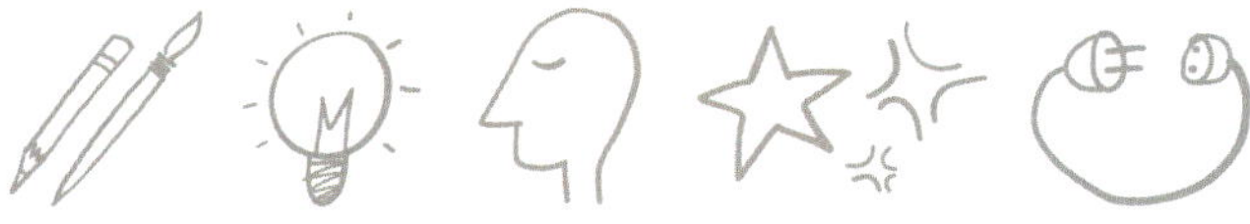

COMBINED ICONS

HOW TO DRAW

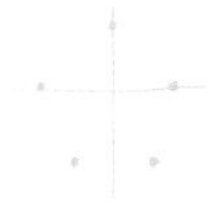

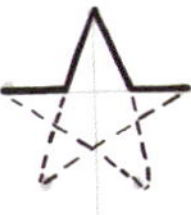

CRITICAL THINKING

BASIC ICONS

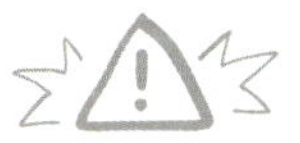
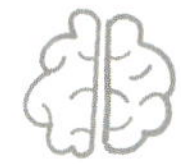
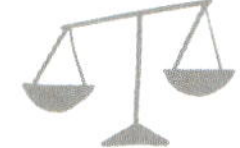

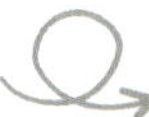

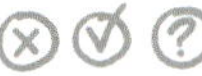

COMBINED ICONS

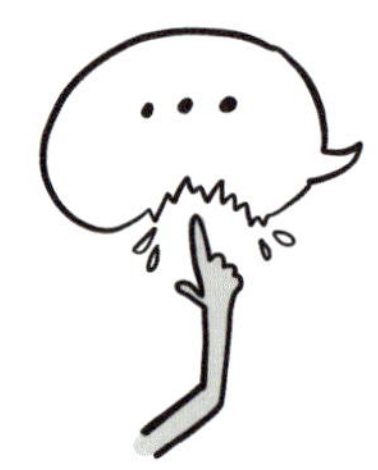
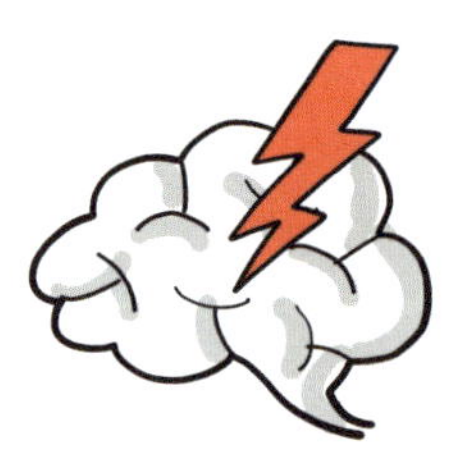
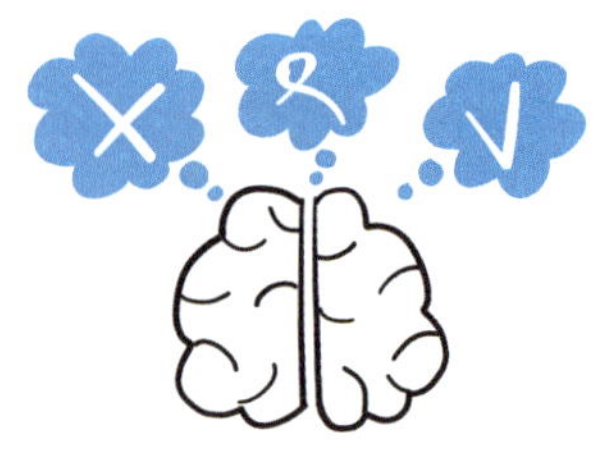

HOW TO DRAW

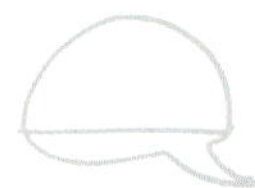
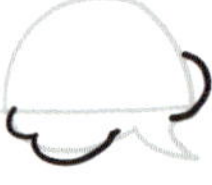

DESIGN THINKING

BASIC ICONS

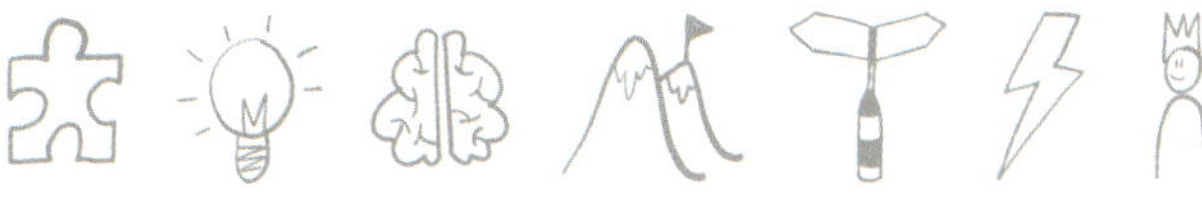

COMBINED ICONS

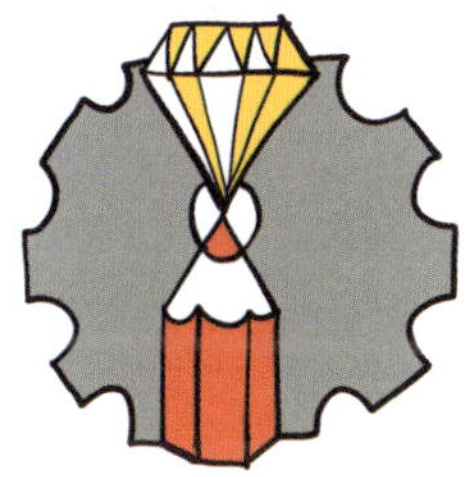

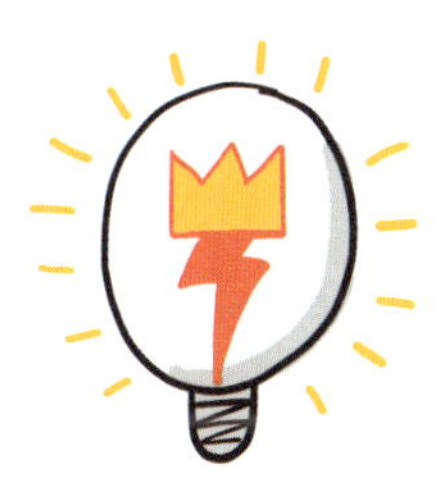

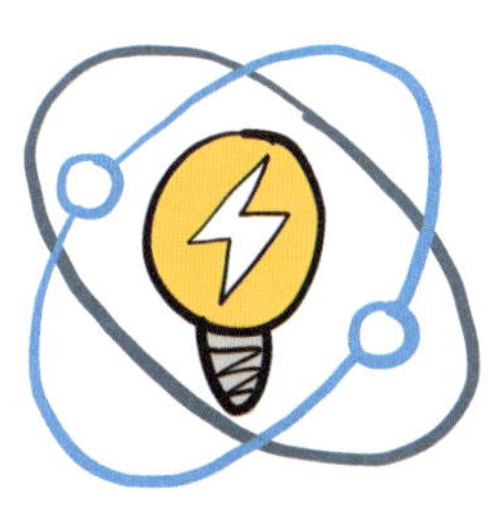

HOW TO DRAW

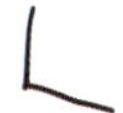

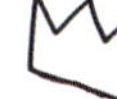

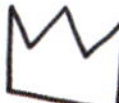

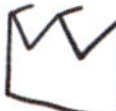

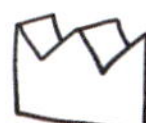

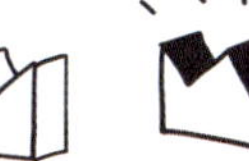

DISCUSSION

BASIC ICONS

COMBINED ICONS

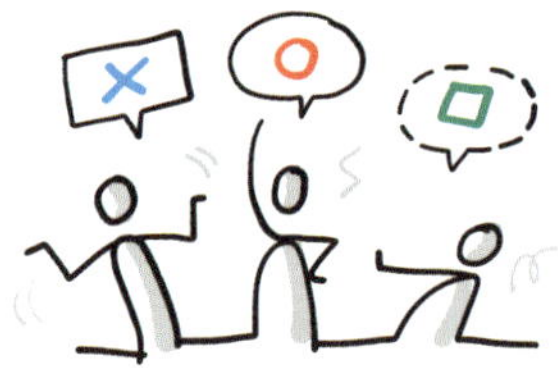

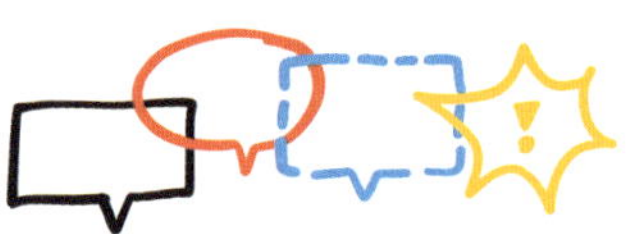

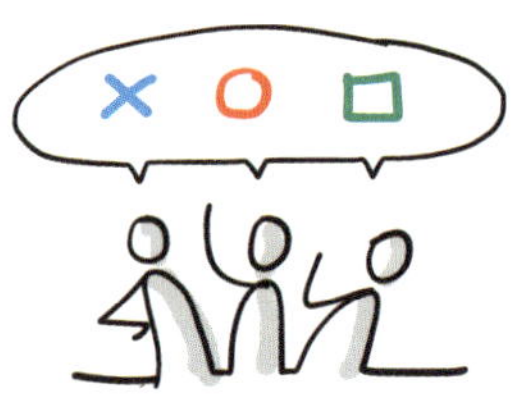

HOW TO DRAW

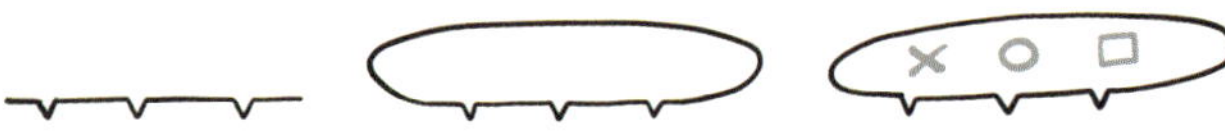

EVALUATION

BASIC ICONS

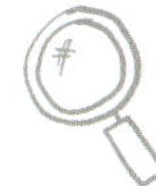
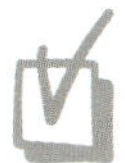

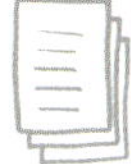
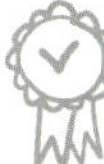
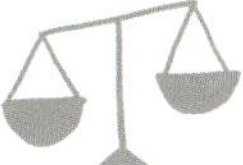

COMBINED ICONS

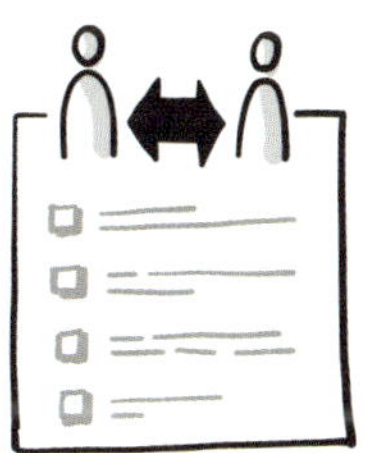
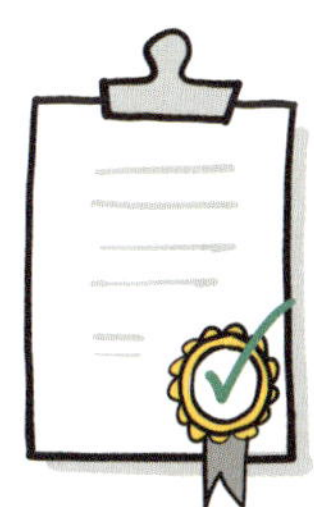
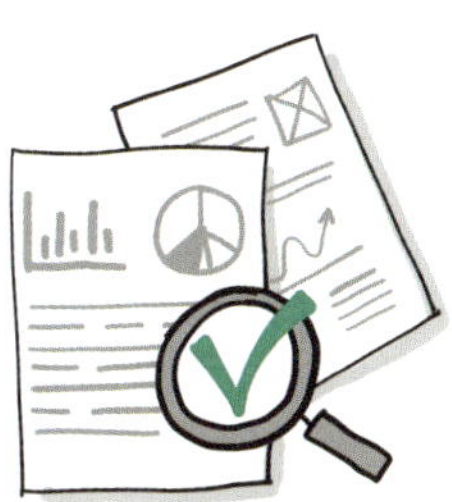

HOW TO DRAW

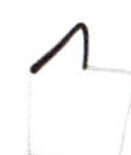
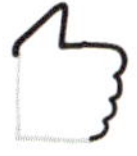
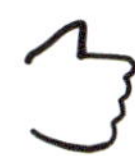
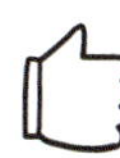
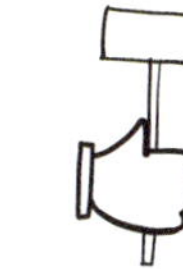
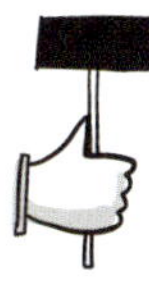

GROUP DYNAMICS

BASIC ICONS

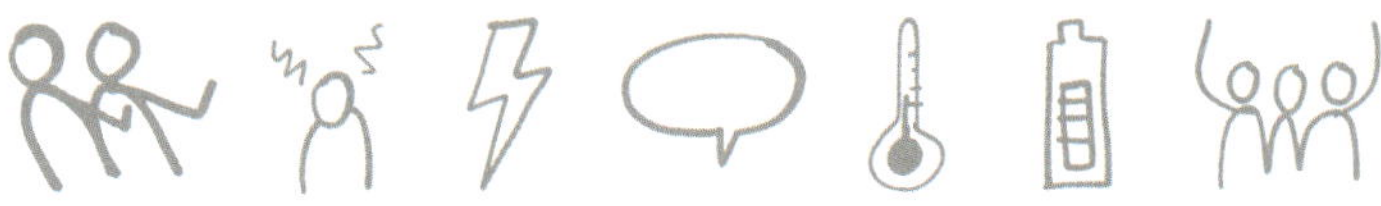

COMBINED ICONS

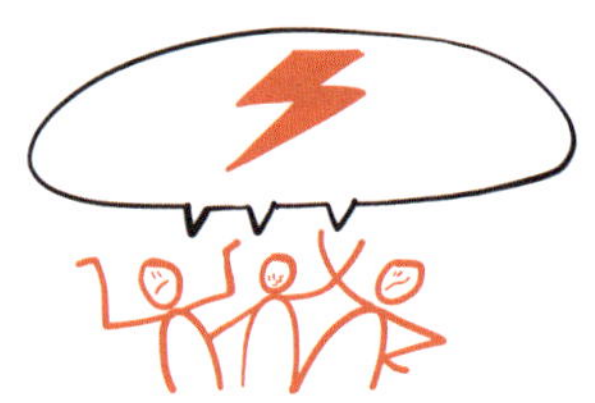

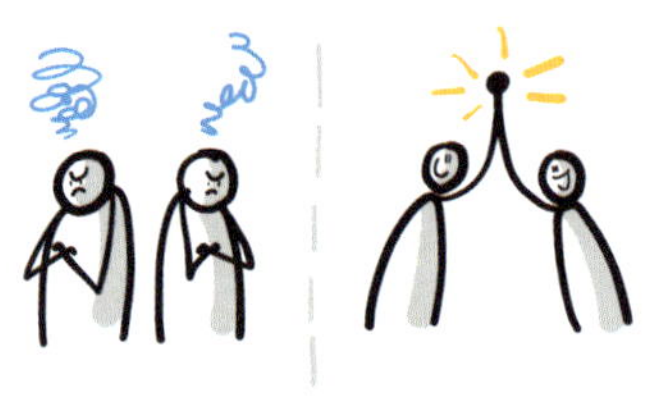

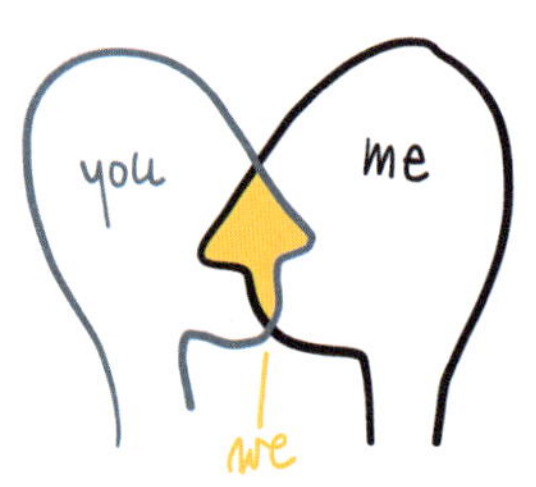

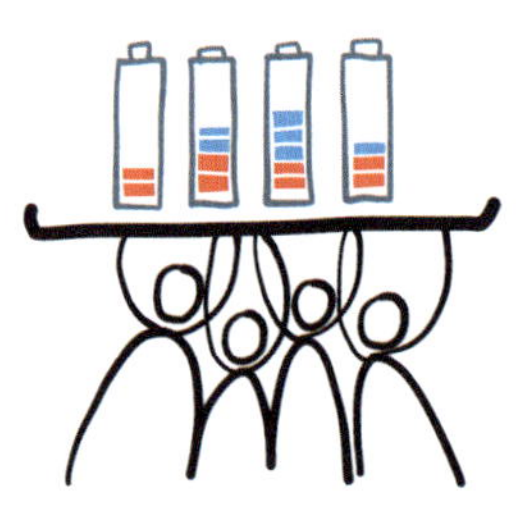

HOW TO DRAW

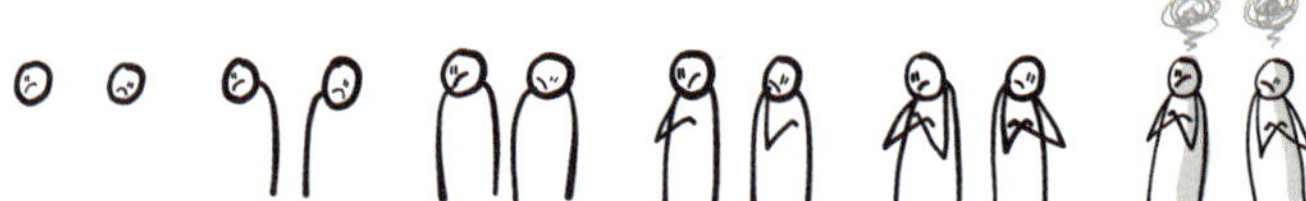

GROWTH

BASIC ICONS

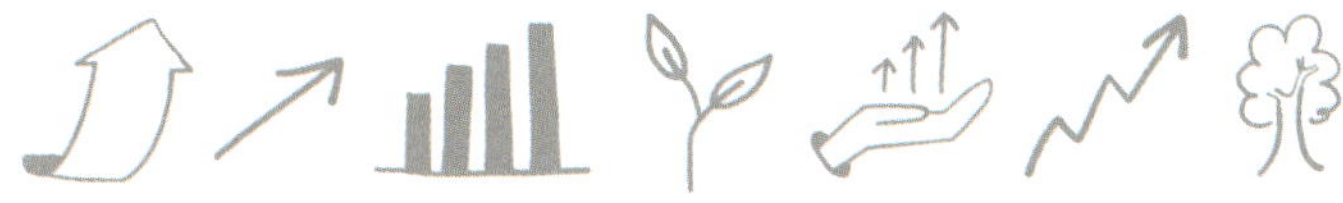

COMBINED ICONS

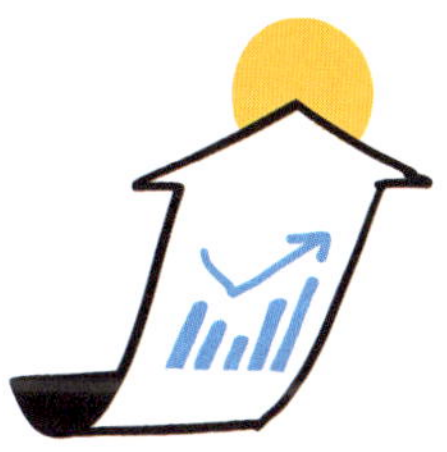

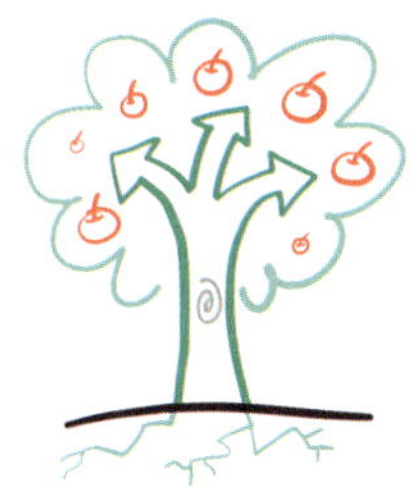

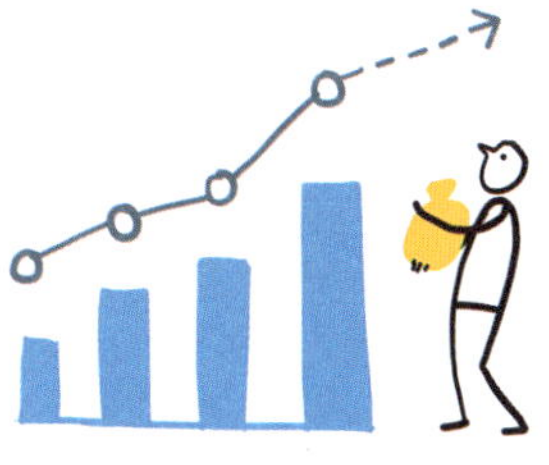

HOW TO DRAW

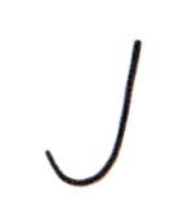

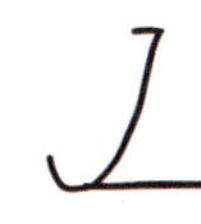

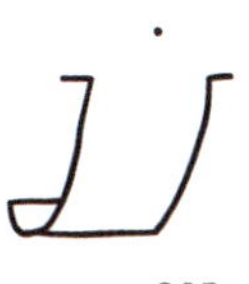

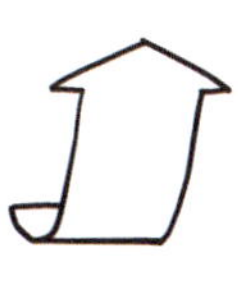

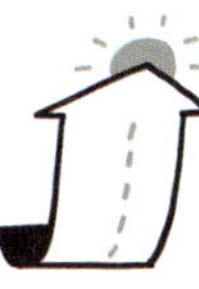

HIERARCHY

BASIC ICONS

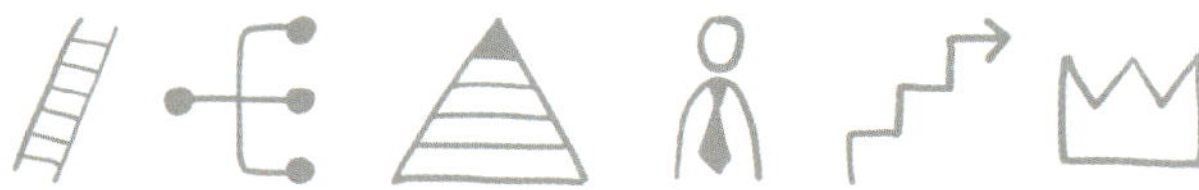

COMBINED ICONS

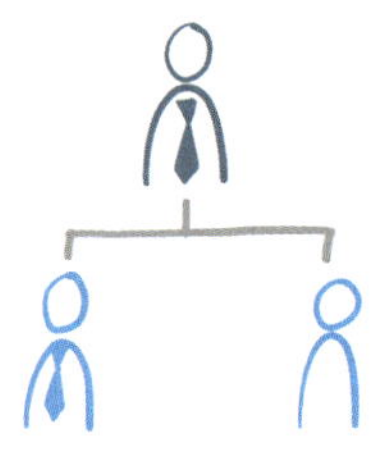

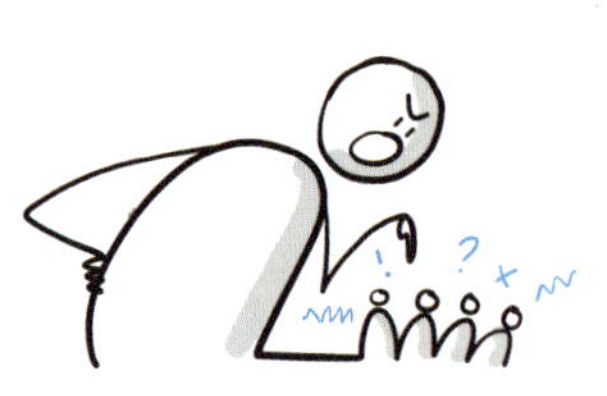

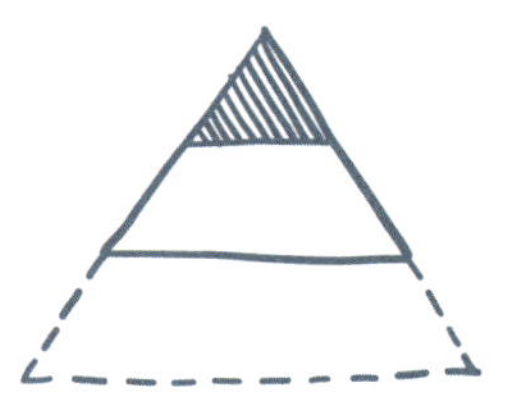

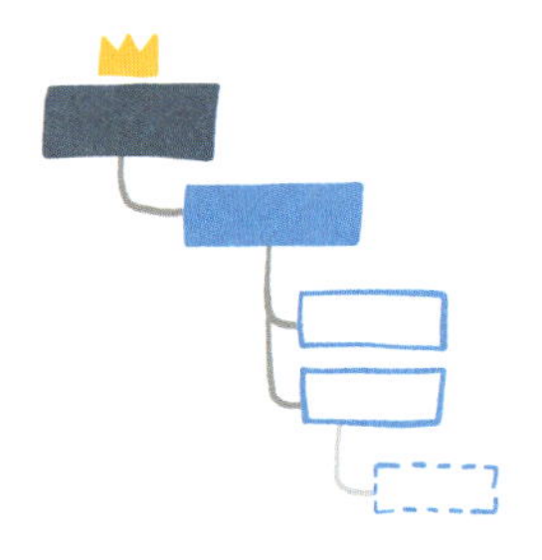

HOW TO DRAW

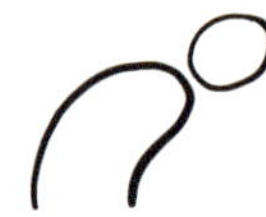

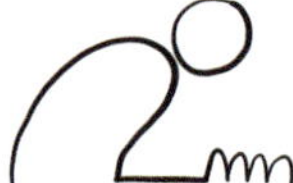

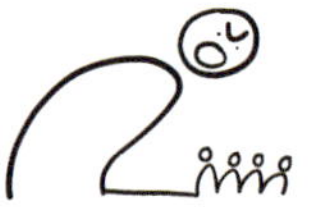

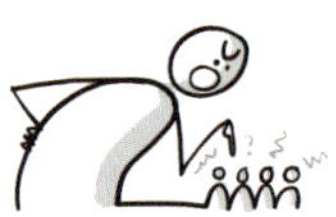

INTERACTION

BASIC ICONS

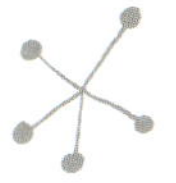
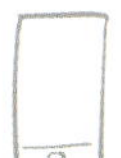
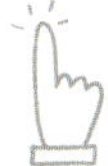
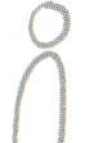
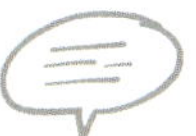
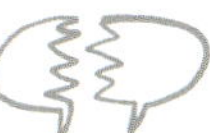
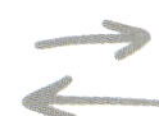

COMBINED ICONS

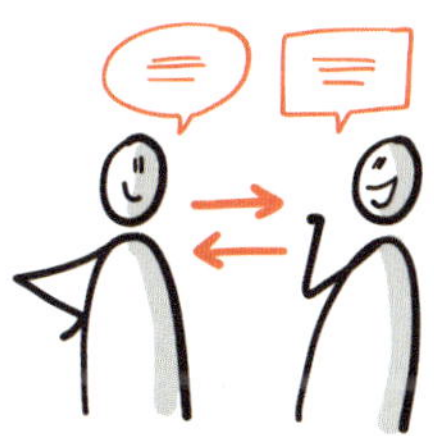
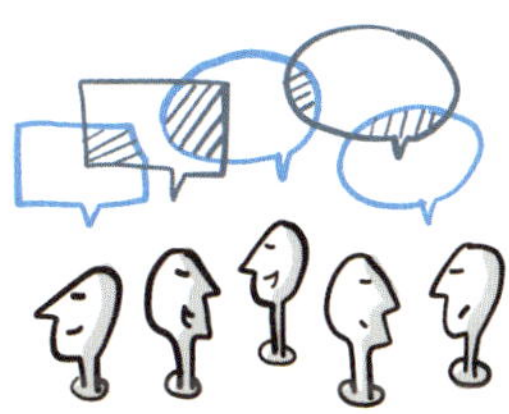
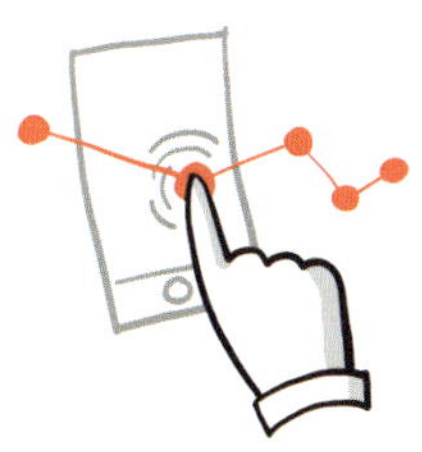
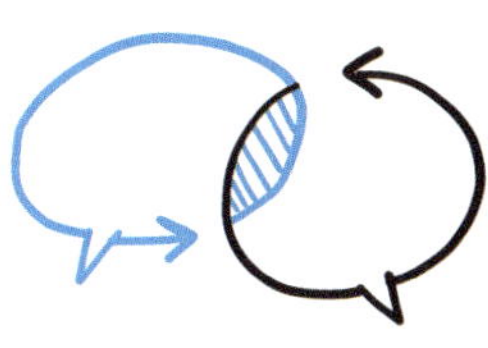

HOW TO DRAW

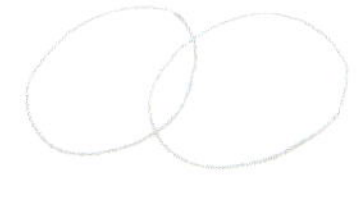
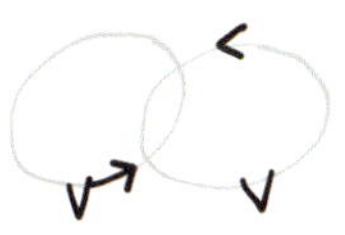
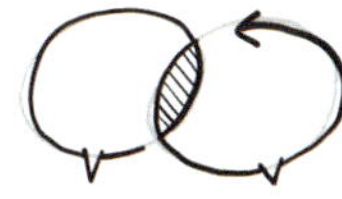

MINDFULNESS

BASIC ICONS

 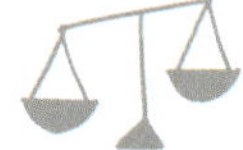 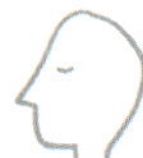 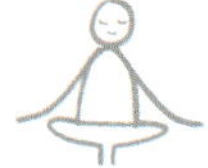 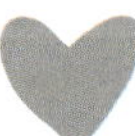 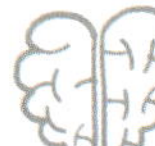 

COMBINED ICONS

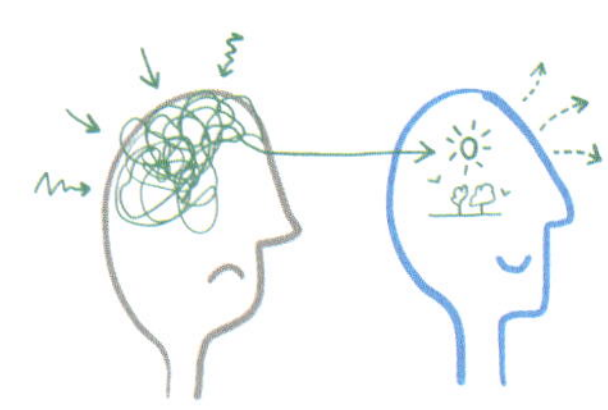

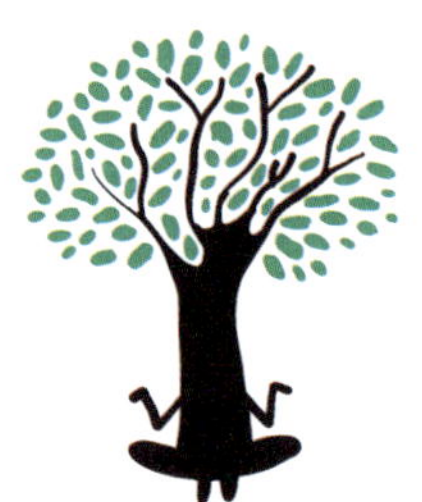

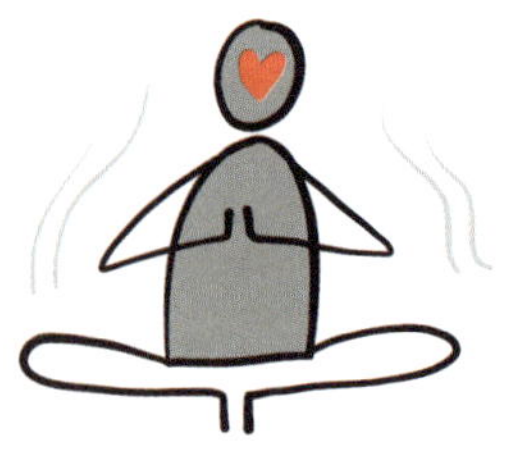

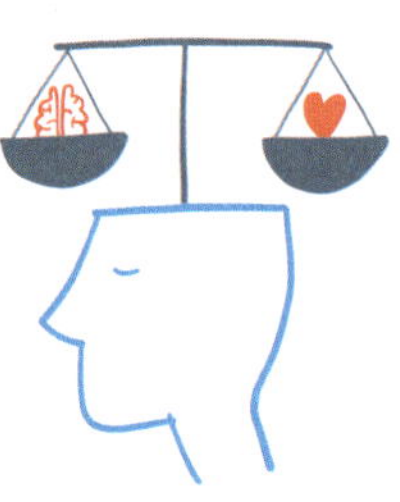

HOW TO DRAW

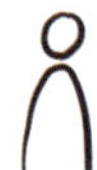 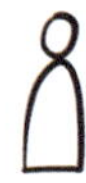 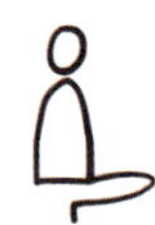 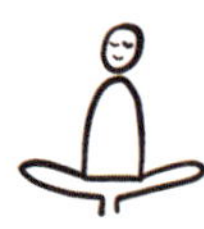 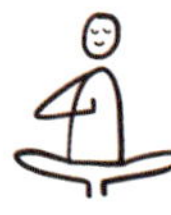 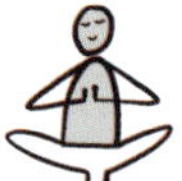

PEER TO PEER (FEEDBACK)

BASIC ICONS

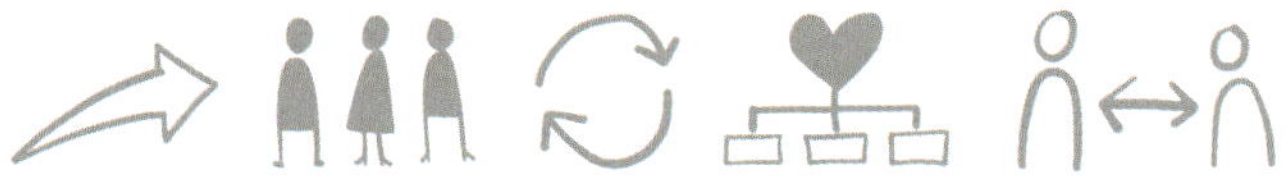

COMBINED ICONS

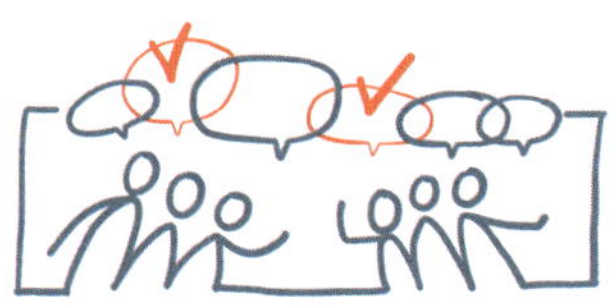

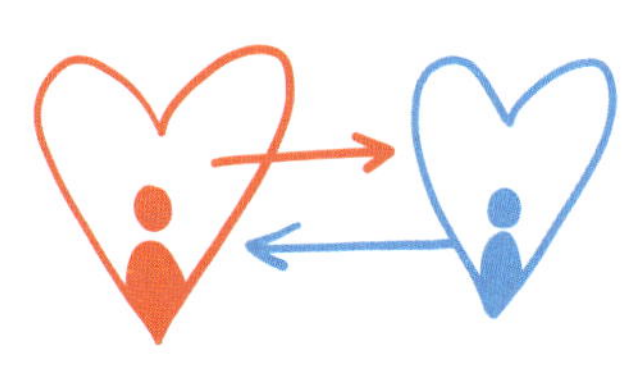

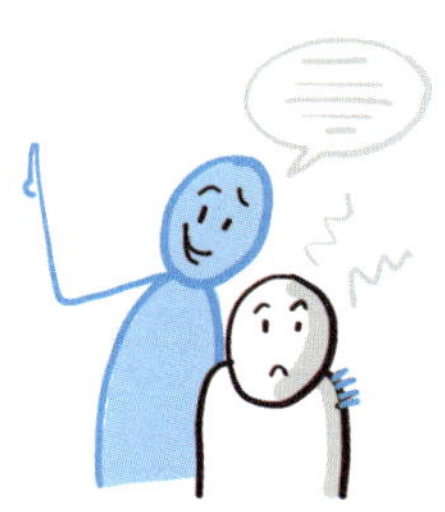

HOW TO DRAW

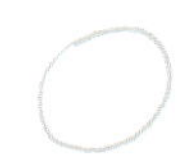

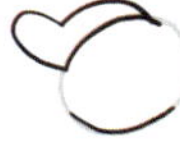

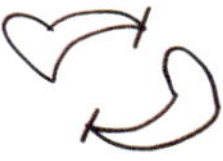

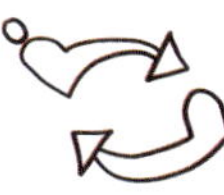

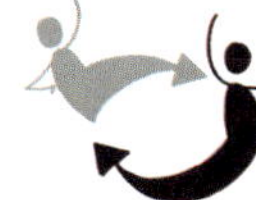

PRIORITY

BASIC ICONS

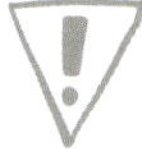
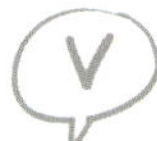

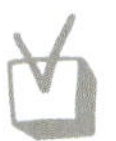
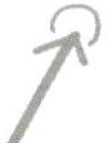
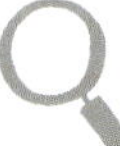
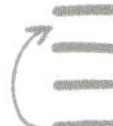

COMBINED ICONS

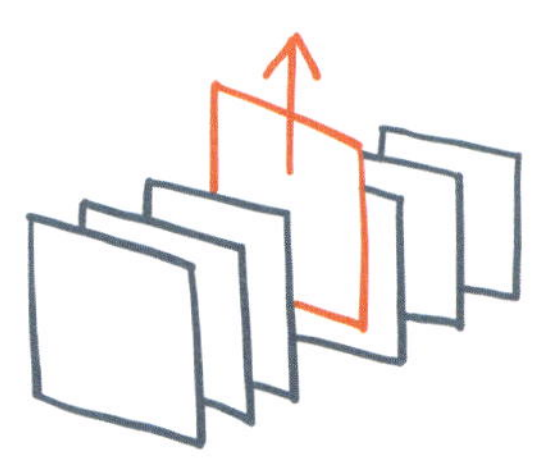

HOW TO DRAW

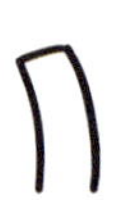
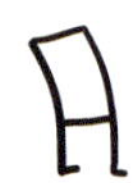
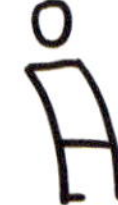
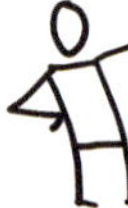
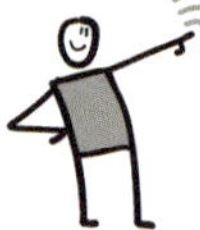

REFLECTION

BASIC ICONS

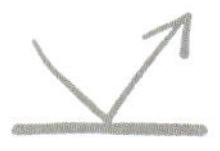
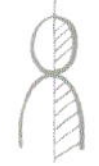
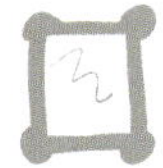
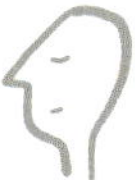

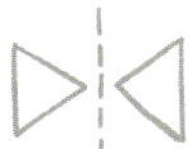

COMBINED ICONS

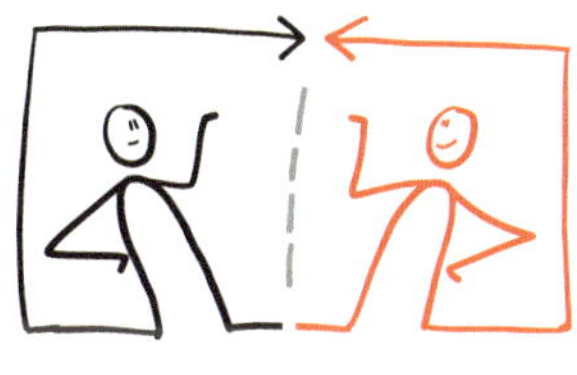
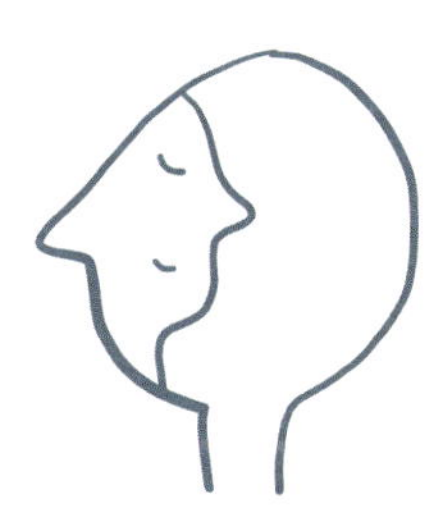
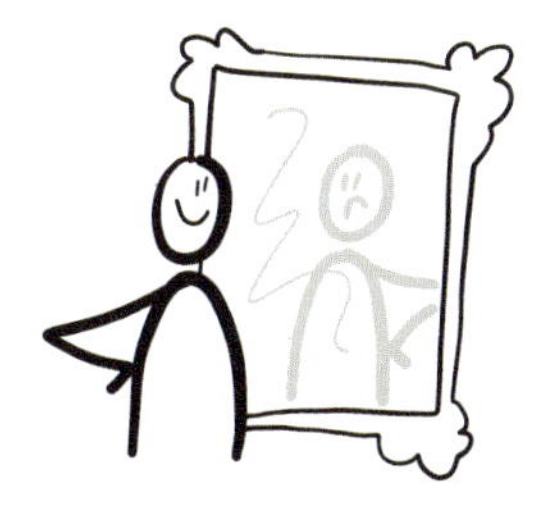
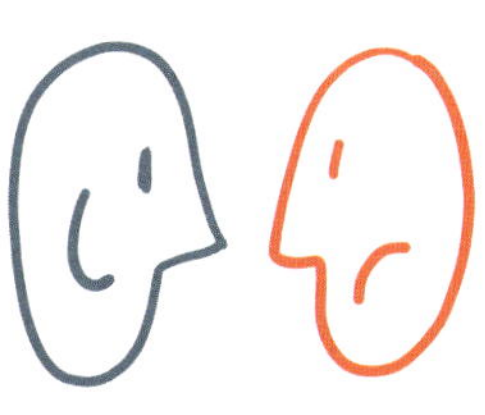

HOW TO DRAW

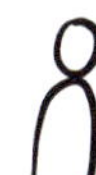
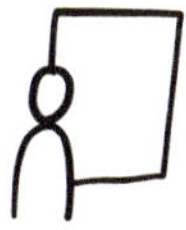
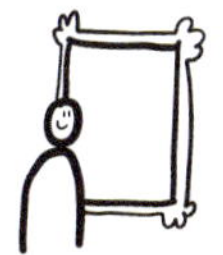
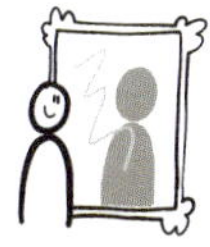

RESEARCH

BASIC ICONS

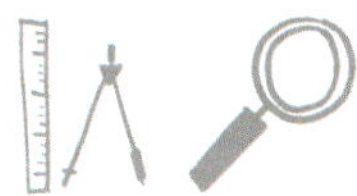
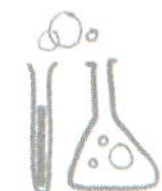
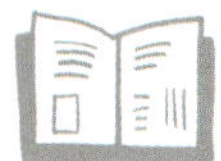
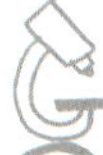
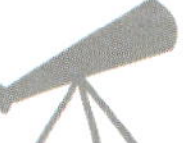
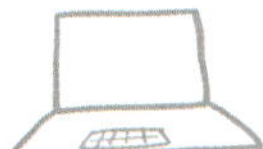

COMBINED ICONS

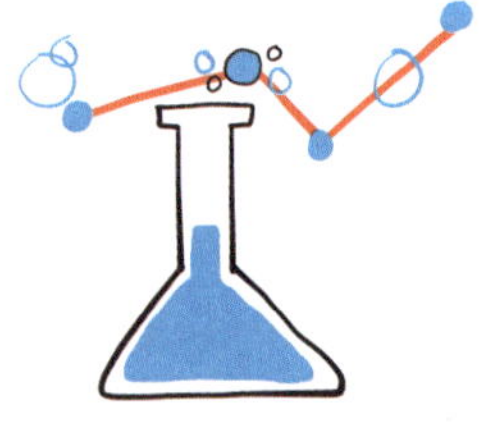
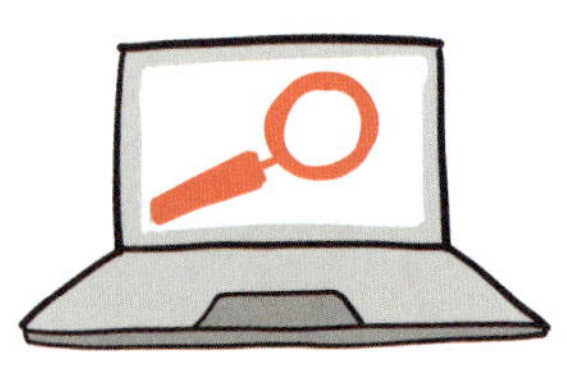

HOW TO DRAW

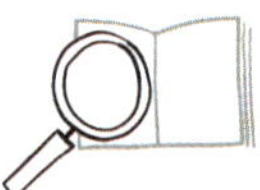

RESISTANCE

BASIC ICONS

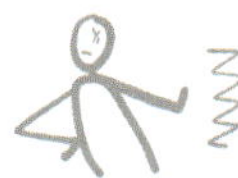
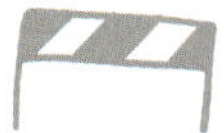
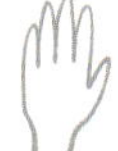
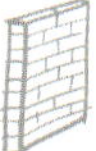
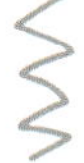
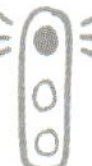
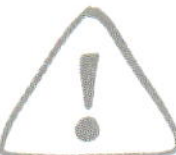

COMBINED ICONS

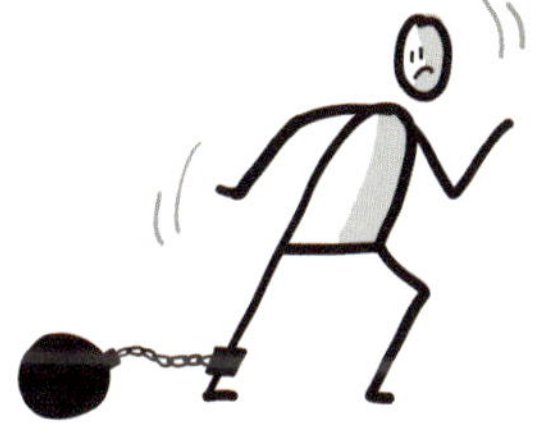
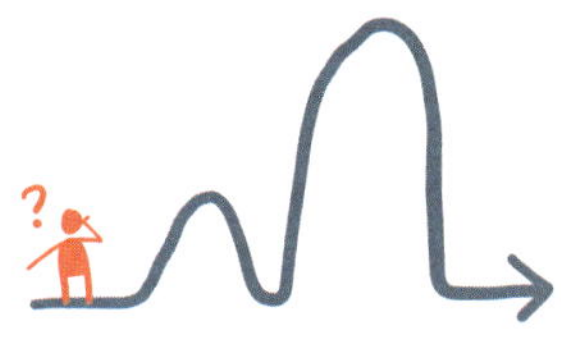

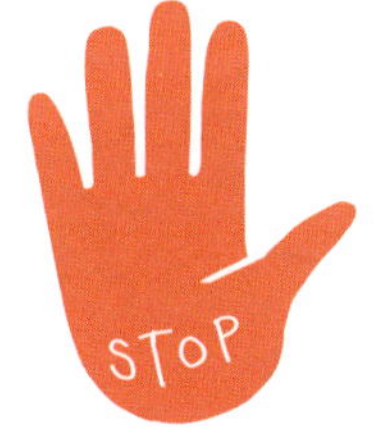

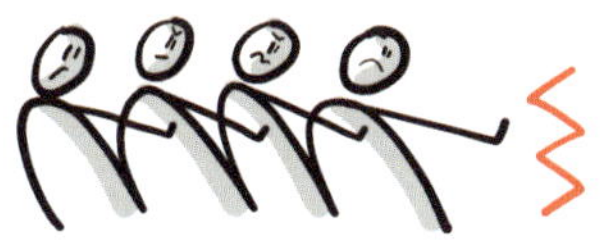

HOW TO DRAW

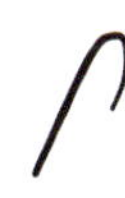
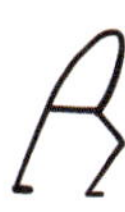
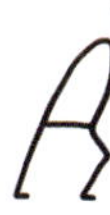
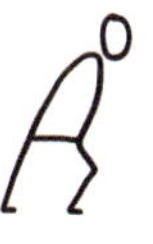
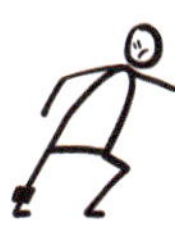
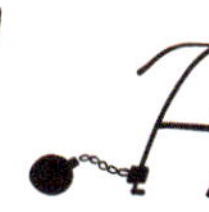

ROLES

BASIC ICONS

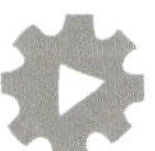
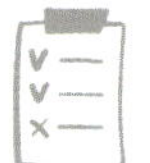
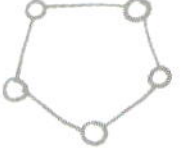
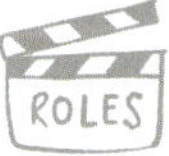

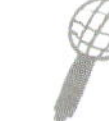
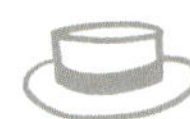

COMBINED ICONS

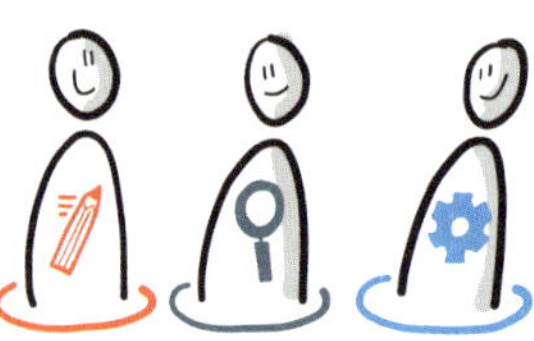
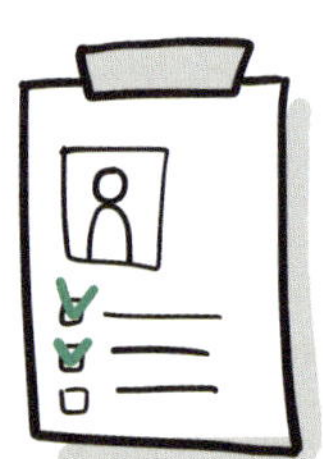
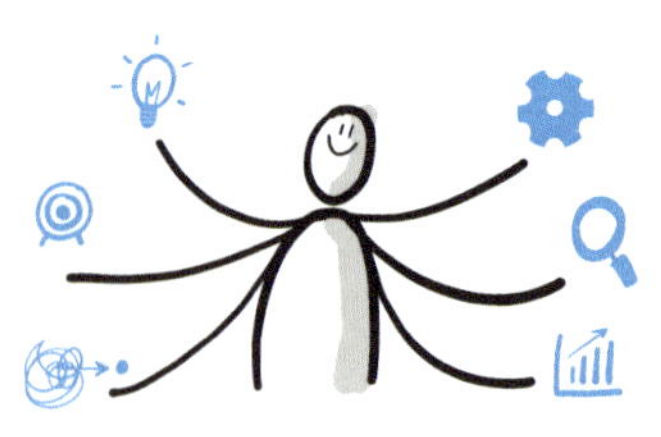
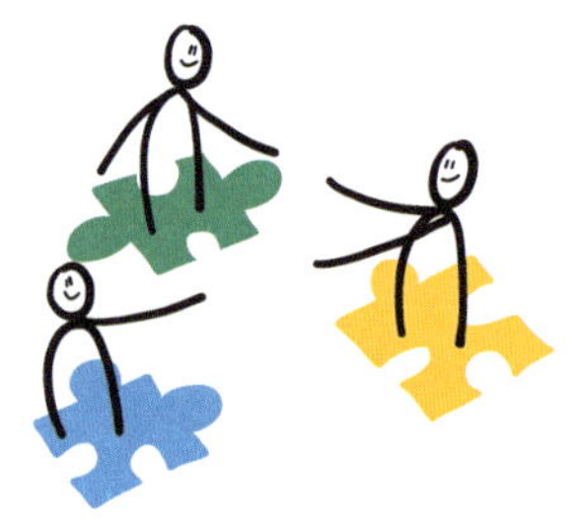

HOW TO DRAW

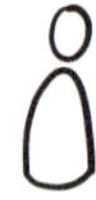
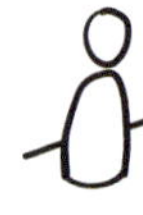
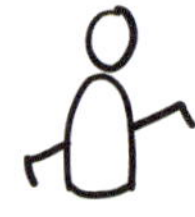
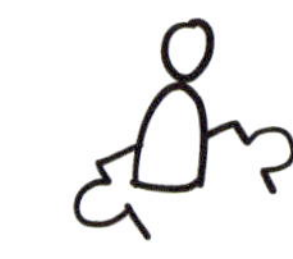

SELF-DIRECTED, SELF-STEERING

BASIC ICONS

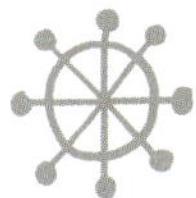
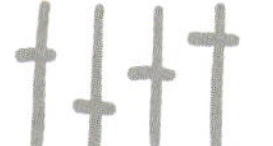
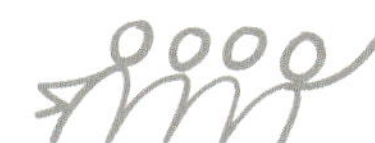

COMBINED ICONS

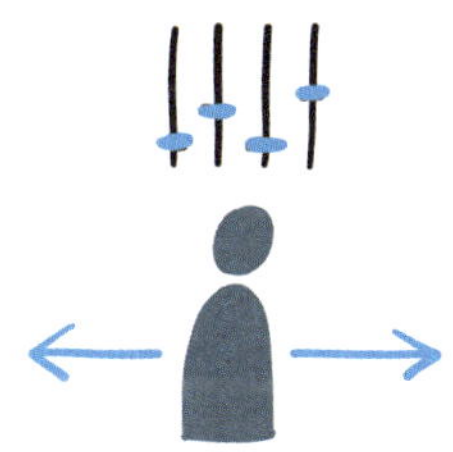
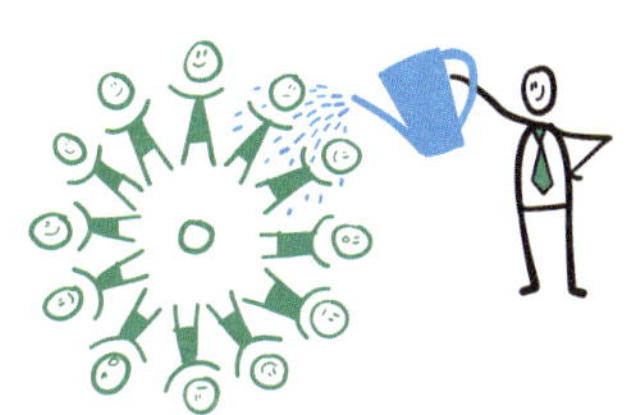
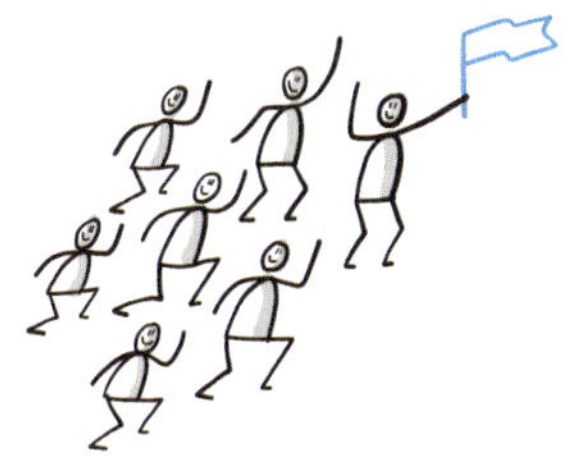

HOW TO DRAW

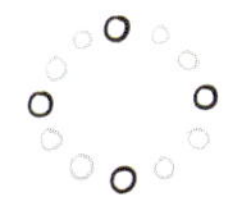
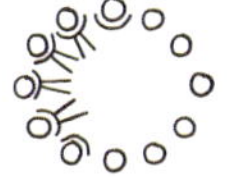
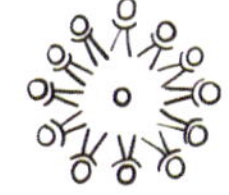

Way of working

SUPERVISED

BASIC ICONS

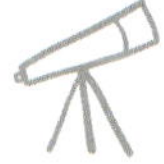 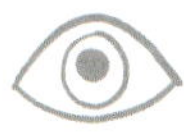 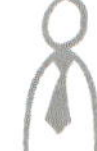 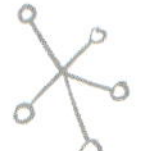  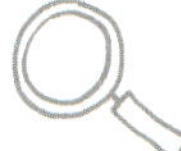 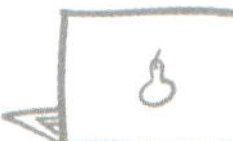

COMBINED ICONS

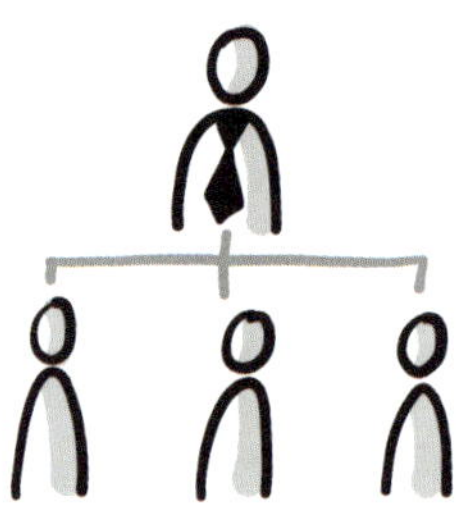

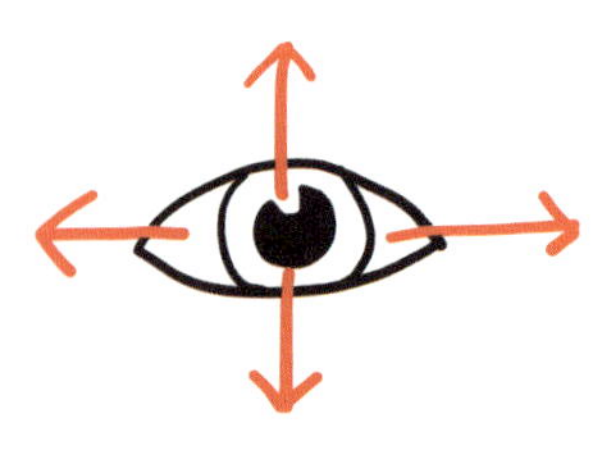

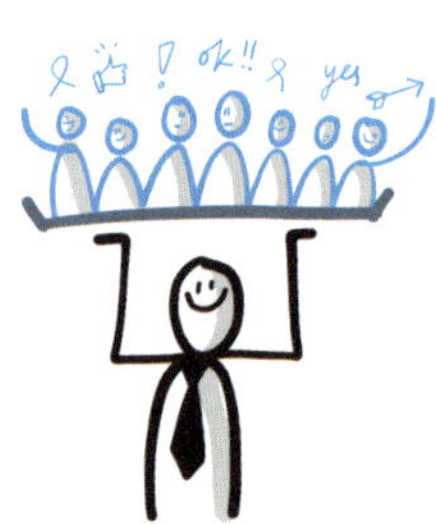

HOW TO DRAW

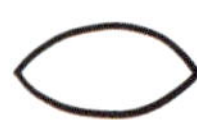 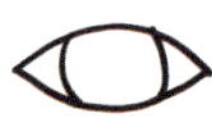 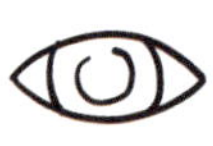 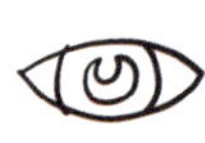 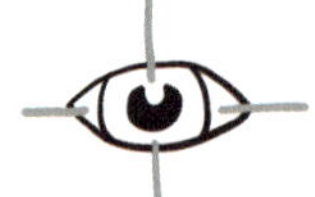

VERIFICATION

BASIC ICONS

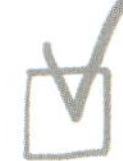
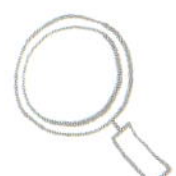
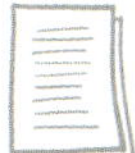
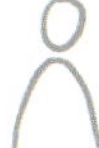
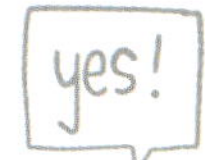

COMBINED ICONS

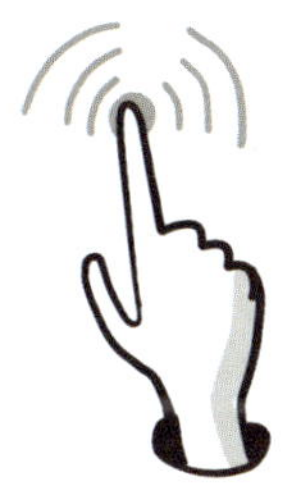
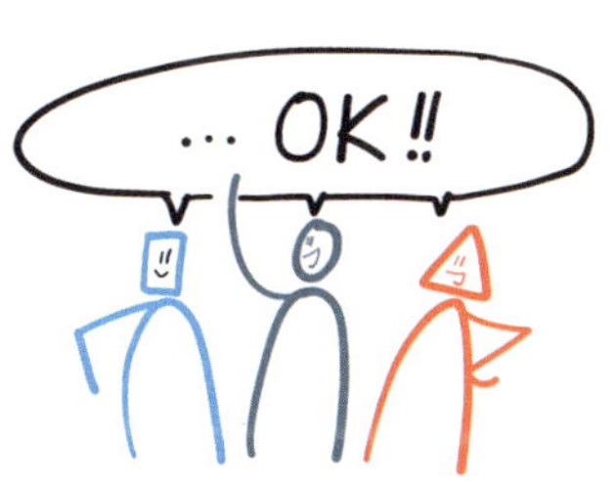

HOW TO DRAW

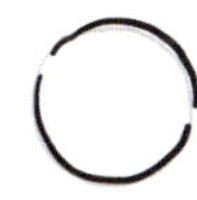
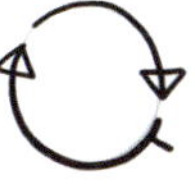
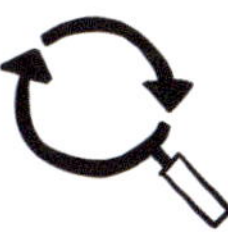

TAKE IT TO THE NEXT LEVEL

Let's look at the potential of a well-designed icon or visual. What can it make happen? What can you do with it? Check Visual Doing chapter 3 and 4 for inspiration.

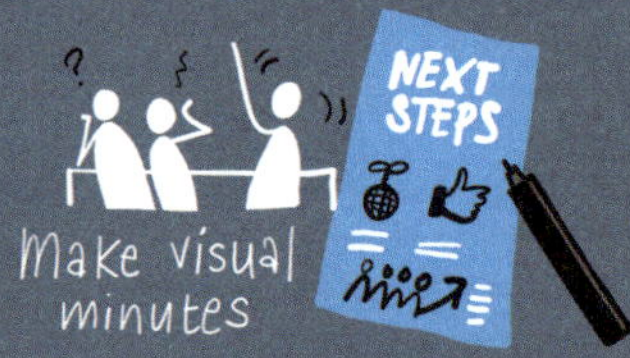

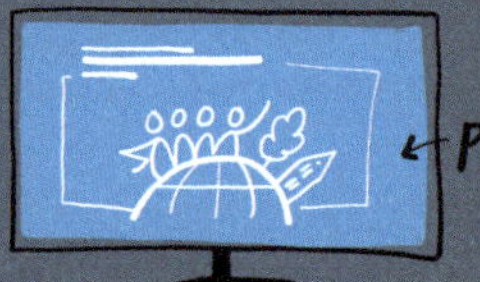

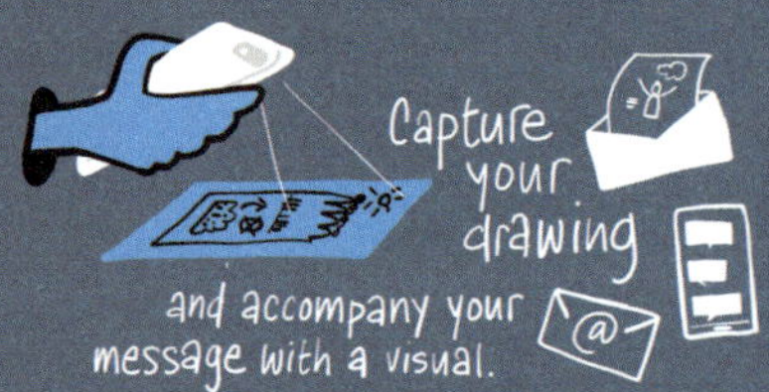

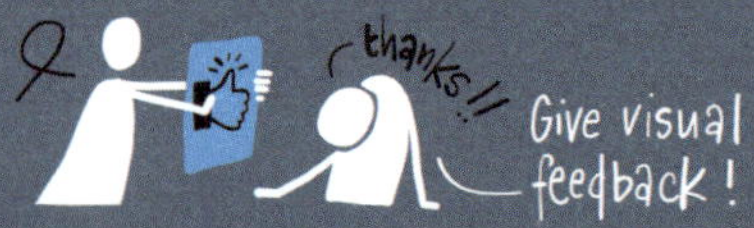

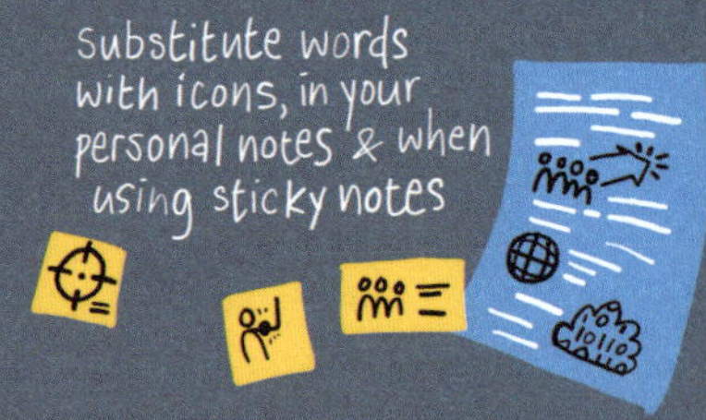

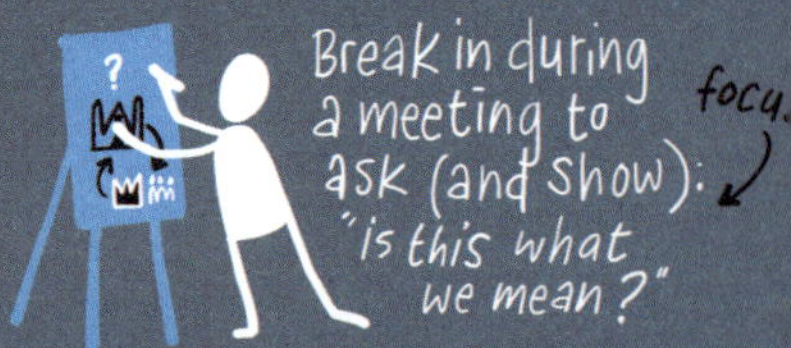

THANK YOU

I can't finish this book without expressing my deep gratitude to all my wonderful colleagues and interns. This book couldn't have been created without all your thinking, writing, sketching, drawing, editing and correcting. It was an absolute pleasure making another book with your help to empower the visual revolution!

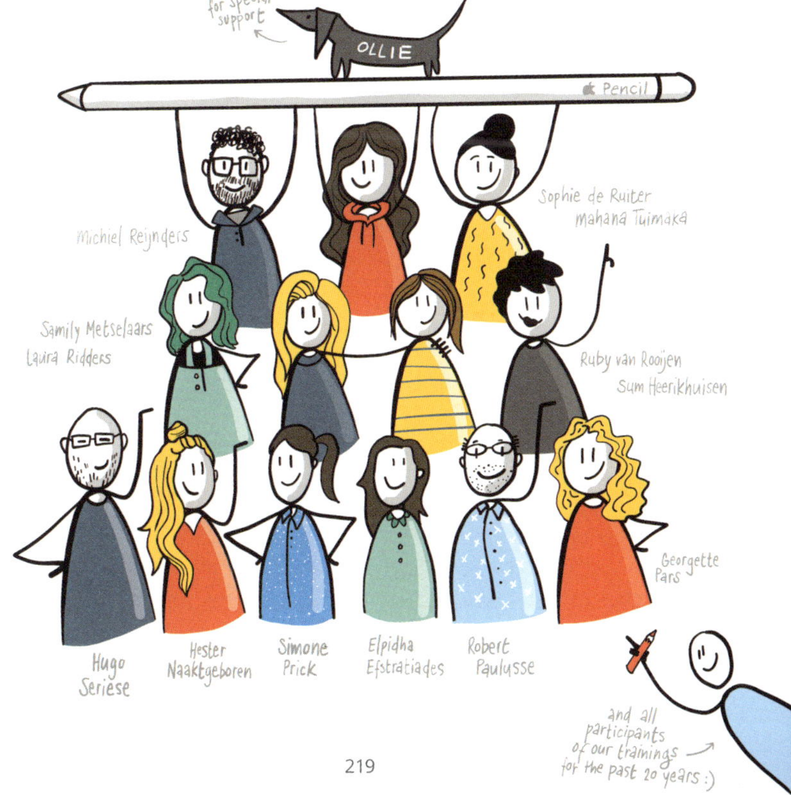

ABOUT THE AUTHOR

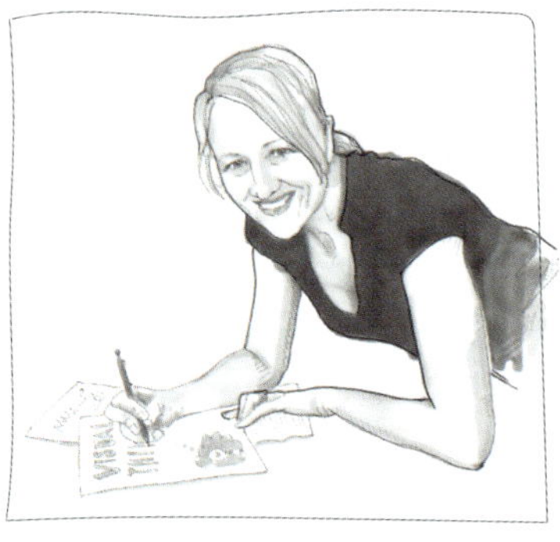

Willemien Brand has channeled her passion for drawing and design into her life's work. After graduating with distinction from the prestigious Design Academy Eindhoven, she became an award-winning industrial designer.

In the late '90s she launched Buro BRAND, a Visual Communication agency harnessing the inventive energy of a team of visionaries who share her passion. Together, they shape ways of visualizing and simplifying complex processes, strategies and information. The longer Willemien and her team worked in the field, the clearer it became to them that drawing and Visual Thinking are powerful tools that strengthen employee engagement and build bridges between businesses and their customers.

Now she and her team from Buro BRAND share this philosophy and passion with companies around the world, inspiring and enabling them to embrace the power of visual communication.

It's a two-way street for Willemien: "Every day I'm able to help other people unleash their creativity and use it to achieve better results in their work, it gives me joy and renews my passion for drawing."

OUR OTHER BOOKS

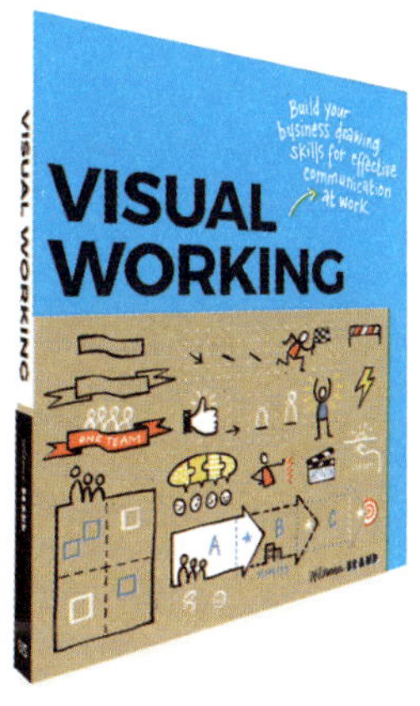

Boost your productivity and collaboration with Visual Working
After the success of Visual Thinking and Visual Doing we now present you the third edition: Visual Working.
This practical workbook guides you step by step in applying business drawing in your daily routine, so you can communicate with images just as easily as with words.
Discover the Five Visual Thinking Types, useful theory to apply to your ideas and concepts immediately. And use the practical tips and tricks to enhance collaboration and communication within your organization.

Visual Thinking With the right mindset and the simple skills this book provides, you can develop your own signature and style and start generating change by integrating visual communication into your business setting.

Visual Doing Visual Doing will improve your visual craftsmanship and broaden your skillset. It's a practical and accessible handbook for incorporating visual thinking into your daily business and communication.

A-Z INDEX

A

B

C

D

E

F

G